MEMORIAL AND BIOGRAPHICAL

RECORD

AN ILLUSTRATED

COMPENDIUM OF BIOGRAPHY

CONTAINING A

COMPENDIUM OF LOCAL BIOGRAPHY,

Including Biographical Sketches of Prominent Old Settlers and Representative Citizens
of Part of the CUMBERLAND REGION OF TENNESSEE, with a Review
of their Life Work; their Identity with the Growth and Development of this
Region; Reminiscences of Personal History and Pioneer Life; and
other Interesting and Valuable Matter which should be
Preserved in History.

ALSO A

COMPENDIUM OF NATIONAL BIOGRAPHY,

Containing Biographical Sketches of Hundreds of the Greatest Men and Celebrities America has Produced
in Various Walks of Life, including Great Statesmen, Lawyers, Jurists, Scientists, Editors,
Poets, Writers, Financiers, Railroad Magnates, Army and Navy Officers, Inventors,
Speculators, Scouts, Merchant Princes, Humorists, Electricians, Educators,
Preachers, Philanthropists, Artists, Manufacturers, Abolitionists,
Explorers, All the Presidents, etc.

ILLUSTRATED.

CHICAGO:
GEO. A. OGLE & CO.
PUBLISHERS, ENGRAVERS AND BOOK MANUFACTURERS.
1898.

Please Direct all Correspondence & Orders to:

Southern Historical Press, Inc.
P.O. Box 1267
Greenville, S.C. 29602-1267

Originally published: Chicago, 1898
Reprinted with new material by,
Southern Historical Press, Inc.
Greenville, S.C., 1980, 1995
New Material Copyright 1980 by:
The Rev. Silas Emmett Lucas, Jr.
Easley, S.C.
All Rights Reserved.
ISBN # 0-89308-191-4
Library of Congress Card Catalog # 80-51027
Printed in the United States of America

COMPENDIUM

OF

LOCAL BIOGRAPHY

COMPENDIUM

OF

LOCAL BIOGRAPHY

OL. S. C. NORWOOD. —Among the most prominent men now living in Bledsoe county who have won an honorable name as a citizen of that county, none is better deserving of representation in a volume of this nature than the gentleman whose name introduces this sketch.

Colonel Norwood was born in the town of Maryville, Blount county, Tenn., February 27, 1822, a son of John and Sarah (Crouch) Norwood. The father was of Irish descent, born in Baltimore of a family of three brothers—one of whom went to North Carolina, one to Alabama and John to Tennessee. From these have sprung large families in each state. Our subject's father, John Norwood, was contemporaneous with Sam Houston, and was a warm personal friend and accompanied

14

him in his campaigns in the Indian wars, and when Houston was badly wounded, he hauled him back to Maryville where they both then lived.

Col. Norwood had no educational advantages in early life, the extent of it being comprised in the old woodback Dilworth spelling book and addition in arithmetic, and what he may have acquired after manhood was by absorption, through a comprehensive, penetrating and discriminating mind upon all questions presented to him. Upon this talent, and enforced by an indomitable energy, he built up an extensive business education or qualification, which gave him the character of one of the most enterprising men of his county. But with his better qualities he possesses others less valuable — that of an extremely nervous, sensitive, impulsive and combative nature, that frequently gives him occasions of great humiliation and pain.

In early life he developed great love

for military tactics, and was promoted to the command of a militia regiment, from which he derives the title affixed to his name. In the year 1856 he was appointed clerk and master of the chancery court at Pikeville, Tenn., and served as such until 1865. This was the first field of his business education, where his natural love and talent for the law was rapidly developed and at the close of the war he was licensed to practice at the bar, with a knowledge and fear of his inability as a public speaker to make a success of his profession, hoping that time and labor would overcome his natural defects. But in a short time he became disheartened and surrendered his profession, for a wider field of activity and constant labor. Into this he entered and found a checkered and uncertain field, but indomitable energy and love for excitement gave him much success in business, mixed with many failures, in all of which his legal knowledge served him admirably. In this field he became an extensive stock dealer, and, also, of general merchandise, and lastly, has done an extensive business in mineral lands, with a large balance sheet in his favor. The last and most fatal error of his life was when, in 1891, he bought twelve thousand dollars of stock in a national bank, whose annual reports showed a prosperous and lucrative business, but in 1893 its discounts and loans proved almost worthless, and the bank failed with the loss of the entire capital.

His business principles were always conducted on the faith and conviction that "the earth is the Lord's and the fullness thereof "; for God hath said, " It is me that giveth the power to get wealth"; that "the Lord buildeth up and He teareth down"; that "the Lord giveth and the Lord taketh away. Blessed be the name of the Lord forevermore." And whilst in the frequent success of business beyond that of many men of like intellect, he always attributed the same to the Lord, and tried to thus acknowledge Him by unstinted acts of charity without ostentation or pride. And when, in his hasty and impulsive business habits, he made grievous mistakes, he humbly submitted without murmur or complaint, saying, "The Lord chasteneth whom He loveth."

He has been a zealous member of the church since 1848, and for the last eight years has devoted his life to the study of the Bible, more directly to the prophecies and revelations. During this time his notes or comments on these portions of the Good Book have been elaborate. From these, in the year 1895, he prepared an article for the Chattanooga "Times," showing, from the Bible, that the world is now in the last days of the gentile dispensations and near the beginning or ushering in of Christ's return for the establishing of his kingdom on earth, and the destruction of all earthly kingdoms or governments. This was to be preceded by a time of trouble such as was never before known or ever will be again. He quoted the words of Christ's declaration of his return, and those of Daniel's prophecies of the same period, and showed that the irrepressible conflict of capital and labor, which is now threatening the disruption and destruction of every intelligent government on earth, was God's immediate agency for the destruction of all nations and governments of earth and for the erection of Christ's peaceable kingdom which shall bless all the nations of the earth and shall be good tidings of great joy, which shall be to all people. This article, by many Bible readers, was regarded as very forcible and timely. Some fifteen years since, Colonel Norwood wrote a long series of reminiscences of the history of Sequatchie valley since 1838, as he knew it. This was interesting and instructive to the older inhabitants as well as the younger, and he has preserved the only copy of this history known, which should be preserved and held sacred by the younger generations. About the same time he wrote a minute history of the life of John A. Murrell, the great western land pirate, after his discharge from the state prison to the date of his death at Pikeville, of his peculiar burial, the disinterring of his body and his decapitation by two medical students. His head was last seen in a museum in Philadelphia, Penn. These articles have lately been reproduced by the Fayetteville "Observer," Fayetteville, Tenn.

In the year 1841, Mr. Norwood was married to Catharine J. Hoodenpyle, daughter of Peter Hoodenpyle and granddaughter of Philip Hoodenpyle. The last named was born and reared in the city of Amsterdam, Holland, and was a graduate of one of the leading universities of the same city. He was a member of a family of great renown, and a descendant of some royal family of the kingdom who had done distinguished service for the crown, both in the army and navy. Evidences of these facts were known and perpetuated in the coat of arms or seal held by Philip at his death.

One of the characters represented on the seal was two single females of the family, who at some critical period of the nation singly and alone successfully held a fort during a siege of the same, and for this patriotic success they were permitted, when marrying, to retain the name of Hoodenpyle. One other device on the seal represented a brother in command of a fleet or ship, who had also performed meritorious acts on the sea. Philip treasured this seal as a memento of the illustrious family from which he descended, and always represented to his children and grandchildren that there was a large fortune at Amsterdam due his naval brother from the crown for the distinguished service performed by him; that his brother was supposed to have been lost on the seas and had died without issue, and the estate would be held for a period of years by the crown and then distributed to his brothers and sisters; that he would likely die before the time or limit expired, after which any of his children could, with the seal or coat of arms, recover his portion of this vast fortune. But in the eventful and destructive events of the Civil war this coat of arms was lost or destroyed. Searching and persistent efforts have failed to discover its existence. Since that time a notice of this estate and inquiry for the heirs of Philip Hoodenpyle was published in one of the journals of Amsterdam, but to this date no effective efforts of recovery have been made.

Mr. Norwood and his wife are now in their seventy-seventh year and fifty-sixth of married life, and are living in the house on the farm where his wife was born and which was her patrimony. In this they hope to die in peace with all mankind, and in that heavenly peace that passeth all knowledge or understanding.

COL. HUGH JAMES BRADY.—This gentleman is a representative citizen of Van Buren county, a man who is widely known and highly respected and whose life affords an example well worthy the emulation of the rising generation. He has served in both the Mexican and the Civil wars, and in the latter he served in the capacity of colonel. He is a man of influence, is highly educated and is recognized as one of the substantial and leading citizens of the Third district, Van Buren county.

Colonel Brady was born in Westmoreland county, Penn., November 11, 1824, and is a son of Hugh Young and Susan (Wanamaker) Brady, both natives of Pennsylvania. The father was a son of James Brady, who is supposed to have been born in the eastern part of Pennsylvania. The latter was a member of the legislature of Pennsylvania. Hugh Young Brady, our subject's father, was by occupation a farmer, a merchant and a miller. He was a member of the Presbyterian church, and, in politics, was a Whig during the early part of his life, but later joined the Republican party. He died in 1866, at the age of eighty-four years. The mother was the daughter of John Wanamaker's father's brother. They were Germans. Her grandmother's maiden name was Frick. They were wealthy citizens of Fayette county, Penn. There was a large family of them, among whom

were Judge Frick, who for a number of years was judge of common plea court of the counties of Westmoreland and Fayette, Penn. Her sister, Sarah, was married to John Kiester, of Mercer county, Penn., an extensive dealer in the Pennsylvania oil field. Another sister, Margaret, married Jesse Kiester, who lived near the Butler county line. Her husband was a farmer, stock dealer and foundry man of Mercer county, Penn. Henry Clay Frick was third cousin to the subject of this sketch. He was general superintendent of the Bessemer steel works of Braddock, Penn., and king of the coke business of Pennsylvania. There is a large estate in Germany due the heirs of the Frick family. Jacob Frick came to take the testimony of our subject's mother at Port Perry, as to the relationship existing between them, but she had been dead fifteen days. Jacob Frick died about three months later, hence the interest in the estate has never been looked after.

In October, 1826, the subject's father and mother separated, and one year later his mother married the grandson of an Irish nobleman, who had run away from his home in Ireland. He came to America and joined the Revolutionary army. He served in the army six years and nine months. The said nobleman married Rebecca Jones, a daughter of a Baptist minister of Scotch descent in western Pennsylvania, after peace was declared. After they were married they settled in what is now Fayette county, Penn. There were six boys and four girls, the result of this union, namely, James, John, Conrad, Peter, the one our subject's mother married, Sam and William, Ibbie, Kate, Mary and Mattie, who are all dead.

The subject's father, Hugh Y. Brady, never married again, and our subject lived with him at home until his majority, except the time he was in the Mexican war.

Captain Sam Brady, the great Indian fighter, and General Hugh Brady, military commander of West Point in 1846, were first cousins to the subject's father as were several other noted Bradys too numerous to mention in this short sketch.

The children by his mother's marriage to Peter Hauer, as above stated, were, John, Conrad, William H., Mary E., Margaret, Amerilla P., Sarah Jane and Nellie, who reside in and near McKeesport, Penn.

Our subject was educated in Greensburg, Penn., and spent his early life helping his father in the store and on the farm.

In 1846, our subject enlisted in Company E, Second Pennsylvania Infantry, for the Mexican war, and participated in many important battles of that struggle, including all the battles around the City of Mexico.

In 1848, he was mustered out at Pittsburg, Penn., after which he returned home and was bookkeeper in his father's store for one year. In 1849, he moved to Indiana county, Penn., built a large sawmill, storehouse, and put in a large stock of goods, and was there engaged in the mercantile business many years; was also shipping lumber to Pittsburg, Penn.

He remained in the latter place until 1861, when he was appointed clerk in the Interior Department at Washington, during Lincoln's administration and was thus engaged until after the second battle of Bull Run. In 1862 he was called home as bri-

gade inspector to assist in raising a regiment. After organizing several he was appointed and commissioned major and was sent with his command to Chambersburg, Penn., where he remained until General Johnson was driven out. The command was then discharged and our subject returned home. In 1863, another call was made for troops and Mr. Brady enlisted and was appointed Lieutenant-colonel of the One Hundred and Seventy-seventh Pennsylvania Infantry, which regiment was enlisted for one year's service. The regiment was organized at Harrisburg, Penn., and sent to Washington, D. C., from thence to Fortress Monroe, Suffolk, Va., and Deep Creek, Dismal Swamp, for the purpose of relieving the Ninety-ninth New York Infantry at Deep Creek. At the latter place he built a fort and commanded a post composed of battery, gun boat, signal station and his own regiment, besides twelve miles of picket line on the extreme left of the Army of the James. His command while stationed there held a very important post, as it was the most available route from Richmond to Norfolk, Va. On several occasions he made important arrest of spies, passing from Norfolk through his line to Richmond with information of plans for fortifications and forces in and around Norfolk and Suffolk. About three days before General Longstreet's advance on Norfolk, Colonel Brady captured a bearer of dispatches and large mail to rebel sympathizers in Norfolk with information that General Longstreet would advance on Suffolk and Norfolk in three days and there would not be a live Yankee left. Immediately Colonel Brady sent a messenger to the general in command at Norfolk with information of

General Longstreet's plans. The general at once telegraphed the government at Washington for five regiments of infantry, which arrived in time to prevent the capture of points aimed at, and General Longstreet was driven back after thirty hours hard fighting. Colonel Brady's command was entirely cut off from the city by Longstreet's advance. His regiment made several raids by way of Albemarle Sound to Roanoke Island. About this time some sixty rebel officers were being transferred from Fortress Monroe to another prison. After being on the Atlantic twenty-four hours the guards, who had charge of the boat and prisoners stacked their arms and were eating dinner, when the rebels, seeing the opportunity, seized the Federals' guns and demanded the surrender of the Federal troops and vessel, which was promptly acceded to. The rebels then changed the course of the vessel and made for Currituck Inlet, landing free men on Virginia soil, taking the guns with them. A small transport, with one six-pounder gun mounted, was sent Colonel Brady at Deep Creek with orders to take sixty enlisted men aboard the transport and pick up ninety by the way of Dismal Swamp Canal and of Currituck Sound and capture the rebel officers, with the remark that it would be a big feather in his cap. He ordered his men ashore in the canal between the Sound and the North landing river. With orders to the captain of the vessel to remain where it was, Colonel Brady went on a reconnoitering expedition with his sixty men. Having no horses the enemy were kept notified of his advance by mounted parties in front— hence it was almost impossible to capture them. Finally at a point where the rebels

made a halt Colonel Brady was so close to them that they took to the swamps leaving their arms and two uniform coats which he took possession of.

At another time he made a raid by way of Albemarle Sound, captured a schooner load of corn and carried it through the enemy's line to Norfolk, Va. While on this same trip he was ordered to the vicinity of Elizabeth City, with positive instructions not to make any attempt to land. His anxiety to capture the city was so great he violated orders and took the place. He made three successful trips by way of Currituck and Albermarle Sounds, notwithstanding two other vessels of ours had been captured. They captured the men who had just succeeded in running the blockade with a large quantity of merchandise. While in command at Deep Creek, Va., Colonel Brady had the support of General Velea, the military governor. He made several other raids in the enemy's country of from twenty to fifty miles, with an escort of sixty men, with his orderly, and without orders from the general command of the department. These raids being, in a general way, successful, notwithstanding that five hundred guerrillas were reported in the counties through which he passed. While in command at Deep Creek Colonel Brady was presented by his regiment with a magnificent sword, belt, silk sash and field glass, as a token of esteem and regard. The sword bore the inscription, on a silver plate: "Presented to Lieut.-Col. Hugh J. Brady, commanding at Deep Creek, Va., April, 1863, by the One Hundred and Seventy-seventh Regiment, Pennsylvania Infantry." This superb testimonial cost the officers and enlisted men some $500 in Philadelphia, from whence it was ordered. At the expiration of his commission Colonel Brady was ordered to Harrisburg to be mustered out, but returned to his home with his troops. He then resumed his former occupation.

Soon there came a call for more troops, and Mr. Brady at once went to Harrisburg, Penn., to get permission from the governor to raise a regiment. Six companies of this regiment he raised in his own county; the balance in Jefferson, Westmoreland and Cambria counties. He gathered them as fast as they could be mustered in. This regiment was sent to Camp Reynolds, near Pittsburg, and from there to Washington, D. C., under sealed orders. From the latter place they went to Virginia and joined General Grant's army. Colonel Brady was ordered to erect a fort above Dutch Gap, on the James river, the place being exposed to eight rebel batteries. Several of his men were killed while working on this fortification. The soldiers named this post Fort Brady, in honor of their leader, and the name was recognized by orders issued by the department headquarters of the Army of the James. Our subject remained in front of Richmond until an advance was made on Petersburg by General Grant. He also participated in the advance on Richmond, and as his regiment was the first to enter the city, by order of Brigadier-General Dent, military governor of Richmond, the regiment was placed on provost duty. On May 22, 1865, by special order of Brig.-Gen. Thomas O. Osborn, Colonel Brady was assigned to command the Third Brigade, First Division, Twenty-fourth Army Corps. On the same day, by command of Major-General Ord, his regiment was detailed for duty at Lynchburg, Va., reporting for duty to General Griggs. On June 11, 1865, by command of Major-General Griggs, the regiment was ordered to rejoin its command at Richmond, Va.

After the close of hostilities, by order of the war department, Colonel Brady's regiment was ordered to Camp Reynolds, near Pittsburg, Penn., to be mustered out and paid. The Colonel then returned to his home and again engaged in mercantile business, which he continued until 1869—when he sold out and went to McMinnville, Tenn., and was there engaged in farming about three years. In January, 1874, he moved to his present large farm of six hundred acres and has since carried on an extensive farming business. From 1876 to 1879 Colonel Brady performed the duty of United States commissioner. Under Grant's administration he was appointed United States storekeeper and gauger and continued in this position until the beginning of Cleveland's first administration. Under Harrison's administration he was appointed deputy collector of internal revenue of the Fifth district of Tennessee and after two years' service as such he resigned to accept the position of United States storekeeper and gauger, which office he held until the beginning of Cleveland's second term of office. He has also been engaged in merchandising at Doyle Station, Tenn., and conducted a drug store at Sparta, Tenn., from 1886 to 1889.

Colonel Brady is a Mason and has twice represented his lodge at the grand lodge of the state of Tennessee, and for forty years he has been a member of the Independent Order of Odd Fellows, having been elected representative of the grand lodges and encampments of Pennsylvania, also Tennessee. Was elected and installed as grand warden of the grand encampment of Tennessee, but refused promotion to the chair of grand patriarch. He was deputy grand master several years and financial reporter of the Knights of Honor. Colonel Brady was elected commander of Gillen post, G. A. R., at McMinnville, Warren county, Tenn., six consecutive years. For the last sixteen years he has been chairman of the Republican county executive committee for VanBuren county, and has represented his party for a number of years as a delegate to the gubernatorial, congressional and various other conventions. As will be seen, he is a life-long, stanch Republican and cast his first vote for Gen. Winfield Scott, the Whig candidate for President.

January 15, 1850, Hugh J. Brady was united in marriage with Miss Henrietta Shields, a native of Indiana county, Penn., born in the year 1836. She was a member of the Methodist Episcopal church and died near McMinnville, Tenn. To this union were born nine children, of whom we have the following record: Anna, wife of Paul Blaunt, Glenwood Springs, Colo.; Margaret J., wife of R. M. Walker, Denver, Colo.; Mary, wife of W. G. Stokes, Denver, Colo.; Hugh Samuel, of the Third district of Van-Buren county, Tenn.; N. Scott, of Denver, Colo.; Henry Clay, of Colorado; Virginia Jane, wife of Dr. I. C. Morgan, Cummingsville, Tenn.; Mike Duffy, of Chattanooga, Tenn.; Bertha Belle, widow of Chas. Caswell, is making her home at Denver, Colo.

After the death of his first wife, Colonel Brady was married, March 9, 1873, to Miss Cherokee Deloniga Wilcher, who was born in Warren county, Tenn., July 20, 1844. She was the daughter of William Waldon and Rebecca (Clark) Wilcher, the former born in 1812, in Warren county, Tenn., and the latter born March 17, 1813, in South Carolina. To the marriage of Mr. and Mrs. Wilcher were born eight children, namely: Thomas, who was a promising young lawyer, and who enlisted in the Confederate army, died at Camp Trusdale while in service on the 1st of September, 1861; George, who was a prominent mechanic at McMinnville, Tenn., afterward moved to Texas, where he died; Fanny, a graduate of the Cumberland Female College, at McMinnville, married Walter Luvane, of Iowa, and died in 1882, and her husband a few years later; Cherokee D., the wife of Colonel Brady; Christeen Pauline, who married Dr. Robert Brown and now lives in Oklahoma; Mary, who died when quite young at McMinnville; Willia who lives in White county, Tenn.; a Anna, who lives in Van Buren county.

To the second marriage of our subject were born four children, as follows:, James M., whose birth took place November 29, 1873. He graduated from Burritt College in 1892 with the degree of B. S. After teaching school a short time in Missouri, he studied law at Sparta and was admitted to the bar in 1893. In 1896 he moved from Sparta to Spencer, where he represents the Union Land, Coal and Coke Company, a large syndicate of wealthy St. Louis parties, who own thousands of acres of valuable mineral land. He has built up an extensive trade and is fast becoming prominent. The second child, Cleo, is the wife of E. S. Haston, a promising young farmer of the Third district of Van Buren county; the others, Tennie H. and Pauline, are students at Burritt College, Spencer, Tenn.

Mrs. Brady is postmistress at Meade, Tenn.

JUDGE JAMES M. STEWART.—This name is borne by a prominent citizen of Dunlap, Tenn., who is the present county judge of Sequatchie county. He is making his present home on the farm on which he was born, and has spent the greater part of his life in the county.

During this time Mr. Stewart has been found standing on the side of truth and justice, and manifesting the true spirit of American progress in his business affairs and in his connection with the advance of civilization, although until 1894 he never aspired to be a public officer. He was born February 10, 1829, the son of George and Martha (Deakins) Stewart. George Steward was born in Green county, Tenn., in the year 1795, and moved with his father to the Sequatchie Valley in the year 1810. His father, William Stewart, was born in Ireland, his parents having emigrated from Scotland to Ireland only a short time prior to his birth. William Stewart was a weaver by trade, and died at the advanced age of seventy-five years, in what is now Sequatchie county, Tenn. Upon migrating to America from Ireland, he first settled in the state of Maryland near Baltimore, remained there only a few years and moved

15

to Washington county, Va., and from thence he moved to Green county, Tenn., and from Green he moved to Blount county, Tenn., and from Blount county, Tenn., he moved to the Sequatchie Valley in the year 1810, settling first in the valley on Indian land on Looney's Creek, which is now in Marion county, Tenn. It being contrary to the law for the "whites" to settle on Indian land, the United States regular soldiers burned his cabin and destroyed his growing crops. He then moved across the Indian line into Bledsoe county, Tenn., near where Dunlap now stands, at which place he ended his days in April, 1834.

George Stewart, a son of William Stewart, was a successful farmer, and died on the 28th day of December, 1887, at the age of over ninety-two years. He married his first wife, who was a native of Washington county, Tenn., in August, 1820, in what was then Marion county, Tenn., and she died in the same county in the month of April, 1834. George Stewart was a member of the M. E. church, South, for about thirty years prior to his death. Politically he was a Whig until the dissolution of that party, after which he identified himself with the Democratic party. Mr. George and wife, Martha Stewart, were the parents of a family of three sons and two daughters, of whom we have the following record: Rev. A. D. Stewart, a minister of the M. E. church, South, and has had charge of a circuit or station most of the time since 1859; James M., the subject of this sketch; Nancy, wife of B. F. Smith, a farmer in Polk county, Ark.; William D., was born April 24, 1831, and died July 28, 1869. He was captain of a company in the Confederate army, in the Thirty-fifth Regiment of Infantry, Tennessee Volunteers, commanded by Col. Ben. Hill, of McMinnville, Tenn.

Judge Stewart was educated in the public schools of the valley, and at the academy at Jasper, Marion county, Tenn., closing his course of study in 1849, after which he taught school two years. On March 1, 1851, he began the sale of goods at Walnut Valley, where he now makes his home, and continued the mercantile business until 1892, with the exception of the years 1862-3-4, when it was impossible to keep store owing to the existence of the Civil war.

In 1867 he moved his store from Walnut Valley to Dunlap. In 1894 he was elected judge of the county court for the term of eight years, by the people of his native county, and has since performed the duties of that office.

On April 3, 1853, Mr. Stewart was united in marriage to Miss Mary A. Kirklen, a daughter of Allen Kirklen. She was also a native of the Sequatchie Valley, and her mother is said to have been the first white child born in the Sequatchie Valley.

Mrs. Stewart died April 21, 1892, the mother of a family of eleven children, viz.: J. A. Stewart, of the firm of Stewart & Alley, of Dunlap, Tenn. Martha L., wife of Rev. W. C. Carden, a minister and presiding elder of the Big Stone Gap District, Va., of the M. E. church, South. George K., a traveling salesman of Chattanooga, Tenn. Daniel R., a farmer of Sequatchie county, and William A., also a farmer in the same county. A. L. is still with his father at the old homestead. Charles A., of Nashville, Tenn., is a traveling salesman.

Byron H., a salesman at Sheridan, Ark. R. Bruce, who is still at the old homestead. Walter Scott, of Chattanooga, Tenn., is a clerk at St. James Hotel. Lizzia A. is a teacher at the Jonesville Academy, Lee county, Va. The family is connected with the M. E. church, South. Socially, Mr. Stewart affiliates with the Masonic fraternity, has been twice master of the lodge in which he holds his membership, and has represented it at the grand lodge. Politically he is a Democrat.

JOHN A. JENKINS, the honored mayor of South Pittsburg, is a man whose well-spent life commands the respect of all with whom he is brought in contact. His fidelity to public duty marks him as a worthy citizen and his reliability in all trade transactions has won him a reputation that is indeed enviable. His well-directed efforts have also brought to him a gratifying success, and he is now the owner of valuable property interests in Marion county.

Mr. Jenkins was born in Jackson county, Ala., August 31, 1840, and is a son of Milton and Sarah (Russell) Jenkins. Milton Jenkins was born in the Pickens district of South Carolina, March 6, 1810, and was the son of Thomas and Mary Jenkins. His father, Thomas, was born July 9, 1769, and died in 1849, aged eighty years, three months and twenty-two days. The mother, born September 10, 1776, died December 17, 1847, at the age of seventy-one years, three months and seven days. Milton Jenkins spent the days of his boyhood and youth in the place of his birth but, on attaining his majority, removed to Jackson county, Ala., where he made his home until his death, which occurred July 26, 1880, when he had attained the advanced age of seventy years, four months and twenty days. His wife, formerly Sarah A. Russell, was a native of Alabama, born November 17, 1818, and died March 14, 1886, sixty-nine years, three months and twenty-seven days old. She was the daughter of Matthew Russell, who was born January 5, 1791, and died February 9, 1832. Thomas Russell, the father of Matthew, was born June 7, 1761, and died July 11, 1850, after attaining the age of eighty-nine years. Matthew's mother was born June 18, 1770, and died January 13, 1861, over ninety years of age.

Milton Jenkins and his wife were devout Christians, both being members of the Methodist Episcopal church, South. In his political views he was a Democrat. The family numbered six children, as follows: Andrew J., born in Jackson county, Ala., October 20, 1838, a resident farmer of Marion county, and of whom a sketch follows this; John A.; Martha, of South Pittsburg, widow of Capt. W. D. McCampbell, who was commander of Company F, Fifty-fifth Alabama Infantry, in the Civil war; T. C., a farmer of Jackson county, Ala.; Grafton and Mary, who died in childhood.

John A. Jenkins acquired his education in the public schools of his native county, and in 1861 he and his two brothers enlisted in the Confederate army; John and T. C. were members of Captain McCampbell's company, of the Fifty-fifth Alabama Confederate Infantry. The subject of this review remained with that command until the battle of Peach Tree Creek on the retreat from Dalton, when he had a part of his left foot shot away. He remained in South Carolina until the close of hostilities, when he returned to his Alabama home. At the battle and surrender of Fort Donelson most of his command were taken prisoners but he succeeded in making his escape. He participated in the engagements at Corinth, Jackson and a great many other battles and skirmishes.

After the war Mr. Jenkins engaged in farming in Jackson county, Ala., until his removal to South Pittsburg. Here he formed a partnership with Shelby Lovelace and engaged in merchandising, meeting with such excellent success that after four years he purchased his partner's interest and for some time conducted the business alone. Later he admitted Reuben Brittain to a partnership, but has now retired from commercial life and devotes his energies to agricultural pursuits. He owns two valuable and highly cultivated farms, one in Doran's Cove, Jackson county, Ala., and the other near South Pittsburg, Marion county.

In 1868, Mr. Jenkins married Miss Lucy, daughter of Thomas Partin, and a native of Tennessee. They have six children. Martha is the wife of Reuben Brittain, and Mary, her twin sister, is the wife of James Brittain, the two husbands being brothers and partners in the largest store in the Sequatchie Valley, the same being located at South Pittsburg. Sarah is at home. Henrietta is the wife of W. R. Ladd, a business man of South Pittsburg. Cora and Harry are at home. The parents hold membership in the Methodist Episcopal church, South, and Mr. Jenkins is a member of the Independent Order of Odd Fellows. His political support is given the Democracy, and in 1896 he was elected mayor of South Pittsburg, in which position he is still serving. His administration is a progressive one, giving general satisfaction to the public. His business career has been crowned with success, owing to his diligence, capable management and enterprise, and he is now one of the substantial citizens of the community.

Andrew J. Jenkins was born October 20, 1838, in Jackson county, Ala., and is the son of Milton and Sarah A. (Russell) Jenkins, sketches of whom are given in connection with that of John A. Jenkins above. He early in life adopted farming as a vocation which he still follows. May 2, 1861, enlisted in Company F, Sixth Alabama Regiment, and for about a year served in the army under General Joseph E. Johnston. Transferred to the Army of Virginia, under the command of General Robert E. Lee, and participated in all the triumphs and vicissitudes of part of the Confederate forces. In the dreadful carnage on Gettysburg's bloody field Mr. Jenkins was wounded, July 3, 1863, in the left leg and has been a cripple ever since.

CAPT. ALEXANDER HOUSTON SANDERS, who was one of the brave boys in gray in the Civil war, doing his duty nobly and unflinchingly on field of battle or in camp, is the man who to-day is serving to the best of his ability, and that ability is of a high order, as sheriff of Grundy county; the man who has ever been found in the foremost ranks of citizens who are devoted to their county's best interests and to the welfare of their fellowmen; in private life and in official positions always laboring for others with an unselfish devotion that well entitles him to the respect which is so freely given him and to a place among the honored and valued residents of Tracy City.

The Captain was born September 20, 1838, in Grundy county, in that part known as Payne's Cove, within a half mile of his father's birthplace, and is a son of Jacob and Martha (Yates) Sanders. The father was born in 1812, and was a son of Solomon Saunders, who after coming to America changed the name to Sanders. The latter was a native of Belfast, Ireland, but at the age of fourteen removed to Cornwall, Ireland, and after his marriage came to the United States, locating at Payne's Cove, Grundy county, Tenn., on account of his fondness for hunting and the abundance of all kinds of game in this locality at that time. Here he continued to live until called from this life at the extreme old age of one hundred and four years and twenty-one days, his out-door life in the woods no doubt lengthening his days. At all times he was stout and rugged, and a year before his death walked a mile and a quarter on a visit to a neighbor. His place of settlement was on the head waters of Elk river. He was a consistent member of the Cumberland Presbyterian church, and was a soldier of the war of 1812, drawing a pension from the United States government, in recognition of his services, until his death. In his family were eleven children, of whom Jacob Sanders, our subject's father, was the oldest son. Like his father, he was a great hunter, and both he and his wife held membership in the Cumberland Presbyterian church, while socially he affiliated with the Independent Order of Odd Fellows. With their family they removed to Lincoln county, Tenn., where both died, the mother in 1866, the father in 1869.

In the family of this worthy couple were twelve children: Andrew, who is employed in a quarry at Sherwood, Tenn. Allie, the widow of John Hunter and a resident of Tracy City. Alexander H., the next in order of birth of those still living. Joseph, a farmer living west of Tracy City. Adaline, the wife of Thomas Johnson, of Franklin county, Tenn. Caledonia, the wife of Mack Meeks, of Tracy City. Mincey died in childhood, and both James and Elzick when about twenty-two years of age. John was a member of the Twenty-eighth Federal Cavalry and was killed at Tracy City during the war. George died at the age of eleven years.

Captain Sander was reared at Payne's Cove and Tracy City, where he attended school to a limited extent, but as his parents were poor his educational privileges were meagre and he was early forced to earn his own livelihood. On the 27th of April, 1861, he enlisted in Company A, First Tennessee Infantry, under Col. Peter Turney, his being the first company and regiment in the state to offer their services to the Confederacy, and there was but few men in the Southern army that fought longer than our subject and with more credit. He was with that command until after the battle of Gettysburg, when he was authorized to return home for the purpose of raising a company, which he did, it being known as Company C, Twentieth Tennessee Confederate Cavalry. He served as captain of his company until forced to surrender on the 2nd of June, 1865, after over four years of arduous and faithful service, during which he was wounded many times. He was in the first and second battles of Bull Run, and the engagements at Yorktown, Seven Pines, Fair Oaks, Fredericksburg, Chancellorsville, Gaines Mill, Slaughter Mountain, Gettysburg and Harper's Ferry, receiving a gunshot through the arm at the last named. In a battle in Madison county, Ala., he had a leg broken by a gunshot; at McMinnville, Tenn., a bullet passed through his chin, at Selma, Ala., he received a bullet in his thigh which he still carries; and in the last named place, while in a hand-to-hand conflict with sabres, his own weapon was cut in two, and thus left defenseless he warded off the blows with his hands until one of his comrades shot his assailant, but his hands were badly cut. After joining the Twentieth Tennessee Cavalry he was with Gen. Bedford Forrest in many engagements.

The war having ended, Captain Sanders joined his father's family in Lincoln county, but soon afterward came to Grundy county, where he has since made his home, and his record as a citizen ranks favorably with that of a soldier, for his career in every respect is above reproach and well worthy of emulation. Without means, he commenced life as a farmer, and is to-day one of the most prosperous agriculturists of his community, owning some very valuable land in different parts of the county. He was married, July 10, 1869, to Miss E. Crabtree, who was born August 16, 1843, a daughter of Walter Crabtree, and they have become the parents of seven children: Robert E., a farmer of Franklin county, Tenn.; Lula, wife of James Bennett, a farmer living near Gorman, Eastland county, Texas; Rebecca wife of John Laxon, a farmer of Grundy county, Tenn.; Delia, Walter and John H., all at home, and Myrtle, who died in childhood.

Religiously the Captain and his wife are devoted members of the Methodist Episcopal church, South, and politically he is a conservative Democrat. Abraham Lincoln was his ideal president, and when the latter was assassinated our subject grieved more over it then if it had been his own father. Fourteen years ago he was elected a member of the county court and most ably filled that position for eight years. 1892 he was elected sheriff to fill the unexpired term of Sheriff Rust, who had died, and he is still discharging the duties of that office with credit to himself and to the entire satisfaction of his constituents.

JUDGE W. A. HAMBY, one of the prominent citizens and political leaders of Cumberland county, was born May 10, 1841. The most of his life has been spent in the vicinity where he now lives and is ably performing the duties of the important office of county judge. He is well and widely known throughout the county, and has made many warm friends both during his private life and his career as a county official.

Judge Hamby's grandfather, Reuben Hamby, was born in South Carolina, and moved from there to Wilks county, N. C., thence to Missouri, from there to Morgan county, Tenn., and from there to Cumberland county, Tenn., in 1830, and settled with his family on Daddys creek. His great-grandfather, whose name was also Reuben Hamby, was a soldier in the marine command, and was wounded at Guilford Court House. By occupation he was a farmer and a hunter, and kept a pack of hounds. From North Carolina he moved with his family to Cape Girardeau county, Mo. There the family were all taken sick, and it is thought they were on their way back to North Carolina, and while passing through eastern Tennessee were pleased with the locality on account of the abundance of game, and located on Daddys creek, in the Eleventh district, Cumberland county. Grandfather Hamby died in Cumberland county at the age of ninety-six years, and his wife, who was in her girlhood Miss Mahala Mitchell, was born in South Carolina and died in North Carolina. He was a member of the Christian church. Their children were: Levi, Andrew, Julius, Thomas and James, who grew to maturity, and Mahala, who died when young. The children are all now dead. Andrew was born in 1800, and died in Cumberland county in 1876. Thomas went to Tarrant county, Texas, and died in that place, and the rest died in Cumberland county.

Andrew Hamby, in later years, lived on a farm four miles east of Crossville, near the Rock Wood road. He was a farmer, and also served as deputy sheriff for many years, but absolutely refused to accept the office of sheriff or other offices in the court house, but took great delight in hunting. He was married in North Carolina to Miss Almira Proffit, who is still living and is eighty-six years of age, and resides on the farm which was the last home of her husband. She is a daughter of Thomas Proffit, of Wilkes county, N. C. They were both members of the Christian church, and Mr. Hamby served many years as deacon of the same. The church built at Antioch, built upon his farm, was the first plastered building in the county, and was for many years used for a school house, and accommodated the largest school on the Cumberland plateau. Mr. Hamby was also instrumental in the building of this church. Politically he was a Democrat. They reared a family of eight children, of whom we have the following record: Thomas F., a shoemaker of White county; William A.; Julius A., better known as " Gunter of Bugtown;" Reuben M. died in 1863 at the Baptist hospital at Knoxville, was a Confederate soldier and served in the Fourth Battalion Cavalry, and had served in the Twenty-eighth Infantry, operating in the states of Tennessee, Kentucky, Mississippi, Alabama and Georgia, and participated in the battle of Shiloh; J. P., the youngest son, died during his term of office as county trustee, in 1878; Amanda died when a young woman; Sarah was the wife of D. L. Hassler, who was captain of Company B, Fourth Battalion Cavalry (Confederate); Albert N. was postmaster at Crossville at the time of his death; he was also a cavalryman in the Confederate army; he was high priest in the Masonic chapter at Crossville, and had represented Crossville lodge and Mt. Pisgah chapter in the grand lodge and grand chapter many times; he was also trustee of Cumberland county one term.

Our subject spent his school days on his father's farm in Antioch, and began teaching school at the age of nineteen and taught twenty-one different schools in Cumberland, Sumner and White counties. In 1874, he was elected county superintendent and performed the duties of that office six consecutive years, and previously held the office of county assessor. In 1889, he was appointed county judge by Governor Taylor, and in 1890 he was elected by the people and commissioned by the governor, and in 1897, was again elected and again received his commission from Governor Taylor. He has also held the office of trustee of institutions of learning, and, in fact, has held some position of trust nearly all his life. He was also a soldier in the Confederate army, enlisting in 1861 in the Twenty-eighth Tennessee Infantry, and was discharged just before the siege of Vicksburg on account of ill health caused by exposure. During the first part of the war he was orderly sergeant but later was promoted to the office of adjutant. He participated in the battles of Yazoo, Fishing Creek and other battles in the vicinity of Vicksburg before the siege of that place, and was in the city during the first part of the siege. He is now assistant adjutant-general on the staff of Gen. W. S. Smith in the Bivouac of United Confederate Veterans.

It was after the war that Mr. Hamby obtained the principal part of his education and taught school to meet his expenses during his course of study. After completing a course of law he was admitted to the bar in 1874 and practiced that profession ever since. He also studied dentistry under Dr. Broyles and practiced dentistry eleven years. He built the hotel now kept by Mr. Rose and operated same seventeen years, and was in the mercantile business with Bell & Company five years. Judge Hamby was married in February, 1869, to Miss Nancy F. Tollett, daughter of William S. and Amanda Tollett. Mrs. Hamby was born August 21, 1850, at the head of the Sequatchie Valley. To this union has been born one son, L. V. L. V. Hamby attended school four years in the state university and graduated at Lebanon, Ohio, and is now the editor of the Pikesville "Reporter." He was married in June, 1894, to Miss Flora Colby, and one son, Stitzel J., has been entrusted to their care.

Judge Hamby and his wife are both members of the Methodist Episcopal church, South. In 1870, he joined the Masonic fraternity, and in 1892, joined the chapter. He was master of the blue lodge two terms, and at different times has held all the positions in the lodge, and is also an official in the chapter. Politically he is a Democrat.

WILLIAM B. GRISSOM.—Among the leading and influential farmers and stock-raisers of Van Buren county who thoroughly understand their business, and pursue the avocation of their chosen calling in a methodical and workmanlike manner, is the subject of this biography. He has throughout his active business career de-

voted his energies to agricultural pursuits with excellent success.

In the house where he still continues to reside, Mr. Grissom, familiarly known as "Buck," was born July 6, 1834, a son of William and Eva (Rhoades) Grissom, the former a native of Tennessee, the latter of North Carolina. They were married in this state and became the parents of ten children, namely: Tolivar, Polly, Celia, Elizabeth, James C., Virginia, Anna, William B., John and Nancy. All lived to be grown and married but are now deceased with the exception of our subject and his brother, James C., who is mentioned below. The parents both died on the old homestead where their two sons are now living. Besides William B. and James C., John also entered the Confederate service during the Civil war and was killed at the battle of Corinth, Miss. Our subject's brother-in-law, Carroll Martin, was murdered August 26, 1894, for his money, which the murderer failed to secure however. At the same time his daughter, Permelia A., and his granddaughter, Permelia Martin, were also wounded.

Mr. Grissom, whose name introduces this sketch, acquired a good practical education in the free schools of the county, and also attended Spencer academy (now extinct) for a few months. Since leaving the school room he has engaged in farming, and he and his brother, James, now own the old homestead, comprising four hundred and fifteen acres of valuable and well improved land. On the 21st of September, 1859, he was united in marriage with Miss Permelia D. Passons, who was born in the Seventh district, Van Buren county, July 17, 1840, a daughter of Major and Anna (Anderson) Passons, the former born February 17, 1791, the latter January 8, 1793. Mrs. Grissom is the youngest of their family of eleven children, the others being Tilford A. and Larkin, both deceased; William J. T., a resident of Hickory Valley, White county, Tenn.; Oliver P., who died in California; James W., who lives in the Second District, Van Buren county; Thomas R., of California; Benjamin F., deceased; Andrew J. and Mary A., who both died when young; Edward T., a resident of the Seventh district, Van Buren county.

During the Civil war Mr. Grissom enlisted at Spencer in Company E, commanded by Capt. M. B. Wood, which was a part of Murray's battalion of cavalry. With his command our subject started for Kentucky, but on reaching the Cumberland river they were ordered back to Murfreesboro, where they were dismounted. They next proceeded to McMinnville, and from there returned to Murfreesboro. Being taken ill, Mr. Grissom was honorably discharged before he had participated in any battle. For two years he served as deputy sheriff of Van Buren county, holding the office at the time of his marriage. He is one of the popular and influential citizens of his community, and is widely and favorably known throughout the county.

JAMES C. GRISSOM was also born in the Seventh civil district of that county December 19, 1829, was educated at Spencer, and during the war enlisted in the same company as William B. Twice he was wounded, being shot in the right side at the battle of Missionary Ridge, and at Peach Tree Creek, July 22, 1864, a shot passed

16

through his lungs, coming out at the small of his back. From this wound he has never fully recovered. He was first confined in a hospital for about a month, and was then sent to the home of relatives in Alabama, where he remained for several months. Besides these wounds, Mr. Grissom was accidentally shot in the thigh by a friend in a bear fight. He was married March 28, 1852, to Miss Anna Boyd, a daughter of Robert and Jane (Logue) Boyd, and to them were born five children: Elizabeth, James B., William R., Lodema G. and Levander L. P. J., who all live near their father. He located on his portion of the old home farm in 1872. He is one of the prominent and representative citizens of the community, has served as tax collector one term, and is a pronounced Democrat in politics.

———

HARVEY HENDRIX, a public spirited and enterprising member of the farming community of Sequatchie county, has devoted the greater part of his life to agriculture, in the pursuit of which he has been very fortunate, and is the proprietor of one of the fine farms of the Sixth district.

Mr. Hendrix was born February 16, 1837, in what is now the Sixth district of Sequatchie county, Tenn., near where he now lives, a son of Gabriel and Mary (Hicks) Hendrix, both parents being natives of eastern Tennessee. Gabriel Hendrix moved to what is now Sequatchie county with his parents when he was quite young, grew to manhood, was married and spent nearly his whole life in that community. He died in the valley April 15, 1851. He was a son of Squire Hendrix, who is supposed to have been born in eastern Tennessee, and moved from thence to Missouri and died there. Mary Hicks Hendrix, the mother of our subject, was a descendant of the famous Borden family, who in colonial days settled in Virginia, near where Staunton now stands. One of this family sent his majesty, the king of England, two bull buffalos as a present. In return the king granted him a tract of land ten miles square, and the town of Staunton was afterward built upon this tract. Our subject has received a portion of this estate but considerable more is yet due him.

Harvy Hendrix is the fifth in the order of birth of a family of eight children, of whom he is the only one now living, and whose names in the order of their birth are as follows: Malvina, Delilah, James, Elijah, Harvey, Mary, Elijah and Lemuel. Our subject was educated in the public and subscription schools but never attended college. He was married January 21, 1858, to Miss Mary Ann Pickett, who was born in Sequatchie county, Tenn., in 1839, daughter Jesse and Margaret (Farmer) Pickett, and the fourth in the order of birth of a family of eleven children, of whom we have the following record: John, deceased; Nancy, deceased; Delilah, wife of Robert Hoodenpyle; Mary Ann, wife of our subject; James, deceased; Selah, deceased; Sarah, deceased; Martha, wife of Henry Layne; Minnie I., deceased; William, a farmer and merchant, at Sunnyside, Tenn., and Joseph, deceased. Mr. and Mrs. Hendrix are the parents of a family of eleven children, viz: John S., deceased; Mary, deceased; Sarah E., deceased; Laura B., wife of Joseph Rogers, who lives near Daws post office; Lemuel L., deceased; William, deceased; Adam married Miss Vina Summers; Jacob, who is living at Winslow, Ariz.; Martha, wife of Erby Gates; Luke, deceased; James, still living with his parents.

Our subject has become one of the well-known and widely respected citizens of Marion county. His financial interests are of an extensive nature; he owns a large tract of land and is a very successful farmer. Thrifty, industrious, and withal a man of economical habits, he has accumulated a comfortable fortune as a result of an active and successful career. He is a man of excellent business qualifications, possessed of broad ideas, and enjoys the confidence and esteem of a large circle of friends. Mr. Hendrix served for a time in the war, enlisting in the fall of 1864, under Colonel Goings, in the Sixth Tennessee Regiment of cavalry and operated near his home. He was in none of the important battles as he was taken sick soon after his enlistment and was discharged for disability. Politically he is a Democrat, but has never aspired political honor.

———————

ALTON TERREL PEAY, M. D.— This gentleman has a high standing as a physician and surgeon, not only among the people but among his medical brethren, and, although he has not yet completed the ascent of the sunny side of life, he has become well known throughout the county as a skillful operator and an honest and painstaking medical practitioner.

In tracing the life of our subject, we

find that he was born in Warren county, Tenn., April 20, 1863, a son of Thomas Terrel and Sarah E. (Winfrey) Peay, the father born in Rutherford county, Tenn., February 29, 1812, and died in August, 1896, and the mother born in Virginia and died in Warren county, Tenn., in 1867, and is buried in Nashville. Thomas Terrel Peay, our subject's father, was reared on a farm and educated in the public schools of Rutherford county. He was married five times. He first married Miss Nancy Kelton, and two children were born to them: Mattie and Nancy, deceased. Mrs. Nancy Peay died, and Mr. Peay subsequently married her sister, Margret, and two children, Emma and Tommie, were born to them, the younger of which is now dead. After the death of his second wife, Mr. Peay was united in marriage to Mrs. Sarah E. King, who was, in her girlhood, Miss Sarah E. Winfrey. He first husband was a Mr. Cobb, and to this union was born one child, William, who died at the age of thirty-five years. Mr. Cobb died and his widow married Mr. King, and three children were born to them: Alonzo, John and Sarah E. Mr. King died, and she then married Thomas Terrel Peay, the father of our subject, and two children were born to this union: Maggie, wife of James Sanders, and Alton Terrel, the subject of our sketch. After the death of Dr. Peay's mother, the father married his fourth wife, Mrs. Nancy D. Jarrett, and, after her death, he married Mrs. Mary Guinn. By occupation he was first a merchant at Readerville, Tenn., following that business for ten years in connection with the work of controlling a large farm. He then sold out everything on account of ill health and moved to Warren county, bought a farm there which he operated, and engaged in merchandising at the same time. Later he built a grist mill, which he controlled for twenty years. About one year before he died he discontinued all the lines of business in which he was engaged, except farming. He died in Warren county, Tenn., and is buried at Vervila cemetery.

Dr. Peay, the subject of this sketch, received his primary training in the public schools of the district in which his boyhood was spent. He then entered the Vanderbilt University at Nashville, Tenn., and completed the medical course in that institution in 1889 and began practice at once. For one year he practiced in the vicinity of his home, and then went to Jasper, Marion county, and practiced there one year. He then served one term as physician at the Inman branch prison under Gov. Bob Taylor. After making his home at Inman for six years he moved in 1895 to Whitwell, where he still makes his home and base of operations. On September 11, 1897, he formed a partnership with Dr. David Carah Shelton, a sketch of whom will appear on another page of this volume, and the firm now enjoys an extensive and profitable patronage.

On December 7, 1886, our subject was united in marriage to Miss Lillie G. Johnson, daughter of C. M. and Catharine (Davis) Johnson. Mrs. Peay was educated at Burksville, Ky. To this union have been born six children, five of whom are now living and make their home with their parents. Their names in the order of their birth are as follows: Mattie, Alton M., Fred J., Robert, Catharine, deceased, and Myrtle.

Dr. Peay is a Master Mason, holding his membership at Altine lodge, Sulphur Springs, Tenn., and his wife is a member of the Methodist Episcopal church, South. Politically he is a Democrat but has never aspired a public office.

Dr. Peay is one of the members of the brass band at Whitwell, Tenn., it being the only brass band now in Sequatchie valley.

HON. WILLIAM ROBERSON RANKIN.—The subject of this sketch may be truly classed as one of the leading citizens of his county. He has for some time been numbered with the agriculturists of Marion county, and in prosecuting his farm work is very progressive in his ideas, and ready to take advantage of every turn of the tide to improve his circumstances. For the past few years he has been making a specialty of high bred stock.

Mr. Rankin was born in Jasper, October 5, 1835, a son of Hon. David and Zilpah (Roberson) Rankin, the former a native of Greenville, Tenn., born February 17, 1799, and the latter a native of Bledsoe county, Tenn., and born near Pikeville, September 19, 1809. David Rankin went to Marion county, Tenn., when a boy, with his parents, and settled in the Sequatchie valley, where his father soon died. He was reared on a farm, and for some time was employed as clerk in a store. He later entered the mercantile business on his own account in Jasper, was very successful, and became quite wealthy, and the owner of a large amount of land in the Sequatchie valley, and Rankin Cove was afterward named in his honor. He was a self-educated man, and always took an active interest in political matters. He was justice of the peace and clerk of the circuit and county court of Marion county for a number of years, and in 1845 he was elected to the legislature and again in 1847, serving two terms, or four years. At the time of his death, September 16, 1862, he was clerk and master of the chancery court at Jasper. He was a Master Mason, holding his membership in the lodge at Jasper, and often represented that society at the grand lodge. His wife died October 26, 1882, and both were members of the Presbyterian church. They were the parents of a family of eleven children, viz.: Caroline L., Peter T., Mary A., James R., deceased, William R., Margaret R., Lafayette R., deceased, Eliza R., deceased, David Byron, John L. and Samuel R., both deceased.

William Roberson Rankin, the subject of this sketch, was educated in the public schools of Jasper and the Burritt College at Spencer. He spent only two years in the latter place, however, when he was compelled to leave school on the account of failing health. He afterward entered the law school at Lebanon, Tenn., but discontinued that before completing his course, returned to his home and read law under George J. Stubblefield, in McMinnville. He began the practice of law in Jasper in the year 1860, and in 1864 he went to Nashville, Tenn., and practiced law there until 1870. He then returned to Jasper, and in 1876 moved to his farm in the Seventh district, five miles east of Jasper, and has since made that his home. He has a beautifully situated and well-improved farm and has for a number of years made a specialty of fine stock raising, and probably has done as much as, or more than any other one man toward improving the stock in that community. He has an elegant home situated in Rankin Cove, which was named in honor of his father. Politically he is a Democrat and on that ticket was elected to the legislature in 1861, and served one term. He is a Royal Arch Mason and holds his membership at Nashville.

July 18, 1865, Mr. Rankin was united in marriage to Miss Louise J. Stockell, who was born in Nashville, Tenn., June 14, 1843, the daughter of Captain William and Rachael (Wright) Stockell. To this union have been born six children, of whom we have the following record: David R., born May 24, 1867, who lives near Chattanooga, married Miss Burta Childress, June 23, 1897; William S., born October 2, 1869, died January 3, 1883; Charles W., born April 22, 1872, single, is living in Chattanooga; Mary L., born March 4, 1874, married Frank C. Gladney, of Arcadia, La., July 21, 1897; Albert R., single, born May 16, 1876, lives near Chattanooga ; and Thomas Turley, single, born December 22, 1878, is living with his parents. The entire family are members of the M. E. church, South. Mr. Rankin is not now practicing law, but is devoting his entire time to his farm and his stock. As a citizen he is loyal in his adherence to the principle of right government, and as a friend and benefactor he has gained an enviable reputation. His financial career has been reasonably successful, and he has planted himself firmly in the esteem and confidence of his fellow citizens. He is the friend of education, and his highest ambition has been to educate his children and qualify them for good citizenship.

JOHN R. ANNIS is one of the popular and well-to-do citizens of Bledsoe county. He is a man of much energy and ambition, and in the various lines of business in which he has been engaged he has invariably met with at least fair success, and has become well and widely known and made many friends. He was born in Kingston, Roane county, Tenn., August 8, 1850, the son of Robert R. and Martha (Love) Annis.

It is not known whether Robert R. Annis was born in Scotland or in Virginia. He removed with his mother to White county, Tenn., in the year 1810, or when he was fifteen years of age. His mother died soon after, and Robert, as soon as he became old enough, secured a position as stage driver, and followed that occupation for forty years, working on different lines. When he married he was living in Kingston, but at the time of his death, which was in the year 1865, he was making his home in White county. His father was a Scotchman by birth, and his mother was Irish. He had one sister, who emigrated to Missouri before the war. His wife, who was a native of Hawkins county, Tenn., died when quite a young woman. They were the parents of a family of six sons and two daughters, of whom we have the following record: William F., who was a soldier in the Northern army, in Kilpatrick's command of Walford's cavalry, and is now living in Henry county, Ky.; John R., the subject of this sketch; Fannie E., who is in San Francisco, Cal.; Daniel C.; Henry, who was a Union soldier in Blackburn's regiment, and was killed after the war; Elizabeth died at the age of two years; George died in childhood; and Sam was a printer at Louisville, Ky., at the time of his death.

John R. Annis spent the greater part of his boyhood with his father on the mail route, and learned to read from the placards along the route. After arriving at manhood he, also, was a stage driver for several years. He spent four years on the route from Kingston to Sparta, over the Cumberland mountains. He then made a trip to Indiana, Arkansas and Texas, and returned to eastern Tennessee and located in Washington. He next made his home for a time in Kingston, and from that place moved to Sparta, but in 1877 or 1878 he located in Pikeville. About the year 1885 he opened a blacksmith shop in the latter place, and has since operated that business. In connection with it, however, he has had several mail-route contracts, one of which is the one from Lafayette, Ga., to Chattanooga, Tenn., and he now has the contract from Pikeville to Cross, S. C., and one from Crossville to Rockwood. He has also had charge of the Bledsoe county poor farm for four years. In all of his various lines of work Mr. Annis has been very industrious, progressive in his ideas, and ready to take advantage of every turn of the tide to improve his circumstances. Politically he is a Democrat.

April 12, 1885, Mr. Annis was united in marriage with Miss Laura White, daughter of William White, and granddaughter of Daniel White, and the family circle has been completed by the presence of a family of four children, upon whom they have seen fit to bestow the names of Robert R., Alfred H., Martha and Ethel.

———

J W. HAMBY is a well known and influential agriculturist of the Eighth district and resides in Grassy Cove. Mr. Hamby was born September 5, 1850, in Cumberland county, Tenn., and is a son of James M. and Mary (Dyer) Hamby. His father was a native of North Carolina, where he was born October 19, 1818. Mr. Hamby was a farmer and stock raiser, and when a young man went to Cape Girardeau county, Mo., where he remained for some time. He then returned to Tennessee and lived for three years in Roane county, then moved to Cumberland county and located near the head waters of Yellow Creek. He successfully cultivated the soil for many years on different farms in Cumberland county. In 1861 he joined the First Tennessee Federal Infantry, and served two years, participating in many battles. He was twice married, his first wife being Miss Mary Dyer. Upon her death, he married Miss Matilda Vassey. He was a member of the Christian church and a Republican in politics. Mr. Hamby died March 2, 1886, in Crossville, Tenn. He was the father of thirteen children, ten of whom are living: George W. lives in the Twelfth district of Cumberland county. E. C., deceased. Reuben is a resident of Roane county. Mahala J. is the wife of Josiah Patton, of Cumberland county. J. E. is a farmer, of Crab Orchard, Tenn. Sarah A.

is married to W. C. Nance, of Roane county. T. T. resides in the Seventh district of Cumberland county. J. W., our subject, is next in order of birth. L. A. is now farming in the Sixth district of Cumberland county. James M. is a farmer of the Twelfth district of Cumberland county. Martha E. is the wife of John Q. Burnes, of Crossville, Tenn. Mary E., deceased, was the wife of J. B. Nance, of Roane county, Tenn. Martin B., the youngest son, died November 22, 1887. Our subject spent his early days in Cumberland county, where he lived upon the farm with his father. When twenty-three years old he settled upon a farm in the Sixth district, near Fox Creek. Four years later he removed to a place in the Fifth district, four miles north of Crossville. He remained there until 1890, and then secured his present farm, which he has since cultivated very successfully. He is, politically, a Republican, and in 1888 was elected sheriff of Cumberland county, holding that office for three terms, as long a time as he was permitted by the state law. He has also been a school director in the Sixth district, and a road commissioner in the Fifth district. He is a member of the Sons of Veterans and the Masonic fraternity, having served as senior warden one year in the latter fraternity. In religious matters he affiliates with the Christian church.

Mr. Hamby married Miss Mary Ann Derrick, a daughter of William and Elizabeth Derrick. She was born in Cumberland county, Tenn., but spent most of her early life in Oregon. Mrs. Hamby died on the 19th of August, 1894. She was the mother of twelve children, five of whom, George O., Richard M. and three infants, are deceased. Those living are: Frances G., a teacher; Robert S., Louisa Savanah, Alice E., Isaac Reuben, James Q. and Henry Evans. Mr. Hamby married again, on the 24th of July, 1895, his second wife being Miss Mary J. Renfro, a daughter of Robert A. and Lucinda Renfro. She has borne her husband no children.

HON. JOHN HAMILTON GUNN, the representative of Warren, Franklin, Marion and Grundy counties in the state senate, was born in Coffee county, Tenn., near Hillsboro, April 5, 1843, and is a son of Thomas L. and Sallie (Reynolds) Gunn. The father was born and reared in Wilson county, Tenn., and afterward moved to Coffee county, and made that his home until his death, which occurred in 1896, when he was seventy-five years of age. The mother was born in Coffee county, and died in 1894, at the age of seventy-one years. Our subject's grandfather, John Gunn, served in the Revolutionary war. Mr. and Mrs. Thomas L. Gunn were the parents of a family of seven sons and three daughters, five of whom are living: Jesse, John Hamilton, Thomas, William R. and Thirzie. The deceased are: Henry, Elijah Joseph, Sarah Frances and Mary.

Our subject received his preliminary training in the public schools in which he spent his boyhood. He left the schoolroom to join the Confederate army, and after the close of the war, he finished his education in the Beech Grove Academy. In April, 1861, he joined the first company and the first regiment that organized in the state, and he was the smallest boy in the regiment with the exception of Captain William Donalson, of Company A, First Confederate Infantry. Mr. Gunn served in this command until the surrender of Lee at Appomatox. He participated in the battles of Seven Pines, the Seven Days' Combat, Gettysburg, Wilderness, Richland, Pittsburg, and many others. At Pittsburg his company opened the fight, and at Gettysburg his company took a leading part and a great many of his comrades were captured. For eighteen months, during the latter part of the war, Mr. Gunn served in a corps of sharpshooters. He was taken prisoner at Petersburg, but was soon exchanged.

In January, 1868, Mr. Gunn was united in marriage to Miss Selina Josephine Patton, a native of Grundy county, and a daughter of General A. E. Patton. She died September 21, 1894, at the age of forty-seven years, and April 27, 1897, Mr. Gunn married Cora Carroll, daughter of Hon. J. K. P. Carroll, of Franklin county, Tenn. To his first marriage were born seven children, six of whom are now living, viz.: Ida, wife of John T. White, died at Sewanee, and the six who are still living are making their home with their parents, and their names appear below in the order of their birth: Thomas E., Henry H., John H., Myrtle, Mamie and Cora. At the time of his marriage, our subject began farming on the place he still occupies and has been very successful. He had nothing, whatever, in the way of earthly possession with which to start the battle of life when he returned from the war, as his father had lost everything by the conflict, and what he now has has been attained by his own industry and economy. He has served as justice of the peace of the county, chairman of the county committee several terms, and has also held some of the school offices. In 1890 he was elected to the lower house from Grundy and Marion counties and served on many of the important committees. In 1896, he was elected to the state senate, and in that capacity served on fifteen different committees. He is a member of the Been Creek society of the Separate Baptist church, and socially, he is a a member of the Pelham lodge of the Masonic fraternity, has been master of the lodge several times, been its treasurer, and has three times represented it at the grand lodge. Politically he is a Democrat.

HENRY BLACKLOCK, superintendent of the "Blacklock" foundry, at South Pittsburg, Marion county, was born in Darlington, England, October 13, 1863. Mr. Blacklock is the fourth son of the. Rev. Joseph Hayton and Amelia Eliza (Galpin) Blacklock. The family is of Scotch-English descent, on the father's side, from Ayrshire and Edinborough, and on the mother's from the Galpins of Somersetshire, England. When the railway movement, inaugurated by the late George Stephenson, gave an immense impetus to the iron trade Mr. Blacklock's grandfather, Jonathan Blacklock, Esq., became sole manager of the Taff-Vale iron works at Pohty-Pridd, owned by the late Rowland Forthergill, of Hensil castle, and under his able direction these works attained distinguished celebrity for the excellence of its product. His only son, the Rev. J. H. Blacklock, was educated privately, became a member of the London University, an associate of the Royal College of Preceptors, and the holder of a first-class certificate of merit from her majesty's committee of council on education. Mr. Blacklock adopted the profession of teacher, for some years under the English government, and later as the principal and proprietor of a middle-class school in connection with the University of Durham. Leaving Darlington the family located in Clapham, London, where the father continued his professional teaching. When the Rugby colony was organized, by the late Thomas Hughes, the distinguished author of "Tom Brown's Schooldays," the family emigrated to America, bought a farm, and devoted themselves to agriculture. Through the personal influence of the late Bishop Quintart, Mr. Blacklock entered the priesthood, laid the foundation of the parish at Rugby, became the first rector of Christ church, South Pittsburg, the assistant rector in St. Paul's parish, Chattanooga, with special charge of Grace Memorial Mission church, and the present rector of St. Luke's Memorial church, Cleveland, Tenn., where he has resided for more than six years. The Rev. J. H. Blacklock is now one of the oldest clergymen in the diocese. Changes by transfer or death have given him this position.

Socially the Rev. J. H. Blacklock is a Master Mason and a Royal Arch Mason, having joined these fraternities in England. His family consisted of eight children, five of whom are living, and of

17

whom we have the following record: Charles H., a bookkeeper for the Tennessee Coal, Iron & Railroad Co., at Birmingham, Ala.; Arthur H., a bookkeeper at Whitwell, for the Tennessee Coal, Iron & Railroad Co.; Henry, the subject of this sketch; Frank M. is an electrician with the Niagara Power Co.; Alexander G., Austin, Texas, M. A. of the University of the South, is just completing a course in law at the University of Texas. The deceased are as follows: Hayton M., who died at the age of twenty-nine years, was an accountant for the Tennessee Coal, Iron & Railroad Co.; Harold F., who died at the age of twenty-seven years, was a certificated locomotive engineer; Walter and Harry, our subject, were twins. Walter died in infancy.

On December 17, 1892, Mr. Blacklock was united in marriage with Miss Catherine Warren Bostick, who was born in South Pittsburg and is the third daughter of the late Dr. Joseph Bostick, a distinguished local physician. Dr. Bostick joined the Confederacy and was gazetted aid-de-camp on the staff of the late General Cheatham, with the rank of captain. In this position Captain Bostick conducted himself with conspicuous courage, and with a true soldier's care for the lives and comfort for the men under his charge. The writer has frequently heard from the lips of old comrades still living, many enthusiastic testimonials to the Doctor's worth as a man—a physician, and an officer.

Mr. and Mrs. Blacklock are devoted members of the Episcopal church, of which Mr. Blacklock is a vestryman. He is also a member of the Knights of Pythias. Politically he is a Democrat, but is not a strict partisan and usually uses his elective franchise and his influence in the support of the candidate best qualified for the position he seeks.

JUDGE CHARLES H. CARPENTER is a noted attorney of Dunlap and a gentleman who holds a conspicuous position, not only as a member of the bar of Tennessee, but also as a citizen and officer of Sequatchie county. He was born in Centre county, Penn., December 25, 1842, the son of Samuel P. and Jane H. (Harris) Carpenter, the former of whom was born in Germantown, Philadelphia county, Penn., in 1814, and died in Philadelphia, in 1883; and the latter died in 1894, at the age of seventy-nine years, at the home of her oldest son, William H. Carpenter, in Clinton, Missouri.

Samuel P. was a son of Charles Carpenter, who died in 1855, at the home of his daughter at Johnstown, Penn. Our subject's mother, Jane H. (Harris) Carpenter, was a granddaughter of William Harris, a wealthy ship owner of Philadelphia, and a merchant of that place. He was a son of Isaac Harris, a surgeon in army during the Revolutionary war and attended Baron De-Kalb when the latter was wounded at the battle of Red Bank. The Harris family were Virginians, and upon migrating from there, they settled in Pitts Grove, N. J. Their ancestry can be traced back to the time of the assembly of Westminister, when one of the family participated as a member of the assembly and his name appears on its

records. Samuel P. Carpenter, our subject's father, was in the wholesale drug business subsequent to the year 1848. Prior to this, however, or about 1840 or 1841, he engaged in the iron and mercantile business in Centre county, Penn., and continued his interests in that line, in connection with his other branches of business, until his death. Mr. and Mrs. Samuel P. Carpenter were the parents of a family of seven children, four of whom are now living: William H., of Kansas City, Mo.; Kate V., of Philadelphia; Charles H., the subject of this sketch; and Nellie, wife of William Spear, living near Clinton, Mo. The deceased were: Annie M., wife of J. M. Thompson, of the state college of Pennsylvania; Frank, a minister of the Methodist church, died in Philadelphia; and Mary Mariam, who died in Clinton, Mo. William H. was a soldier in the Civil war, serving in Company D, Ninety-first Pennsylvania Volunteer Infantry.

Judge Carpenter graduated from the public schools of Philadelphia in 1858, and then entered the employ of the mercantile house of J. F. Dunton & Co. May 28, 1861, he enlisted in Company E, Third New Jersey Volunteer Infantry, which was a part of the famous Sixth Army Corps of the Army of the Potomac. He participated in many engagements, in fact, all in which the Army of the Potomac was engaged except Fredericksburg. Among them we mention the following: First battle of Bull Run, Gaines Mill, West Point, seven-days' battle before Richmond, second battle of Bull Run, Frederick, Md., Salem Church, Gettysburg and the skirmishes preceding and following, Rappahannock Station, and Grant's advance to the Rapidan and Cold Harbor.

He was mustered out at Trenton, N. J., June 24, 1864, after serving over three years in the ranks without receiving serious wounds. In September, 1864, Mr. Carpenter went to Nashville, and January 8 of the following year he went to Chattanooga, where he made his home until October, 1865. He then removed to Dunlap, Tenn., and, in partnership with John Alley, opened a store under the firm name of Alley & Carpenter, and did business in that town until September, 1868. He went from there to Jasper, in the employ of Redfield & Co., with whom he remained one year, and then organized the Jasper Agricultural Works. This institution manufactured wagons and farm implements, and of this he was general manager until 1871. He next went to Nashville, Tenn., and traveled for eighteen months in the employ of Fishel & Bro. In 1872 Mr. Carpenter moved to Clinton, Mo., and engaged in the lumber business until 1875, at which time he sold his yards and returned to Dunlap, Tenn., and entered into business in partnership with William Rankin. In 1878 Mr. Carpenter discontinued this connection to accept the office of clerk of the circuit court of Sequatchie county, which he held for twelve years. During this time he read law and was admitted to the bar in 1882. In 1892 he was appointed county judge, and served for two years. In 1897 he was appointed United States commissioner for Sequatchie county. A gentleman of the highest character, possessed of an excellent education and a wide knowledge of men and the world, no man in the county has taken a more prominent place in general matters than has the subject of this sketch.

He has interested himself heartily in all matters pertaining to the building up of the village and the entire county, and has rendered valuable aid in the affairs of local government. As an attorney he has become well known, not only as a gentleman well versed in law, but of fine education, mentally gifted and courteous, and has practiced before all state and federal courts.

November 2, 1868, our subject was united in marriage with Miss Lila Vaught, daughter of Dr. J. B. Vaught, and granddaughter of Jonathan Polk. To this union have been born two children: Mrs. I. R. Huddlestone and Mrs. W. P. Clack. The family are members of the Cumberland Presbyterian church, and our subject is a member of the Knights of Pythias and also of the Masonic fraternity. Of the former lodge he has performed the duties of past chancellor and delegate to the grand lodge, and of the latter he has been secretary of the Royal Arch chapter. Politically he is a Democrat, and represented his district in the Chicago national convention of 1892, which nominated Grover Cleveland for president.

———

CARROLL H. CLARK.—In the respect that is accorded to men who have fought their way to success through unfavorable environments we find an unconscious recognition of the intrinsic worth of a character which can not only endure so rough a test, but gain new strength through the discipline. The following history sets forth briefly the steps by which our subject, now one of the leading general merchants of Spencer, Van Buren county, overcame the disadvantages of his early life.

Mr. Clark was born February 26, 1842, at Carthage, Smith county, Tenn., but was brought to Van Buren county, in 1846, by his parents, James and Rebecca (Sanders) Clark, who located on the mountain side, near Laurel Cove, where they developed and improved a farm. The father was also a native of Smith county, born in 1817, and was a son of Benjamin Clark, who was born in Virginia and died in Van Buren county, Tenn. James Clark was a farmer and stock raiser by occupation, and was a Democrat in politics. He died on Caney Fork, Van Buren county, in 1866, and his wife, who was born in De Kalb county, Tenn., in 1816, passed away at the home of her son, A. M. Clark, in Spencer, in 1886. Eight children were born to them, of whom three are still living: Carroll H., of this review; Martha, now the wife of C. W. Mooneyhan, of De Kalb county; and A. M., a merchant of Doyle, White county, Tenn. Those deceased are Manson, who died in 1861; Samantha, who married Mark Mitchell and died in Laurel Cove, Van Buren county; Samuel K., who died before the war; James Nelson, who died in Van Buren county, and Bethena, who died in the same county when a young woman.

Carroll H. Clark obtained his primary education in an old school house, which was minus floor and chimney, and for a time pursued his studies under the direction of Rev. Patrick Moore, who is still an honored resident of Van Buren county. Later, he attended the York Academy, in Spencer, walking four miles to school; but while a student in that institution the Civil war broke out, and he laid aside his text books to join the Confederate army. As a private, he enlisted in Company I, Sixteenth Tennessee Infantry, under Colonel John Savage, and came out of the service bareheaded and barefooted, but entitled to a lieutenant's commission. At the battle of Perryville, he was wounded by a gunshot which came near ending his life, and on account of his wound was unable to take part in the battle of Murfreesboro. Later he participated in the battle of Chickamauga, both days; was with Johnston on the retreat through Georgia, taking part in all the battles, and on the 22nd of July, 1864, was again wounded in front of Atlanta, a musket ball passing through his left arm. On leaving the hospital, he joined his command in North Carolina, after a long tramp, and was at Jonesboro, that state, when they surrendered, April 26, 1865.

Mr. Clark's capital at the close of the war consisted of a world of energy, which has been the means of bringing to him success, as he had no money to aid him. Returning to his old home, he bought a small piece of land, and, in connection with its cultivation, he taught some small schools. In 1874 he was the people's choice for sheriff of the county, and so acceptably did he fill the office that he was re-elected in 1876. Two years later he was elected circuit clerk, and, in 1882, was re-elected to that position, the duties of which he discharged with promptness and fidelity. On the expiration of his second term he was appointed deputy and served in that capacity for a few years, after which he was deputy clerk and master for ten years. For four years he has also been a member of the county court, and, during President Cleveland's second administration, was postmaster of Spencer for four years and one month. His official career was ever above reproach, always leaving office as he had entered it—with the confidence and good will of the entire community. In his political views Mr. Clark is a Democrat. In he 1894 embarked in merchandising in Spencer, and is now successfully engaged in that business.

On the 17th of October, 1867, Mr. Clark married Miss Keziah Mooneyhan, who was born in Van Buren county, April 10, 1850, and died September 9, 1897, leaving three children, namely: Charles M., a farmer of Van Buren county; and Frank S. and Robert Y., both at home. A son and a daughter are deceased—Clenney, who died in childhood, and Daisy at the age of six years. Mr. Clark is an active worker in and prominent member of the Christian church at Spencer, in which he is now serving as secretary and treasurer.

JOHN SIMMONS.—The agricultural element that has been so largely instrumental in the upbuilding of Bledsoe county is finely represented by this gentleman, one of its native-born citizens. He has a valuable farm on Cumberland mountain, eight miles from Pikeville, and he is recognized as one of the leading farmers and prominent citizens. Mr. Simmons was born four miles below Pikeville, in the Sequatchie Valley, February 25, 1855, the son of Matthew and Clementine (Stipes) Simmons.

Matthew Simmons was also born in Bledsoe county, Tenn., and was killed at his home during the Civil war, when about thirty years of age. He was a son of Thomas Simmons, who was also probably a native of Tennessee. Clementine Simmons is a daughter of John Stipes, who was of Scotch and Irish descent. After the death of her first husband, she was united in marriage to Jesse Lawson, who is also now dead. She is now an invalid and is making her home with the subject of this sketch.

John Simmons moved with his parents from his native home to the Lowry farm, above Pikeville, and from there to the mountains. He was still a young boy when it became necessary for him to do for himself and his mother. He learned the blacksmith trade, at which he worked for some time and then bought a farm of two hundred acres which he still owns. After his marriage he moved to his present home, near Pikeville. Mr. Simmons is a self-made man. Starting in life with nothing, and throughout it all having depended upon his own resources and his own energy, businesslike prudence and sagacity have won him a comfortable fortune. He is enterprising, intelligent and progressive and every enterprise calculated to benefit his locality receives his earnest support and encouragement. He is a man of high moral character, strict business integrity and is highly respected by all who know him. Politically he is a Republican.

August 26, 1881, Mr. Simmons married Miss Elizabeth Frady, a daughter of General Frady, and their wedded life has been blessed by the advent of a family of nine children, as follows: James Thomas, Avis, Maudie May, Alexander, John H., George

W., Mary, Ethel Lou and Foster Lee. Mrs. Simmons is a member of the Baptist church.

THOMAS S. RICHARDS, a druggist and enterprising merchant of South Pittsburg, belongs to that class of representative citizens who take an active interest in the development of the communities with which they are connected and lend an active support to all measures for the general welfare. He holds an enviable position in commercial circles by reason of his straightforward dealing and his strict conformity to the ethics of business life. His many excellencies of character have gained him high regard and it is with pleasure that we present the record of his upright career to our readers.

Mr. Richards was born on the east side of the valley about two miles below Dunlap in Sequatchie county, then a part of Marion county, December 30, 1835, and is descended from good old Revolutionary stock, his great-grandfather, Ransom Smith, having been one of the heroes who fought for the independence of the nation. The paternal grandparents of our subject were Stephen and Dorcas (Braden) Richards, and the former was a soldier in the war of 1812. They made their home in what is now Sequatchie county, residing on the Jonathan Hatfield farm, and the grandfather was one of the successful agriculturists of the neighborhood. Both he and his wife were members of the Cumberland Presbyterian church.

Harvey Richards, the father of our sub-ject, was born on the east side of the valley, in Sequatchie county, in 1813, and died in January, 1862, on a farm in Marion county, now owned by J. F. and R. C. Richards. He had two brothers, James M., who died in Benton county, Arkansas; and Claiborne, who died in Yell county, Arkansas. Harvey Richards carried on agricultural pursuits and was a prominent citizen, who held public office throughout the greater part of his manhood's years. In politics he was a Democrat, and both he and his last wife were members of the Methodist Episcopal church, South. He married Dorcas Smith, who was called to the home beyond in 1855, and in 1862 Mr. Richards went to visit his son Stephen, who was in the army at Bowling Green, Ky., but as a result of exposure he died soon after at his home. This worthy couple were the parents of eight children, seven of whom are now living: Stephen, a farmer of Weatherford, Texas, who during the Civil war was an officer in B. H. Hills' regiment in the Confederate service; Mary S., wife of E. O. Stafford, and a resident of South Pittsburg; James F., who was a member of Starnes' Confederate regiment, and is now farming on the old home place in the northern part of Marion county; W. D., who was also a member of the same regiment and is now a miner, probably living in Colorado; Elizabeth, who resides on the old homestead; R. C., who is a farmer there; and George H., who died in childhood. After the death of his first wife, Harvey Richards married Nancy Lewis, who still survives him.

The subject of this sketch was reared on his father's farm and assisted in its cultivation until he had attained his majority, when he began farming on his own account. Soon after the war he located in Deptford, where he rented land for a time and then purchased a tract, which he operated for a time, when he sold part of that property to the company who laid out the town. About 1879 he opened his drug and grocery store in South Pittsburg, where he has since been located. He is doing a good business, and has a well stocked store, while by his earnest desire to please his patrons and by his honorable, straightforward business methods he has secured a very liberal patronage. For a time he was associated in a partnership with Dr. R. C. McCurdy and others, but with this exception has always been alone in business.

On the 11th of April, 1861, Mr. Richards married Miss Sarah Elizabeth Beene, a daughter of Owen R. and Martha Beene. She was born in Marion county, on the 1st of September, 1842, and by her marriage has become the mother of five children, as follows: Lulah Belle, wife of J. S. Deakins, who is connected with the Battle Creek Coal Company; Nettie Lee, wife of George E. Deathridge, who is associated in business with J. G. Prigmore; Anna Beene, wife of W. C. Houston, of the Battle Creek Coal Company; Martha Dorcas, wife of J. B. Phillips, of the Battle Creek Coal Company; and Harvey Russell, at home. Mrs. Richards is a member of the Primitive Baptist church. Mr. Richards belongs to the Masonic fraternity and both are highly respected people, having the warm regard of many friends. In his political views our subject is a Democrat, and on that ticket was elected a member of the first city council of South Pittsburg, and has also served

as mayor of the city for one term. His administration of the affairs of the office was progressive, and characterized by a business management that was very effective. He has always been deeply interested in the welfare of the city and does all in his power to promote its interests and advance the general welfare. He has achieved success in commercial circles by earnest purpose, indefatigable energy and keen discrimination and stands to-day among those who enjoy the public confidence by reason of an honorable life.

JAMES MOSES PROCTOR, one of Cumberland county's prominent and influential citizens, and the present postmaster at Crossville, was born near Knoxville, at the Crosby house, which was a fort in the early history of Tennessee and was used by Crosby as a dwelling house at the time he assisted Sevier in making his escape from imprisonment in North Carolina.

Mr. Proctor is a son of Hiram and Martha Ellen (Fryar) Proctor, natives of Buncombe county, N. C., and Knox county, Tenn., respectively, and are now living five miles north of Crossville. The father, Hiram Proctor, went to Tennessee when but a boy of eighteen, and was married in Knox county. Soon after the birth of our subject, they removed to the state of Illinois and lived one year near Carbondale, and during the latter part of the war they moved to Boyle county, Ky., and lived there about two years, and moved to Cumberland county in 1868, where he and his wife are still living, at the age of about seventy, and will soon celebrate the fiftieth anniversary of their wedding. Mr. Proctor joined the Missionary Baptist church when quite young, and, about twenty years ago, he began the ministry, and has had charge of some church work ever since. Politically he was formerly a Whig, but is now identified with the Republican party. The Fryar family are of Irish descent. James Fryar, our subject's grandfather, was a soldier in the Revolutionary war and located in Knox county, Tenn., in an early day.

James Proctor, the subject of this sketch, is the oldest of a family of five children, two sons and three daughters. His brothers and sisters were as follows: William N., who died in boyhood; Elizabeth, wife of Henry Duncan, a farmer and carpenter of Cumberland county; Martha J., wife of Elijah Dickenson, a farmer of Cumberland county; Della, wife of William Tabor, also a farmer of Cumberland county. Mr. Proctor was reared in a vicinity where there were very few schools, and during his lifetime has only enjoyed the privilege of attending an institution of learning about six months, yet he has been a student all his life. In 1877 he moved to Gallatin county, Ill., and worked on a farm near Shawneetown during one summer, and then returned to Tennessee.

In January, 1878, Mr. Proctor was united in marriage to Miss Mary Francis, a daughter of Ben Tanner, of South Carolina. Mrs. Proctor was born in Cumberland county, near Crab Orchard. To this union have been born six children, five of whom are living: Edward E., Adolphus Wayne, who died in infancy; James W.; Minnie G.; Clara R.; and Jessie. At the time of his marriage, Mr. Proctor commenced farming five miles north of Crossville. In 1880, he was elected justice of the peace, and later was elected in the eleventh district, serving in all eight years. In 1888, he was appointed postmaster at Crossville, and about the same time commenced dealing in real estate which led up to the study of law, and in 1891, he was admitted to the bar. He was once nominated, on the Republican ticket, for the office of representative of the eighth district without his knowledge, and, although there was little or no chance for his election, he entered the race and gave his opponent an unexpectedly small plurality. In June, 1897, he was again appointed postmaster of Crossville, having been out of the office during Cleveland's administration. He is public spirited, enterprising and in all matters pertaining to the upbuilding and strengthening of good local government, and tending to the welfare and improvement of Crossville and Cumberland county, he has always proved a valuable factor. He has always sanctioned and given material aid in the development of financial matters which tend to the better establishment of the business of the city. He is a member of the Missionary Baptist church at Crossville and socially is affiliated with the Royal Arch Chapter, and is now serving his third term as master of Crossville lodge, No. 483, A. F. & A. M., and was for two years high priest of Mt. Pisgah chapter, No. 143. He was selected as one of the delegates to the St. Louis convention from the Fourth Tennessee district and was one of the original "McKinley men" in Tennessee.

A NDREW J. LOCKHART, a prominent
and representative citizen of Grundy
county, living two miles northeast of Tracy
City, was born in that county, January 10,
1837, and is a son of John C. and Sallie
(Walker) Lockhart. The birth of the father occurred in Buncombe county, N. C.,
but during childhood was brought to Tennessee by his parents, who settled in Grundy
county at the head of the Collins river.
His father was James M. Lockhart, a son
of Andrew Lockhart, who was a soldier in
the Revolutionary war, and the latter had
a son who also took up arms against the
mother country, participating in the war of
1812.

John C. Lockhart was reared on the
Collins river, but afterward removed to the
mountains, where he continued to engage
in agricultural pursuits until life's labors
were ended. He was one of the most
prominent and influential men of his community, and for a number of years was a
member of the county court. He died in
1879, at the age of sixty-five years, having
long survived the mother of our subject,
who passed away in 1840, at an early age.
His second wife, who bore the maiden
name of Cynthia Bailey, is still living at
the age of seventy-three years, and now
makes her home in Sequatchie county, Tenn.
He was a Democrat in politics, and was an
active and faithful member of the Primitive
Baptist church, for many years serving as a
minister. By his first marriage he had two
sons, George W., a physician now living in
Arkansas; and Andrew J., of this sketch.
The children born of the second union were
James M., a farmer of Grundy county;
Mary, wife of Archibald Dykes, of Marion
18

county, Tenn.; Thomas B., who was for
many years an official of Grundy county,
and now a resident of Indian Territory;
Nancy J., deceased wife of J. W. Orange,
a prominent citizen of Grundy county,
whose sketch appears elsewhere in this
work; and Melinda, who married Lucian
Bain and died in Warren county, Tenn.

The subject of this sketch obtained a
fair education in the school at Altamont,
and was thus well fitted for the responsible
duties of life. In May, 1861, he joined the
boys in gray as a member of Company H,
Fourth Tennessee Cavalry, under Captain
Glover, and was in the service until the
close of the war, participating in many
raids, skirmishes and battles, including the
engagements at Fishing Creek and Murfreesboro. Just before the battle of Chickamauga he was taken prisoner, sent to Camp
Chase, Ohio, and later to Rock Island, Ill.,
where he was confined until hostilities had
ceased. Before this he had been a prisoner
in Nashville for two months, and in all was
a prisoner of war for over two years.

On his return to the south he spent one
year in Trigg and Christian counties, Ky.,
and then came to Sequatchie county, Tenn.,
locating near Dunlap, where he engaged in
farming and in the manufacture of brick.
He also served as trustee of that county for
one year, and took quite an active interest
in public affairs. As a brick mason, he was
for many years in the employ of the Tennessee Coal, Iron & Railroad Company,
and has made his home in Tracy City since
1885, being numbered among its valued and
honored citizens.

In Sequatchie county Mr. Lockhart was
united in marriage with Miss Elizabeth

Pankey, who was born in that county February 29, 1844, a daughter of Thomas Pankey, and they have become the parents of four children, namely: Albert Sydney Johnston, a miner of Tracy City; Sallie, wife of John W. Carick, also a miner of that place; and Milton Dixie and Frank Cheatham, who are similarly employed. William V. died in infancy. The parents are earnest and consistent members of the Primitive Baptist church, and Mr. Lockhart is now serving as deacon and clerk of the Oak Hill church. Politically he is identified with the Democracy, and socially affiliates with the United Confederate Veterans.

JOSHUA C. SMITH, one of South Pittsburg's wide-awake and popular business men, is the manager of the Tennessee Coal, Iron & Railroad Company's store. He was born on a farm near Sparta, White county, Tenn., June 6, 1856, and is a son of Carroll and Katie (Bradley) Smith.

It is thought that Carroll Smith, our subject's father, was born in North Carolina. He died about the year 1857, and at about the age of forty-five years. The mother was born at Crossville, Cumberland county, Tenn., in 1821, and is now residing in Montague county, Texas. In 1858, after the death of her husband, the mother, in company with friends, took her family and started for the state of Arkansas in an ox wagon. The family made their home in Van Buren county, Ark., until 1876, when the mother, our subject and some of the other members of the family went to Boone county, in the northwestern part of the state of Arkansas.

She afterward moved to Montague county, Tex. Her family consisted of nine children, seven of whom are still living, and of whom we have the following record: William, a farmer in Van Buren county, Ark.; Andrew, a farmer in Van Buren county, Ark.; Silas is a farmer in Montague county, Tex.; Henry is a farmer in Van Buren county, Ark.; D. M. is an attorney of Montague county, Tex.; Mary, the widow of Lee Lloyd, is now living in Boone county, Ark.; Joshua C., the subject of this sketch. The deceased are Jane, who was the wife of Frank Maxwell, died in Boone county, Ark.; and Kurg, a farmer by occupation, died in Boone county, Ark., in 1897.

Joshua C. Smith, the subject of our sketch, was educated in the public schools of Van Buren and Boone counties, Ark., and at a very early age he began earning his own living. In 1881, he returned to White county, Tenn., and for a short time was employed by some saw mill people in Warren county. Two years later he went to Crossville, Tenn., and opened a store there, but, after continuing in business for three years on the credit system, was unable to make collections and consequently was obliged to close his business. Afterward, however, he paid all of his debts in full. After discontinuing his business at Crossville he went to Sparta, White county, Tenn., and was there employed by England Bros., in their store at that place for three years. He next went to Montague county, Tex., and was in a store there for two years, after which he returned to Tennessee, and entered the employ of the Tennessee Coal, Iron & Railroad Company, and served in their store at Whitwell as a salesman. Four years later he was promoted to the position of manager of the company's store at South Pittsburg, the position he now holds. Mr. Smith is a man of sterling qualities, superior business ability and has learned the various details of his business by years of varied experience. In public and social life, also, he is held in the highest respect and esteem, and while living in Cumberland county the Democratic party chose him for their candidate for sheriff, and although the county was very strongly Republican, he was defeated by but a very small majority.

May 24, 1893, Mr. Smith was united in marriage to Miss Sallie Vincent, a daughter of Dr. A. F. Vincent, of Manchester, Coffee county, Tenn., where she was born, and to this union one daughter, Hyder, has been born. Mrs. Smith is a member of the Missionary Baptist church, and our subject is a member of the fraternity of the Knights of Pythias and is an officer in his lodge. He also affiliates with the Woodmen of the World lodge. Politically he is a Democrat.

EPHRIAM H. THURMAN.—Sequatchie county is not without its share of well-regulated farms, the income from which form so large a part of the wealth of the Sequatchie valley. One of these carefully cultivated tracts of land belongs to the gentleman whose name introduces these paragraphs. It is located in the Sixth district and the owner has furnished it with buildings of substantial construction and of good design.

Mr. Thurman was born December 23, 1844, the son of Ephriam and Rosa (Rogers) Thurman, who reared a family of fourteen children, nine sons and five daughters. The names of the sons are as follows: James, Wesley, Stephen, Isaac, Oliver M., Joseph, John, George G. and Ephriam, the subject of this sketch and the only son now living. The daughters were, Lucinda, Eliza, Martha, Rosa and Lettie, of whom Rosa is the only one now living. Our subject was reared on a farm, and, upon the breaking out of the Civil war, he enlisted in Company C, Twelfth Regiment of Tennessee, in the Union army. He served in this capacity until the close of the war in middle and western Tennessee, but was engaged in none of the prominent battles. He was discharged at Nashville, Tenn., in 1865, after which he returned to his home in Sequatchie county and, for a short time, he resumed his studies in the district school. Throughout his entire career his principal occupation has been that of a farmer, although he has done some teaming and selling goods. As a farmer he is thrifty and frugal and has become one of the prominent and well-to-do citizens of the district and has accumulated considerable means. He is a man of excellent ability and thoroughly understands the details of his occupation. He enjoys the advantages of a fair education, is a pleasant and courteous gentleman and makes friends wherever he goes. He is a man of the highest character, and is esteemed as a warm friend and a loyal citizen by all who know him.

September 1, 1892, Mr. Thurman was united in marriage to Miss Martha Britton, daughter of John and Sarah J. L. (Peters) Britton, and their home has been blessed by the presence of a family of three children: Rosa B., Mary J. and Martha Lou. Mr. and Mrs. Thurman are both members of the Christian church, and the former is performing the duties of deacon of the society in which they hold their membership. Socially he affiliates with the Grand Army of the Republic.

HON. ANDREW JACKSON McELROY, long a well-known and prominent business man of Van Buren county, was born April 24, 1820, at Rock Island, in what was then Warren county. Later that district became a part of White county, subsequently was made a part of Van Buren county, but is now again a part of Warren county. His parents were Andrew and Martha (Shropshire) McElroy, the former of Scotch-Irish descent, and the latter of English lineage. The father was born in Oglethorp county, Ga., and in 1820 removed with his family to Tennessee, locating at Caney Fork. Six years later he took up his residence at the present home of our subject, and conducted the old public house or tavern on the state road, leading from the southwest to the east, at which place they entertained many congressmen and other men of note who were travelling to Washington. Andrew McElroy here became the owner of 640 acres of land, which at the time of his purchase was improved only with a log cabin and an orchard. He carried on farming and stock raising throughout the remainer of his days and placed his land under a high state of cultivation. His

death occurred in June, 1864, at the age of seventy-three years, and his wife, also a native of Oglethorp county, Ga., died August 19, 1868, at the age of eighty-two. They were buried by the side of the road on the old home farm, almost directly in front of where their residence once stood.

Mr. McElroy, of this review, was the third in order of birth in their family of six children. Only two are now living, the other being his sister Eliza, widow of James Sparkman and a resident of Sparta. Those who have passed away are Louvana, who became the wife of John Sparkman and at her death was buried in the family cemetery; John, who died in Georgia in childhood; James, who was a twin brother of Eliza and was killed by a fall from a horse, his remains also being interred in the family graveyard; and Martha, wife of Thomas Witt, who died on the home place and was buried there.

Andrew J. McElroy was educated in the district schools of the neighborhood and at the age of twenty-two began teaching in his home district, where he followed that profession for four or five terms. Soon after the organization of Van Buren county, he was chosen justice of the peace, but when people began to call him squire he resigned the office. He served for two years as sheriff, for a similar period as county trustee and for sixteen years as circuit clerk, during which time he studied law and fitted himself for practice at the bar. He was in the circuit clerk's office at the time the Civil war was inaugurated and putting aside his duties there he responded to the call of the South, remaining in the service until the close of hostilities. He belonged to General Dibrell's command, participated in the battle of Simpson's Mills, and was taken prisoner at Sparta, but was soon released. The following week he was again captured, but was only held a prisoner for three days.

Mr. McElroy lost all he had during the war save the land which he owned, but with characteristic energy, upon his return home, he began the task of retrieving his lost possessions. In 1869 he was admitted to the bar and has since engaged in the general practice of law in all the state courts. He has the power of keen and close analysis, which added to a careful preparation of his cases has won him many successes before court and jury. In addition to his professional duties he is engaged in farming and stock raising and in this finds a profitable source of income.

In his political predilections Mr. McElroy has been a life-long Democrat, and is a recognized leader of the party in Van Buren county. In 1884 he was elected a member of the state senate, in which he served for two years with credit to himself and satisfaction to his constituency. He was a member of the committees on finance, judiciary and railroads and was chairman of the state department committee, and his comprehensive knowledge of jurisprudence ably fitted him for the framing of the laws of the commonwealth.

In the month of February, 1845, Mr. McElroy married Jane Webb, who was born in White county in 1825, and died December 10, 1867, leaving three children who are now living: Louvina, who is the widow of Daniel Davis and resides on her father's farm; Sarah, widow of William L.

Acuff; and Andrew J., who is also living on the farm. The members of the family now deceased are James K. Polk, who died September 29, 1870, and who would have been twenty-one years of age the following day; Martha became the wife of John Davis and died in 1890; Eliza died May 29, 18 , at the age of fifteen years; William C., who was born December 14, 1861, and followed farming, died July 19, 1885. Mr. McElroy was again married September 5, 1869, his second union being with Martha Doyle, who was born Saturday, December 31, 1842, in White county, Tenn. She was the daughter of Merrill Doyle, and the widow of John Greer, who died in White county. Mr. and Mrs. McElroy are members of the Antioch Christian church, in which he has served as an official. He is a member of the Masonic lodge of Spencer and of the Independent Order of Odd Fellows. Fidelity to duty in all the relations of life has won him the respect and confidence of those with whom he has come in contact and he well deserves mention among the representative citizens of Van Buren county.

LEANDER T. BILLINGSLEY is a well-known and respected citizen of Bledsoe county, whose home and base of operations is situated not far from the village of Billingsley. His principal occupation is that of a farmer, although he has taught a few terms of school since locating at his present home. He was born October 20, 1843, the son of John Billingsley.

The father of our subject was a son of

Captain Samuel and Mary Billingsley. The Captain was a soldier in the Revolutionary war and was once wounded during that struggle. He afterward moved to the Sequatchie valley and died in Bledsoe county. He was a member of the Missionary Baptist church, and a charter member of the first Masonic lodge in Bledsoe county. He died in the year 1816, at the age of sixty-nine years, and his wife passed away in 1838, at the age of eighty-five years. John Billingsley was first married October 10, 1802, and the same year he and his bride started from North Carolina on a blind pony to find for themselves a home. They finally reached the Sequatchie valley with a cash capital of one dollar and twenty-five cents. The valley was then one large cane brake, but they located on the farm which Mrs. Harris now makes her home, cleared a strip of ground, and put in and cultivated a crop with their pony. During the spring of the following year this animal fell and broke its leg, so the second crop was put in and cultivated with a young bull. Arising from these humble circumstances under which he began life, he became one of the wealthy and prominent men of eastern Tennessee, and at his death John Billingsley's property was valued at eighty-five thousand dollars, an example of what can be accomplished by push and energy and an immoderate amount of patient, persistent effort. For forty years this gentleman was a member of the county court, and a part of this time he was chairman of this body. He also represented his county in the state legislature. He died in the Sequatchie valley, May 25, 1856, at the age of seventy-six years, and his first wife died

in 1829 at the age of forty-three years. To this first marriage were born ten children, nine of whom lived to rear families, and one of whom, Elizabeth, wife of James Rankin, is still living. Of the sons, Samuel was a Baptist preacher, Calvin was a farmer, and A. B. Billingsley and J. D. Billingsley were very prominent Christians.

September 13, 1831, John Billingsley was married to Jane Hoodenpyle, daughter of Phillip Hoodenpyle, born in Raleigh, N. C., April 21, 1812. She died in Bledsoe county, Tenn., in September, 1894. To this last union were born nine children, all of whom lived to rear families, and eight of whom are now living: Mary T., widow of Reuben Rankin; P. M., a farmer of Marshall county, Tenn.; Amanda, wife of John Rankin, of Pikeville; Hixey, wife of Jesse Hall, died in Pikeville; Viola, widow of William Farmer; Leander T., the subject of this sketch, owns the old home, is farming and trading in stock; the wife of T. A. Reynolds; Sarah, wife of Frank Hutcheson; and Eva J., wife of John Swafford.

Leander T. Billingsley attended the Sequatchie College eight months after the war. June 16, 1861, he joined Branham's battalion of cavalry, and one year later he joined Company F, Second Tennessee Cavalry, Confederate. He participated in the battles of Fishing Creek, Stubensville, Ky., Murfreesboro, Chickamauga, and several other battles; and his command was in Kentucky to relieve Morgan, when our subject rode eleven days and nights. Mr. Billingsley's clothes were cut several times by passing bullets, but he was never wounded. He was taken prisoner by Michigan troops at Smith's Cross Roads, now known as Dayton, Tenn., and was taken to Sale Creek, Chattanooga, Nashville, Louisville, Camp Morton, Ind., and Camp Delaware, and from the latter place he was released at the close of the war. He then returned to his home in Bledsoe county, Tenn., and began farming on the old Billingsley farm, but later he moved to his present home. December 23, 1873, our subject was united in marriage to Miss Mary E. Worthington, daughter of James Worthington. Mrs. Billingsley was born May 27, 1849, and died April 1, 1890. To this union were born seven children, five of whom are still living: Samuel W., now a United States soldier in Cuba; Flora, deceased; John, Lula, Grover and Leander S., all living at home; and Mary Della, deceased. Mr. Billingsley was married again February 9, 1898. The family is connected with the Christian church. Politically Mr. Billingsley is a stalwart supporter of the Democratic party, and for twelve years has held the office of justice of the peace.

WILLIAM BLACKSTONE McDANIEL.—The family name of our subject is one which has long and honorably been associated with the history of Tennessee, and it is now worthily worn by W. B. McDaniel, who ranks among the most prominent and esteemed residents of Marion county. He was born in Yancey county, N. C., near Burnsville, May 9, 1831, and is a son of Rev. Goodson and Naomi (Young) McDaniel. His father was born in Warren county, Tenn., August 19, 1803, and

died February 23, 1887, on Sand Mountain, Ala., after a long and useful life. His father, David McDaniel, was a native of Virginia, and about the year 1780 was married and removed to Tennessee, locating on Hickory creek, in Warren county. In 1813 he removed from there to Old Bolivar, Ala., which was then an Indian domain. He attempted to raise a crop, but this was a serious infraction of the Federal law at that time, and his crop was destroyed by regular soldiers. He, however, succeeded in making his escape, but his place was watched for some time in the hope of capturing him. His wife, during that period, would hang out a sheet if it was safe for him to venture home, but if the soldiers were near the sheet was taken in, and he was thus warned to keep in hiding. After a time he got a permit from the nation to open a blacksmith shop, which gave him a right to remain, and in connection with that industry he also engaged in raising stock. Not long afterward, however, he came to Tennessee, locating on land that is now a part of South Pittsburg, and there made his home until his death. He and his wife now sleep in the cemetery at South Pittsburg.

Goodson McDaniel was their fifth child. His father was in limited circumstances, and under great disadvantages he acquired the education which he was so anxious to receive. He first received his preliminary education near South Pittsburg, and then attended school at Brainard, an old Indian mission school. Later he engaged in teaching in the Sequatchie valley, and at Nicojack was engaged in instructing the children of Holt, a Cherokee Indian. Again he attended school in order to perfect his own education, and through his earnest effort and by extensive reading he became a well-informed man. He was endowed by nature with strong mentality, and his abilities, both natural and acquired, made him one of the leading men of his section of the state. In early life, probably before 1820, he joined the Methodist church, and in 1823 became connected with the Holston conference, of which he was a member at the time of his death, though his relation therewith had not been continuous. Gov. William J. Brownlow did his first church work under the Rev. McDaniel, and they continued life-long friends, in spite of their political differences.

Mr. McDaniel continued his labors in the ministry throughout his entire life, and experienced all the hardships of the circuit rider in sparsely settled districts. The last circuit of which he had charge was Black Mountain, in North Carolina, where his duties were particularly difficult on account of the wildness of the country, but he never shrank from any task, no matter how much hardship it might involve. His was a consecrated, noble life, and the world is better for his having lived. During his residence in North Carolina, from 1829 until 1838, he was not connected with the Holston conference.

Rev. Goodson McDaniel was united in marriage with Miss Naomi Young, daughter of Wesley Young, who was drowned in the Catawba river in North Carolina. By her marriage she became the mother of six children, of whom two died in infancy, while four are still living, namely: William B.; Mary L., a resident of Marion county; Rachel L., wife of William Owen, of Se-

quatchie City; and Nancy E., wife of George W. Moore. The mother of this family was also a devout Christian, holding membership in the Methodist church. She was killed April 29, 1842, by a falling limb of a tree, and the father afterward married Rachel B. Longacre, an educated lady and a teacher of prominence, who died just before the war. They were married in Wytheville, Virginia. For his third wife, Goodson McDaniel chose Mrs. Elizabeth Cagle, a widow who is now living in Rising Fawn, Ga. After his first marriage he located in North Carolina, where he remained until 1838, and in connection with his ministerial duties he carried on farming. In that year he came to Marion county, Tenn., locating on the south side of the river in the Eighth civil district, on land that belonged to his daughter, Mary L. McDaniel. There he resided for four years, and in 1842 removed to the farm now occupied by George W. Moore, near McDaniel chapel. In 1859 he again joined his old conference and took charge of the Trenton circuit, which included the corners of Alabama, Georgia and Tennessee, and consisted of eighteen appointments. In 1860 he was stationed at Cleveland, Bradley county, where he remained for one year. He then continued on the farm until 1862, when he removed to Sand Mountain, Jackson county, Ala., making his home there until his death. From 1844 until 1848 he taught in the old Sam Houston Academy, at Jasper, and his wife was a teacher in the same institution. He was an able educator as well as minister, and was a supporter of every interest that tended to elevate humanity. He gave his political support to the Whig party and was opposed to secession. Socially he was a Royal Arch Mason and was an earnest advocate of the temperance cause, by example and precept supporting that measure. On one occasion he was offered the degree of D. D. by Emory & Henry College, but did not accept it, willing to labor in the service of the Master, without honors bestowed by men. He built at his own expense, in 1857, McDaniel chapel, which was named in his honor, but it was destroyed by the Federal troops in the Civil war; however, it has since been rebuilt by Mr. G. W. Moore, and stands as a monument to the upright life of Mr. McDaniel. His influence is immeasurable, but the memory of his noble life remains as a blessed benediction to all who knew him and is enshrined in the hearts of his many friends who loved him for his unostentatious yet godly life.

William B. McDaniel, whose name introduces this review, acquired the greater part of his education in the Sam Houston Academy, from 1844 to 1848. Before this, however, he had received instructions from his father, who then taught the Gilliam school. Later he studied under Absalom Bly, and in 1842–3 attended a school taught by his father at Coal City, and in 1843–4 at Rice Place, where Inmann is now located. Thus provided with good educational privileges, he was well fitted for the practical duties of life, and is accounted one of the intelligent and valued citizens of the community in which he resides.

Since 1852 he has resided upon his present farm, and in that year raised his first crop there. He owns three hundred acres of valuable land on the south side of the Tennessee river, and to its care and cultiva-

19

tion devotes his energies, having made it one of the best farms in the district. He is progressive and enterprising and the many improvements on the place indicate his careful supervision. His labors were interrupted, however, during the Civil war, for in the fall of 1861 he joined the Tennessee state troops, and on the 1st of January, 1862, became a member of Rankins' company, Stearns regiment of Confederate troops, which command was attached to the army of General Forrest. He participated in many engagements, and after the battle of Chickamauga was detailed to do scouting duty in his own neighborhood. He was taken prisoner October 14, 1863, while at the home of G. W. Moore, and sent to Camp Morton, Indianapolis, where he was held until May, 1865. In politics he has always been a stalwart Democrat. In 1842 he united with the Methodist church, and is now a member of the board of trustees of McDaniel chapel. Socially he was a Mason until after the war and has held membership in the Grange and the Farmers Alliance. Almost his entire life has been passed in Marion county, and his circle of friends is almost co-equal with the circle of his acquaintances.

———

REUBEN S. HAMBY, who is postmaster and a general storekeeper at Hebbertsburg, is one of Cumberland county's best known citizens. Mr. Hamby was born February 13, 1843, and is a son of Levi and Sarah (Norris) Hamby, both natives of Wilkes county, N. C., where they were married. Levi Hamby was born in 1803 and went to Tennessee with his father in 1830. When about seventy-seven years old he settled upon the farm which is now owned by our subject. He was a farmer and hunter by occupation, and improved this property in an excellent manner. He was a Democrat in the early days, but after the war a Republican. Both he and his wife were members of the Christian church, in which the former was a deacon. They had seven children, five of whom are now living: G. N., who is a farmer of the Seventh district; Frankie, wife of John Potter, a farmer, of Morgan county, Tenn.; Elizabeth, who is married to C. P. McNeal, a farmer, who resides on Yellow creek; Reuben S., the subject of this sketch; Sarah, the wife of J. W. Mitchell, also of Yellow Creek. Those deceased are Hebbert and James H. Hebbert died in 1875. He was a soldier in the First Tennessee Federal Mounted Infantry, and served three years in the late war. He took part in every battle in which his command was engaged, and was honorably discharged upon the expiration of his term of enlistment. The town of Hebbertsburg was named after him. It had been known as Yellow Creek postoffice, but was re-named Hebbertsburg in 1865. James H. was also in the same company during the war, and received a wound at one time which nearly proved fatal. He survived, however, and was discharged at the same time as his brother. His death occurred in the early '70s. Reuben spent the early days of his life in the Seventh district of Cumberland county, where he was educated. He was still a very young man when, August 20th, 1861, he enlisted in Company E, First Tennessee Federal

Infantry, at Camp Dick Robinson, Ky., under Col. Byrd. He reached the camp by going through the mountains from his home, in order to escape the enemy's pickets. The First Tennessee, which was soon afterwards mounted, was captured by the Confederates, but the prisoners were exchanged and our subject went to Camp Chase, Ohio. He was not long afterward taken ill with white swelling, which incapacitated him for army service. He was accordingly discharged and returned to his home. Upon his recovery he engaged in farming, upon the place where he now resides, which is in the Seventh district, but a short distance from Hebbertsburg. At that time he had little money and the prospects were far from encouraging, but by his perseverance, energy and industry he has since secured one of the finest and most modern farms in the county, comprising four hundred acres and is now in very easy circumstances. Mr. Hamby is a Republican in politics, and, with the exception of the office of postmaster at Hebbertsburg, which he has held for sixteen years, never occupied a public position. He has never desired office, and has been frequently been compelled to decline most flattering nominations, which were often equivalent to election.

In 1867 Mr. Hamby married Miss Martha J. Farmer, a daughter of Enoch and Susan Farmer. Mr. and Mrs. Hamby are the parents of thirteen children, one of whom, Ona, died in infancy. The others are living. Noah, the eldest, resides in Morgan county, Tenn. Franklin lives in Cumberland county. Laura is the wife of John Aytes, a farmer of the Seventh district, of the same county. Dexter and Albert are at home. Lulu is the wife of Jack Adkins, of Morgan county. Cora is married to W. J. Smith, a farmer of the Seventh district, while Nora is at home and Flora is the wife of Joe Smith, of Cumberland county. Alvin, Ivory and Charles are at home. Mr. Hamby and his wife are members of the Christian church, in which he is a deacon.

SAMUEL WERNER, Sr., comes from the beautiful land of the Alps, and the strongest and most creditable characteristics of its people have been marked elements in his life and have enabled him to win success in the face of opposing circumstances. He possesses the energy and determination which mark the Swiss race, and by the exercise of his powers he has steadily progressed, and has not only a handsome competence, but has commanded universal respect by his straightforward business methods. For several years he has been prominently identified with the business interests of Tracy City, and is now quite extensively engaged in the manufacture of all kinds of building material, furniture, etc.

Mr. Werner was born in Switzerland August 23, 1832, and in that country his parents, Jacob and Annie (Bendel) Werner, spent their entire lives. The father, who was a brick and stone mason, fell from a house while at work, and was killed, at the age of sixty-four years. He had served in the Swiss army, and both he and his wife were consistent members of the Lutheran church and most highly respected people. She died when our subject was a mere child, leaving four children, the others being as follows: Isaac, who was a carpenter by trade, came to the United States and located in Virginia, but at the end of seven years returned to Switzerland, where he subsequently died; Henry, a brick and stone mason, died in his native land; and Jacob also died in Switzerland during boyhood.

At an early age Mr. Werner, of this review, began learning the carpenter's trade in his native land, receiving most thorough instruction. After he had mastered the business he worked at the same in many of the countries of Europe, including France, Italy and Germany, and while in the first named he learned to speak the French language. After working at his trade for many years he was made foreman of a car shop in his native land—a most responsible position, which he creditably filled for ten years; or until coming to the United States, in 1868. For five years he made his home in New York city, and then came to Tennessee and bought a farm in the Swiss colony. During the eight years of his residence thereon he and his family cleared away the heavy growth of timber and placed the land under a high state of cultivation. He then purchased a place near Tracy City and improved it, in the meantime entering the employ of the Tennessee Coal, Iron & Railroad Company at that place, as a pattern maker, and working for them for a number of years. In 1890 he started his saw and planing mill on a small scale, but as his trade has increased he has enlarged his business facilities, and now manufactures not only all kinds of building materials, but all kinds of furniture as well. In the mill alone employment is furnished to from twenty-five to thirty men, and he is now doing a large and profitable business. His home is near his mill, and surrounding him are his children who are married. He owns some of the choicest residence property in Tracy City, as well as quite a number of first-class tenement houses. He has built up an extensive trade in neighboring towns, and everything he does is done in a practical, businesslike manner that at once commands the confidence of the public and the respect of his fellow citizens.

Mrs. Werner, who bore the maiden name of Elisabeth Kramer, is also a native of Switzerland, and five of their seven children were born in that country. Elisabeth is at home; Annie is the wife of E. Scharer, of Tracy City; Henry is in the mill with his father; Mary is the wife of L. Church, of Tracy City; Bertie is the wife of Henry Schild, a wagon maker of the same place; Ernest is a machinist of Macon, Ga.; and Samuel, Jr., is sawyer in the mill. The family hold membership in the Lutheran church, and are widely and favorably known. In politics Mr. Werner is a Republican. His mill is surrounded in a most convenient manner by his dry houses, ware rooms, stables, etc., all of his own planning, and it is safe to say that Grundy county has no more competent, painstaking and reliable business man than he whose name introduces this sketch.

CALVIN CRITDON ANDERSON, one of the most prosperous and substantial agriculturists, as well as one of the leading citizens, of the Thirteenth district, Marion county, Tenn., was born there on the 9th of April, 1859, a son of Joseph and Elizabeth (Riggle) Anderson. During the Civil war the father enlisted in the Confederate service, and after serving a short time all trace of him was lost, since which time nothing has ever been heard of him. The mother then went to live with two brothers, Daniel and Calvin Riggle, and now finds a pleasant home with our subject. She was born in the Seventh district of Marion county, and by her marriage became the mother of two children, the older being Mary, who died when young.

Mr. Anderson was educated at Hales Chapel, in the Thirteenth district, and among his schoolmates was the young lady who afterward became his wife, their courtship commencing while they were students at that institution. Mrs. Anderson, formerly Miss Georgiana Hale, was born in the Thirteenth district, and is a daughter of Washington and Rebecca (Girdley) Hale, in whose family were seven children, namely: Hattie, deceased; Georgiana, Maggie, Mary, Martha, Jennie and Eliza. The father died about fourteen years ago, but the mother is still living, making her home upon a farm in the Thirteenth district. The marriage of Mr. and Mrs. Anderson was celebrated February 13, 1889, and five children grace their union: Estill A., Leola E., Rebecca, Joseph and Clida, all at home.

Mr. Anderson inherited five hundred acres of fine farming land in the Thirteenth district, two hundred acres of which is in the Tennessee valley bordering on the river, and is most valuable property. Farming and stock raising have been his life work, and the success that has crowned his efforts shows that he made no mistake in choosing his calling. His place is one of the most beautiful and attractive to be found in this region, and is a credit to the industry, enterprise and able management of the owner.

Politically Mr. Anderson is a stalwart Democrat, casting his first presidential vote for Grover Cleveland in 1884. In 1896 he was elected justice of the peace at a special election held on account of the former official having resigned, and is now acceptably serving in that position. He has also filled the office of school director since August, 1896, and has discharged his official duties with a promptness and fidelity worthy of all commendation. He is emphatically a man of enterprise, positive character, indomitable energy, strict integrity and liberal views, and is thoroughly identified with the welfare and prosperity of his native county. In religious belief both he and his wife are Methodists.

SETH JOHNSON is the circuit clerk of Sequatchie county. He is a native of the county and was born near where the iron bridge spans the river, June 26, 1848, the son of Francis and Lucinda (Johnson) Johnson. The father was born in the valley about the year 1802, and died in 1862. The mother was born in Roane county, and is still living on the old homestead.

Francis Johnson was one of the early settlers of the valley and helped to remove the Indians from thence to the Ocoee purchase to the Indian territory in 1837. During the first year of the Civil war he joined Captain Stewart's company in the Confederate army. He was appointed a non-commissioned officer and participated in the battles of Shiloh and Corinth. He died at Columbus, Miss., where he is buried. He left a family of four sons and six daughters, eight of whom are now living, as follows: Martha, wife of J. E. Farmer; Sarah, wife of W. E. Kell, Chattanooga; Daniel, a farmer; Seth, the subject of this sketch; William, a farmer; Mary, wife of Z. T. Baker; Lou, wife of Harmon Hinch, a farmer of Lincoln county, Tenn.; G. F. S., of Sequatchie county, Tenn.; Nancy, who died at the age of ten years; and Addie, wife of W. H. Kell. Both Mr. and Mrs. Kell are now dead.

Seth Johnson attended the schools in the district in which he spent his boyhood, and finished his education in the Sequatchie College when Professor Moore had charge of that institution. After finishing his course of study he taught a few terms in connection with his farm work, and also was engaged in selling goods at the Iron Bridge for seven years, but his principal occupation has been that of a farmer. Mr. Johnson has also found time to serve the citizens of his adopted district and county in the capacity of several of the important offices and in every instance he has proved himself a faithful and efficient officer and well worthy of the confidence reposed in him. He was elected sheriff of Sequatchie county and served two terms, or four years. He was for many years a member of the county court, and served as chairman of that body for ten years, or until Judge Carpenter took the chair. In 1897 he was appointed to his present office of clerk of the circuit court. Mr. Johnson is also an attorney, having been admitted to the bar in 1892. Politically he is a Democrat.

August 29, 1871, Mr. Johnson was united in marriage to Miss Lucinda Leona Cannon, a native of Sequatchie county, Tenn., and their wedded life has been blessed by the advent of a family of four children, viz.: A. G., who is connected with the state service at the new penitentiary; Emma L., still living with her parents; L. Josephine, wife of J. R. O. Deakins; and William S. B. Socially Mr. Johnson is a Mason and has three times represented the lodge in which he holds his membership in the grand lodge.

WILLIAM CARROLL HASTONS, for many years prominently connected with the public affairs of Van Buren county, is still one of its most honored and highly-respected citizens, and makes his home in District No. 3, where he owns a large and valuable farm under excellent cultivation and well improved. He was born here March 2, 1829, and on the paternal side is of Dutch descent, his grandfather, Daniel Hastons, being scarcely able to speak English. At an early day he came to Tennessee, locating in Van Buren county, near the spring now known as Hastons' Big Spring, where he purchased the land now owned by our subject. In his family were thirteen children, all now deceased.

The parents of our subject, David and Margaret (Roddey) Hastons, were probably natives of Virginia, and became well-to-do farming people of this county, where they owned a fine place of two hundred acres. Both were active and faithful members of the Cumberland Presbyterian church, and, before a house of worship was erected in their community, services were often held in their home. Politically, the father was an Old-line Whig. Their family numbered twelve children, namely: Wiley B., Daniel, Ollie, Thomas C., Malinda, David M., Peggy, James, Nancy, Isaac, Lucinda, and William C. All have passed away with the exception of our subject and Lucinda, who is now the widow of Abraham Trodglen, of Warren county, Tenn. The parents both died before the war, the mother preceding her husband three or four years, and their remains were interred in the Big Fork cemetery.

The only educational advantages William C. Hastons received were such as the local schools of his day afforded; but his training at farm work was not so meager, and he early became a thrifty and industrious farmer. He was married, December 3, 1848, to Miss Jane Denney, who was born in Van Buren county, April 27, 1829, a daughter of William and Patty (Burnett) Denney. They became the parents of the following children: Charles T., who married Miss Ellet Morgan and lives in White county, Tenn.; Maggie, wife of Dr. Shepherd, of Yell county, Ark.; David L., who married Miss Tabitha Davis and lives in Hickory, White county; William C., who married Lobelia Morgan and is now deceased; Sarah and John, both deceased; Sophia, wife of Frank Davis, of Van Buren county, living near her father's old home; and Mollie, deceased. The mother, who was a consistent member of the Methodist Episcopal church, departed this life August

1, 1886, leaving many friends, as well as her family, to mourn her loss.

In 1863 Mr. Hastons was a member of the militia of Tennessee, called by Colonel Stanton, and was stationed for a time at Fishing Creek, after which he returned home. He is a stalwart Democrat in politics, and has taken quite an active and prominent part in public affairs, filling the offices of constable, deputy sheriff for fourteen years, sheriff for two years (being elected in 1860), justice of the peace for the long period of thirty-four years, and chairman for eight years. He faithfully and satisfactorily discharged every duty devolving upon him, and his public and private career are alike above reproach. In religious connection he is a member of the Methodist Episcopal church.

NASE SWAFFORD, ex-chairman of the county court of Bledsoe county, was born within two hundred yards of his present home. He is a farmer by occupation and owns and occupies a pleasant and valuable tract of land near Melvine, where he is pursuing the even tenor of his way, gaining worldly goods and enjoying the comfort of a happy household and home.

Mr. Swafford is a son of Thomas Y. and Hannah (Hankins) Swafford. It is thought that Thomas Y. Swafford was also born in the Valley. He lived on the farm on which he died for about fifty years. He was a very successful farmer, a Republican in politics and died June 2, 1880, at the age of seventy-four years, and his wife died January 6, 1881. They were the parents of a family of twelve children, five of whom are now living: Mariah, wife of William Mc-Clennan; Nase, the subject of this sketch; Lieutenant Sam; Thomas and A. H., all of whom are living on different parts of the old home farm. The deceased are: William died on the home farm. He was a soldier in the Northern army. James, also a soldier in the Northern army, was killed at Crossville. Polly died in infancy. Martha Jane died when quite young. Ursaline. Clara U. died in childhood.

Nase Swafford, the subject of this sketch, was born in December, 1840. He spent his school days in Bledsoe county and finished his education at the academy at Pikeville. His entire life has been spent in Bledsoe county, and, in fact, on the farm on which he was born. His wife, who bore the maiden name of Miss Marcissa Worthington, was one of his schoolmates. She was born August 21, 1842, the daughter of Robert Worthington, became the wife of our subject June 7, 1862, and died December 4, 1893. They were the parents of a family of twelve children, eleven of whom are now living, and of whom we have the following record: Sam and Ursaline, at home; Robert, of Greenville county, Tex.; James, at home; Dorris; Thomas D.; Joe; William; Hannah died in childhood; Nettie; Dona and Mollie.

Although Mr. Swafford is living on a portion of his father's vast estate, he has put upon his share all of the improvements that now add so much to its appearance and value. In 1862 he erected his home, and since then has set out an orchard and put up all structures that will add to the convenience of carrying on the work of the farm. In 1868 he was elected sheriff of Bledsoe county and held that office four years. In 1882 he was elected justice of the peace and has held that position continuously ever since. He has also served three very successful terms as chairman of the county court of Bedsoe county. Politically he is a Republican. He is a pleasant neighbor, genial, warm-hearted, and has an agreeable family.

A ZARIAH DORTON is a prominent citizen of Cumberland county, and one of the most progressive, enterprising and successful agriculturists of the Eighth district, where he lives. Mr. Dorton was born in Rhea county, Tenn., August 2, 1839, and is the son of Joseph and Rebecca Dorton, whose maiden name was Davenport, natives respectively of Scott and Russell counties, Virginia. They were married in their native state and soon afterward came to Tennessee, settling in Rhea county. From 1840 until 1856 they resided in Bledsoe county, but in the latter year, the county of Cumberland was created out of part of the former and Mr. Dorton's possessions lying within the boundaries of the new county he became quite prominent in its earlier official life, and was for one term a trustee. Here he and his wife lived until called away by death. Joseph Dorton died at his home in the Eleventh district, in 1890, aged about ninety, and his wife followed him to the grave one year later, aged ninety-one. Mr. Dorton was a farmer by occupation, and a great admirer of horses. He was politically a Republican. Both he and his wife

were members of the Methodist church. They had nine children, but one of whom, our subject, is now living. Moses, the eldest, was killed by guerrillas during the war. Sidney Jane died in Cumberland county, as did Dealthea, who was a young girl at the time of her taking off. James M. was a soldier in the Second Tennessee Federal Infantry, Company D, being its first lieutenant. He was taken prisoner in Hawkins county, Tenn., November 6, 1863, and was carried with the rest of the prisoners toward the Confederate prison, but escaped near Wyeth Hill, Va.

He joined his command twenty days later, and not long afterward, in February, 1864, he was again taken prisoner, in Grassy Cove, Cumberland county, by guerrillas, but was released by them the same day, though not until he was reduced to a destitute condition. In the following April he was appointed provost marshal at Maysville, Blount county, but in September of the same year was again captured by the Confederates. Once again fortune favored him, and he escaped, after four days, and with difficulty made his way to the Federal camp at Knoxville, where he remained until mustered out of the service. After his discharge he returned to Blount county, and there carried on farming until his death, in 1870. Mary was the wife of Elijah Ford, of Cumberland county; she died in 1861. Joseph died when a child. Martha, who was the wife of Wade H. McFall, of Rhea county, died in the early '70s. Azariah was educated in Cumberland county, and on the 14th of August, 1861, left home, dodged the Confederate pickets by going through the mountains, a distance of about two hundred miles, but in such a circuitous course that it took some sixteen days, and enlisted at Camp Dick Robinson, Ky., in Company D, Second Tennessee Federal Infantry, afterward mounted. He served as a sergeant, and took part in many battles, among which may be mentioned Mill Springs, Stone River, siege of Knoxville, Blue Springs, Wildcat Gap, Cumberland Gap, and others, some twenty-seven in all. At Maryville, in Blount county, Tenn., he was made a prisoner for five days, and then released. At another time, November 6, 1863, his company was captured in Hawkins county, but he and two of the soldiers had been cut off from the others and they escaped. Mr. Dorton had many thrilling encounters and enough wonderful experiences during his war service to make a very interesting little volume, were they to be preserved in writing, and it is indeed surprising how he ever survived them all. After serving from September 1, 1861, to October 6, 1864, in the Federal army, he was mustered out at Knoxville, Tenn., and returned to Cumberland, and for several months was connected with the Home Guards there. After the war Mr. Dorton became a farmer in the Fourth district of Cumberland county, near the head of the valley. He remained there but a short time, and then went to Spring City, in Rhea county, and then back to the old farm in the Eleventh district, where he lived until 1879. In that year he removed to Rockwood, and in 1883 bought his present farm, upon which he has resided since. The place is well improved, with excellent buildings, barns, granaries, etc., and is without doubt one of the model farms of the district.

20

Mr. Dorton is a Republican, and for two years was a justice of the peace in the Eleventh district. He was also county assessor for four years. He is a Freemason, and a member of the G. A. R. post at Crossville, of which he has been vice-commander.

On the 11th of January, 1866, Mr. Dorton married Miss Carrie Emeline Brown. She was born in that part of Bledsoe county which has since been annexed to Cumberland, November 22, 1839, and is a daughter of Jesse and Carrie Brown. Mr. and Mrs. Dorton are the parents of five children: Lorena Mowbrey, living at home; Betty Brady, now the wife of Thomas Brady; Thomas B., at home; Lovada DeRosett, the wife of Zachariah DeRosett; and Ollie Anne, living at home.

RUDOLPH MARUGG was born at Klosters, Canton Graubunden, Switzerland, June 27, 1859. In 1873, when fourteen years of age, he came with his father's family to Tennessee and located at Gruetli, in Grundy county, where he resided until 1893. During the latter year he moved with his family to Tracy City, the place of his death, which occurred April 22, 1896.

Rudolph received the common-school education of his native land, which on arrival in this country was supplemented with a few months' country schooling and a term in the University of Tennessee at Knoxville.

For many years he had charge of the public school at the Swiss colony at Gruetli, which he taught in both the German and English languages. He took an active interest in politics and was an uncompromising Democrat. Rudolph Marugg was a prominent member of the Grundy county court for many years. He was best liked where he was best known. He was a man of deep convictions and outspoken in his views. At the time of his death he was a member of the I. O. O. F. and the Royal Arcanum lodges.

In 1884 he was married, at Gruetli, to Miss Anna Heer, who with six children survive him.

BENJAMIN J. BAILEY was born in Wilson county, Tenn., November 15, 1833, a son of Thomas and Nancy (Bennett) Bailey, the former born in North Carolina, November 15, 1890, and died December 23, 1864, and the latter born in southern Georgia in 1797, and died August 11, 1884. Both moved to Marion county, Tenn., in childhood with their parents, were married there and reared a family of eleven children, upon whom they bestowed the following names: Louisa, Cynthia, William, John, James, Malinda, Benjamin J., Martha, Lawson, Almira and Jane. Three of this family, William, James and Almira, are now dead. Our subject's great-grandfather was the first of the family to settle in America, and his son, our subject's grandfather, was Thomas Bailey.

Our subject was educated in the public schools of the district in which he spent his boyhood and worked on a farm until sixteen years of age and then commenced railroad work for the Nashville & Chattanooga company, and was thus engaged for six years. He then returned to his home in Marion county, Tenn., and September 14, 1854, was united in marriage to Miss Emily West, who was also born in Marion county, January 3, 1840. This union has been blessed by the presence of a family of ten children, of whom we have the following record: Margaret J., widow of James Tharp; Nancy, wife of R. E. Davis, a farmer of Marion county, Tenn.; Mary M., wife of George Ealey, who died November 25, 1884; Benjamin C., died October 23, 1888; Amanda; wife of William Holaway, died December 25, 1896; Esther, wife of W. Brown Haloway; James H. married Esther Burnett, and is a blacksmith by occupation; Adam K.; and William E. and John D., both of whom are still living at home.

After his marriage, Mr. Bailey bought a farm which he made his home from 1855 to 1870, and then sold out and went to Missouri, from thence to Arkansas, and then back to Tennessee. He then bought his present farm and has since made it his home. Since then he has opened up the Inman coal mines, and built the railroad from Victoria to the mines, and for three years was engaged in raising ore. He built the railroad incline at Whitwell and ran the coal down the mountain for twenty-two months, but since that time has devoted the most of his time to farming. Socially he affiliates with the G. A. R. fraternity, and he and his wife are both members of the Methodist Episcopal church. Politically he is a Republican, but his first presidential ballot was cast in favor of James Buchanan. He has served as constable of the district and once served as deputy sheriff of Marion county.

Mr. Bailey was also a soldier in the Civil war, joining the Union army, September 7, 1864, and served until June 30, 1865, in the Sixth Tennessee mounted troops under Captain Hurd. He operated for a time in Tennessee, and then went to Dalton, Ga., thence to Resaca, and from there to Nashville, Tenn., but was in none of the larger battles.

MARTIN MARUGG, one of the most prominent and influential citizens of Tracy City, Grundy county, Tenn., where he is successfully conducting a well regulated store. He is endowed with excellent business qualifications, a character of the highest order, and it can safely be said that there are few more energetic or wide-awake men among the younger member of the business population of Grundy county, than the gentleman whose name heads this sketch. He was born in Klosters, Switzerland, in 1861, and is a son of Christian and Anna (Brosi) Marugg, the former of whom was born in 1829, and the latter in 1828. They were married in 1856. Christian Marugg was a merchant in his native land, and was also extensively interested in agriculture in that country. Both the father and grandfather of our subject were president of the district and also held many other positions of trust and honor in their native land. Christian Marugg came to the United States in 1869, and traveled through twenty-eight states, for the purpose of finding a good location with suitable climate, etc., and finally selected Grundy county, Tenn. He returned to his native land in the same year, and in February, 1873, he came with his family and forty others, and located at what is now known as the Swiss Colony, in Grundy county. He made that place his home until 1888, when he, his wife and two of the children returned to Switzerland, where he is engaged in looking after his landed interests. Christian Marugg and family are members of the German Reformed church. While in America he affiliated with the Democratic party. There were five children in the family, three of whom are now living, and of whom we have the following record: Barbara is the wife of John Sabild, a sketch of whom will be found on another page of this volume; Martin, of whom this article is written; George, a merchant of Jasper, Ala., who accompanied his parents when they returned to their native land, but subsequently returned to the United States; Christina was the wife of Henry Nett, and died in Switzerland; and Rudolph, deceased, of whom a sketch will be found below.

Martin Marugg attended the schools in his native land, and, after coming to the United States, attended school at Altamont. Later he supplemented this with a course in the Eastman Business College at Poughkeepsie, N. Y., which fitted him with a thorough business and elementary education. After he had finished his schooling he became assistant bookkeeper and station agent at Tracy City, for the T. C. I. & R. R. Co., a position which he held for three years. During the time that he acted in the above capacity he learned the art of telegraphy, and then spent a portion of the next two years at Chattanooga, where he later on became connected with the Chattanooga "Evening Democrat," and was engaged on newspaper work. Mr. Marugg then located at Nashville, where he secured work on the German paper "Anzeiger Des Sudens," as manager for about one year. After selling his interest in the above paper he located at Gruetli, where he assisted in his father's store for a while. He then went to Birmingham, Ala., where he worked on the "Age-Herald" and from there to Montgomery, in the same state, where he worked as compositor on the "Advertiser." In October, 1888, he returned to Gruetli to take charge of the store prior to his father's return to Switzerland, and in 1891, he removed to Tracy City, where he established the New York Auction store. He has devoted his entire time to his business at this place, and has succeeded in building up an extensive and profitable trade. In 1895 he and others started a telephone line between Tracy City and Beersheba Springs, and since then they have organized the Dixie Telephone Company, of which he is manager. This company has telephone connection with many of the neighboring towns in the vicinity of Tracy City and has just completed an exchange of one hundred and ten subscribers in Tracy City. The subject of this sketch is also one of the incorporators and at present vice-president of the Grundy County Bank.

December 21, 1888, Martin Marugg was united in the holy bonds of wedlock with Miss Elizabeth Schild, a daughter of Peter Schild. She was born in the Canton of Berne, Switzerland, and came to the United States with her parents when she was but three years of age. There has been two children born to bless this congenial union: Brosi and Elsie. Mr. Marugg has always taken an active interest in local political matters, and was a member of the Grundy county auditing committee from 1889 until 1897. Politically he affiliates with the Democratic party, and in his religious life he is a communicant of the German Reformed church. Socially he is a member of the Knights of Pythias, and has represented his lodge in the grand lodge. He also belongs to the Royal Arcanum, which he has also represented in the grand lodge, and is a member of the Swiss Relief Society of Nashville. He is active, intelligent and progressive and every enterprise that is calculated to be of benefit to the community at large receives his earnest support and encouragement.

L EWIS P. BREWER, a public-spirited and enterprising member of the farming community of Sequatchie county, has devoted his entire life to agriculture, in the pursuit of which he has been very fortunate, and is the proprietor of as good a farm as can be found within the limits of Sequatchie county, his home being situated near the village of Mountairy.

In tracing the history of the life of our subject, we find that he is a native of Sequatchie county, which was, at that time, a part of Marion county. He was born October 13, 1831, a son of Lewis P. and Tabitha (Shadrick) Brewer, both of whom were natives of this part of Tennessee. The father died when our subject was ten years of age, or about the year 1841, and the mother died since the war. Their home was for many years on a farm, near Dunlap. They were the parents of a family of five children, of whom we have the following record: Betsy, wife of Henry Russell, a farmer near Jasper; Sallie, of Arkansas; Polly Larramore; Elijah, who died soon after the war; and Lewis P.

Our subject was educated in the district school near Dunlap. After the death of his father the care of the family was left to him and he found it no easy task, as his wages were twenty-five cents per day. Before the war, however, he became possessed of a farm in the Fifth district, Grundy county. He then married and made his home on his farm in Grundy county until about the year 1897. In 1861 he enlisted in the Federal army, and served one year. The principal engagement in which he engaged during this time was the battle of Sheldons Hill. After leaving the army, he returned to his home in Grundy county and there plied the vocation of a farmer until he moved to Sequatchie county, his present home. He is an enterprising and progressive man, and although his start on the road to fortune was beset by a great many difficulties, the courage and fortitude which were dominant traits in his charactor made him equal to every emergency. Patience, too he has always had, contenting himself with diligent, persistent effort and then awaiting the ticking of fortune's wheel for results.

In about the year 1855 Mr. Brewer was united in marriage to Miss Mary Alls, who was born in Marion county, Tenn., in 1840, and to this union have been born a family of twelve children, ten of whom are now living, as follows: William, a farmer near Jasper, Tenn.; Lewis, a farmer on the mountains of Grundy county; Elizabeth, wife of Stephen Brown; Alex, a farmer of the Fifth district, Grundy county; Maggie and Sidney, at home; Rachael, wife of Isaac Turner, Whitwell, Tenn.; Sallie, wife of William Brown, Whitwell, Tenn.; Vesta and Abbie, at home. The two deceased are Benjamin, who died at the age of four years, and an infant. Mrs. Brewer is a member in good standing of the Missionary Baptist church, and our subject is connected with the Grand Army of the Republic. Politically he is a Republican.

BENJAMIN FRANKLIN ASHBURN is a public-spirited and enterprising member of the farming community in Marion county. Although he has done considerable merchandising and worked for a time at tanning, he has devoted the greater part of his life to agriculture, in the pursuit of which he has been very fortunate, and is the proprietor of one of the fine farms in the Third district, where he is making his home and base of operations.

Mr. Ashburn was born on the farm on which he now lives September 14, 1830, a son of Joshua Thompson and Mary G. (Foster) Ashburn, the former born January 3, 1801, in Granger county, Tenn., and the latter was born in Bledsoe county, Tenn., in 1802. Joshua Thompson Ashburn was a son of Martin Ashburn. Our subject's father settled in the Sequatchie Valley, in Marion county, Tenn., when a young man.

He was married in Bledsoe county, Tenn., built the house in which our subject now lives and made that his home until 1850. He then moved to another house on the same farm, and made that his home until his death. His wife died in March, 1857, and is buried at Red Hill cemetery. The father subsequently married. Mrs. Nancy Horn, who died in 1884, and is also buried in Red Hill cemetery. He was an elder in the Cumberland Presbyterian church, was the owner of a large tract of land, and died at his home in 1883. To his first marriage were born ten children, of whom we have the following record: Martin, deceased; Elizabeth, deceased; James, deceased; William, deceased; Benjamin F., the subject of this sketch; Anderson T., deceased; Isaac H., deceased; Sarah O., wife of J. M. Price, a farmer of the Third district; Mary C., widow of Mordica C. Claim, a farmer of Sequatchie county, Tenn.; Martha, wife of W. L. Andes, a farmer of the Third district.

The subject of this sketch was educated in the public schools of Marion county, and afterward taught school for several terms. He bought a portion of his father's farm, just before the war, made that his home and engaged in merchandising at Victoria for five years, and then sold out and went to Whitwell. After operating a mercantile business at that place for six years, he sold out the business and turned his attention to farming. Before the war he started a tannery at his home, and continued the same for a time after the close of the war. In 1863 he enlisted in the Confederate army, under Captain Corn and Colonel Howard, and operated in Kentucky and Tennessee,

returning to his home just before the close of the war and resuming his farming. Politically he is a Democrat, and both he and his wife are members of the Cumberland Presbyterian church, and Mr. Ashburn has served that denomination in the capacity of elder. He is a Master Mason, a man who is held in the highest respect and esteem wherever he is known and has a large circle of warm friends. He has always made his home on the farm he now occupies, even when he was merchandising in Victoria and Whitwell.

August 15, 1854, Mr. Ashburn was united in marriage to Mary Price, who was born in the Third district, Marion county, Tenn., January 7, 1831, a daughter of Charles and Susie Hawkins, and their home has been blessed by the presence of a family of eight children, as follows: Charles married Miss Amanda Andes and is living at Whitwell; Thompson, a Cumberland Presbyterian minister, married a Miss Marlo, and is now living in Evansville, Ind.; Early married Miss Mollie Vinsane, and is making his home in Whitwell; John M., a dentist at Nashville, is still single; William F. married Miss M. Condra and is living in the Third district, Marion county; Ida, wife of Charles Bell, of Bonair, White county, Tenn.; Alice, wife of N. B. Moore, a dentist at Whitwell, Tenn.; and Lucy, who is still living with her parents.

———

LIEUT. GREENBERRY JOHNSON is one of the public-spirited citizens of the First district, Van Buren county, to whose energy and foresight that locality is indebted for many improvements. While Mr. Johnson, as a prosperous business man, has given close attention to his private affairs, he has never forgotten or ignored that bond of common interest which should unite the people of every community, and he is always ready to promote progress in every line.

In De Kalb county, Tenn., Mr. Johnson was born September 18, 1832, a son of Squire and Lavina (Hill) Johnson, the former a native of De Kalb county, the latter of White county, Tenn. The paternal grandparents, Allen and Nancy (Whitely) Johnson, are supposed to have been natives of Virginia, but their marriage was celebrated in De Kalb county. All his life the father of our subject followed the occupation of farming, and was a very energetic, enterprising man. · He gave his political support to the Democracy. He and his wife both held membership in the Baptist church and died in that faith in Van Buren county, the father September 6, 1873, the mother July 15, 1888. They now sleep side by side in the cemetery at Laurel Creek church, Van Buren county. Greenberry is the oldest in their family of eleven children, the others being as follows: John L., deceased; William R.; Samuel M.; James M.; Francis M.; Nancy K. and Lavina J., both deceased; Wesley; and Squire and Sarah, both deceased.

Greenberry Johnson was educated in the schools of Antioch, and before the war successfully engaged in teaching for three sessions. In 1861 he enlisted in the Confederate army at Spencer, and was commissioned first lieutenant of Company I, under Captain York, in Colonel Savage's regiment,

The command first moved to Camp Tronsdale, near Nashville, thence to West Virginia, and, after the battle of Cheat Mountain, proceeded to Port Royal, S. C. They also went to Corinth, Miss., but did not get there in time to take part in the battle at that place. There the regiment, which had enlisted for one year, was reorganized and James Worthington was made first lieutenant of Company I, after which Mr. Johnson returned home, and, with Capt. M. B. Wood, organized a company for T. B. Murray's cavalry battalion. Two months after entering the service they were dismounted and sent to Murfreesboro, but arrived too late for the battle. At Shelbyville they remained until the following spring, and then went to Chattanooga, where our subject was detailed to go home and gather up the stragglers. While engaged in this duty he was taken ill with fever and was captured and paroled by the Federal forces, taking no more active part in the war.

On the 8th of February, 1865, Mr. Johnson was united in marriage with Miss Angeline Russell, who was born in Van Buren county, September 28, 1844, and died March 26, 1876. The children born to them were Flora, now the wife of Murphy Hillis, of the First district, Van Buren county; Albert L., who married Mattie Cravens and lives in Van Buren county; Mary Maud, who became the wife of J. B. Grissom and died February 3, 1898; and Beatrice, who died when about three years old. Mr. Johnson was again married, October 4, 1876, his second union being with Mrs. Mary C. Dyer, who was born in White county, Tenn., October 30, 1839, a daughter of Elijah and Melvina (Halterman) Denton. The only child born of this union, Vodra Smith, died at the age of five years.

In 1868 Mr. Johnson located upon his present farm in the First district, and now has about four hundred acres of highly-cultivated and well-improved land, on which are found the noted Big Bone cave and also the Arch cave. He has probably done more than any other man to improve the grade of hogs in the county, and is justly ranked among the most progressive, reliable and wide-awake farmers of his community.

In his political affiliations Mr. Johnson is a Democrat, and was elected to the office of county court clerk, which position he held for three years, resigning at the end of that time to enter the army. For about a quarter of a century he has been justice of the peace, which position he now holds, and ten years of that time has served as chairman of the county court, while for twenty-five years he was also postmaster of Rocky River, an office that has since been discontinued. In 1876 Mr. Johnson was elected to the office of county superintendent of public instruction, which position he held for two years. When he came into office he found the schools financially embarrassed, teachers having to wait one and two years for their pay. While in office Mr. Johnson organized a system by which the schools of Van Buren county have ever since been able to pay their teachers at the end of the term. He has also served as a trustee of Burritt College since 1878, he having given as much or more time and money than any man in the county toward the erection of the same. This college has sent out many able ministers of the gospel of the Christian faith, as well as physicians,

lawyers, judges and statesmen. Mr. Johnson's public service has been most exemplary, and his private life marked by the utmost fidelity to duty. In the Christian church he and his estimable wife hold membership, and in the social life of the community occupy an enviable position.

THOMAS WILLIAM MORRISON, one of Bledsoe county's wide-awake and industrious citizens, is making a good support by plying the trade of a painter, and is incidentally laying aside something for a rainy day. He was born near Kingston, Roane county, Tenn., January 12, 1857, and is a son of William D. and Deborah (Holmes) Morrison, the former born in Roane county and died in the same county in 1887, at the age of sixty-four years; and the latter born in Greene county, Tenn., and died in Roane county in the year 1867, at the age of about forty-five years.

William D. Morrison was a son of John Morrison, who was a native of Virginia. The latter moved to Roane county, Tenn., and settled on Riley's Creek. He was a soldier in the contest known as the Creek and Seminole war, and was under the command of General Coffee, who had command of the Tennessee forces. He served thus in the years 1812 and 1813. He died March 17, 1864, toward the close of the late war at the age of sixty-nine years. William D. Morrison made his home on Riley Creek during the most of his life, and for a time previous to the Civil war was drill-master in the militia. Early in the year 1861 he joined Forrest's cavalry and was in every engagement in which that noted body participated, but escaped without wounds. He was taken prisoner in the western part of Tennessee by Colonel Byrd, who was in command of an eastern Tennessee regiment. The Colonel was an intimate friend of Mr. Morrison and for that reason soon released him. After the war Mr. Morrison was a member of the Cumberland county court for a number of years. Politically he was a Democrat, and was a member in good standing of the Baptist church. After the death of his first wife in 1867, he was united in marriage with Caroline Jones, who is still living, making her home in the state of Missouri. Eight children were born to the first marriage, of whom we have the following record: Margaret, wife of Mr. James, a resident of Clark county, Ark.; Gideon P., a farmer of Harrison county, Mo., Lydie E. wife of W. T. Ware, a farmer of Clark county, Ark.; John A., a farmer of Clark county, Ark.; Thomas William, the subject of this sketch; George W., a farmer in Arkansas; Mary, who died in infancy; and Francis, who, also, died while quite young. To the last marriage were born six children, five of whom are now living: Columbus A., Josephine, Eliza, Bryant and Joseph. Jack died at the age of twelve years.

Our subject spent his boyhood in his native county. He was educated in the Oak Hill Academy and taught one term of school, and then began to learn the trade of house painting, in the vicinity of Kingston. In 1877 he removed to Pikeville, Bledsoe county, where he began his business and soon built up an extensive patronage, working in nearly every district in the

21

Sequatchie Valley. For about one year, in 1880–81, he followed his trade in Chattanooga. Mr. Morrison has become one of the prominent and well-to-do citizens of Bledsoe county, and has accumulated considerable means as a result of his thrifty and systematic habits. He is a man of excellent ability and understands thoroughly the details of his occupation as a painter and also the business of paper hanging which occupies a part of his attention. His home is one of the most conspicuous in the neighborhood of Pikeville, being situated on the side of one of the foot hills of the Cumberland mountain, overlooking the Sequatchie Valley and about one hundred feet above the town. Politically Mr. Morrison is a Democrat and has become one of the leaders in the local affairs of that organization.

In the year 1877 our subject was united in marriage with Miss Sarah E. Hale, a daughter of Lemuel Hale, born at Hickman, Ky. To this union have been born nine children, who bear the following names: John L., who is his father's assistant in his business; Lemuel H., Margaret A., Frank Edison and Nellie A., now living; Ella D., Robert, Mary and Henry died in childhood. Mrs. Morrison is a member of the Methodist church.

JOHN LEMUEL MINTER, a representative and influential citizen of Marion county, who owns and occupies a good farm two and one-half miles southeast of Jasper, is a native of Tennessee, his birth occurring at Lynchburg, Moore county, April 24,

1844. His parents, Anthony and Nancy (Price) Minter, were both natives of North Carolina, born on Tar river, probably in Buncombe county, but when young went to Mississippi, and in Tishomingo county, that state, were married. The maternal grandfather, William Price, died in Mississippi, but the death of Richard Minter, the paternal grandfather, occurred in Jasper county, Ga. About 1843 Anthony Minter and his wife came to Tennessee, and after living for a time in Moore county, and at Wauhatchie, Hamilton county, took up their residence in Jasper, Marion county. The father was a successful merchant, but by aiding friends he lost heavily, and finally disposed of that business, removing to a farm at Sorrel's Mill, on the Sequatchie river. He leased the mill, which he operated while his sons cleared and improved the farm. Anthony Winter, during the Civil war, was in the Confederate army and was killed at Petersburg, Va., when the breastworks were blown up by General Butler, in the summer of 1864. His wife died at Rome, Ga. In their family were seven children, five sons and two daughters, of whom only three sons are now living. John L. is the eldest; James is a farmer residing near Rome, Ga.; and Robert lives near his brother, in that state. Those deceased are William, who was one of the county officials of Floyd county, Ga., where his death occurred; Thomas, who was killed on the Nashville & Chattanooga railroad while in the employ of that company; Julia Ann, who married William Beck and died near Cave Spring, Ga.; and Sarah J.

During his boyhood Mr. Minter, of this review, attended school to some extent in Jasper, but when the Civil war broke out in 1861, he was working at Monticello, Ga., where he enlisted in Capt. Lee Lane's company, of the Fourteenth Georgia Confederate Infantry, remaining in the service until hostilities ceased. He participated in the second battle of Manassas Junction, and the engagements at Seven Pines, Williamsburg and Fredericksburg, besides many others. At Gaines Mill he was wounded in the foot and had a finger shot off, while another shot passed through his shoulder, all happening so close together that it was impossible to tell which wound was received first. After being confined to the hospital for some time, he was engaged in guarding prisoners at Macon, Ga., and then returned to his home in that state.

For two years after the war Mr. Minter lived in Rome, Ga., and at the end of that period returned to Jasper, Tenn., where he was employed in the mercantile establishment of Redfield & Co., followed by service with the following firms: S. B. Deakins, G. S. Deakins, W. B. Mitchell and A. A. Coppinger. He then purchased his present farm, two and a half miles southeast of that city, it being the place on which his father located on retiring from mercantile pursuits, and which our subject helped to clear during his boyhood. He has met with decided success in his farming operations, and is now regarded as one of the most substantial and reliable citizens of the community.

On the 8th of June, 1875, Mr. Minter was united in marriage with Miss Eliza A. Lewis, a daughter of Rev. Charles Lewis, and to them have been born the following children, all living with the exception of

Roddy, who died in childhood. The others are Samuel D., Scott, James, Charles, Harley, Herchal and Lilly May.

The Democratic party has always found in Mr. Minter a stanch supporter, and on that ticket he was elected county court clerk in 1874, although the county usually had a large Republican majority. This fact plainly shows his popularity and the confidence and trust reposed in him by his fellow citizens, and that this confidence was not misplaced is also evidenced by the capable and satisfactory manner in which he performed the duties of the office, gaining for him a re-election on the expiration of his four years' term. He was also elected justice of the peace to fill a vacancy caused by the death of Chairman William Bennette. After serving in that position he was employed as salesman for six years by Roddy Brothers at Tracy City. It was through his influence that the first bridge was built across the Sequatchie river at Sorrel's Mills, as he made up half the cost and the county paid the balance. He has always been an enterprising, public-spirited citizen, giving his support to every object which he believed calculated to benefit his county or state, and is therefore deserving of honorable mention among the valued and useful citizens of the community. Socially he is a prominent member of Olive Branch lodge, F. & A. M., and also the Knights of Labor.

THOMAS S. PARHAM is a prosperous, enterprising and highly respected agriculturist of the Fourth district, Cumberland county. Mr. Parham was born in the above mentioned county on the 3rd of February, 1863, and is a son of John and Elizabeth Parham, both natives of Tennessee also. His father was a prosperous farmer, and shipped stock to Atlanta and other southern cities. He came to be rated as wealthy, and at one time made a large amount of money, but evil fortune and business reverses came at last, and he lost nearly all of his possessions. His father, who was well known as "Grandfather Jack" Parham, was the first member of the family to settle in the valley of the Sequatchie, where he lived for many years. John Parham was shot to death by a man named John Bradley in the year 1865. Bradley was a southern sympathizer and Parham was an equally ardent supporter of the north in the late war. A feud was started, with the result that John Parham suffered death at the hands of Bradley and Bradley, who, after an absence of sixteen years, returned and went gunning for a son of Parham, was himself killed. Mr. Parham was a justice of the peace for a number of years, and held other local offices. Mrs. Parham, his wife, is still living. Her maiden name was Elizabeth Brown, and she was born June 11, 1815, the daughter of Jessie and Cary Brown. Mrs. Parham, who is still living, is the mother of eight children, two of whom, Martha, who was the wife of Capt. J. C. Hinch, of Roane county, and Sallie, who married I. N. Thurman, of Bledsoe county, are deceased. The latter was at Pikeville with her husband at the time, seeing to the education of her children. The children now living are: James L., a farmer of Osage county, Mo.; W. J., a farmer of the Fourth district, Cumberland county; Emeline, the wife of Lieut. Sam Swofford, of Bledsoe county, Tenn.; John W., a farmer residing near Seattle, Wash.; J. F., clerk of the circuit court of Cumberland county, and a resident of Spring City, Rhea county; and Thomas, the subject of this sketch. Mrs. Parham now makes her home with her children and is a member of the Hickory Grove Methodist Episcopal church. Thomas was educated in the common schools of Cumberland county and at Grant Memorial University, at Athens, Tenn. Since the age of twelve he has supported himself, and has engaged in many ventures and different kinds of business, being at various times a logger, mill sawyer, storekeeper, distiller, etc., and later was in the lumber business at Spring City for two years. When the town of Jewett was established he set up a sawmill there and for eighteen months he and his brothers, Johnson and J. F., cut lumber for the Tennessee Lumber Company, getting over one million feet from the Bear Den mountains. He now owns the old family homestead and carries on farming there. He has been very successful and now has one of the best country places in Cumberland county. In political matters he is a Republican.

Mr. Parham married Miss Laura Acuff, a daughter of Martha Reid, of Cumberland couuty, on the 31st of July, 1893. Mr. and Mrs. Parham are the parents of two children, Frank D. and Isa.

L AWSON HILL NORTHCUT.—Fortunate is he who has back of him an ancestry honorable and distinguished, and happy is he if his lines of life are cast in harmony therewith. Our subject is blessed in this respect, for he springs from a prominent family. He is a native of Grundy county, born April 5, 1840, in the house where he still resides, and is a son of Gen. Adrian and Sarah (Cope) Northcut. The father was a distinguished officer of the Mexican war, and remained in the service from 1845 to 1848, participating in all the engagements from Matamoras to Mexico City, as captain of Company A, in Colonel Campbell's regiment. After the close of the Mexican war he became prominently identified with the political life of the state, and served in the legislature for eight years, two in the senate and six in the lower house. He was highly esteemed, and looked upon as one of the most active members, and made hosts of friends. At one time he gave the general assembly an oyster supper to show his generosity. The grandfather, John Northcut, was a soldier of the war of 1812, and died at New Orleans soon after the battle at that place, in which he had taken part. He was a native of Lee county, Va., and from the Old Dominion removed to Warren county, Tenn., about 1806 or 1808. By occupation he was a farmer.

The subject of this sketch acquired a good education in the academy at Altamont. During the Civil war he espoused the cause of the Confederacy, and in May, 1861, as a non-commissioned officer, he joined Captain Patton's company, Peter Turney's regiment, which was mustered in as the First Tennessee Confederate Volunteer Infantry. He participated in the battle at Fair Oaks, Va., and in the seven-days' battle before Richmond, where he was wounded. While home on a furlough, July 4, 1863, he was captured and sent as a prisoner of war to Camp Chase, Ohio, later to Camp Douglas, Chicago, and from there to Point Lookout, Md., where he was finally released June 24, 1865. Fortunately he was never seriously wounded. His father lost almost all his property, valued at $15,000, during the war, but our subject ably assisted him in building up his farm, remaining with him until the father's death. He then took charge of the estate, and also cared for his mother until she, too, was called to her final rest. Upon the old homestead he still continues to reside, while devoting his time and attention to the cultivation of the farm and to stock raising. The place is pleasantly situated seven miles northwest of Altamont, and, being under a high state of cultivation, forms a most attractive spot in the landscape of this region.

On the 1st of March, 1871, Mr. Northcut was united in marriage with Miss Mary E. Moyers, who was born January 10, 1851, seven miles east of McMinnville, Tenn., and is a daughter of Thomas Moyers. The Moyers family came to Warren county from Jefferson county, E. Tenn. The children born of this union are Thomas A., Johnathan D. and Errett A. The parents are earnest members of the Christian church, in which Mr. Northcut is now serving as elder. He is an honored member of Alto lodge, No. 478, F. & A. M., which he has represented in the grand lodge, and in which he has served as master. Politically he is a supporter of the Democracy, and has taken quite an active and prominent part in local political affairs. For four years, from 1880

to 1884, he acceptably served as justice of the peace, and in 1883 and 1884 was one of the leading members of the state legislature, ably representing the district comprised of Grundy and Marion counties, and serving on several important committees. As a citizen he meets every requirement, and manifests a commendable interest in everything that is calculated to promote the county's welfare in any line. He is a pleasant and genial gentleman, and is very popular, having a most extensive circle of friends and acquaintances, who esteem him highly for his genuine worth.

JAMES KELLY DAVIS, an energetic and progressive farmer, residing in the Seventh district of Marion county, two miles east of Jasper, was born in the Sequatchie Valley, near Sulphur Springs, Marion county, November 30, 1837, and is a son of Robert Earl C. and Amanda (Carmack) Davis, both born near Abingdon, Va., the former May 24, 1820, and the latter September 24, 1825. When young they came with their respective parents to the Sequatchie Valley, and after their marriage they located upon the place where the mother still continues to reside. The father died August 8, 1885, and was buried in the family cemetery upon the old home farm. In politics he was a Democrat, and in religious belief was a Cumberland Presbyterian. The six children that constituted his family were as follows: one who died in infancy; John L., who makes his home in the Third district of Marion county, near Whitwell; Robert E., in the fifth district, near Whitwell; James K., of this sketch; William E., a farmer of Arkansas; and Mary J., deceased.

Mr. Davis, of this review, was educated in the public schools of Marion county, and upon the home farm grew to manhood. On the 12th of May, 1881, he led to the marriage altar Miss Nettie Duke, who was born in the Third district of Marion county, February 15, 1863, and is a daughter of Edwin and Mary (Holloway) Duke, the former a native of North Carolina, the latter of Sequatchie county, Tenn. The father died November 28, 1886, but the mother is still living, and now makes her home with her son Charles. She is a faithful member of the Methodist Episcopal Church South, of which her husband was also a member. In their family were seven children, namely: Mattie, Joseph, Joshua, Thomas, Charles, Nettie and Nelson. Mrs. Davis was reared in Marion county, and was educated in the common country schools.

After his marriage, Mr. Davis located upon his father's farm, which he operated for a few years, but in 1895 purchased his present place, and has since devoted his energies to its cultivation and improvement. He is a Master Mason, belonging to the lodge at Sulphur Springs, Marion county, and is an ardent Democrat in politics.

WILLIAM E. SNODGRASS. — This name is borne by a prominent citizen of Pikeville, Bledsoe county, who has spent his entire life in the eastern part of Tennessee. Mr. Snodgrass is an attorney-at-law by profession, and has held a number of important offices in the county. He has become well known as a gentleman well versed in law, mentally gifted and courteous, and has been a potent factor in the political and legal life and welfare of Bledsoe and surrounding counties. He was born August 5, 1857, a son of Dr. Thomas and Eliza (Evans) Snodgrass.

Doctor Snodgrass represented White county in the legislature before the war. His sympathies were for the Union during the years of dispute as to the justice of slavery, and it caused him no discomfort to see his own slaves liberated. He had a brother who was a captain in the Confederate army, and several others who held minor offices or were in the rank, and one or two were killed during their service. He made his home in Sparta for a long time, operating a large cotton factory, selling goods and practicing law and medicine. About the year 1878 he moved to Crossville, Tenn., for his health, and has since been engaged in the practice of law and medicine in partnership with his son, C. E. Snodgrass, in that city. His wife, Mrs. Eliza (Evans) Snodgrass, is a daughter of Colonel Sevier Evans, who fought in the war of 1812. She was born in White county, Tenn. Doctor and Mrs. Snodgrass are the parents of a family of eleven children, ten of whom are now living, viz.: Sevier, a physician in Texas; Judge David L., chief justice of the supreme court of the state of Tennessee; Jennie, wife of R. H. Swafford, of Crossville; Lou, wife of V. Carrick, of White county; William E., the subject of this sketch; Mattie, wife of W. C. Baker, of Crossville; Susie, who died at the age of eighteen; C. E., a prominent attorney of

Crossville; Tom, of Crossville; James T., of Crossville; and Annie May, wife of Judge E. G. Tollett, of Oklahoma.

William E. Snodgrass attended the academy at Sparta and the Burritt College at Spencer. After completing his course of study he taught school for a time, and then began to read law in his father's office and was admitted to the bar at Crossville, in 1884. In 1885 he was united in marriage to Mrs. Addie L. Norwood, daughter of Colonel S. B. Northrop, and soon after move to Bledsoe county, and has since made that his home. He was appointed state's attorney for the counties of Cumberland, Van Buren and Bledsoe to collect the back tax, and held that office until his task was completed. Mr. Snodgrass has built up for himself an extensive practice, and has long been recognized as one of the leading members of the Bledsoe county bar. Thoroughly learned in the law, always a student as well as a practitioner; with not only a quick but a comprehensive mind, earnest in his convictions, able in his assertion of them; devoted to the interests intrusted to his keeping, he has few superiors as a well equipped practitioner. Mr. and Mrs. Snodgrass have five children, whose names in the order of their birth are as follows: Nannie, Burt, Eliza, Tom and Ed.

ANDERSON CHEEK GRAYSON.—The commonplace duties of daily life, trivial though they may seem to the casual observer, demand for their proper fulfillment the same admirable qualities of character which in a higher degree and under other circumstances attract universal notice and approbation. However it may seem to the superficial mind, our rural communities furnish an excellent field for the development of the traits which go to the making of good citizens and one purpose of this work is the preservation of records which show the innate worth and dignity of such a life.

Among the leading and representative agriculturists of Marion county is Mr. Grayson, who was born December 23, 1841, on the farm near Whitewell where his brother Houston now resides, and is a son of Henry and Nancy (Hixon) Grayson, and grandson of Joseph and Elizabeth (Brazil) Grayson. The father was born in Anderson county, Tenn., November 2, 1799, and during his childhood was taken by his parents to Bledsoe county, locating in the neighborhood of Stephen's chapel. Later the family came to Marion county, Joseph Grayson entering seventy acres of land, upon which Byron Hudson now resides, and there his death occurred, while his wife died on a farm near the Burnette school house. He was of English descent, and by occupation was a farmer and blacksmith.

On the 11th of September, 1820, in Bledsoe county, was celebrated the marriage of Henry Grayson and Nancy Hixon, the latter of whom was born in Greene county, Tenn., July 22, 1799, and when a child of six was taken by her parents to Bledsoe county. After their marriage they removed to what is now Sequatchie county, but later took up their residence on the farm in Marion county where our subject's birth occurred and in 1857 located on the farm where he is now living. Here both departed this life, the father November 9, 1879, the mother November 10, 1881. During his younger years Henry Grayson engaged in blacksmithing and wagonmaking, but later in life gave his entire time and attention to agricultural pursuits and the milling business and also served as justice of the peace for a while. Politically he was first a Whig and later a Democrat, and religiously inclined to the Christian church, while his wife was a devoted member of the Cumberland Presbyterian church.

Anderson C. Grayson is the youngest in the family of nine children, the others being as follows: Pleasant, a farmer of the Third district of Marion county; Louisa, wife of Joseph Burnette, who lives on the farm where she was born; William H., who is living retired in Whitwell, Marion county; Patrick H., a farmer on the west side of the Sequatchie river in the Third district; James M., a farmer and ranchman of Texas; Sarah C., wife of William Cowan, of Texas; Houston, who lives on the old homestead; and Joseph, who died in infancy.

In the schools near his childhood home, Anderson C. Grayson obtained his education, remaining with his parents until after the Civil war had broken out. In December, 1861, he volunteered in the Confederate service under Captain Rankins and Colonel Starnes. His brother, Patrick H., also fought on that side, but his brothers, Pleasant and William, joined the Federal army, while Houston remained at home. Pleasant was a member of Gov. Andrew Johnson's body guard at Nashville. For a time Andrew Grayson was stationed near Nashville and later at Rogersville, East Tennessee, as the advance guard of Gen. Kirby Smith. He took part in a number of battles and

skirmishes in Kentucky under Colonel Scott, of a Louisiana regiment, who was acting brigadier, notably that of Richmond and the capture of Frankfort, and assisted in raising the Confederate flag over the state capitol at the latter place. He was also at the battles of Redmound and Thompson's Station, Tenn., and in the engagement on the Columbia Pike, when with Lieutenant Havron's command they covered the retreat of Gen. Braxton Bragg from Tullahoma, when Colonel Starnes was killed. He was with General Forrest in the pursuit and capture of Colonel Stuart with all his men, near Rome, Ga. He was, also, with his company at Chattanooga and on Chickamauga's bloody field, and in the fall of 1863 was the last Confederate to leave the heights of Strings Ridge, he having been on picket duty there, north of the Tennessee river. His command was then detailed to remain in Lookout Valley to watch the movements of the Federal army, but he was soon after captured near home, remaining a paroled prisoner until the close of the war. While his company was stationed in the valley Lieutenant Havron and a squad, composed of our subject and others, seven in all, crossed the Tennessee river, passed through the enemy's lines, pillaged their wagons and made their escape. The next day they captured four prisoners, but at night two of the latter escaped, but they carried the two others across the river and turned them over to the headquarters of General Bragg. The first year of the war Mr. Grayson served as a sergeant, but afterward was a private, fighting gallantly and fearlessly for the cause he believed to be right.

Returning home, he gladly took up the

more peaceful pursuits of farm life, and since the war has successfully operated the farm on which he still resides. He also conducts a mill which his father erected many years ago at Standifer Cove, and is also engaged in bee culture and is noted for the production of a fine grade of honey. He is to-day numbered among the most substantial and reliable business men of his community.

On the 6th of May, 1869, Mr. Grayson married Miss Josephine L. Barber, who was born July 27, 1851, a daughter of William R. and Nancy M. (Real) Barber. They now have eight children, namely: Florence N., wife of Frank Kelly, a merchant of Whitwell; Lawrence H., who married Lilla M., the daughter of Prof. W. H. Wilson, and who is a partner of Mr. Kelly in business; and Lula F., Ella Elizabeth, Mattie Electa, Irvin Anderson, Alva Josephine and Mina Agnes, all at home with their parents except the first named. Mr. and Mrs. Grayson, with their six oldest children are members of the New Hope Cumberland Presbyterian church and take an active and prominent part in its work. He is now serving as ruling elder and clerk of the session. The family is one of social prominence, is widely and favorably known, and at their hospitable home they delight to entertain their many friends. Mr. Grayson is a Democrat in politics and a member of the New Hope Masonic lodge.

DR. GEORGE REAL, Mrs. Grayson's maternal grandfather, and a well-known physician and minister, was for many years an honored and prosperous citizen of Sequatchie Valley. He was born in Virginia in 1794, and was, on the paternal side, of German origin and the maternal of English extrac-

22

tion. In White county, Tenn., he married Esther Pilson, also a native of Virginia, born in 1800, and from that county they removed to the Sequatchie valley, residing on quite a number of different farms, including one on Brush creek, in what is now Sequatchie county. He became quite an extensive dealer in real estate, and when a young man also commenced the practice of medicine and engaged in preaching, first in the Methodist church and later in the Missionary Baptist church. As a physician he was highly successful, and remained in practice until nine years before his death, when he suffered a stroke of paralysis. He was a soldier of the war of 1812; was a Democrat in politics, but not an extremist or in sympathy with secession, but after the war commenced he favored the Confederacy. As a minister he labored earnestly and long and was a great revivalist in his day. After a long and useful life, free from every suspicion of evil, he passed to his reward in 1887. His first wife, Mrs. Esther (Pilson) Real, had died in 1851, and he later married Jemima Smith, whose death occurred in 1888. Of the nine children born of the first union, only four are now living: Hannah, wife of Lawrence Pitts, of Hamilton county, Tenn.; Edward B., a minister in Texas; Nancy M., the mother of Mrs. Grayson; and George W., a farmer, who went west before the war. Those deceased are Susan, the eldest, who married Samuel King and died in Bradley county, E. Tenn.; Elisabeth, who married Benjamin F. Brown, moved to Texas and there died; William and Peggy, who died in childhood; D. Hardman; and Esther M., who died at the age of fifteen years. By his second marriage Dr. Real had three children, of whom Mary M., wife of James Nelson, died at Dayton, and the others died when young.

William R. Barber, Mrs. Grayson's father, was born in Kentucky. While a young man he came to Tennessee, where he married Miss Nancy M. Real. By trade he was a saddler. During the war he entered the Federal service as a member of Company L, Tenth Tennessee Infantry, and while serving as a member of Governor Johnson's body guard at Nashville, Tenn., died February 11, 1865. His widow, who is a lady of education and refinement, has remained true to his memory, and now makes her home in Sequatchie county. She is a devout member of the Methodist Episcopal church.

WILLIAM R. PAINE, chairman of the county court of Van Buren county, takes a leading and prominent part in public affairs, his large acquaintance and unbounded popularity giving him an influential following, while his shrewd judgment of men and affairs make his counsel of value in all important movements.

Mr. Paine was born May 18, 1837, near Rock Island, about on the line between Van Buren and Warren counties, and is a son of Charles and Martha (Medley) Paine. The father was born near Augusta, Ga., and with his father, Charles Paine, Sr., came to Tennessee, locating first in Grainger county, but afterward coming to what is now Van Buren county, but at that time formed a part of Warren county. On the Cumberland mountains they developed a farm, Charles Paine, Sr., being interested in agriculture during his entire life. He was a soldier of the war of 1812, and died when our subject was a mere child.

Charles Paine, Jr., also a farmer by occupation, died in Laurel Cove, in 1863, at the ripe old age of eighty-four years. He was twice married, his first wife being Sallie Paine, a native of Warren county, Tenn., by whom he had six children, but only one is now living, John, a resident of Texas county, Mo. Those deceased are Lewis, who died in Giles county, Tenn,; Elizabeth, who married Thomas Massey and died in Illinois; Orlenia, who became the wife of David Martin and died in Missouri; Mary Ann, who married G. W. Thomison and died in Missouri; Nancy, who married Tandy Slatten and died in Van Buren county, Tenn.; and Sallie, who died in childhood. After the death of the mother of these children, Charles Paine, Jr., weeded Martha Medley, a native of Tennessee, and to them were born five sons and three daughters, of whom the living are as follows: B. W., a farmer of Van Buren county; William R., the subject of this sketch; J. T., an agriculturist of Van Buren county; W. S., a farmer and Baptist minister of White county, Tenn.; Melvina, wife of R. T. Thomison, a farmer of Warren county; and Louisa, widow of Samuel Baker, and a resident of Van Buren county. Those deceased are H. C., who was a member of the Sixteenth Tennessee Confederate Infantry, under Colonel Savage, and was killed at the battle of Jonesboro, Ga.; Eliza, who married Caleb McBride and died in Warren county; and Charles, who died at Rock Island, the same county.

The schools of Van Buren county furnished William R. Paine his educational advantages, and he remained at home with his father until the outbreak of the late war. In May, 1861, he enlisted in Captain York's company, Colonel Savage's regiment, and took part in many important engagements, including the battles of Perryville, Ky., Murfreesboro, Chickamauga, Rocky Faced Ridge near Ringgold, Ga., Resaca, Adairsville, Altoona, Marietta, Kenesaw Mountain, Peach Tree Creek near Atlanta, Ga., Jonesboro, Ga., Franklin and Nashville. He was with J. D. Cummings all through the service, and at Murfreesboro was wounded by a gunshot.

Mr. Paine was married, January 24, 1865, to Miss Sophronia Mitchell, who was born in Van Buren county, January 11, 1842, and died November 19, 1876, in Houston county, Tenn., while the family were returning to this section of the state from their recent home in Texas county, Mo. The children born of this union were James T., a farmer of Van Buren county; Calista, wife of John Thomison, who is engaged in farming on our subject's land; H. O. and W. C., who are both with their father; J. S., a farmer, who died in Van Buren county, at the age of twenty-six years; and Julia, who died in childhood. On the 28th of May, 1881, Mr. Paine was united in marriage with Nancy McDaniel, a native of Warren county.

After the war Mr. Paine taught four fall terms of school in this region, and in 1871 removed to Dent county, Mo., where he successfully followed the same profession for four years. On account of the ill health of his family, he then returned to Tennessee, and was soon afterward elected justice of the peace, an office he had creditably filled prior to his removal to Missouri. In 1882 he was elected a member of the county court and has since held that position with the exception of the years 1889 and 1890, when he resigned. His fellow citizens appreciating his worth and ability again called him to that office, and in January, 1897, and again a year later, was elected chairman of the court. He was instrumental in establishing the post office at Paineville and is numbered among the valued citizens of his community, taking an active interest in everything which will advance the public welfare. Since casting his first vote for James Buchanan in 1856, he has been a pronounced Democrat in politics. Fraternally he is a member of the Farmers Alliance and also belongs to the Masonic lodge at Friendship. At the age of seventeen he joined the Baptist church, but since 1858, has been an active and prominent member of the Christian church at Crane Hill.

WILLIAM S. LAMB, of Dunlap, is the present sheriff of Sequatchie county. He was born on the east side of the valley and has spent the greater part of his life in Sequatchie county. He has always taken a prominent part in public matters and has attained an enviable reputation as a respected citizen and an able officer. He was born March 26, 1856, the son of Joseph H. and Louisa (Barker) Lamb, both natives of Sequatchie county, the former born in April, 1834, and died August 8, 1875, and the latter born August 12, 1836, and is still living on the old homestead.

Our subject's grandfather, Hugh Lamb, upon removing to Tennessee, located three miles east of the present site of Dunlap, and died there when Joseph was a small boy. Joseph Lamb was educated in the public schools of the district in which he lived. Early in the war he joined Stewart's company of Confederate guards, and, after serving for a time in that capacity, he joined the home guards and was appointed one of the officers of that body. After the war he served one term as clerk of the county court. He was a charter member of the Masonic fraternity, Sequatchie lodge, No. 339, and he and his wife were both members of the M. E. church South. They were the parents of a family of ten children, five sons and five daughters, of whom four sons and four daughters are now living, as follows: John A., M. D., a well-known physician of Dunlap; William S., the subject of this sketch; Addie, wife of Daniel Stewart, a farmer of Sequatchie county; Malinda, wife of J. H. Kell, a farmer near Dunlap; Martha, wife of William Stewart, who is living on the old Stewart homestead; Hugh is in Chattanooga in the employ of the Southern Railroad Company; Lizzie, wife of Byron Farmer, a state official at Inman; Joseph H. is with his mother; Alex and Mary Ann both died in childhood.

William S. Lamb spent his boyhood with his mother and was educated in the district schools. On December 22, 1875, he was united in marriage with Miss Docia Smith, daughter of Dr. Smith, and their wedded life has been blessed by the advent of a family of nine children upon whom they have bestowed the following names: Allie, Annett, Carrie, Lou, Joseph S., Grace, Earnest, Ina and Hal. Mr. Lamb began farming at the time of his marriage, and, in 1886, he bought his present farm, which is situated near Dunlap. His first public service was that of constable of the Fourth district, and, after serving one term in that capacity, he was elected sheriff of Sequatchie county. He served three successive terms and was repeatedly re-elected. The following term he served as deputy sheriff and was then again elected sheriff, in which capacity he is now serving his sixth term, a record not equaled in the state of Tennessee. Mr. Lamb is a well-informed man, being particularly well versed on topics of economy, and is widely and favorably known as a citizen devoted to his county's best interests. He is a potent factor in the prosperity enjoyed by Sequatchie county and has been of great assistance in developing and extending its agriculture. His is the record of an upright life, and an influence for good in the community, with whose highest interests his name is associated. He is a Mason, holding his membership with the Sequatchie lodge, No. 339, and has performed the duties of master of the lodge and has represented it four times at the grand lodge. Politically, he is a stalwart and zealous Democrat.

WILLIAM ANDERSON GRISWOLD, who is living at Wagon, Grundy county, Tenn., is the pioneer miller of the county, and one of the most extensive land owners in the vicinity. He was born January 30, 1832, near Altamont, in what is known as Grundy county. His parents, Stephen M. and Sarah (Purdom) Griswold, were natives of, the former of Connecticut and the latter of North Carolina. Stephen M. Griswold grew to manhood in his native state, and first visited this part of Tennessee as a traveling salesman, handling clocks, etc. He settled here and turned his attention to farming and saw-milling, and became very prosperous, as he succeeded in accumulating large tracts of land in and around Altamont. He was very prominent in the local political affairs of the county before the war, and was county court clerk at that time. He was a Whig in his political views. He died in 1882 at the advanced age of eighty-four. He was married in Coffee county, Tenn., to Miss Sarah Purdom, who came with her parents from her native state to Tennessee, when she was a child, and who died at Altamont. They were members in good standing of the Christian church, at which they were regular attendants. Stephen M. and Sarah (Purdom) Griswold were the parents of thirteen children, five of whom are now living, and of whom we give the following: William A., of whom this article is written; Mary, the wife of Joseph Sweeton, of Tracy City, Tenn.; Nancy E., the wife of Robert Sanders, who was clerk and master of Grundy county for years, resides at Altamont; Lucy, wife of Abner Street, a miner of Tracy City, Tenn.; Sophia Jane, widow of Peter Long, making her home in Rockwood, Tenn.; David, living in Georgia; George, Altamont, Grundy county, Tenn.; Wiley P., who died in Kentucky; S. V., who was a farmer and liveryman at Mc-

Minnville, one of the firm of Griswold & Houchen, who died in the latter place, and DeWitt, who was a soldier in the Confederate army under Peter Turney, and died while in the service.

William A. Griswold received his education at the Altamont Academy, and at the age of twenty-two he devoted his attention to saw-milling. He has followed that calling ever since, with great success, and by strict attention to business he has succeeded in amassing sufficient to insure him a comfortable income during his declining years. He moved from his place near Altamont to his present location in Hubbard's Cove, ten miles from Altamont, First district of Grundy county, some years ago. He is one of the prominent men of the district and one of its largest land owners. His holdings amount to some fifteen thousand acres of land including a fine valley farm, sawmill and planingmill, with all the machinery that enters into the manufacture of lumber. He is also the owner of a good gristmill. Mr. Griswold took an active part in the erection of the school house and church.

On April 8, 1860, William A. Griswold was united in the holy bonds of matrimony with Miss Martha Jane Warren, daughter of John Warren. There have been twelve children born to bless this union, eleven of whom are living, viz.: James, a carpenter of Tracy City; Thomas, a farmer of Hubbard's Cove; Isaac, also a farmer of Hubbard's Cove; Norman, lives on Collins river in Grundy county; David, makes his home near his father; and is the postmaster at Wagon, Grundy county; George resides near the parental home; Charlie, in Coffee county; Claude, Vanie and Lily (the latter twins), at home, and Leonard, who died at the age of sixteen. Mrs. Griswold died on September 3, 1897, at the age of sixty-three. Mr. Griswold is a member in good standing of the Christian church, as was his respected and lamented wife. Politically he he affiliates with the Democratic party. He is a man of the strictest integrity, honorable and upright in all his dealings with his fellow citizens, and highly respected for his many sterling traits of character.

E VANCE HINCH, one of the well-educated, ambitious and wide-awake young men of Cumberland county, is now living in the Fourth district, near Burke postoffice.

Before entering into the details of the life of the gentleman whose name heads this article, a short sketch of the history of his ancestors will be in order. John Hinch moved to Bledsoe county, the part of which that is now Cumberland county, and located near the head of the valley, on the place now owned by Thomas Patton, and lived and died on this farm. His son, William Hinch, is still living and resides in the Eleventh district of Cumberland county, where he has spent his entire life in the pursuit of agriculture. His son, Craven Hinch, was born in 1849, and now lives in the Fourth district, Cumberland county, at the head of the valley, near where the creek flows from under the mountain, where he owns a fine farm. He was married to Miss Mary Morris, a daughter of J. D. Morris. Mr. Morris was formerly one of the success-

ful farmers of the valley. Mr. and Mrs. Hinch are members of the M. E. church, South, of which he is also an officer. Politically, he is a Democrat. Of their family of eight children, we have the following record: E. Vance, the eldest of the family and subject of this sketch; Minnie A.; Virgil, still living at home; Gustave; Vezola; Venus; Herman; and Vernom, who died at the age of ten years.

E. Vance Hinch was born November 20, 1873, was educated in the public schools of the vicinity of the place of his birth, and began teaching at the age of eighteen years to earn money to complete his education. In 1895-6 he attended the university at Harriman. He is a very popular young man and is looking forward to a bright and prosperous future.

WILLIAM McNABB, a representative farmer of Marion county, is pleasantly located in the Sixth district, on the banks of the Tennessee river, where he is maintaining his place among the progressive and intelligent men around him, engaged in agricultural pursuits. Upon that farm he was born July 10, 1844, a son of David and Margaret (Long) McNabb. On coming to this state with his parents, the father first settled in Meigs county, but later came to Marion county, locating on the north side of the river when the Indians still occupied the south side. With the early development of this region he was prominently identified, was a successful farmer, and also owned and operated the McNabb coal mines, boating the coal down the river to market.

In his political views he was a Republican. David McNabb was born March 2, 1811, and died in Marion county, February 8, 1880, and his wife, who was a native of the county, born February 28, 1811, passed away June 24, 1884, honored and respected by all who knew them.

Of their nine children, seven are still living, namely: Jane, the wife of Andrew Lawson, now a resident of Midlothian, Texas; Alexander, a farmer of the Sixth district of Marion county; John, who operates a farm on the south side of the river in the same county; Rachel, who married William Anderson, but both are now deceased; Silas, a farmer of the Sixth district; Annie, wife of Lewis Carlton, of Ætna, Mont.; David, who was a member of the Fourth Tennessee Federal Cavalry and died in Nashville; and William.

The subject of this sketch was educated in the schools of the Sixth district, and was reared to habits of thrift and industry. Feeling that his country needed his services, he laid aside all personal interests in July, 1863, and enlisted in Company I, First Tennessee Federal Infantry, but was afterward transferred to the Tenth Regiment, with which he served until the close of the war. On his return home he commenced farming on the farm at Mullin's Cove, on the banks of the Tennessee, where he still lives, and has demonstrated his skill and ability as an agriculturist, the well tilled fields yielding bountiful harvests.

In February, 1865, Mr. McNabb was united in marriage with Miss Louisa Sexton, a daughter of Joseph Sexton, born July 10, 1844, and they became the parents of the following children: Curry, who is now working in the McNabb mines; Isabel, wife of Thomas Ridge, of Fairmount; John, David, Finis, George and Tommie, all at home; and Margaret and an infant, deceased. The wife and mother was called to her final rest August 25, 1892, and Mr. McNabb was again married April 31, 1893, his second union being with Miss Sarah Ellis, who was born February 15, 1847. She is a daughter of William Ellis. She is a devoted member of the Methodist Episcopal church, and Mr. McNabb is an ardent Republican in politics, taking a deep and commendable interest in public affairs.

JONATHAN H. H. BOYD is a widely-known citizen of the First district of Sequatchie county, and the owner of a very large grain and stock farm and nursery, and is doing a very extensive business in forest and decorative trees and shrubbery. He was born in Roane county, Tenn., February 11, 1861, and is the son of Fernando C. and Elizabeth J. (Winchester) Boyd.

Fernando C. Boyd was born in Anderson county, Tenn., March 16, 1840, and by occupation was a farmer and cooper. At the breaking out of the Civil war he went to Kentucky and made his home there until 1868. He then returned to Tennessee and located in Bledsoe county, and one year later went to Sequatchie county. He there bought a small farm and worked very hard to pay for it, but died before this task was completed. The date of his death is March 13, 1871. He was a member of the Missionary Baptist church, and in politics was a stanch and enthusiastic Republican. His wife was born November 2, 1837, in Roane county, Tenn. She had seven brothers, all of whom except one served in the Union army during the war. Fernando Boyd and his estimable wife were the parents of a family of four children, of whom the subject of our sketch is the oldest. The second in the order of birth is Daniel Dueast, a farmer and veterinary surgeon living in Sequatchie county; Ballinger Right, a farmer near Cagle; and John Campbell, a teacher of public schools and a farmer, whose home is also near the latter town.

Jonathan H. H. Boyd, the subject of this sketch, only attended school about four months, but has always been a student of nature, and it has been his privilege to make the acquaintance of and be recognized by a number of the popular naturalists. He started in this work by writing to the " Farm Journal," of Philadelphia, with a view to finding out the nature of the calycantheus, which had poisoned so many cattle in that section of Tennessee. He had also written to several farm journals, but the one named is the only one that gave any definite information. Emerson E. Sterns, Robert G. Eccles, of Brooklyn, N. Y., and others became interested and were instrumental in bringing our subject into public notice. Mr. Sterns wrote for a bushel of the pods of the plant, and Mr. Boyd gathered and expressed them, and for this he received five dollars, the first of his experience in gathering and selling seeds, which has since been his principal occupation. Later Mr. Sterns paid our subject a visit of several weeks, and during this time taught him the names and uses of all the trees and plants indigenous to the locality. While Mr. Boyd makes a specialty of trees, shrubs and seeds native to that part of the country, and furnishes larger nurseries with stock that they cannot produce, he receives stock from China, Japan, France, England, and also gets cacti from Mexico. He exports stock to France, England, Germany and many other countries both of the new and old world, and his trade is steadily increasing year by year. His home for a time was the farm that his father bought upon locating in the county, and which, after his father's death, with the help of his devoted mother, he improved and cleared of debt. He afterward bought a farm ten miles north of Dunlap, and later sold out and bought his present large place, which is situated in the Second district, eleven miles northwest of Dunlap. Mr. Boyd has always taken a keen interest in politics, and has become one of the leaders in the affairs pertaining to his district and county. For ten years he was postmaster at Cagle.

May 15, 1889, Mr. Boyd was united in marriage with Miss Ersey M. Johnson, of Van Buren county, Tenn., and two children, Fernando Campbell and James Reed, were born to them. Mrs. Boyd died November 15, 1892, and May 20, 1893, our subject was married to Miss Edna Tate, a native of Warren county, Tenn., and two children have been born to this union—Mary and Athelia M. The four children are all living with their parents.

ELDER RICHARD LEEK GILLEN-TINE, of Spencer, is prominently connected with both the material and moral development of Van Buren county. He has occupied his time with agriculture and mercantile interests, and has also given an active service to the cause of Christianity, laboring earnestly for the uplifting of his fellowmen. Such a life contains many lessons of inspiration and encouragement that may be profitably followed.

Elder Gillentine was born in Van Buren county, January 28, 1852. His grandfather, Nicholas Gillentine, was probably a native of Ireland, and on coming to America located in Virginia. Some years later he removed to upper East Tennessee, subsequently took up his residence in White county and thence removed to the western part of the state. He was a typical pioneer, delighting in the experiences that one has in subduing a wild region, and finding on the frontier ample opportunity to follow his chosen pursuits of hunting and farming. Nicholas Gillentine's family consisted of the following children: John, Terry, Elizabeth, Margaret, Polly, Richard, Martha, Nicholas, Jane, Susan, Rachel, Sarah and William.

Squire John Gillentine, the father of our subject, was probably a native of Virginia, and was born November 16, 1797. He was married May 2, 1816, to Polly Martin, who was born in 1790, and died September 22, 1822. Their children were Nicholas M., who went to Texas many years ago and was killed by the Indians; Macajah T., a resident of Warren county, Tenn.; Clementine, who became the wife of James Maloy, and died in Van Buren county; Patsy, widow of John Stewart, and a resident of Kentucky; Rachel, wife of William Meyers, of White county, Tenn.;
23

and Jane Terry, who married Lawson Seitz, and both are now deceased. The father of this family was again married, November 27, 1824, his second union being with Margaret Parker, who was born May 9, 1804. They had eight children: Arthur P., who died in childhood; John W., who died in Kentucky; Ellen, who resides with our subject; Harrison C., postmaster at Gillentine; George W., who died in childhood; William M., also deceased; Elizabeth, wife of Newton Camp, a farmer of White county, Tenn.; and Richard Leek. With the development of Van Buren county Squire John Gillentine was prominently identified. He was educated here, was one of the first settlers of the county seat and built the second house in Spencer. He carried on merchandising there and for nine years was a partner of John Stewart in that business. For many years he held the office of justice of the peace and was chairman of the county court for a long period. Deeply interested in the cause of education, he was one of the promoters of Burritt College and was the first president of its board of trustees. When a young man he belonged to the Hardshell Baptist church, but was dismissed from that organization because he permitted the Separate Baptists to hold meetings at his home. He then joined the latter denomination, but at the time of his death was a member of the Christian church. During the war he spent two years in Monroe county, Ky., and after his return to Tennessee was elected a member of the board of claim commissioners of Van Buren county. In politics he was a Whig, and later became a Republican, his sympathies being with the Union during the Civil war.

His last years were spent on the farm near Gillentine post office, which was named in his honor. His death occurred July 2, 1870, and an honored and upright man this passed to his reward.

Richard L. Gillentine, of this review, continued to make his home with his father until the latter's death. He attended school in the county during his boyhood, but his education was much interrupted, his terms of attendance not being longer than three months at a time. Later he pursued his studies in Monroe county, Ky., for two terms. After his father's death he took care of his mother and sisters, the mother passing away July 22, 1895. For twenty years he devoted his energies to farming and for a time owned a farm lying just in the rear of Burritt College. In 1890 he took up his residence in Spencer, from which point he continued his agricultural pursuits until 1893, when he began merchandising. After eighteen months, however, he sold out, but again the following year opened a store, and on the 1st of January, 1898, formed a partnership in this enterprise with J. T. Walker. Since October, 1897, he has conducted a store in Cummingsville. He is an enterprising, progressive merchant and his well-appointed mercantile establishment receives from the public a liberal patronage, which is well merited by reason of his honorable business methods and his courteous dealing.

On the 3rd of September, 1874, Elder Gillentine wedded Miss Mary, daughter of Logan Seitz, a prominent citizen of Van Buren county. She was born March 31, 1853, and by her marriage has become the mother of nine children, namely: Logan S., John S., Matilda, Thomas H., James A., Margaret E., Sallie, Mary and Bessie. With the exception of the youngest all are now connected with Burritt College, in which Matilda is an instructor in music, while Logan S. is a member of the graduating class of 1898 and is superintendent of public schools of the county. For many years Mr. Gillentine has served as school commissioner and is now one of the trustees of Burritt College. He does all in his power to promote the cause of education, and his labors have been very effective. In politics he is a Republican and is now serving as postmaster of Spencer by appointment of President McKinley. When seventeen years of age he united with the Christian church and at twenty-four was ordained as an elder therein, since which time he has preached in almost every church of the denomination within fifty miles of Spencer. He now has charge of the churches in Spencer, Antioch, Bethel and Jericho. He is a man of broad humanitarian principles, kindly and charitable, and his influence for good throughout the community is far reaching.

DR. ZEBULON MONTGOMERY PIKE MORRIS, the able and popular editor of the " Pikeville Banner," was born on the Cumberland river, in Dickson county, Tenn., August 12, 1832, the son of Joseph and Lucy (Stewart) Morris.

Joseph Morris was a native of Virginia, and was probably a soldier in the war of 1812. He was a farmer and died in Dickson county, Tenn., when about fifty years of age, and his wife died during the same year. His wife was a native of Dickson county, Tenn., and a daughter of Andrew Stewart, who was born in Virginia and died in Dickson county, Tenn., at the age of one hundred and five years, or in the year 1847. He was a soldier in the Revolutionary war, and was in Philadelphia when Zebulon Montgomery Pike was shot, and saw the affair. When our subject was born Mr. Stewart insisted that he should be named Zebulon Montgomery Pike Morris. Mrs. Lucy Morris was born in Dickson county, Tennessee.

The subject of our sketch is the only survivor of a family of five children, whose names in the order of their birth are as follows: Andrew, John, Zebulon Montgomery Pike, Thomas and Ann; the youngest three were reared by their grandfather. Zebulon was educated at Jacksonville, Ala., leaving school in 1854, and began the study of medicine under the preceptorship of Dr. Maut Bell. He then read medicine for Dr. John B. Craig and, of course, received the same benefit as did Dr. Craig. He was afterward taken to DeSoto county, Miss., by his brother, and he made that his home until he graduated from the medical course. During the seasons 1859–60 and 1860–61 he attended the lectures at the University of Nashville and graduated in 1861. After leaving the college he spent but two days at home and then enlisted in the Twelfth Tennessee Confederate Infantry, and was commissioned lieutenant of Company A, of that regiment. He served in that capacity until the reorganization at Corinth. At the battle of Shiloh he received a gunshot wound in the shoulder and was sent home

on a furlough until his wound could heal. His command was then reorganized and when he returned to the field he joined Van Dorn's command as a private soldier, serving in that capacity until Van Dorn was killed at Spring Hill. He was then placed under Gen. W. H. Jackson and served until April 16, 1865, when that command surrendered at Selma, Ala. The principal battles in which he participated were: Shiloh, the battles of the Georgia campaign, Atlanta, Lovejoy's Station, near Atlanta, Franklin and Nashville. He was also in many other minor engagements, aggregating about one hundred. He received several slight wounds but was not absent from the army with the exception of the one furlough mentioned above.

At the close of the war he settled at Newbern, Tenn., without a cent in his possession, except a quarter given him by a Federal soldier as a parting souvenir, his property being destroyed during the war and slaves emancipated, but he began the practice of his profession and soon became established and was realizing a comfortable income. Five years later he went to Lowell, Washington county, Ohio, and resumed his practice there, losing his health in the colder climate and from exposure consequent to his profession. In 1884 he went to Trenton, Dade county, Ga., from ill health abandoned the medical profession, and was there until 1889. He then went to Jasper, Marion county, Tenn., and after residing there two years, located in Pikeville and established the " Pikeville Banner " and has since been engaged in the publication of that paper. In 1866 Dr. Morris was united in marriage to Miss

Nora B. Hallett, daughter of Orrellane and Lucy Hallett. Mrs. Morris was born in Lower Salem, Ohio, about the year 1840. Her uncle, B. T. Blake, was an educator and went south before the war and took his niece with him that she might attend the school over which he presided. She afterward graduated from a convent at Wheeling, W. Va., and was engaged in teaching at Newbern when she became the wife of the subject of this sketch. To this union have been born three children: George B., who died in 1867; Joe H. is his father's assistant in the management of the "Pikeville Banner," and Musa May. The Doctor and his wife are both members of the Cumberland Presbyterian church, and he also affiliates with the Masonic and I. O. O. F. fraternities. Politically he is a Democrat.

J OHN SEXTON.—Throughout the greater part of his life this gentleman has been a resident of Marion county, and his name is inseparably connected with its agricultural as well as its public interests. He is a man of intrinsic worth, esteemed in all the relations of life, and has been prominently identified with the growth and prosperity of this section of the state.

Mr. Sexton was born October 3, 1843, in the Sixth district of Marion county, a son of Joseph and Martha Jane (Higdon) Sexton, natives of Polk county, Tenn., where their marriage was celebrated. On coming to the Sequatchie Valley they located just below Dunlap, but only remained there a short time as that section was Indian land. Their next home was on the south side of the Tennessee river in what is now the Sixth district of Marion county, the father making a few improvements upon the land now owned by John Cummings. At the end of two years they removed to the north side of the river, where the following four years were passed and then spent two years in Alabama. For the same length of time they made their home in Tishomingo county, Miss., and then returned to the Sixth district of Marion county, Tenn., where they lived for four years. A short time was then passed in Hamilton county, Tenn., and after again living in the Sixth district of Marion county, they returned to Hamilton county in 1858, remaining there until 1863. In the latter year the father again took up his residence in Marion county, where he departed this life in 1867, at the age of fifty-eight years. His wife had passed away in 1854, aged forty-six. By occupation he was a farmer and wood workman, and in politics was an ardent Democrat.

In the family of this worthy couple were thirteen children, but only four are now living, namely: Caroline, wife of Alexander McNabb, a farmer of Kelly's Ferry, Marion county; John, of this sketch; Blackburn, a farmer and miner at McNabb mines; and George W., an agriculturist of Clay county, Mo. Those deceased are Mary, who wedded Thomas Hale and died in Marion county; Celia Ann; Sallie Ann; James, who died in Marion county many years ago; Joseph and Wilson, who also died in that county; Martha; and Louisa, who married William McNabb and died in Marion county.

John Sexton secured his education in the public schools of Hamilton county, where most of his boyhood was passed. True to his early teaching, he enlisted, in October, 1862, in Company H, Fourth Georgia Confederate Cavalry, and served as sergeant of his company until August, 1863, when he was detached on courier service under Gen. D. H. Hill. Later he was with General Walker's escort. He and his command were afterward detailed as scouts under General Johnston, and was subsequently with General Hood until the close of the war. He was in many important engagements, including the battles of Ashville, War Trace, Tullahoma, Chickamauga, and was with the command from Dalton to Atlanta, and in the battles of Franklin and Nashville. At the close of the war he had nothing left but a poor horse and a ragged uniform. Nothing daunted, however, with his characteristic energy, he commenced farming and getting out timber, and is now one of the prosperous and well-to-do citizens of the community.

On the 26th of May, 1867, Mr. Sexton was united in marriage with Miss Mary Hartman, a daughter of John Hartman, and they have become the parents of eleven children, but only five are now living: Mary E., at home; Thomas J., a farmer of the Sixth district of Marion county; Nancy J., wife of Silas Powers, of the same district; and Sallie and Joseph, both at home. Those who have already crossed the dark river of death are William, George, James and Samuel. The wife and mother is an earnest and faithful member of the Methodist Episcopal church, South.

Mr. Sexton exercises his franchise in support of the men and measures of the Democratic party, and as the candidate of his party he was elected sheriff of Marion county in 1886, acceptably serving in that position

for two years. Throughout life he has made the most of his opportunities, has accumulated a handsome property, and his career illustrates what can be accomplished through industry, perseverance, good management and a determination to succeed. He has not only won success financially, but has also gained the high regard of all with whom he has come in contact.

JAMES W. FARMER, one of Cumberland county's most prominent and influential agriculturists, resides in the Seventh district. Mr. Farmer was born in Knox county, Tenn., October 14, 1835, and is a son of Enoch and Susan (Canten) Farmer, both natives of Ashe county, N. C. They were married in North Carolina and soon afterward went to Tennessee, settling on Hickory Creek, twelve miles northwest of Knoxville. They removed later to Morgan county, and made their home in that part which afterward became Cumberland county. Enoch Farmer died there in 1888, at the age of about seventy-five. His wife is still living, and lives with her children. Mr. Farmer tilled the soil for a living, and prior to the war had a small farm, which was ravaged by both sides during the memorable struggle. He was a church member for many years, as was his wife. They had thirteen children, eleven of whom are still living. Our subject, who was the eldest, was but three years of age when his parents removed to Cumberland county. He spent his early days upon the homestead there and assisted his father in managing it. When about twenty-five he began farming for himself in the woods. During the war he also suffered great hardships, and saw his capital melt away before the onslaughts of the numerous foraging parties, but he got himself together after peace was declared, went to work with renewed vigor, and is now able to declare himself successful once more. While the war was in progress Mr. Farmer assisted many men to get from the mountains to the Federal lines in order to enlist, and was always an ardent sympathizer with the Federals. He is a Republican in politics, and was formerly a Whig.

In his twenty-fourth year Mr. Farmer married Miss Permelia D. Kindred, who was born in Cumberland county, February 17, 1843, and was a daughter of John H. and Susan Kindred. Mrs. Farmer died May 31, 1897, leaving ten children, three sons and seven daughters. Two of the sons are in Texas, one in Fannin county and the other in Navarro county. One of the daughters is in Colorado and another in Morgan county, Tenn. All of the other children live in Cumberland county. The family are members of the New Home Christian church, near Hebbertsburg, with which they have been connected since 1866.

WILLIAM LAY is the owner of one of the fine farms of Marion county, his valuable and highly cultivated tract of land being conveniently situated about five miles from Jasper. Its well-tilled field and substantial improvements indicate his careful supervision and progressive spirit, and he is numbered among the leading agriculturists of the community. His success is largely due to his own efforts and he has therefore justly won the proud American title of a "self-made man." The study of biography yields to no other in point of interest and profit. It tells of the success and defeat of men, the difficulties they have met and overcome, and gives us an insight into the methods and plans which they have followed so as to enable them to pass on the highway of life many who started far ahead of them in the race. The obvious lessons therein taught would prove of great benefit, if followed, and the example of the self-made man should certainly encourage others to press forward.

In his business career Mr. Lay has won the success which ever crowns industrious and well-directed effort. He was born near Tazewell, Claiborne county, Tenn., May 7, 1847, and is a son of John and Mary (Odell) Lay. His father was also born near Tazewell, in Big Valley, and died in Campbell county, Tenn., in 1861. The grandfather of our subject, David Lay, died in Big Valley, at the very advanced age of about one hundred and eight years. He was an industrious farmer, and aided in the cultivation of his land almost up to the time of his death. He always raised his own tobacco, and in his last years hoed his little crop while sitting in a chair. His wife died at the age of about ninety-six, and about the same time her husband passed away. He was a Whig in politics, and his religious views harmonized with the doctrines of the Baptist church.

John Lay followed farming throughout his active business life and was a worthy and highly esteemed citizen. About 1851 he removed from Claiborne county to Campbell county, Tennessee, where he spent his remaining days. In connection with the cultivation of his land, he there operated a still. He was an advocate of the Union cause during the Civil war and was a man of honest convictions, true to his belief of the right. His wife, who was a member of the Missionary Baptist church, was born near Speedwell, Tennessee, and died at the home of our subject, in 1896, when sixty-seven years of age. In their family were ten children: Lavisa, wife of James Brown, of Arizona; Elizabeth, wife of J. H. Carnutt, of Arizona; David, who is living on the old home farm in Campbell county; William; Elijah, of Arizona; Elisha, twin brother of Elijah and a resident of Oklahoma; John, who is also living in Arizona; Mary, deceased; Rhodie, wife of Charles Wells, of Campbell county, Tenn.; and Nancy, widow of Ballard Lindawood and a resident of Fincastle, Tenn. The oldest son of the family, David Lay, served in the Union army as a member of the Sixth Tennessee Infantry.

When his brother went to war, the care of the mother and her younger children devolved upon the subject of this review, who nobly discharged the duties thus resting upon him. During the years of her widowhood his mother usually made her home with him, and his filial devotion repaid her for her care of him in youth. Mr. Lay was educated in the common schools and his life has always been a busy and useful one. In 1867, he went to Indiana, living first in Lebanon and afterward in Stanton. He spent three years in that state, devoting his energies to farming and the timber business,

and later he occupied the position of weigher in a mine. In 1870 he took up his residence in Campbell county, Tenn., and a year later came to Marion county. For eleven years he engaged in farming near Victoria, and then purchased his present desirable property at Rankin's Cove, about five miles east of Jasper. There he carries on business with excellent success, making a specialty of stock-raising.

On the 14th of December, 1873, Mr. Lay was united in marriage to Miss Louisa Jane, daughter of G. W. Brown. She was born in Campbell county, Tenn, in 1850, and by her marriage had ten children, nine of whom are living, as follows: John, at home; James, deceased; George, Sarah, Alice, Lizzie, Janie, America, Willie and Celia, all yet under the parental roof. The parents are consistent and leading members of the Methodist Episcopal church at Sardis, in which Mr. Lay is serving as trustee. He is also a valued and prominent member of Altine lodge, A. F. &. A. M., which he has represented in the grand lodge. He exercises his right of franchise in support of the men and the measures of the Republican party, and is deeply interested in the welfare of the community, giving to all measures for the general good the aid and co-operation of a loyal and public-spirited citizen.

JAMES F. RUST is an engineer on the Tracy City branch of the Nashville, Chattanooga & Saint Louis railroad. Mr. Rust was born in Rutherford county, near Murfreesboro, January 10, 1853, a son of

Isaac and Margaret L. (McElroy) Rust, the former born in Washington county, Va., near Abingdon, January 8, 1805, and died December 23, 1877, and the latter born February 17, 1817, and died April 17, 1870.

Isaac Rust, our subject's father, was twenty-one years of age when he left his home in Virginia and traveled for a time in Georgia, Louisiana, and some of the other southern states, and then settled on a farm in Rutherford county, Tenn. He moved to Grundy county in 1854. In religious views, he and his wife were both Methodists and she was a member of that denomination. Politically Mr. Rust was a Whig originally, but later he joined the ranks of the Republican party. Like many others in this section of Tennessee, he lost very heavily from the war. He was in sympathy with the Union cause, and strongly opposed to secession. He participated in the Florida war, and his oldest brother was a soldier in the war of 1812. His death was caused by lockjaw which resulted from a wound received in his foot.

Isaac Rust was of Scotch descent. His father, John C. Rust, came from Scotland to help the Colonists in their struggle for independence from Great Britain, and was a sergeant in the Colonial army. He was wounded at the battle of Camden and carried the British ball to his grave. After the war, he came with General Lafayette to America, to the colonies in Virginia. Of this family, Isaac Rust, our subject's father, was the only one to settle in Tennessee. He reared a family of ten children, only three of whom are now living, and of whom we have the following record: Samuel R., a farmer and miner living three miles east of Tracy City; James F., the subject of this sketch; and Margaret, wife of E. C. Green, a farmer of Grundy county. The deceased are: Martha Burnett, wife of John Burnett, died near Pelham, Grundy county, Tenn.; Melinda, wife of George W. Roberts, died in Texas; John C. died while serving as sheriff of Grundy county; Isaac N., also an employe of the railroad company, died in Tracy City; Mary, wife of John Burnett, Jr., died near Pelham, Tenn.; Harriet F., wife of Isaac Tucker, died in Tracy City; and William H., who also died in Tracy City.

When our subject was still a child he moved with his parents to Grundy county, Tenn., and settled near Pelham. Here he grew to maturity and was educated. At the age of seventeen years, or in the year 1870, he left home, went to Tracy City, and entered the employ of the railroad company in the capacity of brakeman. Three years later he became fireman, and after serving in that capacity for nearly three years, he was made engineer, August 13, 1879. Ever since he first entered the employ of the company, he has worked on this branch, and has worked there longer than any other man employed in that section.

On November 10, 1875, Mr. Rust was united in marriage to Miss Lena J. Sims, who was born July 18, 1855, in Warren county, Tenn., a daughter of J. T. Sims, a veteran of the Mexican war. To this congenial union have been born two children, Della L. and Frank S. Mr. Rust is a member of the Methodist church, South, and is a trustee of the society in which he holds his membership, but his wife, although not a member of any denomination, endorses the discipline and policy of the Christian church. Our subject is also a member of the A. F. & A. M., the Knights of Pythias, the Independent Order of Odd Fellows, the Royal Arcanum, the Knights of Honor and Brotherhood of Locomotive Engineers. Politically he is identified with the Democratic party, but usually uses his elective franchises in the support of the candidate best qualified for the office he seeks, regardless of party lines.

WILLIAM O. JONES, editor of the South Pittsburg "Republican," and timekeeper for the Tennessee Coal, Iron & Railroad Co., is one of the energetic and wide-awake men among the younger members of the business population of the thriving town of South Pittsburg.

Mr. Jones was born near Centerville, Hickman county, Tenn., October 13, 1870, a son of Patrick R. and Matilda E. (Radcliff) Jones. The father was born in Nashville, Tenn., September 26, 1849. The mother was probably born in Hickman county, Tenn., in the year 1845. They were married in Vernon, Hickman county, and made their home in that locality until 1895, when they moved to South Pittsburg, Marion county, Tenn. They are both members of the Christian church. Politically, Mr. Patrick Jones is identified with the Republican party, but formerly was a Democrat. He is of Scotch descent, and his father, Barnett Jones, is still living and is making his home in Hickman county, Tenn. He is a farmer by occupation, and is about

24

eighty-seven years of age, having been born in Halifax county, Va., in 1818.

William O. Jones, the subject of our sketch, is the oldest of a family of six children, and the names of his brothers and sisters are as follows: John, who is a moulder in the employ of the Blacklock foundry; Ewell T., who is an assistant in the laboratory of the Tennessee Coal, Iron & Railroad Co.; Jesse, in the employ of the Eagle Pencil Co., at South Pittsburg; Maud and Reece, at home. Our subject spent his boyhood at Warner, and was educated in the public schools of that place and at home. Since locating in South Pittsburg he has done some teaching in the night schools. After completing his study he entered the office of the Southern Iron Co., at Warner, Hickman county, Tenn., in the capacity of assistant bookkeeper, and was thus engaged for six years. Six months of this time, however, he was at Goodrich as timekeeper. He then worked eighteen months as timekeeper for the Round Mountain Furnace Co., and, on severing his connection with this firm, entered the employ of the Tennessee Coal, Iron & Railroad Co. as timekeeper, and is still holding that position. March 16, 1898, in partnership with Mr. W. F. McDaniels, he leased the South Pittsburg "Republican," and since that date our subject has performed the duties of editor of that paper in connection with his work for the Tennessee Coal, Iron & Railroad Co.

March 11, 1890, Mr. Jones was united in marriage with Miss Minnie A. Blocker, daughter of Thomas and Josephine (Nicks) Blocker, and their union has been blessed by the advent of two children, Horace and

Edwin. The younger died in infancy. The family is connected with the Christian church, in which our subject is a deacon. He is also a member of the fraternity of the Knights of Pythias, and in politics is identified with the Republican party.

PROF. WILLIAM WILSON.—Sequatchie county has been the home and scene of labor of many men who have not only led lives that should serve as an example to those who come after them but have also been of important service to the community through various avenues of usefulness. Among them must be named Prof. Wilson, who passed away on his farm seven miles below Dunlap, October 30, 1897, after a life of industry, and rich in those rare possessions which only a high character can give. For many years he labored with all the strength of a great nature and all the earnestness of a true heart for the bettering of the world about him; and when he was called to the rest and reward of the higher world his best monument was found in the love and respect of the community in which he lived for so many years.

Prof. Wilson was born in Meigs county, Tenn., June 29, 1847, and completed his literary education by his graduation from Burritt College in Spencer, Van Buren county. For two years thereafter he successfully engaged in teaching at Masonic Hall, Sequatchie county, and then in connection with his brother David, engaged in mercantile business in Georgetown for some time. On selling out he turned his attention to farming, and also taught school for three years at Masonic Hall and for the same length of time at New Hope, being one of the most popular and efficient teachers of the county. His political support was always given the men and measures of the Democratic party, and in religious faith was a Cumberland Presbyterian. He was a Master Mason, and being one of the most prominent and influential members of his lodge, he was thirteen times chosen to represent it in the grand lodge of the state. He was a kind and indulgent husband and father, and his memory will be a sacred inheritance to his children; it will be cherished by a multitude of friends.

In 1870 Prof. Wilson was united in marriage with Miss Lizzie Bennett, who was born in 1849 on the farm in Sequatchie county, where she still continues to make her home. She is a daughter of Burrell and Lizzie (Lamb) Bennett, and was well educated in the schools of Pikeville and at Sequatchie College. She is a cultured and refined lady, and a prominent member of the Baptist church. The family is one of prominence and includes the following children: Lilla, now the wife of Lawrence Grayson, a merchant of Whitwell, Tenn.; Bennett, an attorney of Chattanooga; and John, Mattie and Samuel, who reside with their mother on the old homestead in the Sixth district of Sequatchie county.

MARTIN LUTHER HARRIS, one of the most prominent young men of Marion county, a leader in educational and political circles, was born February 7, 1869, in Sequatchie Cove, on the little Sequatchie river, and is a worthy representative of one of the honored and highly respected families of the county, his parents being William and Nancy (Tate) Harris.

The father was born in Knoxville, Tenn., some sixty-five years ago, a son of William and Martha (Roddy) Harris, who were from Virginia, and from Knoxville, this state, who removed to Dade county, Ga. Subsequently they took up their residence on the Cumberland mountains in Marion county, Tenn., and later lived in Dickson's Cove, where the grandfather of our subject died March 10, 1875, his wife March 17, 1878. Both were earnest and faithful members of the Baptist church, while in politics Mr. Harris was formerly a Whig and later a Republican. By occupation he was a farmer and miller, operating mills in Georgia and on the Little Sequatchie river.

In the family of this worthy couple were twelve children, eight sons and four daughters, the latter being Elizabeth, who married John Allen, of Rising Fawn, Ga., and died during the Civil war; Martha, wife of William McCoy, who lives on the Cumberland mountains in Marion county; and Caroline and Melissa, who live with a brother in the same county. The family has always been a very patriotic and loyal one, the eight sons having been among the boys in blue during the war, valiantly fighting for the old flag and the cause it represented. Of these, Martin, the eldest, died in Tracy City, Tenn.; Samuel is a farmer of Marion county; James, also an agriculturist, died near Tracy City, in Marion county; William, our subject's father, is the next in order of birth; John was taken prisoner in Marion county, and died in Andersonville during his incarceration; Andrew, who also served in the Federal army, is now a carpenter at Victoria, Marion county; Cowan, a carpenter and farmer, died in Dickson's Cove soon after the war; and Marshall was killed at the battle of Murfreesboro.

William Harris accompanied his parents on their various removals, and obtained his education in the schools of Knoxville and Georgia. Agricultural pursuits then claimed his attention until June, 1862, when he laid aside all personal interests and enlisted in the Second Kentucky Federal Cavalry, in which he served until the close of the struggle, participating in the battles of Missionary Ridge and Chickamauga. Later he was with General Sherman in the advance on Atlanta and the celebrated march to the sea, and was present at the surrender of General Johnston in North Carolina. Although he took part in many important battles and skirmishes, and several times had his clothes pierced by bullets, he was fortunately never wounded. During his service he was in eleven different states. At the close of the war he returned to Sequatchie Cove, where he engaged in farming until 1881, when he and his family removed to their present place of abode on Sequatchie river in the Fifth district of Marion county. In 1860 William Harris married Miss Nancy Tate, who was born in Sequatchie Cove, September 5, 1845, a daughter of William Tate, and they have become the parents of ten children, namely: Cowan, a farmer of the Fifth district; Martin L., of this sketch; Sherman, a resident of Vanndale, Cross county, Ark.; Mary, wife of George White, a farmer of the Third district of Marion county; Martha, at home; Marshall, also a farmer of the Third district; and Sheridan, James, Jane and Amanda, all at home with their parents. The father is a stanch supporter of the principles of the Republican party, and both he and·his wife are worthy members of the Looney's Creek Methodist Episcopal church, their earnest Christian lives winning them the respect and confidence of all who have the pleasure of their acquaintance.

In the public schools near his childhood home, Martin L. Harris began his literary education, and at an early age he became a successful and popular teacher. After following that profession for a time he entered the college at Lebanon, Ohio, where he pursued the classical and scientific course, graduating in 1896. Early in life he learned that knowledge is the key with which the poor boy anywhere can open the storehouse of the world and cull its choicest fruits, and he resolved to obtain an excellent education. He paid his own way through school, not only paying his tuition, but also buying all books necessary with the exception of a ten-cent blue back spelling book. For forty-five months he has engaged in teaching school, a part of the time at Tracy City, and since his return from college has taught at Victoria and Oak Grove. After graduating at Lebanon College, he took a law course in the Cumberland Presbyterian University at Lebanon, Tenn. He is now the nominee of the Republican party for the office of circuit clerk of Marion county, a position he is well qualified to fill, and if elected will undoubtedly prove a most efficient and reliable official, as in the discharge of all duties he is prompt, energetic and painstaking. In religious con-

nection he is a member of the old Ebenezer Cumberland Presbyterian church, and socially is identified with the Masonic Order.

REV. LAWSON SAFLEY, a Baptist minister of prominence residing in the Eighth district, VanBuren county, is a native of Tennessee, his birth occurring at Shellsford, Warren county, April 21, 1848. His grandfather, Jesse Safley, who, with his wife, came to this state from North Carolina, on foot, was among the earliest settlers on Collins river, and he and his family' have borne a prominent part in the upbuilding and development of this section. By occupation he was a farmer, and formerly was a member of the Baptist church. He died in 1862 when well advanced in years.

The parents of our subject, Anderson and Myra (McGregger) Safley, were also farming people and were held in high esteem by all who had the pleasure of their acquaintance. The father, who was born on Collins river, in Warren county, died near Rock Island, that county, in 1885, when past the age of seventy years, and the mother departed this life at the age of sixty-nine. They reared to man and womanhood a family of nine children, in which they took a just pride, for all occupy honorable and useful positions in society. During the Civil war, one son, Jasper, joined the Sixteenth Tennessee Infantry, and died at his home while still in the service. The others are still living, viz.: Cynthia, wife of T. J. Patton, of Warren county; Ann, wife of Nathan Bouldin, a prominent citizen of Spencer; Marion, a farmer of Warren county; Spencer, a farmer of Bell county, Texas; Lawson, of this sketch; Nancy, wife of I. T. Green, of Warren county; Laura, wife of Gaiterd Chism, a farmer of White county, Tenn.; and D. A., who married Melinda Simmons, and is engaged in agricultural pursuits in Warren county.

Lawson Safley spent his school days in Warren county, and acquired a good practical education which has well fitted him for life's responsible duties. From his first home he removed to Cane Ridge and later to Laurel Creek, remaining with his parents until 1871. He was married September 22, 1871, to Miss Jerusha Thomas, who was born on their present farm in the Eighth district, VanBuren county, May 31, 1846. Her father, Isaiah Thomas, came with his people to this region from Kentucky, and in VanBuren county he and his father both died. Mr. and Mrs. Safley have an interesting family of six children, as follows: Jephtha A., who is a graduate of Burritt College and is now a successful and popular teacher near Utica, Miss.; T. J. and Myra, who have also engaged in teaching and are now attending Burritt College; Permelia, also a student at Burritt College; Charles Remus and Lawson I., at home.

Mr. and Mrs. Safley began their domestic life upon the old Thomas homestead, where they still continue to reside. Both have long been active and influential members of the Baptist church at Friendship, in which he became an official a few years after joining. In 1874 he began preaching for that denomination, and has since had charge of various churches, including the one at Friendship, Crane Hill, New Hopewell, Wayside, and Philadelphia, Grundy county. His labors in the ministry have been very effective and productive of great good to the communities with which he has been identified. He is a man of thoughtful, earnest purpose, who wins the confidence and high regard of all with whom he comes in contact. In politics he is a Democrat, and in his social relations is a Mason, belonging to the lodge at Friendship.

WILLIAM A. BARBER, clerk of the county court of Bledsoe county, is a man of progressive, enlightened views, and his standing as a citizen and an officer in the county is well known. There are few more energetic or wide awake men and he is deservedly held in high esteem and respect by his fellowmen. He was born in Whiteside county, Ill., May 5, 1858, a son of Edward H. and Ina (Kennedy) Barber, the former born in Vermont, in the year 1819, and the latter on the island of Saint Helena, in the year 1837.

When Edward H. Barber was eighteen years of age he went to sea in a whaler and spent nineteen years on the ocean and during the latter part of his career he served in the capacity of captain of the vessel. During this time he circumnavigated the earth three times and visited nearly all of the known countries of the world. While visiting the island of Saint Helena, he met the lady who became his wife. Her people had migrated thence from England before Napoleon was taken there as a prisoner. They were married on the island and soon after went to the United States and settled in Whiteside county, Ill. From there they moved to Indianapolis, Ind., and in 1874, he moved his family to the mountains of Bledsoe county, Tenn., where they bought land and have since made their home. Before going to sea, Mr. Barber learned the woodworking trade and of recent years he has followed that vocation. Early in the year 1862 he enlisted in Company D, Seventy-fifth Illinois Volunteer Infantry, and was commissioned lieutenant of the company. He participated in the battles of Perryville, Murfreesboro and others, and at the battle of Perryville he was severely wounded and was discharged on the account of his injury. He is a member of the G. A. R. and formerly affiliated with the Masonic and I. O. O. F. fraternities, while he and his wife are both members of the Methodist Episcopal Church, South. Politically he is a Republican. To this union were born children, of whom six are now living, and of whom we have the following record: William A., the subject of our sketch; Helen C., wife of Thomas Pearson, of Stanton, Mich.; Edward C., Brownville, Tenn.; George W.; Ina E., wife of John Wilson, of White county; one who died in infancy and Frank W.

William A., the subject of this sketch, was educated in the public schools of Indianapolis, and moved to Tennessee with his parents. December 20, 1877, he was united in marriage to Miss Sarah B. Seals, a native of Bledsoe county, and a daughter of James Seals, and their wedded life has been blessed by the presence of a family of three children: James E., Mamie E. and Carrie E. Mr. Barber spent one year on a farm in the Eleventh district and then moved to Pikeville and began the wood working

trade, and five years later he opened a blacksmith shop in connection with his wood shop. For five years he was bookkeeper on the Herbert stock farm, and has held many positions of trust. In 1894 he was elected on the Republican ticket to the office of clerk of the county court and has proved himself a trustworthy and efficient officer. He is loyal and determined in his adherence to the right and to his friends, and is one of the most important factors in the development and growth of the social and financial interests of the county.

CAPT. ROBERT CRAVENS SWAN, who resides in the Eighth district, near Grassy Cove, is one of Cumberland county's most prominent and highly-respected citizens. Captain Swan was born in Rhea county, Tenn., December 19, 1829, and is a son of Thomas Buckingham and Margaret H. (Cravens) Swan, the former a native of Blount county, Tenn., and the latter of Greene county, in the same state. Thomas Swan was a mechanic and millwright by trade, and assisted in developing the iron interests of Roane county in the Hindes. or Tennessee valley, in what are now known as the Rockwood mines. He also carried on farming, and was a colonel of Tennessee militia after removal of Indians. When the Indians were being removed from East Tennessee to the Indian territory he was a captain in that service. He settled in Cumberland county in 1848, and erected a mill on Daddys creek. This mill is not now in existence. He was also postmaster at Maple Springs, and was very well known thereabout. He was a Whig, and later a Republican, and a member of the Methodist Episcopal church, as was also his wife. The Swans are of Scotch-Irish origin, and Buckingham island belonged to our subject's great-grandfather, Thomas Buckingham. The Buckinghams were from Virginia, and the Swans from Maryland, and were among the earliest settlers in East Tennessee. Our subject was the second in a family of eight children, two of whom, Samuel and John R., the latter of whom was a soldier in the Civil war upon the Union side, are deceased, as are James and Thomas, who died in infancy. Those living are Robert Cravens, our subject, Elizabeth, Nancy F. and Mary E. Elizabeth resides in Evansville, Rhea county. Nancy is the wife of G. W. Dawson, of the Fifth district, Cumberland county. Mary is the wife of John A. Renfro, ex-sheriff of Cumberland county, and an inhabitant of the Fifth district. John R., a soldier in the late war, was a corporal in Company D, Second East Tennessee Federal Volunteer Infantry, and with his company was captured by the enemy near Morristown, E. Tenn., in November, 1863, and imprisoned on Belle Isle, Va., where he suffered severely from hunger and cold through the winter, and later was removed to Andersonville, Ga., where, in August, 1864, he died. In his honor the G. A. R. post at Crossville, Tenn., was named.

Our subject spent his early days in Roane and Cumberland counties. He remained with his father until the breaking out of the war, when, early in 1861, he organized a company of Federal troops and started across the mountains for Camp Dick Robinson, Ky. The company was there mustered in on the 1st of September, of that same year, as Company D, Second Tennessee Infantry. Though there were not enough men in his squad to fill out the company, some other volunteers were added and the requisite number secured in a short time, and the company organized with John Boles captain and R. C. Swan first lieutenant. After serving for a few months Captain Swan resigned, but remained with or near the army until his failing health compelled him to seek rest, which he found at a noted summer resort, Sublimity Springs, Ky. He subsequently was with his old company at the battle of Mill Springs. At one time he was almost captured by the enemy. This was at Cumberland Gap. His father and a friend were taken at that time. The former remained a prisoner for several days. Lieutenant Knight, another friend of our subject, had a narrow escape from a Confederate prison at the same time. After the war Captain Swan resumed mill work, superintending the rebuilding of the mills at Sublimity Springs, Ky., and a short time later established the resort known as Rock Castle Springs, three miles below Sublimity Springs, on Rock Castle river. This is in Pulaski county, Ky., and is noted for its beautiful scenery, fine buildings, delightful climate, etc. In 1870 the Captain went to Independence, Kans., and engaged in the general merchandise business there. After the lapse of a year he returned to Cumberland county and took possession of his old homestead, which he had retained. He now lives in the valley. Before the war he lived for a time at Cascade Mills, in White county, Tenn., where he kept a general store. He is at the present time engaged in farming, at which he has been very successful. Captain Swan is a Republican politically. He is connected with the Masonic fraternity, and is a charter member of the local G. A. R. post.

On the 10th of June, 1862, the Captain married Miss Kate Webb, who was born at Stanford, Ky., October 10, 1843, and is a daughter of Pleasant F. and Amanda Webb, both natives of Boyle county, Ky. Captain and Mrs. Swan are the parents of nine children, seven of whom are living: These are: Edwin, now at home; John R., of the firm of J. R. Swan & Bro., Crab Orchard, Cumberland county, Tenn.; Muggis A. is at home with her parents; Samuel Josephus is a clerk in the Crab Orchard store and postoffice; George W., Arthur G. and William A., all at home. Those deceased are: Ida M., who was the wife of R. R. Miller, a soldier in one of the Indiana regiments during the war; and Clara, who died when an infant.

WILLIAM ANDERSON HAYNES, one of Tracy City's substantial and enterprising business men, is one of the leading merchants of that place. He was born in Grundy county, Tenn., not far from the present town site of Tracy City, October 1, 1851, and is a son of E. M. and Clerecy Eveline (Wooten) Haynes.

E. M. Haynes was born in North Carolina in 1816, and moved from thence to Tennessee with his parents when about four years of age. The family settled in Marion county, in the Sequatchie Valley, and there his parents died. Mr. Haynes went

to the mountains when about eighteen or nineteen years of age, entered the employ of Mr. Benjamin Wooten, and for his services for one year he received fifty dollars. With the laudable wish to do better and improve his worldly prospects he determined to start out for himself, so, after his marriage with the daughter of his former employer, he cleared a farm for himself within a mile of Tracy City. Here he and his estimable wife reared a family and he is still a resident of the county. His wife, who bore the maiden name of Clarissa Eveline Wooten, was born about the year 1819, and died in September, 1895. The elder Mr. Haynes is a member of the Primitive Baptist church, while his wife is strongly attached to the Methodist church. Mr. Haynes was a member of the county court when this was still a part of Marion county. In politics he has always been a Republican, and was an ardent advocate of the principles of that party when its members in this county numbered less than half a dozen. The family is of German and English descent.

E. M. Haynes reared a family of seven children, five of whom are living, and of whom we have the following record: William Anderson, the subject of this sketch; Henry F. is a miner at Tracy City; Perry D., also a miner at the same place; John F. is tax assessor for the coal district; Mary J., wife of Ben Leverton, of Cowan, Tenn. The deceased are: Mary Elizabeth, wife of Theophilus H. Hall, died at Tracy City; and Joseph B., who was shot in Grundy county by the revenue officer, although he was not connected with the illegitimate manufacture of alcoholic liquors.

William A. Haynes, the subject of this

sketch, received his schooling before the war at Belmont. Soon after the war he began coal mining and was thus engaged for fifteen years. He then went into the mercantile business and has been identified with the commercial interests of Tracy City since that time. In February, 1870, he went to Earlington, Ky., and from there to Spottsville, Ky., and was in that state until the middle of the summer of that year, and then went to Washington, Ind., and worked in the mines at that place for four years. While in this last named place, he was married, January 31, 1872, to Miss Annie E. Buzan, who was born in Indiana, in April, 1849, a daughter of Elza Buzan. To this congenial union have been born two sons, Walter Thomas and Oliver Perry, both of whom are now partners in the store. Two other sons were born to them, one of whom, Edward Madison, died while quite young; and the other, William Etter, died in infancy. Mrs. Haynes is a member of the Methodist church. Her husband affiliates, socially, with the Knights of Pythias fraternity, and politically he is a Republican.

ELISHA TATE is one of the extensive land owners and successful farmers of Marion county. Often do we hear it said that success is the result of advantageous circumstances, but a careful study of the lives of successful men shows that it is the outcome of industry, well directed effort, perseverance and sound judgment, and such is the case with Mr. Tate, who started out in life empty-handed, but has steadily
25

worked his way upward to a position of prominence.

He was born on Battle Creek, Marion county, July 24, 1832, and is a son of John K. and Rachel (Alsup) Tate, the former born in Greene county, Tenn., in 1792, the latter in Grainger county, this state, in 1796. The paternal grandparents were David and Comfort (Knox) Tate, and the family is of Irish lineage. The parents of our subject were married in Grainger county, whence they removed to Jackson county, Ala., and later took up their residence on Gizzard creek, Marion county, Tenn., where the father died December 20, 1853. His wife passed away March 4, 1870. They were members of the Methodist Episcopal church, and at an early day services were frequently held in their home. The father was a Whig in his political predilections, and served as justice of the peace for many years and as trustee two years. In his family were the following named children: Edward, deceased; Rev. Samuel, a farmer and minister residing on Battle creek; James M., deceased; David, probate judge of Jackson county, Ala.; Abigail, widow of Berry Winn, and a resident of Jackson county, Ala.; John K., an agriculturist of Marion county; Elijah D. and Elisha, twins, the former now deceased; Comfort, wife of William Rolston; and Margaret, twin sister of Comfort and wife of Spencer Anderson.

The father of our subject engaged in teaching school to some extent, and during his youth Elisha Tate pursued his education under his direction. After his father's death he provided for his mother until her demise and thus discharged his filial duty, repaying her for her care of him in childhood. He has made farming his life work and about a quarter of a century ago purchased a part of his present farm. As his financial resources increased he added to this from time to time, until his landed possessions aggregate about fifteen hundred acres at the head of Battle creek. He has a fine spring of pure water at his door and a good cave in which to store fruit and vegetables for winter consumption. His business career has been a prosperous one, and to-day he is the possessor of a handsome competence acquired entirely through his own efforts. His business methods are honorable and straightforward and thus has he won the confidence of those with whom he has had trade transactions. His eldest son, Ransom, is also a worthy citizen, who is now engaged in the operation of a sawmill.

In 1872 Mr. Tate was united in marriage with Miss Jane Coppinger, daughter of Alex. Coppinger, and a native of the Sequatchie valley, born January 6, 1848. Mr. and Mrs. Tate became the parents of eleven children, seven of whom are living: Susan, wife of Forrest Parmley, who resides near Tracy City; Rachel, wife of Jack Martin; Elijah D., Austin, Frankie and David, all at home. Those who have passed away are Florence, John K., James and Ellen.

Early in 1862 Mr. Tate responded to the call of the south and joined the Confederate service as lieutenant of Capt. Alley's company, of the Thirty-sixth Tennessee Infantry. Later he was transferred to Company L, Fifth Tennessee Infantry, and during his service participated in the battle of Stone River and other important engagements. He has served as a member of the the county court for eight years, and in the discharge of his official duties is ever prompt and faithful. In politics he votes independently of party ties, supporting the candidates whom he thinks best qualified for office. He and his wife hold membership in the Oak Grove Methodist Episcopal church, in which he is serving as steward, and their well-spent lives have gained them the warm regard of a large circle of friends.

STARLING TRIED SMITH, M. D., of Dunlap, Sequatchie county, is well known as a physician who has a high standing, not only among the people, but among his medical brethren. He was born and reared in this vicinity, and the greater part of his life has been spent in the eastern counties of Tennessee, where he has become well known and has established a high reputation as a skillful operator, and an honest and painstaking medical practitioner.

Dr. Smith was born near Georgetown, in what is now James county, Tenn., April 11, 1839, a son of Payton and Nancy (Welch) Smith. Payton Smith was born in Virginia, in 1809, and died at his old home in James county, Tenn., in 1876, and his wife was born in Russell county, W. Va., in 1813, and died at the age of sixty-seven years. They both moved with their parents to Claiborne county, Tenn., after they had grown up, and were married in that county. In 1836 they moved to the Ocoee purchase, where they bought an improved farm from the Indians. This farm consisted of two acres of cleared land, furnished with two log cabins with dirt floors. To this they added quite a tract of adjoining land, which they cleared and improved, and on which they lived, reared a family, and where they both died. Politically, the father was a Democrat before the war, but afterward affiliated with the Republican party, and for two terms performed the duties of bailiff. They were both members of the Missionary Baptist church. Payton Smith was a son of Josiah Smith, a Virginian by birth, and of Irish and Scotch parents. He was a farmer and lived to be very old, and died in Hamilton county, Tenn. Nancy Smith was a daughter of John Welch, who was born in the north of Ireland of Scotch parents. He came to America with his father, and was an American soldier in the Revolutionary war. Payton and Nancy Smith were the parents of a family of nine children, eight sons and one daughter, as follows: Leroy, a blacksmith, living in southeastern Missouri; Starling Tried, the subject of this sketch; Elihu Francis was a farmer and died at Jasper, Marion county, Tenn.; John H. lives on the old homestead; George W., a soldier in the Fourth Confederate Cavalry, was killed at Pulaski, Tenn.; William J., a physician and farmer, died in Bledsoe county, Tenn.; Mary I. was the wife of Caldwell Anderson, and died at Shellmound, Marion county, Tenn.; James B. is a farmer in southwestern Missouri; and Samuel J. is a farmer in Oklahoma.

Dr. Smith, the subject of our sketch, attended school at the academy at Georgetown, completing his course of study at the age of sixteen years and began teaching. He taught one term in Hamilton county, and thereby secured means by which he attended the medical college, which from his early boyhood had been his desire and intention. For some time he studied medicine under Dr. J. L. Yarnell, a graduate of the Jefferson School of Medicine, and Dr. Thomas H. Roddy, a graduate of the University, Nashville. In 1857 he went to Nashville and entered the University of Tennessee. Our subject began the practice of medicine at Birchwood, Hamiliton county, Tenn., and was there two years. In March, 1860, he went to Dunlap, hung out his shingle and has since been a practitioner in that place. Early in the war, Dr. Smith's father was forced into the Confederate service, although his sympathies were with the Union, but our subject fully endorsed the cause of the South and tendered his services to the Confederate government. He became assistant surgeon in the Thirty-sixth Tennessee Infantry, and was stationed with his command at Cumberland Gap, for six months, after which he returned to the Sequatchie Valley. In August 1863, Crittenden's Federal command was in the valley, and upon his retiring he left many of his sick men in the care of Dr. Smith. Our subject afterward became surgeon of the three companies of home guards organized in the valley. After the war, or during the years 1866-67, he returned to the University of Tennessee and graduated in medicine. Soon after the war he was elected clerk of the circuit court and served for a term of four years and has been one of the leaders in public matters, especially those pertaining to education. He is the present pension examiner at Dunlap, and has held that position for some two years.

July 12, 1856, Dr. Smith was united in marriage with Miss Ama L. Matthews, daughter of Harlin Matthews, who moved to McMinn county, Tenn., from North Carolina. To this union have been born thirteen children, of whom we have the following record: Theodosia, wife of W. S. Lamb; Delilah Isabel, wife of James T. Hixson, of Hamilton county; John L. B. is a farmer at the foot of the mountains; William H. is a farmer of Sequatchie county; George P., a farmer living near Dunlap; Mary, deceased, was the wife of H. C. Farmer, a merchant at Daus; Florence, at home; James B., M. D., a graduate of the University of Nashville, is located at Hixson station; Nancy, wife of Horace Deakins, of Marion county, Tenn.; Hetty, wife of James Barker, mail agent on the Chattanooga and Pikeville mail route; Polk B., Mattie and Sallie are at home. Socially, Dr. Smith casts his lot with the Masonic fraternity, and, since the age of fourteen years, he has been a member of the Missionary Baptist church. Politically he is a Democrat.

PROF. WILLIAM NEWTON BILLINGSLEY, A. M.—This name will be readily recognized by many of the citizens of Van Buren and surrounding counties, and especially by the students and educators of that community, as that of the president of the Burritt College at Spencer, Tenn.

Professor Billingsley's parents were John M. and Hannah D. (Myers) Billingsley. The father was born in Kentucky, November 19, 1805, and died May 16, 1883. He was a minister in the Christian church and also worked at teaching and farming. John M. was a son of Samuel A. Billingsley. Samuel A. Billingsley was the son of Samuel A. Billingsley, Sr., who, with his brother, Cyrus, migrated from Wales, shortly before the Revolutionary war, and the former settled in that part of Virginia which is now a part of Kentucky, and the latter settled in Georgia. Our subject's mother was born in Jefferson county, Tenn., a daughter of John C. Myers, and her mother's maiden name was Miss Snoddy. Mr. and Mrs. Samuel A. Billingsley, our subject's grandparents, reared a family of eight children, all of whom are now dead, and whose names in the order of their birth are as follows: Mary, Rebecca, Sallie, John M., Betsey, Jonathan, Matilda and Joseph. John M., the father of our subject, was married three times. His first wife bore the maiden name of Miss Melie Metcalf, and was born in White county, Tenn. To this union one child, Cyrus, was born. He grew to manhood and was married just before the breaking out of the Civil war to Miss Betty Plumlee. He then joined the Confederate army, but was wounded at Perryville, Ky., and returned to his home and began teaching school. He died soon after, in the year 1865, from the effects of his wounds. His mother died when he was quite young, and the father was married, November 19, 1843, to Miss Hanna D. Myers, and three children were born to this union: David and Mary died in infancy, and William Newton, the subject of this sketch. Mrs. Hannah Billingsley died April 9, 1867, and the father subsequently married Miss Mariah Dickerson, a native of Virginia, and one child, Virginia, was born to them. She is now living in White county, Tenn.

Prof. William Newton Billingsley, the subject of this sketch, was born near Pikeville, Bledsoe county, Tenn., November 9, 1853, but at the age of two years he moved with his father to Van Buren county, Tenn. His primary training was received in the public and private schools of this county and in Union Academy in White county. He afterward attended Burritt College four years, from which institution he graduated in 1872, receiving the degree of A. M. He at once began teaching in Eaton Institute, White county, and has been actively engaged in the educational work for twenty-six years, all of the time teaching ten months of the year except while serving as superintendent of public instruction for White county, which position he filled with marked ability for two terms, or from January, 1887, to January 1891. While superintendent of White county schools, he was an active member of the State Association of Public School Officers, of which body he had the honor of being president. Under his supervision the schools of White county were graded and a uniform series of text books adopted. He also raised the standard of teachers qualifications and in other ways improved and strengthened the educational interests of his county. He held state or county institutes in his county at which were enrolled annually more than one hundred teachers. The fact that Prof. Billingsley has taught at only three different points in all these years is a strong evidence of his rare ability as an educator.

His first work was at Eaton Institute, where he taught two and a half years, which position he resigned to accept the principalship of Onward Seminary, where he taught for fourteen years.

In 1889, the day on which he was thirty-six years old, Prof. Billingsley was elected president of Burritt College, his alma mater, and has now performed the duties of this office for nearly nine years. The outlook was anything but flattering at first, as the school had been neglected, but President Billingsley soon turned the tide and now has a faculty of seven active teachers and an enrollment of nearly two hundred.

HENRY CLAY GREER, a public-spirited and enterprising member of the farming community of Bledsoe county, has devoted the greater part of his life to agriculture, in the pursuit of which he has been very fortunate, and is the proprietor of as good a farm as can be found within the limits of Bledsoe county, his farm being situated in the Seventh district.

Mr. Greer was born in Grassy Cove, March 1, 1839, the youngest son of a family of eight children born to Weatherston S. and Mary (Kyle) Greer. After attending the public school in his district he completed his education at Burritt College and the University of Tennessee. He taught school for a short time in connection with his farm work. He inherited a part of his farm from his father and bought the balance of his two-hundred-and-fifty-acre estate. In the spring of 1861, he enlisted in the Confederate army and was mustered in at Knoxville, Tenn., under Col. William Brazelton and Capt. W. T. Grass as a private soldier. But soon after the organization of his battalion he received a captain's commission, and was assigned to duty in the commissary department, which commission he resigned at the end of his first year's service, and returned to the ranks and did duty there to the close of the war, with the exception of a part of the last year of the war, during which time he was adjutant of his regiment. He was first sent to Cumberland Gap, where he spent the fall and winter. His command was with Bragg's army through Kentucky and at the battle of Murfreesboro, after which they were transferred to the armies defending East Tennessee and Virginia. He was with Longstreet for a time after the siege of Knoxville, Tenn., and served the latter part of the war with the armies operating in the valley of Virginia and southwest Virginia. He surrendered at Jonesboro, Tenn., about the first of May, 1865. After this Mr. Greer returned to his home in Tennessee, where he resumed his farming and stock raising interests, and since that time he has devoted his attention to that line of work.

January 3, 1861, Mr. Greer was united in marriage with Miss Hortense Randals, a native of Mississippi, where she was born June 29, 1842, the daughter of James and Lucinda A. (Mayberry) Randals. To this union have been born a family of thirteen children, whose names in the order of their birth are as follows: Arethusia, Wed S., James R., Moses, Dion A., Kyle, Elizabeth, Emma, Sylvester, Lucinda, Clute, Flora and Rice S. Of this family, one child, Kyle, is now dead. Mr. and Mrs. Greer are members of the Church of Christ at Bethel, and he is a Master Mason. Politically he is a Democrat and cast his first presidential vote for John Bell. He held the office of county surveyor for eight years, was school director for several years and is at present justice of the peace. Every office to which he has been elected was unsought by him, and he has held none that relieved him from the necessity of hard manual labor on his farm to support his fast increasing family, and give them a fair business education.

CAPT. JOSEPH CAIN, the well-known mine foreman at the Whitwell mines, Marion county, for the Tennessee Coal, Iron & Railroad Co., is a man whose sound common sense and vigorous, able management of his affairs have been important factors in his success, and with his undoubted integrity of character have given him an honorable position among his fellowmen.

Mr. Cain was born January 15, 1862, in Mold, Flintshire, North Wales, Great Britain, a son of John Henry and Mary (Morris) Cain, the former also a native of the British Isles, and the latter an American by birth, although of English parentage, who later returned to England where she was married. Our subject was reared to manhood in the place of his birth. At the early age of eight years he commenced working in the mines in the northern part of his native country, and was subsequently employed in different mines throughout England and Wales. As he made a thorough study of practical mining in all its various departments, he became an expert workman and well fitted to take entire charge of the mines. His employers recognizing his ability at first appointed him deputy foreman, and later foreman, a position he filled with credit to himself and to the entire satisfaction of the company. Coming to the Unite States, he located in Marion county, Tenn., in 1887, and has since been in the employ of the Tennessee Coal, Iron & Railroad Co. Soon after entering their service he was appointed mine foreman, a position he has most capably filled ever since, and the system now in use in these mines was inaugurated by him. He introduced the split system of ventilation, the first of the kind used in the Tennessee coal districts, and has made many innovations in the former methods employed in these mines, his excellent knowledge of the business enabling him to make many useful and practical improvements. He has entire charge of the inside working of the Whitwell mines, where employment is given to three hundred and twenty-five diggers, or a total working force of four hundred and fifty souls.

At the age of eighteen years, Mr. Cain was married to Miss Annie Elizabeth Roberts, who was also born at Mold, Flintshire, Wales, and they have become the parents of six children: Joseph, Jr., Edith, Maggie, George, Annie and Laura. The parents are worthy members of the Methodist church, South, and Mr. Cain is now serving as secretary and trustee of the Mt. Olive church, which has recently been erected after a hard struggle, in which he bore an important part. He has always been an active worker in both church and Sunday-school, and is now teaching a class of young

men in the latter organization. Fraternally he affiliates with the Knights of Pythias and the Masonic order, Woodmen of the World and Regents of the White Shield, while politically he is identified with the Democratic party. He deserves great credit for the success that he has achieved in life, it being due entirely to his own individual efforts, for since an early age he has been dependent upon his own resources and has labored early and late. To become efficient in the theory and practice of mining, letting no opportunity pass that would help him to that end, and recognizing the practical advantages resulting in becoming a member of the correspondence school of mines, at at Scranton, Penn., he became one of the first students. This he did as a sure help toward increasing his knowledge and efficiency. All his spare hours, even encroaching on his hours of sleep, are devoted to self-improvement and the improvement of the work under his care.

JACOB M. SIEVER, a prominent citizen of Cumberland county, was born in West Virginia, in Hardy county, or what is now Grant county, October 4, 1854, a son of Moses and Harriet (Smith) Siever.

Moses Siever was born in what is now Grant county, W. Va., April 16, 1828. He was married December 25, 1853, to Harriet Smith, and his death occurred in Jackson county, Kans., May 3, 1888. His wife is still living and resides in Holton, Kans. He was a son of Philip Siever, who was born June 15, 1800, in Rockingham county, Va., and died August 25, 1869, in Grant county, W. Va. He was married August 13, 1822, to Susanna Keplinger, who was born October 3, 1800, and died April 9, 1871. It is believed that Governor Sevier, well known in eastern Tennessee, and a prominent character in the history of that part of the state, is of the same family, and that that branch of the family have changed the spelling of the name from "Siever" to "Sevier." Philip Siever was a successful farmer, and moved with his family to West Virginia, where there was a colony made up of the Siever, Lentz, Keplinger and other families. This colony established a church in what is now Grant county, W. Va. Both Philip Siever and his son, Moses Siever, were stanch advocates of the principles of the Republican party. Moses Siever belonged to the state troops organized to protect their homes during the late war. In November, 1874, the family moved to Marysville, Union county, Ohio, and in February, 1881, moved to Jackson county, Kans. He belonged to the registration board during reconstruction days in West Virginia. Mr. and Mrs. Moses Siever were parents of ten children, eight of whom are living, and of whom we have the following record: Jacob M., the subject of this sketch; Mary Ann, wife of James Poling, a liveryman, of Holton, Kans.; Philip H., an attorney of Alvord, Texas; George W., railroad agent of the Rock Island road at Arkalon, Kans.; Margaret, living at home; John W., who died March 26, 1889, just as the train was pulling into Vandalia, Ill., while on his way home from a visit to Tennessee and Ohio, being twenty-six years old; Lloyd, a prominent business man of Holton, Kans.; Albert, express agent on the Rock Island

railroad; Charles M., principal of schools at Hoyt, Kans.; Lettie Adellia died December 11, 1886, in her fifteenth year.

Our subject was educated in the high school at Maysville and at the age of eighteen years, began teaching and taught in the common schools of his native county for a number of years, and after moving to Tennessee he taught two terms. For twenty-three years he has been a practical surveyor, and has done a great deal of the official surveying in West Virginia. In 1887 he moved to Cumberland county, Tenn., and located on the farm on which he now lives, and has since put on all the improvements, and in April, 1890, he was elected surveyor of Cumberland county, and re-elected in 1894, and has done surveying in every part of the county. In 1888, he was elected justice of the peace, re-elected in 1894 and has ever since been a member of the county court. He has several times been urged to resign the surveyor's office and accept that of chairman of the county court, but has always refused. In 1887, Mr. Siever opened a general merchandise store at Winesap which he has since successfully conducted, and has built up a profitable trade. Eight years ago, he was appointed postmaster of that village and performed the duties of that office, in conjunction with the business of that store. During Cleveland's administration a Democrat from Bledsoe county took charge of the office, but after the present administration began, Mr. Siever was again appointed. He is also school commissioner of the Third district.

September 27, 1877, our subject was united in marriage to Miss Mary A. Cosner, of Grant county, W. Va., and they are now the happy parents of a bright, interesting family of nine children, all of whom are living and making their home with their parents, viz: U. S., Myrtie T., Guy W., Cora, Bessie H., Amy M., Ollie, Moses J., and Violet.

Mr. and Mrs. Siever were members of the United Brethren church while in Virginia, but when they moved to Tennessee, they joined the Free Will Baptist church, and Mr. Siever is the present clerk of the Laurel Creek church. Politically he is a Republican, and is now a candidate for county judge of his county.

JOHN W. ORANGE—Prominent among the energetic, far-seeing and successful business men of Tracy City is the subject of this sketch. His life history most happily illustrates what may be attained by faithful and continued effort in carrying out an honest purpose. Integrity, activity and energy been have the crowning points of his success, and his connection with various business enterprises and industries have been of decided advantage to the community, promoting its material welfare in no uncertain manner.

Mr. Orange is a native of Prussia, Germany, born near the Saxon and Hanover line, April 16, 1839, and is the only child of John and Annie (Gerbod) Orange, also natives of Prussia. The father made sheep raising and farming his life work and was fairly successful in his business ventures. He died in 1853, at about the age of sixty years, and his widow subsequently married

26

Frederick Schneider. She was born about 1818, and died about 1879.

The public schools of his native land afforded our subject his educational privileges, and at the age of fourteen years he commenced learning the baker's trade. Two years later he left home as he could not agree with his step-father, and came to America, the sailing vessel on which he took passage being seventy-three days in crossing the Atlantic owing to continuous storms, but he finally reached Baltimore in safety. There he worked at his trade for a time, and after spending a few months in Cincinnati, Ohio, he went to Butler county; that state, where he worked on a farm and learned to speak English. Subsequently he returned to Cincinnati, and from there went to New Orleans, where he was located at the inauguration of the Civil war. In the spring of 1861 he entered the Confederate service as a member of Company C, First Louisiana Infantry, under Captain King and Colonel Clayton, and was in that command for one year. Later he joined the Eighth Confederate Cavalry, and when cut off from that command at Sparta, Tenn., he enlisted in the Fourth Tennessee Cavalry, from which he was afterward cut off. He took part in many engagements, including the battles of Fort Pickens, Fla., Shiloh, Perryville, Ky., and many skirmishes, but fortunately he was never wounded nor taken prisoner.

After the war Mr. Orange located in Grundy county, Tenn., but later removed to Sequatchie county, and from there to McMinnville, Warren county, where he was engaged in the bakery business for about a year. He then went to Marion county, and from there moved to Tracy City, where he has since made his home. The greater part of his time and attention have been devoted to farming, but he has also taken contracts for coal, furnished prop timber for the mines, and has been interested in mining operations in different ways. He is a man of sound judgment and good executive ability, and in business affairs has met with excellent success.

On the 23d of June, 1863, Mr. Orange was united in marriage with Miss Nancy Jane Lockhart, who was born in Grundy county, September 23, 1844, a daughter of John C. Lockhart, and died April 23, 1893. Of the twelve children born to them ten are still living: A. L., a miner; J. C., a miner at Bon Air, White county, Tenn.; W. S., a miner at Hartshorn, Indian Ter.; James H., of Bessemer, Ala.; Fred, a miner connected with the Tennessee Coal, Iron & Railroad Co., at Tracy City; Alice, wife of W. L. King, a miner at the latter place; Hester, wife of Frank Hobbs, a miner of the same place; Lilly, Samuel and Barney, all at home; Mary, who died at the age of seven months; and Nannie, who died at the age of fourteen months.

Mr. Orange speaks English as fluently as a native, born American, and is one of the most valuable and useful citizens of his adopted county. He is an earnest member of the Primitive Baptist church, and an ardent Democrat in politics.

CHARLES A. JUSTIN, boilermaker for the Tennessee Coal, Iron & Railroad Company, at South Pittsburg, was born in Sullivan county, N. Y., August 12, 1855, a son of Philip J. and Mariah (Miller) Justin.

Philip J. Justin, our subject's father, was born in Germany. He grew to manhood and learned the blacksmith trade in the fatherland. He worked at his trade for a time in Germany and also in a number of places in France, and while in the latter country learned the French language. When about twenty-eight years of age he emigrated to the United States. He landed in New York and lived in that state until just before the war, when he moved to Clark county, Ohio. From there he moved to Franklin county, Tenn., where he turned his attention to farming. He died in Marion county, Tenn., April 11, 1896, at the age of eighty-four years. His wife was born in Poughkeepsie, N. Y., and they were married in the Empire state. She also died in Marion county, Tenn., January 17, 1894. They were both members of the Methodist church, and socially he affiliated with the Masonic fraternity. In politics he was a Republican. They were the parents of a large family of children, seven of whom grew to maturity, as follows: Mary, the wife of D. L. Buckner, of Franklin county, Tenn.; Arthur, a blacksmith and making his home and base of operations in New York; George M., was a blacksmith by occupation, and died in Franklin county, Tenn.; Charles A., the subject of this sketch; Frank, a boilermaker living in South Pittsburg; William, in the grocery business at Atlanta, Ga.; and Flora, wife of J. P. Armstrong, express agent at South Pittsburg.

Charles A. Justin, the subject of our sketch, was reared in Franklin county, Tenn., and when a boy was much given to fox hunting. At the age of twenty-one years, he began learning the trade of boiler-making and in 1878 was employed by the Tennessee Coal, Iron & Railroad Company, and has been in their employ the most of the time since. For a time, however, he was in Birmingham, Ala., working on the furnaces at that place and was also in Chattanooga, Tenn., for a time. He has also taken contracts to unload the iron ore from the barges on the Tennessee river.

May 12, 1894, Mr. Justin was united in marriage with Miss Nannie McCarthy, daughter of Eugean and Ellen McCarthy. Mrs. Justin is a native of the state of Maryland, but was reared in Chicago, Ill. She is a member of the Catholic church. Mr. Justin is a pleasant neighbor, genial, warm-hearted, and has a cheerful home. As a citizen he is loyal in his adherence to the principles of right, and as a friend and benefactor he has gained an enviable reputation. Politically he is a Republican.

OSCAR T. KELL, one of Sequatchie county's prominent and enterprising citizens, is the present register of deeds of that county. He was born June 10, 1866, the son of W. E. and Emily (Tatum) Kell. The father, W. E. Kell, was born in the Sequatchie valley, a son of Robert Kell, a native of Virginia. The family was one of the first to settle in the valley, and is closely related to the Barker family. Robert Kell died in the valley. W. E. Kell was a farmer by occupation, and was for many years a member of the county court. He is still living, and is making his home with his children; his wife died August 27, 1895. They were both members of the Cumberland Presbyterian church, and W. E. Kell still holds the office of deacon of the society in which he holds his membership. Socially he affiliates with the Masonic fraternity, and in politics he uses his elective franchise and his influence in the support of the candidates of the Democratic party. They were the parents of a family of six children, four of whom are now living, of whom the following is a record: Sarah Elizabeth, who died in infancy; James H., a farmer of the Fifth district, Sequatchie county; W. H., also a farmer of the Fifth district, Sequatchie county; Mary M., wife of O. R. Martin, a farmer of Hamilton county; Oscar T., the subject of this sketch; and Ada A., who died at the age of sixteen years.

Oscar T. Kell, whose name appears at the head of this article, was educated in the Masonic hall, completing his course of study at the age of eighteen years. He was employed for a time in the store of H. T. Kell, at Dunlap, Tenn. From there he went to Tracy City in the capacity of state guard over the convicts at that place for three years. He next began the cattle business, trading and grazing, and afterward discontinued that to engage in the drug business at Dunlap, Sequatchie county, Tenn., which occupied his attention for two years. He then returned to the old home place and lived with his parents until the death of his mother, when the home place fell to him as his share of the estate. Wherever he has been Mr. Kell has always taken an active and wholesome interest in all matters pertaining to the advancement of the better interests of the community in which he has made his home, and in local politics. In 1894 the citizens of Sequatchie county saw fit to confer upon him the duties of the office of register of deeds, which office he now holds, and is a candidate for re-election with no opposition.

September 28, 1892, Mr. Kell was united in marriage with Miss Sarah A. Beckwith. She was born in Washington, Kans., September 28, 1873, and their home has been blessed by the advent of two sons, Neil Paul and Oren Stewart. Our subject and Mrs. Kell are both members of the Methodist church South, and he is a member of the Masonic fraternity. Politically he is a Democrat.

JOHN J. SPARKMAN, a representative and leading farmer of the First district of Van Buren county, was born December 7, 1857, on the farm where he still continues to reside. His parents, Andrew J. and Elizabeth (Hunter) Sparkman, were also natives of Van Buren county, the former born November 2, 1838, the latter May 8, 1840. The paternal grandparents, John and Lavina (McElroy) Sparkman, were natives of North Carolina and Van Buren county, Tenn., respectively. The father of our subject was a farmer by occupation and served as constable in his district for two years. During the Civil war he entered the Confederate service, was captured near St. Louis, Mo., and was taken to a hospital in that city, where it is supposed that he died. His widow made her home with our subject until she, too, was called to her final rest in February, 1894.

Upon the home farm John J. Sparkman grew to manhood, and attended the public schools of the neighborhood, where he obtained a good practical education. For many years he devoted his attention exclusively to his agricultural interests, but for the past ten years has also engaged in merchandising at Bone Cave and has built up a lucrative trade. He also served as postmaster at that place for about twenty years, but was removed a few months since on account of his advocacy of the free coinage of silver. He has been district constable for six years, and also served as deputy sheriff for two years with credit to himself and to the satisfaction of the general public. In connection with general farming he has been interested in stock raising, making a specialty of fine hogs and poultry, and has been instrumental in improving the grade of the same in Van Buren county.

On the 9th of June, 1881, Mr. Sparkman married Miss Rebecca A. Moore, who was born in VanBuren county, May 12, 1852, and they have become the parents of three children: Andrew J., born April 11, 1882, died April 22, 1888; Mary E., born June 30, 1884, and Emma T., born November 24, 1886, are both attending school. The parents and older daughter are members of the Missionary Baptist church, and the family is one of prominence in social circles.

REV. PATRICK MOORE, father of Mrs. Sparkman, has for over a half century been a tireless worker in the cause of Christianity as a minister of the Missionary Baptist church, and is one of the most honored citizens of Van Buren county, his home being in the Sixth district. He was born in Greene county, N. C., October 17, 1825, a son of Thomas and Rebecca (Stepp) Moore, who were born, reared and married in Virginia, whence they removed to Greene county, N. C., and later to Cumberland county, Tenn., locating in the Crocker Neck neighborhood. Subsequently they removed to Ball's Bottom on Caney Fork, when bears and panthers were still quite plentiful in that region and from there they went to Big Bottom, finally settling near Spencer, Van Buren county. The father died at the age of fifty-three years and was the first person buried at that city. His wife reached the advanced age of eighty-six years. He was probably of Irish parentage, was by occupation a farmer and mechanic, and was a soldier in the war of 1812. In early life Mrs. Moore was a Methodist, but in 1849 joined the Missionary Baptist church, with which she ever after affiliated. Of her six children only our subject is now living; James, a farmer and Baptist minister, died in White county, Tenn.; Amanda and John both died in childhood; Frederick, a brick mason and farmer, died in Warren county, Tenn., at the age of seventy-three; Jane married William Mayfield and died in Fisher county, Tex.

Patrick Moore obtained his literary education in a small free school conducted at Laurel Cove, and while not in school he engaged in farming until twenty years of age, when he joined the Missionary Baptist church and commenced preaching. Ever since he has been a devoted minister of the gospel, and has been the means of bringing many souls to Christ. For one year after his marriage he lived in Warren county, Tenn., the following year made his home at Rocky Run, and then purchased his present farm in Van Buren county, where he has now resided over half a century.

Feeling the need of a better education, Mr. Moore attended Burritt College for two terms after his marriage, and subsequently engaged in teaching on Pine Ridge, in a free school in Spencer, and in his home district. For the long period of forty years he has faithfully served as pastor of the Laurel Creek Missionary Baptist church, and has also had charge of many other congregations, including those at New Hope and Bethel in White county; Macedonia; Greenwood; Shells Ford; Friendship; Hebron; Philadelphia; Grundy; Rutledge Falls; Coffee; Morrison and Blue Spring, both of Warren county. At times he has also served as missionary, was pastor of the church at McMinnville for a time and of a church in the upper part of Bledsoe county, has preached for many miles around his home, and has taken a deep interest in the Sunday School at Laurel Creek Seminary.

Mr. Moore was married on the 5th of December, 1845, to Elizabeth Jane Neal, who was born on Rocky river, in 1829, and died November 6, 1882, beloved by all who knew her. Her father was Charles Neal, and the family came to this county from East Tennessee. Of the thirteen children born to Mr. and Mrs. Moore only four are now living, namely: James M., a resident of Van Buren county; Rebecca, wife of John J. Sparkman, of Bone Cave; Lansford M., a farmer of this county, though formerly a merchant; and Homer, a farmer of Warren county. Those deceased are Amanda and Docia, who died at the home of their parents; Charles, who was married, but died at home; and Richard, who was married and lived in the same neighborhood. In July, 1883, Mr. Moore married Nancy Cunningham, who was born in Irving College, Warren county, December 5, 1849, a daughter of Thomas Cunningham. Four children blessed this union: Claude Fate and Fred Clay, who are still living; and an infant and John, now deceased. Mrs. Moore is also a consistent and faithful member of the Missionary Baptist church.

Mr. Moore has placed his farm under excellent cultivation and in connection with farming he successfully engaged in merchandising for fifteen years at Laurelburg, where he also erected a mill, and did quite an active business as a miller and shipper of grain. He was also instrumental in establishing the postoffice at that place, and for a short time after the war he served as circuit court clerk. Fraternally he is a charter member of the Masonic lodge of Spencer, with which he has affiliated for thirty-five years, and politically he was originally a Whig, but is now identified with the Democratic party. During his ministry Mr. Moore has received thousands into the church, and has married hundreds. His life is exemplary in all respects, and he ever supports those interests which are calculated to uplift and benefit humanity, while his own high moral worth is deserving of the highest commendation.

ROBERT BROWN SCHOOLFIELD, a talented and popular member of the Bledsoe county bar, was appointed circuit court clerk September 17, 1873, when a mere boy, and held said office five years and on 24th day of March, 1882, was appointed clerk and master in chancery of that county, and is at present performing the duties of said office. He did the work of both said offices from September, 1, 1890, to September, 1, 1894. It is safe to say that he has done more than twice the amount of public service than any man in Bledsoe county. He was born five miles below Pikeville, his present home, on the farm now owned by Lee Bros., at Lee Switch, January 15, 1849, the son of William and Mary (Brown) Schoolfield.

William Schoolfield was born in Pikeville, August 31, 1819, and is still living in that town. In 1843, which was before his marriage, he went to Bentonville, Benton county, Ark., but after a stay of three years, he returned to Bledsoe county and has since made that his home. He has served as justice of the peace for many years. By trade he is a blacksmith, learning that business when a young man, and was well adapted to that line of work. For many years he conducted a shop at Pikeville and also for some time at Lee Switch. He and his brother, O. P. Schoolfield, at one time owned the farm on which Lee Switch is now located. He was an excellent farmer and was quite successful in every line of work in which he engaged. He was married April 27, 1847, to Miss Mary Brown, who was born in Sweet Water Valley, Tenn., and moved to Bledsoe county with her parents in an early day, and is also still living. She is a daughter of William L. Brown, whose home was located in the valley, a short distance above Pikeville. They are both members of the M. E. church, South, and he is also a member of the Masonic fraternity, having joined the Temple lodge before the war and became a charter member of the Saint Elmo lodge, No. 437. In politics he was formerly a Whig but is now identified with the Democratic party. William Schoolfield's father, Dr. Aaron Schoolfield, was a Virginian by birth and migrated to Bledsoe county when a young man, and was the first of that family to settle in Tennessee. He died in Arkansas at a very old age. The family is of Scotch descent.

Our subject is next to the oldest of a family of seven children, five of whom are now living. The second in the order of birth now living is Virginia Sawyers, wife of Dr. G. W. Sawyers, now living in the Indian Territory; Edith, wife of Rev. J. R. Walker, a Presbyterian minister at Fresno, Cal.; Dr. H. F. Schoolfield, Sunset, Texas; and W. A., an attorney at Chattanooga. The deceased are: Pocahontas, the eldest, wife of R. E. Alley, of Bridgeport, Ala., died in April, 1886. Lucy Lane, wife of J. G. Lane, of Bledsoe county, died in 1889.

Robert Brown Schoolfield, the subject of this sketch, finished his education at Sequatchie College, which he attended from 1866 to 1869. His favorite study was mathematics. After leaving school he worked on a farm until 1871 and then went to Helena, Ark., and from thence to Austin, Miss. While in Austin he commenced the study of law in the law office of Gen. J. R. Chalmer. After a time he returned to Pikeville,

and entered the circuit clerk's office in the capacity of deputy clerk, under his uncle, T. G. Brown. In August, 1873, Doctor Brown died and Mr. Schoolfield was appointed in his place, serving in all, in that office, five years. Then on the account of ill health he was obliged to discontinue the work for a time. In 1882, without solicitation on his own part, he was appointed clerk and master in chancery and has performed the duties of this office continuously since, being repeatedly re-appointed. He was first appointed by Judge W. M. Bradford, his second appointment was by Judge S. A. Key, and the third by Judge T. M. McConnell. He was admitted to the bar in the year 1875, and, in connection with his other work, has been engaged in the practice of law.

December 29, 1886, Mr. Schoolfield was united in marriage to Miss Lizzie M. Stanfield, daughter of Martin and Eva Stanfield, and a native of Kingston, Tenn. To this union have been born four children: Lurton, Evah, Ray and Worth. Mr. and Mrs. Schoolfield are both members of the Methodist Episcopal church, South, and the former has been the steward of the society in which they hold their membership for many years. He is also a Mason and for a long time has performed the duties of master and several times has represented his lodge at the grand lodge. Politically he is a Democrat.

HENRY W. HILL, one of South Pittsburg's most prominent citizens, was born April 17, 1847, in Appomattox county,

Virginia. He was the son of James and Elizabeth (Garrett) Hill, both of whom were Virginians. To this union were born six children, viz.: Annie Elizabeth, Mary Etna, Leland W., Henry W., Victoria and Robert Fletcher. Three of the brothers and sisters have their homes in Danville and the other two in Lynchburg—cities of their native state. His father was a merchant and had an interest in cotton and woolen factories.

Mr. Hill did not enjoy the privilege of an education at an early age on account of the war—but notwithstanding this—through his great ambition and perseverance he has been successful in business. In 1864 he joined the Confederate army at the age of seventeen and served until April 6, 1865, when he was captured at the battle of Harper's farm, Virginia, and taken to Point Lookout, Md., as a prisoner, and was not released until July of the same year.

When he was quite young he learned the carriage and wagon making trade, but not satisfied with this he abandoned it and became a machinist and soon worked himself up to hold important positions.

In 1870 he was married to Miss Leonora Virginia Coffman, of Virginia, daughter of George and Katherine Coffman. To them were born four children—the oldest and youngest died in infancy and their mother died in 1879. The other two daughters are now accomplished young ladies.

In the fall of 1870 Mr. Hill came to Chattanooga, Tenn., and accepted a position with the Roane Iron Company. In 1872 he became the superintendent of the Chattanooga Iron Works and held this office until May, 1882. Mr. Hill was married again June 5, 1881, to Miss Mary Emma Payne, of Sulphur Springs, Ala., daughter of William O. and Sarah (Simmons) Payne. They resided in Chattanooga until 1882, when Mr. Hill entered the employ of the Tennessee Coal, Iron and Railroad Company, of South Pittsburg, Tenn., and remained with this company until 1892, when he accepted a position with the South Pittsburg Pipe Works, with whom he is at the present.

Mr. Hill and his wife have made for themselves and their two daughters one of the most beautiful homes in the town. They are members of the Methodist Episcopal church, South. He has always enjoyed the complete confidence of his employers and the same confidence of the many men he has himself employed. He is a man of strict integrity, loyal and determined in his adherence to the principles of right and to his friends, careful and methodical in his business habits and carries these characteristics into all the details of life.

———————

ELDER WILLIAM B. BREWER, a popular and respected citizen and member of the farming community of the Third district, Cumberland county, was born near Melvine, Bledsoe county, January 19, 1844, a son of Pleasant and Elizabeth (Seals) Brewer.

Pleasant Brewer was an orphan boy in North Carolina. At the age of fourteen years, he was taken by his kinsfolks to Hawkins county, Tenn., where he grew to manhood, and was married to Miss Elizabeth Seals. After their marriage they moved to the Sequatchie valley. They were members of the Baptist church, in which he was a minister of the gospel, and for many years had charge of a society of that denomination. He died in Bledsoe county, March 5, 1871, aged about sixty-five years. His wife afterward moved to Cumberland county and died there, April 28, 1887, aged about eighty-four years. Of their family of thirteen children, five are now living, viz: John Brewer, a farmer near Cookeville, Putnam county, was a soldier in Company D, Second Tennessee, in the Federal service; Fannie, a resident of Cumberland county; Nancy, widow of Robert Pugh, now living in Putnam county; our subject; and Pleasant Burton, a resident of Cumberland county, was also a soldier in the Federal service. The deceased are: Russell, who died in Bledsoe county at quite an advanced age (he had a son, John E., who was a soldier in the Second Tennessee regiment, and was taken prisoner in Hawkins county, Tenn., and taken to Belle Isle and from there to Andersonville, where he starved to death); Rebed was the wife of G. W. Presly and died in Cumberland county, Tenn.; Eliza was the wife of Jordan Edmonds; Lucinda, the wife of Drew Maynard, died in Kentucky; Margaret, the wife of· John Sweet, of Bledsoe county; David was killed during his service as a Federal soldier; and the rest died while young.

William Brewer, the subject of this sketch, spent his school days in Bledsoe and Cumberland counties, attending some after his return from the war. August 13, 1861, he left home and went to Kentucky, and September 1, of the same year, he enlisted at Camp Dick Robinson, in Company D, Second Tennessee Infantry, and was

27

discharged at Knoxville, October 6, 1864. He participated in several battles, among them Stone River, Murfreesboro, and served one year in the mounted infantry, but was never wounded. At one time a ball passed his forehead so close that it touched him but did not break the skin, and balls often came uncomfortably near, but each time he escaped without injury. After the close of hostilities he began to shift for himself, working at farming in Cumberland county about one year, and in Bledsoe county two years, and then moved from there to Cumberland county in about 1867 or 1868, and located at Brown's Gap, at the head of the valley, in the Fourth district, and about two years later moved from there to his present home.

December 7, 1865, Mr. Brewer was united in marriage to Rebecca J. Webb, widow of Thomas Hall. She was born in Cumberland county in 1845, and to her union with Mr. Brewer have been born eleven children, of whom eight are now living, and of whom we have the following record: Sarah Ann, wife of Houston Miller, a farmer of Cumberland county; Flora, wife of Daniel Schrum; Crocket died at Norwood, Wright county, Mo., in 1890, at the age of twenty years; Emma, who was the wife of Thomas Evans, of Cumberland county, is also dead; William, still living with his parents; Jane, widow of Thomas Burgess, is now living with her parents; Eli, at home; John Benton, at home; Ira, who died in childhood; Gertie, living at home; and Zanie. Mr. and Mrs. Brewer are members of the Primitive Baptist church, joining in about 1872, and Mr. Brewer was ordained October 16, 1892, a minister, and preaches at Mount Union, where he helped establish a society. He is a member of the G. A. R., at Crossville. Politically, he is a Republican.

DANIEL JACKSON ROGERS.—The maturer years of this gentleman have been devoted to the pursuit of agriculture, although the greater part of his life has been spent in the mercantile business. He owns and occupies a pleasant and profitable tract of land in the Third district, Sequatchie county, not far from the city of Dunlap, where, since the year 1891, he has pursued the even tenor of his way, gaining a little of this world's goods to tide him and his companion over the declining years and enjoying the comfort of a happy household and home.

Our subject was born in Bledsoe county, Tenn., August 27, 1831, the son of John and Delilah (Jones) Rogers, both natives of Lee county, Va. The father was a farmer all his life and died in Bledsoe county, Tenn., in the year 1833, and is buried in that county. The mother is also dead, and is buried in Rhea county, Tenn. They were the parents of a family of eleven children, whose names in the order of their birth are as follows: William, Margaret, Rebecca, Frederick J., Mary, Thomas, Elizabeth, James M., John H., George W. and Daniel Jackson, the subject of this sketch. Of this family, the last named is the only one now living. He was born on a farm near the city of Pikeville, and at the age of fifteen years he secured a position as clerk in one of the stores of that city. Two years later he began merchandising on his

own responsibility, in the country, on the present site of the city of Dunlap, and continued in business there from 1851 to the year 1891. He then sold out and moved to the farm he had purchased several years previous, which is situated about two and a half miles east of Dunlap, and has since made that his home and base of operations.

The estimable lady who for many years has had charge of the household affairs of Mr. Rogers, and has shared equally his grief and joy, and loss and gain, was born in Sequatchie county, Tenn., September 20, 1831, and became his wife November 4, 1852. Mrs. Rogers, whose maiden name was Miss Keziah Kirklin, is a daughter of Allen and Louisa (Anderson) Kirklin, the former a native of North Carolina, and the latter of Sequatchie county, born about the year 1808, the first white child born in the Sequatchie Valley. Mr. and Mrs. Kirklin had a family of eleven children, of whom we have the following record: Keziah A., Mrs. Rogers; Mary, deceased; Harriet, deceased; Louanza, of eastern Tennessee; Allen, deceased; Sophia, deceased; John, deceased; James, in the West; and Moses, of Sequatchie county, Tenn. To our subject and Mrs. Rogers have been born seven children as follows: Ellen, wife of William Thurman, of Winchester; Hester A., wife of John Stewart, Pulaski, Giles county, Tenn.; John B., deceased; Mary J., who died in childhood; James S., who now lives in Dunlap, married Miss Lizzie McColough, of Georgia, and they have four children, Hallie J., John M., Daniel J., an infant; Hallie, wife of Frank Dickinson, of Nashville, Tenn.; and Clay, who lives in Dunlap. The latter married Miss Carrie

Rankin, a native of Marion county, Tenn., and one child, Lucile, has been entrusted to their care. Mr. and Mrs. Rogers are members of the M. E. church, South. Socially our subject affiliates with the Masonic fraternity, and in politics he uses his influence and elective franchitr in the support of the candidates of the Democratic party, but has never aspired to a public office.

JEREMIAH TILLMAN WALKER, one of the most prominent men of Spencer, where he is engaged in the mercantile business in partnership with Richard L. Gillentine, under the firm name of Gillentine & Walker, and near where he is also carrying on quite an extensive agricultural business, is one of the wide-awake and well-to-do citizens of Van Buren county. He also has a partnership with his brothers in a store at Stephens Chapel, Tenn.

Our subject was born in Bledsoe county, Tenn., June 18, 1854, a son of James and Rebecca (Billingsley) Walker, both natives either of eastern Tennessee or North Carolina, the former born December 13, 1814, and the latter June 18, 1823. James Walker was a son of William and Mary (Eden) Walker. William was a son of George Walker, who lived in North Carolin, and who was a life-long member of the Primitive Baptist church. James Walker was a farmer and miller by occupation, and is still living and makes his home in the Ninth district in Bledsoe county. Mr. and Mrs. James Walker were the parents of a family of ten children, as follows: William H., Dayton, Tenn.; George W., Winchester, Tenn.; Sarah, wife of James Heard, of Bledsoe county, Tenn.; Malinda, wife of Andrew J. Card, of Abilene, Tex.; Benjamin F. lives in Bledsoe county, Tenn.; Rachel I., wife of A. C. Grear, of Bledsoe county, Tenn.; Jeremiah Tillmann, the subject of this sketch; Thomas J., deceased; Mary D. J., wife of F. A. Johnson, of Sequatchie county, Tenn., and an infant.

Jeremiah Tillman Walker, the subject of this sketch, was educated at Sequatchie College, in Bledsoe county, Tenn., took the English course, graduated and secured a diploma. After finishing his course of study he taught school for about seven years in Marion, Bledsoe and Sequatchie counties. In 1882 he entered the mercantile business at Stephens Chapel, Bledsoe county, Tenn., and was thus engaged until December, 1897, when he moved to Spencer, entered into partnership with Richard L. Gillentine, and has since been engaged in business there under the firm name of Gillentine & Walker. Together with his other lines of business, Mr. Walker has carried on a farming business ever since he started in life on his own responsibility. He is a man of excellent business capacities, having met with eminent success in all the business enterprises in which he has embarked. He is a man of strict integrity, careful and methodical in his business habits, and carries these characteristics into all the details of his life. At whatever lines of business he has been engaged he has made many friends by his push and energy. In politics he affiliates with the Democratic party, and although he has never been an aspirant after political honors, the citizens of his county have seen fit to confer upon him the duties of justice of the peace for three terms.

October 28, 1875, Mr. Walker was united in marriage to Miss Martha M. Beene, a native of Marion county, Tenn., born in April, 1855, a daughter of Elder Samuel and Mary (Kirk) Beene. To this union have been born a family of seven children, upon whom they have bestowed the following names: Allie J., Amy L., Porter S., Brents B., Dessie M., Dora K. and Anna, of whom the last named is now dead. The rest are living at home, and Allie J. is engaged in teaching at Burritt College, Tennessee, and the others are attending school. Both our subject and Mrs. Walker are members of the Christian Church.

HON. JONES C. BEENE.—There are in every community men of great force of character and exceptional ability, who by reason of their capacity for leadership become recognized as foremost citizens, and bear a most important part in the development and progress of the locality with which they are connected. Such a man is Mr. Beene, who is one of the most prominent and distinguished citizens of South Pittsburg, Marion county, and is a worthy representative of one of the honored pioneer families of the state.

He was born September 3, 1844, in Sweeden's Cove, Marion county, whither his parents, Owen R. and Martha (Roulston) Beene, had come in childhood, about 1820, with their respective parents, the former from North Carolina, the latter from Virginia. A member of the Beene family erected the first cabin built in Tennessee, and the first white child born in this state was a Beene, while the first paper published within its borders was printed at Jonesboro by our subject's grandfather Roulston, who afterward removed to Knoxville. Col. James Roulston was a soldier of the war of 1812, an officer of considerable rank under General Jackson at the battle of New Orleans, and he afterward was a prominent member of the state legislature of Alabama. He died in that state. He had received an excellent education in some institution of learning in Virginia, and became a noted geologist. Obediah Beene, our subject's paternal grandfather, was a man of means and influence, who served as justice of the peace in Marion county for forty years.

Owen R. Beene, father of our subject, followed agricultural pursuits throughout life and was a successful business man. He was married to Miss Martha Roulston in 1830, in Kings Cove, Jackson county, Ala., just across the Tennessee state line, and in 1858 they became residents of South Pittsburg, Marion county, where the former died February 22, 1895, aged seventy-eight years, the latter in January, 1898, aged eighty-one. They were active and prominent members of the Primitive Baptist church, and he was a Democrat in politics. In their family were ten children, of whom seven are still living: Mrs. Washington Pryor, whose sketch is given elsewhere in this volume; Mrs. Richards, whose husband, Thomas Richards, is a druggist of South Pittsburg; Jones C.; Mrs. Dr. Lee, of Bridgeport, Ala.; Raleigh, the present city marshal of South Pittsburg; S. J., a contractor and builder of

Memphis, Tenn.; and Mrs. D. C. Death-ridge, of South Pittsburg. Those deceased are Mrs. John G. Kelly; Mrs. William Hall; and Patton Beene, who was killed in 1887.

Jones C. Beene was educated in the schools of Jasper, but at the breaking out of the Civil war, he laid aside his text books to fight for the principles he believed to be right, in June, 1861, joining Company A, Fourth Tennessee Confederate Infantry, in which he served until May, 1865, partici-pating in the battles of Murfreesboro, Mis-sionary Ridge, Chickamauga, and many others. He then proceeded with Johnston to Atlanta, and during his service was taken prisoner, being confined at Nashville for seven months, and finally released through the intervention of Gen. Frank Cheatham and family friends. He attained to the rank of sergeant major, and proved a most fearless and gallant soldier although quite young.

After the war Mr. Beene engaged in farming for a short time, and then com-menced working for the Nashville & Chat-tanooga Railroad Company in the capacity of station agent. Subsequently he was em-ployed as a salesman in a store in Texas for four years, and on his return to Marion county was appointed agent for the Nash-ville & Chattanooga Railroad at South Pitts-burg, a position he most creditably and sat-isfactorily filled for the long period of seven-teen years. For about twenty years he filled the office of justice of the peace and was then elected to the state senate, be-coming a very active and popular member of that august body. He was appointed a member of most of the important commit-tees, and was elected secretary of many of

them, including the one on ways and means. But his most important duty was on the Beene Investigating Committee, which in-vestigated the election for governor, when Evans and Turney were the candidates, de-ciding in the latter's favor. In the councils of his state he took front rank; the meas-ures he advocated always met with warm and cordial support, and he proved a most able and efficient representative of his dis-trict. Mr. Beene has also served as post-master of South Pittsburg for four years, and mayor of the city for two years. On the 11th of November, 1893, he established the "Statesman," which he is still success-fully publishing.

Mr. Beene was married October 1, 1865, to Miss Tennie Eugenia Cotnam, who was born in Jackson county, Ala., and is a daughter of Dr. T. T. Cotnam. Nine chil-dren blessed this union, namely: Joseph C., an engineer on the Nashville & Chat-tanooga Railroad; Russell O., a clerk in the printing department at Washington, D. C.; Claude T., a resident of Shelbyville; Ida Lee, Lena M., Jones C., Jr., and Annie A., all at home; William G., who died at the age of fourteen years; and an infant, deceased.

Mr. Beene takes an active interest in civic societies and is an honored and prom-inent member of the Ancient Order of United Workmen, the Mystic Circle, the Independent Order of Odd Fellows, the Knights of Pythias, and the Knights of Honor. He has always been a stalwart Democrat in politics, and religiously is a member of the Primitive Baptist church, while his wife is a devout Methodist in re-ligious belief. Socially he is deservedly popular, as he is affable and courteous in manner, a good story teller, and possesses that essential qualification to success in public life, that of making friends readily and strengthening the ties of all friendships as time advances.

EPHRAM H. FOSTER, one of Bledsoe county's industrious and prosperous agriculturists, was born in what is now Cumberland county in about the year 1846, the son of William and Nancy (Blaylock) Foster. The father was born in Bledsoe county, Tenn., and died in Alabama when Ephram was a child, and the mother died a short time after at Bridgeport, in the same state. William Foster was a farmer by occupation and left a family of four children, three of whom are now living. Of this family our subject is the oldest. Jonah and Joshua moved from their native county to Douglas county, Mo., and from thence to Fannin county, Texas, where they have since been engaged in farming. The deceased son, Samuel, was also a farmer.

After the death of their parents, the children went to live with their grandfather, Hubbard Blaylock, and here our subject made his home until the breaking out of the war. In February, 1864, he joined Company L, Fourth East Tennessee Cavalry, and served until July, 1865. He was in Tennessee most of the time during his service, and was discharged at Nashville. After the close of the war he returned to Cumberland county, Tenn., but his grandfather had died during the war and he soon went to Bledsoe county and worked for a time as a farm laborer in the Sequatchie Valley.

After his marriage he moved to Cumberland county, and, after making that his home for several years, he returned to the valley where he has since claimed his residence.

February 4, 1868, Mr. Foster was united in marriage to Miss Sarah Hyder. a daughter of Alfred Hyder. She was born in Cumberland county, and died about the year 1878, leaving four children, three of whom are now living, and of whom we have the following record: Nancy, wife of George Sweat, of Jackson county, Tenn.; Thomas and Amanda, both still living at home, and the deceased, William, died in infancy. About the year 1879 Mr. Foster married Clementine Fields, who was born in White county, Tenn., in 1852, the daughter of Isaac Fields, a native of Kentucky. To this union have been born seven children, all of whom are living, and upon whom they have bestowed the following names: James Riley, Rachel Emeline, Jonah, Martha, Sammie, John and Annie. In political matters our subject uses his elective franchises in support of the candidates of the Republican party, but he has never sought a public office. He was once elected justice of the peace without any solicitation on his own part, but resigned after serving a short time.

JOHN F. HAYNES, a highly respected and influential citizen of Tracy City, was born near that place, in Grundy county, on the 22nd of January, 1860, and is a son of E. M. and Clerecy Eveline (Wooten) Haynes. The father was born September 16, 1820, and during his childhood was taken by his parents to Jasper, Marion county, Tenn. When a young man he worked for Benjamin Wooten, whose home was among the mountains, and whose daughter he subsequently married. Since then he has always made his home near Tracy City and has been prominently identified with the agricultural interests of this section of the state. For several years he most acceptably served as justice of the peace, and has always faithfully performed all duties of citizenship. He is a Baptist in religious belief, but his wife, who passed away September 12, 1863, was a member of the Methodist church. His father died in North Carolina.

The subject of this sketch is one of a family of seven children, of whom five are still living and in order of birth are as follows: William A., a merchant; Henry F., a miner of Tracy City; Perry D., also a miner; John F., of this review; and Mary Jane, wife of Benjamin Leverton, an employe of the Nashville & Chattanooga railroad living in Cowan, Tenn. Those deceased are Sarah Elizabeth, who married Theophilus H. Hail and died in Tracy City; and Joseph B., who was killed in 1878 by a revenue officer, James Davis.

John F. Haynes passed his boyhood and youth in much the usual manner of farmer lads, attending the local schools and aiding in the labors of the fields. He continued to assist his father in the farm work until twenty-six years of age, and later worked in his brother's mercantile store for a number of years, after which he turned his attention to coal mining for the Tennessee Coal, Iron & Railroad Company. In 1892 he was elected county assessor, and so capably and satisfactorily did he discharge the responsible duties of that office, that he was re-elected at the end of his four years' term, and is the present incumbent. No trust reposed in him has ever been betrayed, and he deserves and receives the highest confidence and esteem of his fellow citizens. The Republican party has always found in him an earnest supporter of its principles, and he is recognized as one of its leading and most prominent representatives in Grundy county. Socially he is identified with the Royal Arcanum.

On the 25th of November, 1886, Mr. Haynes was united in marriage with Miss Mattie Summers, a native of Grundy county, and a daughter of George W. Summers. They have three children living: Fred Harrison, Harvey Sutton and Clarence Dunn, and one, Minnie Olive, who died at the age of two years. Mrs. Haynes is a member of the Methodist Episcopal church and a most estimable lady.

WASHINGTON PRYOR, one of Marion county's most extensive land owners, and a very prominent farmer and stock raiser, living in the Seventh district, near the city of Jasper, was born nine miles north of that city, November 14, 1824, a son of Green H. and Obedience (Holloway) Pryor, and Green H. was a son of Matthew Pryor.

Matthew Pryor, the grandfather of our subject, and his wife were both born in North Carolina, and he was a soldier in the Revolutionary war. He moved with his family to Tennessee in an early day and settled on a farm in Roane county, and later moved to the Sequatchie valley, settled on a farm and died near Whitwell. Green H. Pryor, our subject's father, was a farmer and stock trader by occupation, and died June 2, 1862, and his wife died a few years before. She was a member of the Cumberland Presbyterian church. They were the parents of a family of twelve children, viz.: Jackson, who is living in Jasper, Tenn.; Sampson, deceased; Mary, deceased; William, a farmer living near Whitwell; John, deceased; Washington, the subject of this sketch; Preston, who died while young; Anderson, deceased; Jeremiah, deceased; Benjamin F., deceased; Eliza, widow of I. P. Alexander, is living with her brother Jackson, in Jasper; and Caroline, deceased.

Washington Pryor, the subject of this sketch, was educated in the valley, in the public schools of the district in which his boyhood was spent, and after completing his course of study engaged in farming. At the breaking out of the war with Mexico he enlisted as a private at Chattanooga, and went with the command to Memphis on flatboats, and from thence to Brazos Island, Camargo, Tampico, and to Vera Cruz in sailing vessels. He participated in the battle at the last-named place, and then moved toward the city of Mexico, taking part in the battle of Cerro Gordo. He was discharged and returned to his home in the year 1847, having served in Haskal's regiment, under Capt. William I. Standefer.

After the close of the war Mr. Pryor returned to his home and began farming and selling goods at Oates Landing. In 1850 he formed a partnership with Mr. Prigmore, and engaged in business for a time under the firm name of Pryor, Prigmore & Co. Our subject then bought out his partner and continued the store alone for several years, and also sold goods in Jasper until the breaking out of the Civil war. During this time he continued his farming operations in connection with his mercantile interests. He lost very heavily by the war, as the soldiers on both sides took his horses, mules, cattle, sheep, hogs and grain, and also robbed his store, burned his fences and plundered his house, and he also lost twenty-four slaves, and was left with nothing but his land. In 1866 he moved to Jasper and stayed one year, and then moved back to his farm near Oates Landing. In 1875 he continued his selling goods at that place, but after a few years he sold out and since has devoted his attention to farming and dealing in stock.

Mr. Pryor has been married three times, first to Miss Ruth Kelly, July 14, 1848, and to this union two children were born, viz.: Sarah G., wife of Samuel Bennett, a farmer near Oates Landing; and William A., deceased. Mrs. Pryor died December 25, 1855, and in February, 1858, our subject was united in marriage to Miss Jane Reed. She died in 1871, and Mr. Pryor was married February 22, 1872, to Miss Mary A. Beene, who was born in Marion county, Tenn., August 16, 1838, daughter of O. R. and Martha (Roulston) Beene. Her grandparents were pioneers of Tennessee. Her grandfather, Col. Joseph Roulston, and his father published the first newspaper published in Tennessee. She is the second child in the order of birth in a family of ten children, and attended school at the Sam Houston Academy at Jasper, and afterward attended the Robert Donnels Institute at Winchester. She was a member of the Primitive Baptist church. To this union have been born two children: Francis K., born February 12, 1873, and educated at the Nashville College for Young Ladies. She is still unmarried and is living with her parents, and is a member of the Cumberland Presbyterian church. The younger child, Andrew W., married Miss Mollie E. Kelly. He is a miller by occupation, and lives but a few rods from his father's home. Politically our subject is a Democrat. He is a Master Mason, holding his membership at Jasper. As a farmer he is thorough and systematic, enterprising and progressive, and has become one of the wealthy and popular men of Marion county. His lands comprise more than five thousand acres.

WILLIAM WHITLOCK, of Hebbertsburgh, is one of Cumberland county's best known and most enterprising citizens. Mr. Whitlock was born near old Philadelphia, Monroe county, Tenn., October 2, 1834. His family is an old one. His grandfather, Robert Whitlock, was born and raised in Union district, S. C., who after his marriage, to Martha Nance, went to North Carolina, where the mother of our subject was born. After some years residence in North Carolina they moved to Jefferson county, East Tennessee. Robert Whitlock spent the declining years of his life in Roane county, of the same state. He was of Scotch descent, a farmer by occupation and a member of the Baptist church.

William entered school for a few months
28

when quite young. But as soon as he was large enough to do farm work, he had to quit school to make a support for himself and mother. In the year 1857 William was married to Mary C. Bowman, December 24, 1857, by Samuel Burnett, Esq. In May, 1858, he began learning the blacksmith trade. He set up a shop in Roane county and remained there until the breaking out of the late war, taking sides with the United States government. There being no Union troops nearer than Cumberland Ford, Ky., he in company with hundreds of his countrymen refugeed and crossed the Cumberland mountains to join the Federal army. He enlisted in Company A, Fifth Tennessee Volunteer Infantry, under command of Col. J. T. Shelley. He was elected by the company as first lieutenant, in which capacity he served until his term of service expired. His company and regiment joined Sherman's army on the fourth day of May, 1864, at Red Clay, Ga.

He was in all the battles from Tunnel Hill, Ga., to the Chattahoochie river; was one of the first men to cross said river and drive the enemy away from their position on the south bank, taking two guns from them. On the 13th of July he was sent back to Marietta, Ga., on fatigue and post duty and remained there until the 10th day of November, when his company and regiment joined Thomas at Pulaski, Tenn., when Gen. Hood was marching on Nashville. He came by the way of Pulaski and forced us to return from Pulaski to Nashville, which retreat was made in good order. He was in the battle at Franklin; established the skirmish line for his brigade at Nashville. He carries one bullet in his left knee as a reminder of our late unpleasantness, but he is satisfied with the results of the war and has no hard feelings toward him who wore the gray, always ready to take him by the hand in friendly greeting. Soon after receiving the wound at Nashville Mr. Whitlock was stricken with smallpox which almost carried him off. He recovered, however, and on the 21st day of April, 1865, he was honorably discharged.

He returned to Roane county and resumed his trade just where he had left off some years previously. He also pursued farming at the same time. In 1869 he bought a farm on the Tennessee river, six miles southeast of Rockwood and lived on the same until 1872. In June of that year he took charge of the blacksmith shop of the Roane Iron Company for about fourteen months. In January (about the 20th), 1873, Mr. Whitlock's first wife was taken with the measles from the effects of which she died on the 30th. In July of the same year he went to Oakdale, Roane county, to take charge of the Oakdale Iron Company's blacksmith shops, which he ran until in April, 1874, the Company having failed and the works were shut down. In May, 1874, Mr. Whitlock was married to Pathena Ellis, daughter of Samuel Kindrick, of Roane county, a well-to-do farmer. In 1879 he went to Cumberland county, took up his residence near Hebbertsburgh, where he now lives. He owns five hundred acres of land, and has a well improved and profitable farm. Mr. Whitlock was the father of two children by his first wife—one girl and one boy. The boy died in early infancy; the daughter is still living. She is the wife of Jas. R. Kindrick, a brother to his present wife. Politically Mr. Whitlock is a Republican of the unswerving kind. He has held a number of local offices, was justice of the peace in Roane county for several years, and in 1882 was elected to the same office in Cumberland county. He was a member of the county court until 1890, when he resigned and was its chairman from January, 1884, to 1889, being twice elected by acclamation. He is connected with the Masonic fraternity and has held various positions in the lodge. He is a member of the Missionary Baptist church. His church is a member of the Big Emory Association. He joined the church in May, 1860, was baptized by his brother, Rev. A. D. Whitlock, in June, following. He has served his church as secretary for a number of years, was ordained as deacon sometime in the seventies and has served his association as its moderator for five years in succession. He is now moderator of the Salem church, though a layman.

———————

DR. ROBERT MORGAN is one of Tracy City's oldest and most efficient physicians. Having begun the study of that profession at a very early age and devoted his entire life to it, he has become very skilled and also very popular and has gained an enviable reputation as an honest and painstaking medical practitioner.

Doctor Morgan was born in Shelbyville, Bedford county, Tenn., October 25, 1832, a son of Moses and Elizabeth (Johnson) Morgan, both natives of Cabarrus county, N. C. They both moved when quite young, with their parents, to Bedford county, Tenn., were married there, and there spent the remaining years of their lives. The father was a carpenter by occupation, and they were both members of the Methodist Episcopal church, South. The father died in the year 1846, at the age of forty-five years, and the mother subsequently married Mr. George Kimbro. She died in 1882, at the age of eighty-two years. Mr. and Mrs. Moses Morgan were the parents of a family of seven children, of whom our subject is the fourth in order of birth, and of whom but three are now living, viz: German B., a farmer living in Bedford county, Tenn.; Dr. Robert, the subject of our sketch; Mrs. Sarah Cox, wife of Thomas Cox, a carpenter of Shelbyville, Tenn. The deceased are: Melissa J., Cornelia, Annie E., and George M.

Doctor Morgan grew to maturity in Shelbyville. He began the study of medicine when a boy from such books as he could obtain, and at the age of twenty-two years he began the practice of his profession in Bedford county. After practicing continuously in that county for twenty-five years, he moved to Tracy City, Grundy county, where he has built up a large patronage and has been very successful. November 17, 1856, the Doctor was united in marriage to Miss Elizabeth Locke, of Bedford county. Mrs. Morgan was born in 1842, a daughter of Weakley Locke. To this union have been born five children, of whom we have the following record: George W., a resident of Grundy county, and a blacksmith and farmer by occupation; Annie, wife of R. N. Blanton, a carpenter of Decherd, Tenn.; Mary, wife of J. W. Berry, of Tracy City, and Martha, wife of Rev. J.

R. Reeves, a Methodist minister of Hickman county, Tenn., are twins. The fifth child in the order of birth is Moses, of Tracy City. The Doctor and Mrs. Morgan are both members of the Methodist Episcopal church, South. In politics, our subject is a Democrat.

———

WILLIAM H. GRAYSON, a prominent citizen of Whitwell, now retired from active business cares, is one of the men who make old age seem the better portion of life. He is an honored son of Marion county, born on the old Ashburn farm, just above Whitwell, April 12, 1826. His father, Henry Grayson, born in Anderson county, Tenn., November 2, 1799, and during his childhood was taken to Bledsoe county by his parents. Joseph and Elizabeth (Brazil) Grayson, who located near Stephens Chapel, whence they later removed to Marion county. The grandfather, who was of English descent, and a farmer and blacksmith by occupation, entered seventy acres of land upon which Byron Hudson now resides, and there he made his home until his death, but his wife died on a farm near the Burnett school house.

During early life Henry Grayson was also a blacksmith and wagonmaker, but later gave his attention to agricultural pursuits and served as justice of the peace. He was married September 11, 1820, in Bledsoe county, to Nancy Hixon, who was born in Greene county, Tenn., July 22, 1799, and when a child was taken by her parents to Bledsoe county. For a time after their marriage they lived in what is now Sequatchie county, then removed to the farm occupied by their son Houston, and in 1857 to the one where another son, A. C. Grayson, now lives. There both died, the father November 9, 1879, the mother November 10, 1881. They are faithful members of the Cumberland Presbyterian church, and he was a Democrat in politics. In their family were the following children: Pleasant, a farmer of the Third district of Marion county; Louisa, wife of Joseph Burnette, who lives on the farm where she was born; William H., of this sketch; Patrick H., a farmer on the west side of the Sequatchie river in the Third district; James M., a ranchman of Texas; Sarah C., wife of William Cowan, of Texas; Houston, who lives on the old homestead in Marion county; Josiah, who died in infancy; and Anderson C., a prominent agriculturist of Marion county.

During his boyhood and youth William H. Grayson pursued his duties in the Burnette school and those at Red Hill and Looney's Creek, thus acquiring a good practical education, which has well fitted him for life's responsible duties. Early in life he learned the blacksmith's trade, which he followed in connection with farming until the Tennessee Coal, Iron and R. R. Company opened up their mines at Whitwell, when he took charge of their blacksmith shop, but after conducting it one year he returned to the farm. Subsequently he and his son opened a shop in Whitwell, doing a general blacksmithing business for four years. The following year was spent upon the farm, but since then he has practically lived retired at his pleasant home in Whitwell, enjoying a well earned rest.

Mr. Grayson was married December 5, 1849, the lady of his choice being Miss Sarah Cowan, who was born in Jackson county, Ala., April 1, 1827. They have three children living, namely: Joseph, who now operates his father's farm in the Third district of Marion county; Esther Louisa, wife of Byron Hudson of the same district; and Samuel H., now a resident of Chattanooga, who was formerly a salesman for Alexander Patton, then in the blacksmith business with his father, and subsequently in the employ of different railroads at Chattanooga as yardmaster, etc. Those of the family now deceased are Francis M., who was born April 13, 1852, and died in 1885, leaving a family; Henry C. and Nancy, who both died in infancy; P. L., who died at the age of twenty-seven years; and Cynthia, who married Thomas Smith and died in Arkansas.

During the Civil war Mr. Grayson's sympathies were with the Union cause, and in September, 1864, he joined Capt. William Pryor's company, which was connected with the foraging department. He was in the Georgia campaign and the siege of Atlanta, and when hostilities ceased was honorably discharged and mustered out at Nashville, on June 30, 1865. He is now an honored member of Spears post, G. A. R., at Sequatchie, and also belongs to the Masonic lodge at Whitwell. He is a pronounced Republican in politics; acceptably served as justice of the peace in the Third district for fourteen years, and several times acted as chairman. In the Cumberland Presbyterian church he and his wife hold membership. For over half a century they have traveled life's journey together, sharing its joys and sorrows, its adversity and prosperity, and now in their declining years enjoy the esteem and confidence of their neighbors and the affection of their children and friends.

ALEXANDER PROWL SMITH. — An honorable position among the farmers of the First district, Sequatchie county, is willingly accorded to this gentleman by his associates. He occupies one of the large and well-developed farms of the county, and is greatly respected in the community where he has spent the greater part of a long and useful life.

Mr. Smith was born in Hamilton county, Tenn., June 28, 1838, the son of Elijah and Nancy (Sawyer) Smith, the father born in 1810, and died in Hamilton county, Tenn., in 1840. They were the parents of a family of five children, of whom our subject is the fourth in the order of birth: Eli T. was killed in the battle of Chickamauga, September 20, 1863, and left a wife and a little daughter; Mary W., deceased, was the wife of James C. Rogers, and left two children living. One child died before her; Elisha K. married Miss Dora Rogers, and four children have been born to them, three of whom are living; Alexander P., the subject of this sketch; Elizabeth, wife of Philip T. Bradfield. They have eleven children. After the death of Elijah Smith, his widow married Martin Hartman and three children were born to them, Elbert, Henry C., and William W., deceased. Our subject's mother died September 6, 1868, in Hamilton county, Tenn.

Alexander P. Smith was reared in Hamilton county, Tenn., and was educated in the public schools of the county and the academy at Fairmount. At the age of eighteen years he began teaching school and followed that vocation for several years, and, at the same time, was engaged in farming. At the breaking out of the Civil war he ran away from home to join the Union army, and, finding the troops at McMinnville, he offered his services but was rejected by the recruiting officer on the account of disability. He then returned to his home where he was employed as a forage master at the foot of Walden's Ridge, Hamilton county. About six months later he again offered his services to the Union cause and this time was accepted. He operated principally in Tennessee and Georgia, participating in many skirmishes but was in none of the great battles. He was discharged at Nashville, June 30, 1865.

January 4, 1866, Mr. Smith was united in marriage to Miss Sarah A. Martin, daughter of Russell M. and Mary (Rogers) Martin, the father a native of McMinn county, Tenn., and the mother a native of Hamilton county, Tenn. They were the parents of a family of twelve children, as follows: Elisha R.; Elizabeth J., deceased; Douglas A.; Sarah A., now Mrs. Smith; Joseph C., deceased; California; James C.; Eliza K., deceased; Allison R.; Susan; Richard A., deceased; and William L., deceased. Mrs. Smith was born June 27, 1846, and was educated in the public schools of her native county, and to her union with the subject of our sketch have been born eight children, viz.: Mary E.; Nancy R., wife of Wyatt Thurman, of Bledsoe county; and Eli L.,

Elbert R., Newton A , Arthur B., John B. and Jesse D. All but the first two named are still living with their parents. Mrs. Smith is a member of the Methodist church. In all matters pertaining to the welfare and the improvement of Sequatchie county, Mr. Smith has proved a valuable factor. He has always sanctioned and given material aid to all matters tending to improve the status or upbuild or strengthen the local government of the vicinity in which he lives. He owns a small but beautiful and valuable farm in the First district. He is a man of excellent business qualities, is genial, warm-hearted and generous, and is highly esteemed by all who know him. Politically he is a Republican.

DUDLEY C. PECK, deceased, was for many years connected with the business interests of Marion county, and his well-spent life won him high regard. He was born in Jefferson county, Tenn., on the 24th of December, 1827, a son of Henry Peck, who resided on Mossy creek, in that county. The father was a farmer by occupation, and in addition to agricultural pursuits operated a carding machine and cotton gin. At his death Jefferson county lost one of its worthy citizens.

Dudley C. Peck was reared in his parents' home and after attaining his majority went to Knoxville, Tenn., where he secured a situation as bookkeeper in a warehouse. He occupied that position for several years and then became clerk on a steamer in the Tennessee river. While thus engaged he formed the acquaintance of Miss Nancy Mayo Kelly, a daughter of Alexander Kelly, and a representative of one of the most prominent and honored families of Marion county. On the 27th of January, 1853, was celebrated the marriage which united the destinies of these young people, and they began their domestic life on the old Oates homestead. Mrs. Peck was born May 20, 1830, in Marion county, and to her husband she proved a faithful companion and helpmeet.

In addition to agricultural pursuits, Mr. Peck devoted his energies to selling goods, and also conducted the warehouse at Oates Landing. Industry and enterprise were numbered among his chief characteristics and his well directed efforts brought him a very comfortable competence. In addition to the labors of private life he acceptably discharged the duties of a member of the county court, and did all in his power to promote the welfare and advance the best interests of the community in which he lived. He gave his political support to the Democracy, socially was connected with the Independent Order of Odd Fellows, and in religious faith was identified with the Cumberland Presbyterians, holding membership in the church of that denomination in Ebenezer. He passed away December 13, 1861, when in the prime of life, and his loss was deeply mourned by many friends as well as his immediate family, for he was a man of sterling worth, whose fidelity to every trust reposed in him gained him the confidence and good will of all.

Mr. and Mrs. Peck had a family of four children: Nancy E., wife of John C. Turner, a farmer residing with Mrs. Peck; Henry A., a representative agriculturist living in the same neighborhood, who served as tax assessor of Marion county for four years, and married Eugenie Hicks, a native of Virginia; Sallie A., at home; and Dudley C., who also resides with his mother and is a member of the county court. Mrs. Peck and all her children are members of the Cumberland Presbyterian church, and the family is one of prominence in the community, enjoying the hospitality of the best homes in this section of Marion county.

ISAAC STEPHENS McREYNOLDS, a prominent and influential farmer and stock raiser whose home is situated in the Sixth district, Bledsoe county, was born in the house which is still his home, September 17, 1845, the son of Samuel and Anna D. (Stephens) McReynolds. The mother was born December 24, 1813, and died March 4, 1873. The father was born in June, 1797, and died February 19, 1865. They were the parents of a family of five children, three of whom are now living, viz: Isaac Stephens, Mattie E., Thomas S., Joseph and Dora. The two last named are now dead. By a former marriage the father has eight children, as will appear in the sketch of Samuel M. McReynolds, on another page of this volume.

Our subject attended the public schools of Bledsoe county, and afterward took a course in the Burritt College at Spencer, working at farm work in connection with his studies. In 1866 he bought a farm of six hundred acres in the Seventh district, Bledsoe county, and made that his home until 1874. In the fall of that year he bought the old home place, in the Sixth district, and has made that his home since. This farm consists of five hundred and ninety-five acres, all first-class land and well-improved. This is the farm on which Mr. McReynolds was born, and his parents are buried upon it, not far from the house.

July 14, 1868, Mr. McReynolds was united in marriage to Miss Virginia Addie Davis, a native of Meigs county, Tenn., born September 5, 1847. She is a daughter of Robert R. and Harriet C. (Boggess) Davis, both natives of Meigs county, Tenn., the former born September 3, 1821, and the latter December 2, 1826, and both still living in their native county. They are the parents of a family of fourteen children, whose names are as follows: Obigah Monroe, Susan Olivia, Virginia Addie, Zachariah Taylor, Vasta Jane, John Boggess, Robert Clinton, Hattie Emaline, Mary Artemecia, Simon Pierce, Gustave Beauregard, William Bruce, Irby Jackson and Thomas Gibson, all of whom are still living except Simon Pierce. To our subject and wife have been born three children, of whom we have the following record: Tulloss Vander, born June 6, 1869, and is married to Miss Myra Hembree. They have three children: Claud Price, Hugh Dallas and Robert. The second son, Samuel Davis, was born April 16, 1872, and married Miss Jennie Huchins. They live in Chattanooga, where Samuel is an attorney. The youngest of Mr. McReynolds family, Bertie Lew, was born September 19, 1885, and is still living with her parents. Mrs. McReynolds was educated at Pleasant Grove Academy, near her former home. Our subject is a Master Mason, and holds his membership in the lodge at Pikeville, and both he and his wife are members of the Missionary Baptist church. Politically, he is a Democrat, but has never sought political honors, although he has held the office of justice of the peace. As a farmer he has been quite successful, and is recognized as one of the leaders and prominent men of the community. He is a loyal citizen, and an earnest and enthusiastic supporter of everything which tends to develop and bring prosperity to the locality in which he has spent his entire life.

D R. ROBERT ALYISON BRECK MOYERS, one of Jasper's popular and leading dentists, was born in Bledsoe county, Tenn., August 28, 1843, a son of Dr. Christopher and Sarah (McGowen) Moyers. The father was a son of James and Mary Moyers, the former of whom is supposed to have been born in Culpeper county, Va., and was of German descent. He moved in an early day to French Broad river, near the mouth of Long creek, in Jefferson county, Tenn., and died there. His wife, Sarah, was the daughter of Pettigrew and Elizabeth McGowen, and was born at Spartansburg, S. C., and died several years subsequent to her husband in Bledsoe county, Tenn.

Christopher Moyers, the father of our subject, was a physician. He was reared in Jefferson county, Tenn., moved to Bledsoe county about the year 1830 and settled on a farm, where he engaged in agricultural pursuits in connection with his medical practice. He bought a large tract of land in the Cumberland mountains and made that his home until his death, which occurred in 1860, after a severe and painful illness. He and his wife were both members of the Cumberland Presbyterian church. They were the parents of a family of twelve children, of whom our subject is the youngest, and of whom we have the following record: James P., deceased; Oliver H., deceased; Mary, living in White county, Tenn.; Emaline, deceased; Nancy, deceased; Sarah, deceased; Thompson, McMinnville, Tenn.; Henry, White county, Tenn.; Darwin and John died in infancy; Terressa, living near Pikeville; and Dr. Robert Alyison Breck. After the death of Christopher Moyers his widow lived with her daughter Terressa, and died while making her home there near Pikeville.

Dr. Moyers, the subject of this sketch, was educated in the public schools of the district in which he spent his boyhood. He did not attend college, as the breaking out of the war put an end to his studies for a time. He accordingly began farming, and was thus engaged until 1867, when he began the study of dentistry. In 1869 he gan the practice of his profession in Pikeville, and practiced there until the fall of 1880, at which time he moved to Jasper, where he has since made his home and base of operations. December 10, 1871, he was united in marriage with Miss Martha J. Hamilton, who was born in Bledsoe county, Tenn., twelve miles above Pikeville, the daughter of Benjamin and Mary Hamilton. To this union have been born two children —Walter E., a school teacher, and Lillie May, a teacher of music. The entire family are members of the Cumberland Presbyterian church, and the Doctor is a Master Mason, holding his membership in the lodge at Pikeville. Politically he is a Democrat, and has always adhered to the principles of that party, but in 1860 was opposed to secession, although he was in sympathy with the southern cause. Dr. Moyers is a man of much energy, and, upon leaving the dental department of the University of Tennessee in 1883, he passed very high in his examinations, and has been very successful in his practice. He is a man of good business qualifications, of the best of character, and is held in high esteem by all with whom he comes in contact.

RICHARD LAFAYETTE FLYNN, a prominent and well known character throughout eastern Tennessee, is now living on the farm on which he was born, which is located in the Third district, Cumberland county, near Lantana post office.

Mr. Flynn's mother moved to Cumberland county when it was known as "White" county, some time between the years 1810 and 1815, and located in the Thirteenth district of White county, now known as the Third district of Cumberland county. His grandfather, John Flynn, was a soldier in the Revolutionary war and belonged to a company commanded by Capt. Fortner, and was a recruit from Virginia. He died in Cumberland county in 1832, at the age of seventy-seven years. By occupation he was a farmer, following that vocation while in Virginia, but upon moving to Tennessee he retired from active business on account of old age. He also worked to considerable

29

extent at the cooper trade, and Mr. Flynn now has a barrel which his grandfather made over one hundred years ago. During the latter part of his life he was a devout member of the Christian church and meetings were often held at his home. His old homestead is still the property of the Flynn family and near where his bones lie will be the last resting place of "Uncle Dick." Grandmother Flynn died in 1837, at the age of seventy-four years.

Richard Flynn attended school three weeks when quite small, although under circumstances of much difficulty. The school was six miles from his home and he had to be carried to and from school by his aunt. He was reared on his grandfather's homestead until twelve years of age, when his mother moved to the upper part of Bledsoe county, and there he grew to manhood and was married, in 1846, to Miss Zilpah Wyatt, daughter of John Wyatt. Mrs. Flynn was born in Buncombe county, N. C., July 7, 1825. After his marriage, our subject located in the woods, opening the farm and building, where Henry Norris now lives, and made that his home for forty years. At the commencement of the war, he espoused the cause of the union and acted as a scout for then Union army, carrying many a dispatch and acting as a guide on many a dangerous expedition. He was once taken prisoner, and had his captors known that he was the famous "Red Fox," he would not have been permitted to escape. He was bearing a message to the colonel of a regiment at Sparta when he met a squad of Confederates who stopped him and the young man who was with him, but by a little strategy and a bold act, he gave them the slip, jumped over a fence and rushed through the brush, and they being on horseback, could not follow. He lost his coon-skin hat in his haste and was permitted to see the troopers tear it to pieces in their rage, and made his escape with only a bullet hole in his coat sleeve. He also acted as guide for the fugitives and for squads of the regular army. He guided Lieut.-Col. D. A. Dorsey and his comrades after they captured an engine on one of Georgia railroads, when they were making their escape from Atlanta, Ga. He also helped collect munitions of war when Rosecrans was pushed into the mountains, and was guide for him from Cumberland, Tenn., through the mountains, thirty miles, and up into Kentucky. At one time he led thirty-seven through the mountains. During the latter part of the war, Mr. Flynn belonged to Capt. J. C. Hinch's company, an independent company organized for the purpose of protecting the country from guerrillas. During the whole four years he led a life of constant exposure and danger, and as he was a constant menace to the enemy, they often made him a mark, but always found him too shrewd and artful, and for his large stock of these endowments he was nicknamed the "Red Fox." John Flynn, an older and only brother of Richard, was taken by guerrillas, while they were in search of Richard and was cruelly murdered January 3, 1865. At the close of the war Richard Flynn was by Governor Brownlow appointed tax collector of Cumberland county, which position he filled to the entire satisfaction of the people.

Mr. and Mrs. Flynn are the parents of nine children, four of whom are now living; John died at the age of eight years; Carroll died in infancy; Elsie died at the age of eight years; Ruth died at the age of five years; Elizabeth was the wife of P. H. Norris, a resident of Cumberland county, and a soldier in the Second Tennessee Union Infantry during the Civil war. She died June 6, 1891. William L., a farmer in Cumberland county; A. L., a farmer living in the Third district, Cumberland county; Thomas S. Flynn married Miss Flora Brown, daughter of J. W. Brown, of Crab Orchard, Tenn. He was county assessor of Cumberland county from 1892 to 1896. He owns the tract of land on which his grandfather lived and died and has built upon it a handsome residence. They are the parents of a bright and interesting family of four children, Clifford C., Whitelow R., Violet and Thomas Wesley. Our subject's youngest son, Philip S., is living with his parents.

Richard Flynn is a member of the Flynn Christian church and has held the position of elder for eighteen years. He grows old gracefully. He is nearing his seventy-third year but time has touched him lightly. Like one of old, his eye is not dimmed nor his natural force abated. Surrounded by numerous descendants and a large circle of friends he waits with serenity the coming of the Boatman to row him to the other shore.

WILLIAM E. HAMILTON, who owns and occupies a lovely farm at Rankin Cove, was born in Jasper, December 15, 1866, is a representative of one of the oldest and most distinguished families of Marion county. His grandfather, John Hamilton, was a native of Virginia, where he grew to manhood and married a Mrs. Weatherspoon. After their marriage they came to the Sequatchie Valley before it was opened up for settlement, it being at that time Indian land, and Mr. Hamilton had his property and crops destroyed by the government soldiers. He remained, however, and bore an important part in the development and upbuilding of this section of the state, being numbered among the honored pioneers and useful citizens. He died on his farm in the Fifth district of Marion county, and his wife passed away a few years later.

The parents of our subject are Elbert K. and Margaret (Carter) Hamilton, and the father still resides in the Fifth district within one mile of his birthplace. The mother was born near Red Clay, Ga., and died November 1, 1894. Their children were as follows: George W., who died in childhood; Eliza; William E.; Cynthia, deceased; Alice; John; and Mary. Elbert K. Hamilton is one of the leading and influential citizens of his community, has always taken an active part in local politics, and at different times has efficiently served as county and circuit clerk, and justice of the peace. He is now a free-silver Republican, and is a member of the Cumberland Presbyterian church. He is a prominent member of Altine lodge, A. F. & A. M., of which he is the present master, and several times he has represented the local organization in the grand lodge of the state.

The early education of our subject, which was acquired in the public schools of Marion county, was supplemented by a course in the Grant Memorial University at Athens, Tenn., and the Sam Houston Academy at Jasper. Naturally he is an expert mechanic, being able to do all kinds of carpentering and blacksmith work, as well as along other lines of trade, and he has made many improvements upon his farm which add greatly to its value and attractive appearance. He is an ardent Republican in politics; socially is a member of Altine lodge, No. 477, A. F. & A. M.; and is identified with every interest for the good of his community or the public welfare.

On the 25th of September, 1889, Mr. Hamilton was united in marriage with Miss Delilah A. Barker, who was born three miles east of Dunlap, in the Sequatchie Valley, and is a daughter of Moses and Alice (Stewart) Barker. Four children bless this union, viz.: Sallie E., Byron E., Alice and John A. Mrs. Hamilton holds membership in the Methodist Episcopal church, and is a most estimable lady.

———

BENJAMIN L. SIMMONS, a prominent citizen of Van Buren county, living in the Fourth district, on Cane creek, near Sweet Gum, needs no special introduction to the readers of this volume, but the work would be incomplete without the record of his life. Being one of the leading men of the community, he has been prominently identified with its industrial, agricultural and political history, and has taken an active part in its upbuilding and progress.

A native of Tennessee, Mr. Simmons was born about seventy-six years ago in White county, and his interests have always been allied with this section of the state.

In early life he engaged in the tanning business, but since the war has devoted his time and attention principally to agricultural pursuits while not serving his fellow citizens in an official capacity. For six years he filled the office of justice of the peace, his decisions being rendered in a fearless and impartial manner, and he has also served as deputy sheriff, and as tax collector of Van Buren county for three terms. Prior to the war he was a Whig in political sentiment, and during that struggle his sympathies were with the Union cause, which necessitated his leaving his home in this county for a while. Since then he has been a stanch supporter of the men and measures of the Republican party. He is an elder in the Cane Creek Christian church, and is one of its most active workers and influential members. He is a prominent member of the Masonic lodge at Spencer, which he has represented in the grand lodge at Nashville, Tenn., and also belongs to the Independent Order of Odd Fellows.

In early manhood Mr. Simmons was united in marriage with Miss Caroline Beaty, a native of White county, Tenn., who died in 1869 at about the age of forty years. Mr. Simmons' father, Joseph Simmons, also a native of Tennessee, was drowned in Cane creek, in 1862, at the age of seventy years.

Of the ten children born to our subject and his wife only five are now living. (1) Charles T., born February 4, 1849, received a good practical education during his boyhood, and upon the home farm grew to manhood. He became a teacher of marked ability, successfully followed that profession for six terms, and also served as county superintendent of public instruction. He was a Union sympathizer during the war, and although too young to enter the regular service, he was for a time with the Federal troops. Since attaining his majority he has been an ardent supporter of the Republican party, has served as deputy sheriff of Van Buren county, and is now postmaster at Sweet Gum. As a life work he has adopted farming, and is meeting with good success in his chosen calling. He is a consistent member of the Christian Baptist church, and is one of the most popular and highly respected citizens of the community. He married Miss Jennie Phifer, a native of Van Buren county, and to them were born ten children, of whom seven are now living. (2) Joseph R., the second son of our subject, was born April 29, 1853, and being an apt student obtained a good education. On starting out in life for himself he engaged in farming, but for the past four years has been interested in merchandising at Sweet Gum, and has built up a large and profitable trade. After studying law, he was admitted to the bar in 1887, and has since successfully engaged in practice in the courts of Van Buren county, winning an enviable reputation along this line. Like his father and brother, he casts his ballot generally with the Republican party, and takes quite an active interest in political affairs. He has also served as deputy sheriff, and has most faithfully and satisfactorily performed every duty devolving upon him, either in public or private life. In the Christian church he holds membership, and socially he is connected with the Masonic lodge at Spencer. He married Miss Emeline Shockley and has two children. (3) Phronia is the wife of

G. W. Lawson, of Warren county, Tenn. (4) Margaret is the wife of Thomas Miller, a farmer living on Cane creek. (5) Benjamin L. is a distinguished physician, now holding a prominent position in the Eclectic Medical College at Atlanta, Ga.

HARRIS BRADFORD NORTHCUT, senior member of the general merchandise firm of Northcut & Sons, and one of the leading business men of Grundy county, Tenn., is a resident of Altamont, the county seat of that county. He was born and reared in this section of Tennessee, and has, throughout his life, been identified with the business interests of that region.

Our subject's father, Gen. Adrian Northcut, was born in Virginia, in the year 1799, and was brought to Tennessee by his father. John Northcut, who located near Irving College, Warren county. John Northcut had been a soldier in the war of 1812 and died on his way home at the close of the war. Adrian Northcut grew to maturity in Warren county, and after making several moves, he settled in the cove which was named in his honor, five miles northwest of Altamont, which was his home for the balance of his life. He was a member of the county court about forty years and never charged the county a cent for his services in this capacity. During the muster of state militia, he served at different times in the capacity of captain, colonel and brigadier-general. In 1846 he raised a company and was appointed its captain and served in the Mexican war. He was a member of the state legislature for eight terms, or sixteen years, and during a part of that time was also a member of the state senate, and wielded a wonderful influence in both houses.

General Northcut was the representative from Warren county, and Isaac Roberts was the representative from Franklin county at the time Grundy county was established, and both men became residents of the new county. They then became leaders of the two parties contending for the location of the county seat. General Northcut proved to be the victor and the county seat was located at Altamont. He then engaged in selling goods at his home for many years. He put up the first store in Altamont, and engaged in the mercantile business, but his principal occupation was driving stock south, at which he accumulated quite a large fortune. He was very hospitable and generous and served as security for many of his friends with the result that he was called upon to pay about half the amount that he guaranteed payment, but in spite of all he was very prosperous and was known as one of the wealthy men of the county. He was not well educated but possessed wonderful forethought, good judgment and business ability. His wife was, in her girlhood, Miss Sarah Cope, and was a daughter of James Cope, a primitive Baptist minister. She was born in Warren county, Tenn., in the year 1807, and died in 1873. The General died in 1869. They were both members of the Primitive Baptist church, and in politics he was a stanch and enthusiastic Democrat, and it was said of him that he would ride a hundred miles to convince one Whig that he was wrong. The General and Mrs. Northcut were the parents of a family of fifteen children, eleven sons and four daughters, five of whom are now living, viz: Lydia Tipton, now living in Fannin county, Texas; Harris Bradford, the subject of this sketch; L. H., a farmer living on the home farm; P. K., a farmer also living on the old homestead; and Mary Walling, whose home is in Texas. The deceased are: John, who died at the old home: Stephen died in Mexico while serving in his command in the war with that country; James, a farmer, died in Warren county; William E., was a trader among the Indians and died somewhere in the West; Archibald died at his father's home; S. H. was a recruiting officer for the Confederacy and was killed in Coffee county, during the war; Lynchia L. was the wife of Colonel Hughes and died in McMinnville; Wootson L. was killed at The Wilderness, Va., May 5, 1864. Elizabeth and George both died in childhood.

Harris Bradford Northcut, the subject of this sketch, was born December 11, 1829, and grew to maturity in Northcut Cove. He attended the public school in the district in which his boyhood was spent, and afterward attended the Altamont Academy. He helped to cut the brush from the town site of Altamont when that town was laid out for the county seat. At the age of twenty-four he began driving stock south, having had several years' experience in that business with his father. In March, 1858, he began selling goods at Altamont and has been engaged in the mercantile business at that place continuously since that date with the exception of an interruption of four years caused by the war. He was a very heavy loser by the war, as he lost all that he had. His store was robbed and burned by the soldiers, and at the close of hostilities he was without means and in debt. During the struggle he was with the Confederate army a part of the time and after its close he returned to his mercantile pursuits again, and gradually retrieved his situation. The firm is now known as H. B. Northcut & Sons.

In 1862 Fannie McCraw, daughter of William McCraw, became the wife of Mr. Northcut. She was born in Hawkins county, Tenn., in June, 1839. To this union have been born three children, of whom we have the following record: Thomas B., a partner with his father and brother in the mercantile business; Mrs. T. A. is the widow of James Moffitt, deceased. She is living with her parents; James H. is also a member of the mercantile firm, and is president of the Dixie Telephone Co. Our subject and Mrs. Northcut are both members of the Cumberland Presbyterian church. Mr. Northcut is a Mason and was instrumental in the organization of Alto lodge, No. 478, at Altamont. He has held all the official positions in the lodge of which he is a member except worshipful master and has represented it at the grand lodge several times. Politically he is a Democrat.

HON. GEORGE W. DAME has spent his entire life in the neighborhood which is now his home and is one of its most honored and valued representatives. He was born on the 10th of December, 1825, and is a son of John and Elizabeth (Oyler) Dame, both of whom were natives of Virginia. The family is of German origin, and the grandfather, George Dame, who was born in Germany, came to the new world in colonial days and served through the war of the Revolution. By trade he was a brick and stone mason, and was a very earnest and consistent Christian man, whose membership was probably in the Methodist Episcopal church. His death occurred in Virginia.

John Dame, father of our subject, was born in Bottetourt county, Virginia, and his wife in Franklin county, that state. At an early day they came to Tennessee, locating in the Sequatchie Valley, and when the war of 1812 came on the father entered the service of his country. On the close of hostilities he walked from Mobile, Alabama, to his home. Later he removed with his family to Kentucky, but not liking that state he returned to Tennessee. The Indians were living in the lower part of the Sequatchie valley when they first came to this state and the region was wild and unimproved. The father learned the tanner's trade in Fincastle in his early life and was following that pursuit at the time of his death, which occurred on the homestead farm in 1867. He had reached the age of eighty-two years, and his wife passed away several years later at the age of eighty-five. In his political views he was a Whig and his sympathies were with the Union cause. Both he and his wife held membership in the Methodist Episcopal church and were people of the highest respectability, having the warm regard of all who knew them. Their family numbered twelve children, only three of whom are now living; Elizabeth, widow of E. Ridley and a

resident of Jackson county, Alabama; Sallie, widow of S. A. Rogers, a resident of Marion county, Tennessee; and George W. Those who have passed away are Valentine, who died in Polk county, Missouri; John, who died in Marion county, Tennessee; Polly, who was the wife of Isaac Kersey and died in this county; Melinda, who was the wife of Saunders Walker and died in Stoddard county, Missouri; Lucinda, who married Isaac Kersey and died in Marion county; Andrew, who died within a mile of his birthplace; Frederick, who was accidentally drowned when a boy; David, who died within a short distance of his birthplace; Daniel, who was drowned in the Sequatchie river.

George W. Dame acquired his education in the neighborhood of his home. One of his earliest recollections is of picking peach blossoms for the little girl that charmed his boyish fancy and who in later years became his wife. They attended the same school, lived in the same neighborhood, and on the 9th of October, 1845, the marriage was celebrated which united the destinies of George W. Dame and Elizabeth T. Rogers. She was the daughter of George Rogers, and was born in November, 1827, within a half mile of her present home. Her entire life has been passed in this locality and for more than half a century she has been to her husband a faithful companion and helpmeet.

Mr. Dame entered upon his business career as an employe in a tan yard, but during the greater part of his life he has carried on farming and stock-raising. His career has been one of industry, enterprise and unflagging perseverance, and in all matters of business his reputation is unassailable.

Mr. Dame is a recognized leader in matters of public interest, and his influence and counsel have been important factors in molding the public progress to goodly ends. During the muster of the militia he served both as sergeant and captain. For the long period of twenty-five years he filled the office of justice of the peace, discharging his duties with marked fairness, promptness and impartiality. He was also chairman of the county court for many years, and in 1868–69 he represented his district in the state legislature. His political support was given to the Whig party in early life and when the war came on he strongly sympathized with the Union cause and became an advocate of Republican principles. He has since voted for the men and measures of that party, and on political questions is well-informed. Socially he is a member of the Masonic lodge in Jasper, and both he and his wife are members of the Methodist Episcopal church, with which they have been identified for more than half a century. Their upright and useful lives exemplify their belief, and their good deeds have won them the love and confidence of all. The career of Mr. Dame has been characterized by devotion to all the duties of public and private life. He is a man of high intellectuality, broad human sympathies and honorable purpose; honor and integerity are synonymous with his name, and he enjoys the respect, confidence and high regard of the entire community. Although he has passed the Psalmist's span of three score years and ten, his is a useful old age, and when he shall have been called to his reward he will leave to his descendants that priceless heritage of the good name which is rather to be chosen than great riches.

Mr. and Mrs. Dame had a family of twelve children, eleven of whom reached mature years and were married: David V.; Sarah E., who became the wife of A. J. Quarrels, and died at the home of her parents; Minerva, who died in infancy; John W., who is engaged in farming in the Seventh district of Marion county; Mary A., wife of George Ramsey; Martha M., who became the wife of James Quarrels, and died in Cole City, Ga.; Nancy J., wife of Alex Rogers; Alex, who is living in Chattanooga; James B., an agriculturist of Logan county, Ark.; Laura, wife of Joseph McBride, a resident of the Seventh district of Madison county; Kate, wife of Sherman Warren, also of the Seventh district; and Estelle, wife of Thomas Smith, of Dayton, Tenn.

David V. Dame, the eldest of this family, acquired his education in the public schools of the neighborhood, and on laying aside his text books began farming on his father's land. He was born on the homestead farm, four miles east of Jasper, December 4, 1846, and during the greater part of his life has devoted his energies to agricultural pursuits. Since 1868 he has resided upon the farm which is now his home, and all of the improvements upon the place stand as monuments to this thrift and enterprise. Industry and energy are numbered among his chief characteristics and his well directed efforts have brought to him a handsome competence which is the merited reward of his labors.

On the 27th of August, 1868, Mr. Dame was united in marriage to Miss Sarah Mitchell, a daughter of George Mitchell, who removed from Alabama to Marion county, and became one of the leading agriculturists of this locality. Mrs. Dame was born in the Seventh district of the county, April 19, 1841, and by her marriage has become the mother of one son, George M., who is still with his parents. Mr. Dame and his son are members of the Methodist Episcopal church, and Mrs. Dame holds membership in the Cumberland Presbyterian church. Their home is noted for its hospitality and the members of the household occupy an enviable position in social circles.

Mr. Dame is one of the most prominent and stalwart Republicans of the county. He has studied broadly the issues and questions affecting the welfare of the country and his views are the result of earnest consideration. He is now chairman of the Republican central committee of Marion county, also of the executive committee, and his able management in the organization of campaign forces has resulted in some notable Republican victories. He is a loyal and worthy citizen who has the interest of his county at heart, and with liberal hand does he contribute to the support of all measures and enterprises intended for the public good. Socially he is connected with the Olive Branch lodge, of Jasper, since 1869, and is a worthy exemplar of that benevolent and time-honored fraternity. In 1876 he represented his lodge in the grand lodge, and again in 1893 and 1894. His career has been marked by the strictest integrity and faithfulness to every trust reposed in him

30

and his record is unclouded by shadow of wrong. He is known as an honorable man, a pleasant, social companion, and a devoted husband and friend. There is also particular satisfaction in reverting to the life history of the honored and venerable gentleman whose name initiates this review, since his mind bears the impress of the historic annals of the state through seventy-five years, and from the fact that he has been a loyal son of the republic and has attained a position of distinctive prominence in the community where he was born and where he has retained his residence to the present time, being one of the revered patriarchs of the community.

WILLIAM H. SMITH.—Among the farmers in the prime of life in Sequatchie county, a good station has been attained by the gentleman above named, whose career has been marked with energy, prudence and persistent effort. His well-directed labors have resulted in the attainment of a good farm on the east side of the Sequatchie Valley, in Sequatchie county, where he is surrounded with those improvements and home comforts which make life enjoyable.

Mr. Smith was born December 12, 1863, the fourth child in the order of birth of a family of thirteen children, born to Dr. and Mrs. Starling Tried Smith, a sketch of whom appears on another page of this volume. He was educated in the public schools of Dunlap, and, after completing his course of study, combined farming and teaching school for a number of years. In political views he is a Democrat, and on that ticket has been elected to several of the district and county offices. He served as constable two years and was sheriff for one term, and has always been interested in and taken an active part in all matters pertaining to the welfare of the community or the strengthening or upbuilding of good local government. Socially he affiliates with the Masonic fraternity.

December 18, 1888, Mr. Smith was united in marriage with Miss Mary L. Henson, daughter of W. R. Henson, whose biography appears on another page of this volume. Mrs. Smith was born in Sequatchie county, October 12, 1866. To this union have been born three children, as follows: Samuel H., born June 30, 1890; Gladdys A., born July, 1, 1894; and Riley H., born December 30, 1897. Mr. Smith is a member of the Baptist church, but his wife is a Methodist.

WILLIAM ALEXANDER PRYOR, one of Marion county's popular and well-to-do citizens, is carrying on an agricultural and horticultural business near the city of Jasper, in the Seventh district. He was born in Marion county, Tenn., September 16, 1837, a son of John H. and Harriet (Williams) Pryor. John Pryor is supposed to have been born in North Carollina, and was a son of William Pryor. Harriet (Williams) Pryor was a native of Virginia. Her father was a direct descendant of Roger Williams, of Rhode Island.

Our subject's parents were married in the Sequatchie valley, and settled on a farm there. In 1838 they moved to Chattanooga, Tenn., where the father followed the cooper's trade until his death, which occurred January 19, 1844. His wife then returned to Jasper and spent the remaining years of her life in that city. She died in May, 1868. They were both members of the Methodist Episcopal church, and in politics the father was a Whig. They were the parents of twelve children, of whom we have the following record: Hayden, deceased; Matthew, deceased; Mary N., deceased; Nancy J.; Juda S., deceased; Betsey A., deceased; Sarah, deceased; Philip G., a farmer living on Looney creek, Marion county; Paul M., deceased; William A., the subject of this sketch; Harriet, deceased; and one who died in infancy.

William Alexander Pryor, the subject of this sketch, was educated in Chattanooga, after which he followed the carpenter trade for a number of years. In 1863 he went to Kentucky to evade the war, but later enlisted in the Union army at Louisville. He was first sent to Nashville, and from thence to Lookout Mountain, where he served on detached duty until the close of the war. He was discharged in August, 1865, and returned to Lookout Mountain, where he had previously lived. In the beginning of the war he was arrested by the Confederate government on account of his sympathy with the Union cause, and was taken to Bridgeport, Ala., and confined for about three weeks. A Confederate soldier then assisted him in making his escape, about eleven o'clock one night in May, while the guard was asleep.

April 19, 1866, Mr. Pryor was united in marriage to Miss Louise Cox, who was born near Jasper, Marion county, Tenn., a daughter of George W. and Tabitha (Pearson) Cox, and their wedded life has been blessed by the advent of a family of four children: Hattie, deceased, was the wife of M. A. Wall; May, wife of R. B. Patton, a moulder living in South Pittsburg; Frederick died in childhood while his parents were living in Texas; and one who died in infancy. Mr. Pryor lived at Lookout Mountain about two years after his marriage, and then moved to Jasper and engaged for a time in the meat-market business, but the most of his time has been devoted to farming. In 1871 he moved to Grayson county, Texas, and, after making that his home about one year, returned to Marion county, Tenn., and began farming there. In 1892 he bought a tract of land three miles east of Jasper, in the Seventh district, and began farming on a scientific plan, making a specialty of small fruit. In this line of work he has been quite successful, and has become one of the substantial and well-to-do citizens of the district, and has accumulated considerable means. He and his wife are both members of the Cumberland Presbyterian church, and he is a member of the Grand Army of the Republic. Politically he is a Republican, but has never aspired to office.

REV. ARTHUR L. PARKER, a well-known and beloved minister of the Missionary Baptist church, lives in the Sixth district, of Van Buren county of which county he is a native. He was born December 26, 1825, in the Third district, and is a son of Arthur and Eleanor (Ballard) Parker, both natives of Grayson county, Va., and the latter the daughter of William Ballard. They were married in the Old Dominion but at an early day came to Tennessee, locating upon a farm now in Van Buren, but at that time formed a part of White county. Throughout life the father followed agricultural pursuits. In 1830 he went to Springfield, Ill., on business, and while there was taken sick and died, his remains being interred at that place. The mother died about 1845, in White county, this state, where she was laid to rest. Both were earnest members of the Christian Baptist church and were held in high esteem by all who knew them.

In the family of this worthy couple were ten children, namely: Andrew K., Elizabeth, Margaret and Samuel, all now deceased; Caroline, widow of Nathan Trogden and a resident of McMinnville, Tenn.; Susan, deceased; Mary, widow of Barnet K. Mitchell and a resident of Nebraska; Arthur L., of this sketch; and Joseph and William, both deceased.

Mr. Parker, of this review, obtained his literary education in the York Academy at Spencer (now extinct), and subsequently engaged in teaching for a time. On the 19th of December, 1849, he was united in marriage with Miss Lodema Worthington, who was born in the Sixth district, Van Buren county, June 22, 1831, a daughter of William and Elizabeth Worthington. Eight children blessed this union, namely: William W., a prominent physician of Smithville, Tenn., who married Violet Sparkman; Mary E., wife of Solomon Sparkman, a farmer of the First district, Van Buren county; Elizabeth K., wife of Isam Hastons, of White county, Tenn., Samuel J. and Lodema Ursaline, both deceased; Theodocia E., wife of Samuel Johnson, of the Sixth district, Van Buren county; Arthur J., who married Ada Sparkman and is successfully engaged in the practice of medicine in Dibrell, Warren county, Tenn.; and Lenora B., wife of Edward Angel, of Spring City, Tenn. Mr. and Mrs. Parker have eighteen grandchildren and five great-grand-children.

Mr. Parker's brother, Andrew K., was the first clerk of Van Buren county, and at his death, after serving six years in that office, was succeeded by our subject, who was appointed to the position in 1847, and most efficiently served his fellow citizens in that capacity for the long period of twenty-five years. In 1853 he located upon his present farm of three hundred and fifty acres in the Sixth district, and in connection with his ministerial labors has successfully engaged in agricultural pursuits, becoming a well-to-do and prosperous citizen. He took no active part in the Civil war, and when peace was once more restored he was not required to take the oath of allegiance. He lost considerable during the conflict.

In 1860 Mr. Parker began preaching as a minister of the Missionary Baptist church, and has since served as pastor of a number of congregations in Van Buren county, and for three years was a missionary preacher. He has been extremely successful in his ministerial work, has brought many into the church, and has been an incessant and un-tiring worker in the Master's vineyard. He has found in his wife an able assistant in all church work, for she is an earnest Christian woman and has proved a true helpmeet to her husband. Politically, he is a Democrat, and fraternally is a member of the Masonic lodge at Spencer. After a pure, honorable and useful life, actuated by unselfish motives, he may rest assured that he has the confidence and respect of all who know him and that the people are not un-mindful of the great good he has accomplished in their midst, and at this advanced age has recently resigned the pastoral care of all his churches and is now giving himself wholly to an evangelist's work with a clear, strong and musical voice witnessing over thirteen hundred conversions in the last six years.

JESSE CARROLL WORTHINGTON, a prominent and well-to-do citizen of Bledsoe county, and one of the leading farmers of the Fourth district, was born at Big Springs, in the Fourth district of Bledsoe county, January 30, 1831.

Mr. Worthington is a son of William and Margaret (Brown) Worthington. The family settled in the Sequatchie Valley in the year 1800, when the Indians still inhabited it, and made their home on the east side of the valley on the land now owned by Jane Worthington. William Worthington, soon after he was married, moved on to the farm now owned by Robert Worthington, which was formerly owned by a cousin, John Worthington. He was twice married and reared a very large family. His second wife was, in her girlhood, Miss Mariah Hutcheson, of Jackson county, and is still living on the old farm. By the first marriage were born twelve children, of whom five, Jesse Carroll, John, William, Rubin and Sarah are still living. Of the children born to the second marriage, five are now living: Mart, Tom, Frank, Eveline and Robert. William Worthington died at Big Springs, in November, 1896, at the age of ninety-two years, and is buried near Big Spring on the farm.

Our subject spent his school days in, Sequatchie Valley. At the age of twenty-one he went to Union Point, Ala., where he was employed in laying track on the Union Point & Columbus railroad. From there he went to Hamilton county, Tenn., and after following the vocation of a farmer for two years, entered the· employ of the East Tennessee & Georgia railroad, working on the Dalton branch of that road, and hauled much of the lumber for the bridge across the Chickamagua. He next returned to Bledsoe county, Tenn., and lived for a time on the farm his brother John now occupies, after which he moved to his present farm. Of the four hundred and fifty-three acres it comprises, two hundred acres is cleared and in a high state of cultivation, and altogether is a very pleasant and attractive home and profitable farm.

In 1854, Mr. Worthington was united in marriage to Margaret Seagraves. She was born in Bledsoe county, Tenn., and died January 8, 1856, leaving one daughter, Margaret, who is deceased. Our subject subsequently married Sarah Shirley, who was born in Bledsoe county, Tenn., and died in 1862. To this union were born five children, three of whom are now living: James, in Kansas; Thomas, in Idaho; and William, in Missouri. The two now dead were Samuel, who died when quite young, and Jennetta became the wife of James Sampson, and died in Arkansas. In 1867 our subject was united in marriage to Mary Jane Shutters, also a native of Bledsoe county.

In 1861, Mr. Worthington joined Company F, Fourth Tennessee Cavalry (Confederate), and was with it when it became a battalion. He was in the battle of Perryville, and was with Hood in Kentucky, and at Cumberland Gap. His only wound while in the service was in his hand which resulted in the loss of a finger.

———

JAMES LONG.—An honorable position among the farmers of the Sixth district, Marion county, is willingly accorded to this gentleman by his associates. He occupies an immense and well developed farm and is operating a very extensive agricultural business, and is greatly respected in the community where he has spent the greater part of his life.

Mr. Long was born in Mullins Cove, Marion county, Tenn., February 11, 1855, and is a son of Henry M. and Sarah J. (McGill) Long. Henry M. was a son of Henry and Zilpha (Stepens) Long. Henry Long moved from Washington county, Va., in 1807, and settled in Sequatchie valley, near Inman, and engaged in farming and dealing in stock for about four years. He then moved to Mullins Cove when he had to cut a road through the timber in order to move his goods to his new home and entered a large tract of land there. He settled near Oates Island and was the first man to move stock into that community. He died there September 16, 1875, at the age of ninety-four years, and his wife died in the year 1860, and both are buried in the cemetery the former selected before his death, on what is now our subject's farm. They were the parents of a family of ten children, as follows: Jackson, Nancy, Mary, Alfred, James M., Susan, wife of Wilford Merritt, near Victoria; Henry M., the father of our subject; Minerva; David and Finetta, all of whom are dead except Susan.

Henry M. Long, the father of our subject, was born in Mullins Cove and was educated in the public schools of that community, and throughout his life followed the occupation of farming and dealing in stock. He died at his home in 1857, and his wife died in June, 1856, and both are buried at Wahatchie. Both were members of the Cumberland Presbyterian church. The mother and her daughter, Tennessee, both died on the same day of congestive chill, and both are buried in the same grave. Mr. and Mrs. Henry M. Long were the parents of a family of four children, of whom we have the following record: Tennessee, deceased; Maloy, a farmer in northwestern Louisiana; Balaam, a farmer living near Victoria, has been married twice. His first wife was Miss Mary Jackson, and after her death he married her sister, Hester Jackson. The fourth and youngest of this family is James, the subject of this sketch.

James Long received his primary training in the public schools of the district in which he spent his boyhood and supplemented it with a course in the Sequatchie College, near Pikeville, which is not now in operation, and also the Hiwassee College. He was married November 25, 1875, to Miss Rhoda E. Greer, who was born in Grassy Cove, October 9, 1855, and was educated in the same schools with our subject and their courtship began while they were in school. Mrs. Long taught school a few terms before her marriage. To this union have been born ten children, upon whom they have bestowed the following names: Cora M., Henry C., Moses M., Richard M., Susan O., James B., Flora T., Wed R., Cecil C. and William A., of whom, Moses M., the third in the order of their birth, is dead. The nine living are still making their home with their parents. Mrs. Long is a member of the Christian church.

Mr. Long owns a part of his grandfather's old farm, and in all has a tract of about one thousand three hundred acres. He settled where he now lives in 1892. Politically he is a stanch and enthusiastic Republican, and on that ticket he was elected justice of the peace in 1895. In the same year, also, he was appointed postmaster at Oates Island, and has since served in that capacity, keeping the office in his home. He is a man of good business ability, and, as a farmer, has been very successful and is recognized as one of the leading and influential agriculturists of the community. During the Civil war the Long family was in sympathy with the Federal cause.

WILLIAM O. KEARLEY, county trustee of Cumberland county, was born December 3, 1859, and is the son of Columbus and Sarah (Rector) Kearley. Columbus Kearley was a son of William Kearley, who was a native of North Carolina and moved from thence with his mother to Tennessee in 1810, and located at the head of the Sequatchie valley, in what is now Cumberland county, and made that his home until his death. He was born in 1799 and died in 1886. Politically, he was a Whig, a Union man and a Republican, and was a member of and an officer in the Methodist church. Columbus Kearley, like his father, has spent his whole life on the farm. In 1870 he was elected clerk of the county court, and ably performed the duties of that office four years. Our subject's mother was born in Putnam county and died in Cumberland county in 1889. To Mr. and Mrs. Columbus Kearley were born ten children, five sons and five daughters, six of whom are now living. One son, James, died at the age of twenty-two; and three daughters, Nancy Jane, the first and eldest of the family, died in infancy; Annie, the wife of T. J. Parks, a farmer in Cumberland county, died at the age of thirty-five years; and Sarah died at the age of seventeen years. Of the six now living, we have the following record: M. L. Kearley, a farmer near Crossville; John, also a farmer near Crossville; Ben, a printer by trade, has worked in many newspaper offices and is now connected with the Pikeville ''Reporter''; Alice and Ellen, living at home; and the subject of this sketch.

Mr. William Kearley was educated in the common schools of his district, and subsequently taught school at Flynns, Hale Chapel, Flat Rock and Lantana. After leaving the work at the last named place, he entered the Grant Memorial University, at Athens, Tenn., after which he taught at Glen Alice, Roane county, and Flat Rock,

in Cumberland county. He was married in 1888 to Miss Letitia Brown, daughter of J. W. Brown. She is also a native of Cumberland county. To this union have been born four children, one son and three daughters: Seward, Pearl, Laura and Grace.

Since his marriage, Mr. Kearley has made the Third district his home. He attended school for a time after his marriage, at the same time working for the support of himself and his wife and to defray his school expenses. In 1890, he was appointed county superintendent of Cumberland county by the county court to finish an unexpired term. In August, 1896, he was elected to the office of county trustee, the duties of which still occupy his attention, and he is proving himself a well-qualified and efficient officer. Politically, he is a Republican. Mr. Kearley is a member of the Blue lodge at Crossville, and he and his wife are members of the Christian church.

WILLIAM RICHARD McREE, M. D., one of Marion county's popular and efficient physicians, was born in Soddy, Tenn., May 23, 1863, a son of Robert Clark and Mary A. (Anderson) McRee, the father born in Soddy, Tenn., in 1836, and the mother born at Sunnyside, Tenn., in 1840. Robert Clark McRee was the son of Robert Clark McRee, Sr., who was born at Charlotte, N. C., and moved to Soddy in an early day, and assisted in removing the Indians from that section to their reservation in the Indian Territory. He died at his home in Tennessee in 1878.

Robert Clark McRee, the father of our

subject, received his primary training in the Mobry School, and afterward studied law with Judge Hopkins, of Atlanta, Ga. He commenced the practice of law in 1866, at Chattanooga, and was thus engaged for four years. He then became connected with the Soddy Coal Co., and, after working in their employ for four years, he severed his connection with the company to accept the office of judge of Hamilton county and served one term, or eight years. He was then appointed coal oil inspector at Chattanooga, and served in that capacity two years. In 1894 he retired from public life and has since devoted his time to agricultural pursuits on a farm situated two miles east of the village of Soddy, which has been his home since he settled in Hamilton county. He was also a soldier in the Civil war, enlisting in the Confederate army early in the war and served until its close. He was married in 1861, to Miss Mary Anderson, daughter of Col. Josiah Anderson who was stabbed to death on the account of his extreme Southern sympathies. They are the parents of a family of eleven children, of whom the subject of our sketch is the oldest. The second in the order of birth is Josiah A. McRee, M. D.; Nannie died while young; Thomas died while young; Lizzie, unmarried; Alma, wife of Thomas R. Sangster, an attorney living in Chattanooga, Tenn.; Anna, deceased, was the wife of James E. Davis, now of Sherman, Texas; Hugh C., a physician; and Iris, Dugal and Park are still unmarried. The parents are both still living. They are Old-School Presbyterians, and socially the father is a Master Mason, holding his membership in the lodge at Soddy.

Dr. William Richard McRee, the subject of this sketch, was educated in the common schools of Soddy, the University of Tennessee, and King College at Bristol, Tenn. He also attended the lectures at the Vanderbilt University, at Nashville, Tenn., graduating in 1887 with the degree of M. D., and began practice the following year at Whitwell, where he still makes his home and base of operations. The life of Dr. McRee since locating in Whitwell has been one of continued successes in every direction and in every line in which his faculties have been directed. He is prominent in the social circles of the village and vicinity. In matters tending to the general welfare and to develop the business and social interests of his adopted town he has taken a hearty interest and has aided materially in various ways in the upbuilding and strengthening of good local government. He is a member of the Knights of Pythias, the Independent Order of Odd Fellows, the Modern Woodmen of the World and the White Shield. He is also a member of the Old-School Presbyterian church. As a man and citizen he is highly respected, and as a physician and surgeon he stands at the head of his profession and has built up an extensive and profitable practice. Politically he is a Democrat.

JAMES D. WILEY, the well-known mine foreman at East Fork and Bryant Ridge mines, at Tracy City, is a native of Grundy county, Tenn., born August 30, 1853, and is a son of Thomas A. and Elizabeth (Harrison) Wiley, the former born in Franklin county, this state, in 1833, the latter in Grundy county, in 1837. The paternal grandfather, Peter Wiley, was a native of North Carolina and one of the pioneer settlers of Franklin county, Tenn., where he married Evelina Long, whose birth occurred in Virginia. He located near Alto, and died within two miles of his place of settlement, at the age of seventy years. He was a farmer by occupation, and was a soldier of the Mexican war. His wife spent her last days in Kentucky and there her death occurred. They reared a family of thirteen children, among whom was Thomas A. Wiley, our subject's father, who was a trader and stock-dealer, and at different times was also interested in other business. In his political affiliations he was a Democrat, and in religious belief a Methodist, holding membership in the Methodist Episcopal church, South, at the time of his death, which occurred at Sewanee, Tenn., about fifteen years ago. His wife survived him for some time, dying at the same place June 15, 1894.

Their children were James D., of this sketch; Frances, wife of J. M. Castleberry, of Sewanee; William H. and Jefferson D., both miners of Tracy City; Melinda, wife of I. N. Stewart, a carpenter and builder of Winchester; Elizabeth, a dressmaker of Sewanee; Alice, widow of George Kurl and a resident of Sewanee; Martha, wife of H. C. Harrison, a miner of Tracy City; Thomas A., who died at the age of three years; and Nancy, who died at the age of thirteen.

James D. Wiley obtained a good practical education at Fayetteville, Lincoln county, Tenn., in what was then a splendid school taught by Hal Dickinson. On lay-
31

ing aside his text-books, at the age of sixteen years, he turned his attention to farming, and, being the oldest son, he took charge of the home farm two years later, as his father removed to Sewanee on account of ill health. There he engaged in gardening for about three years, and after his removal to Tracy City, in 1872, he was in the state service as guard for the same length of time. Later he engaged in braking on the railroad, and was employed in a business house in Tracy City for a time, after which he became interested in mining. He has steadily worked his way upward from track man, becoming familiar with every department of the business, until he now holds the responsible position of mine foreman. He is one of the most faithful and trusted employes of the company, and the confidence reposed in him has never been betrayed. As a public-spirited citizen he takes an active interest in the upbuilding of his town, and was a director of the Grundy Building & Loan Association, the first organization of the kind formed in this community.

On the 27th of January, 1877, Mr. Wiley married Miss Ellen Farrell, daughter of Patrick and Margaret Farrell. She was born May 10, 1859, and with her husband holds membership in the Methodist Episcopal church, South, in which he is serving as chairman of the board, steward and Sunday-school superintendent. He is a prominent member of Brice Thompson lodge, K. P., and which he has also represented in the grand lodge of the state. He also belongs to the Independent Order of Odd Fellows, the National Union and the Royal Arcanum, and politically is identified with the Democratic party, though he usually votes for the man whom he considers best qualified to fill the office, regardless of party affiliations. He has been a member of the school board, and in all the relations of life has been found true and faithful to every trust reposed in him.

WILLIAM ALEXANDER PRYOR, JR.—The motto "merit always commands its reward" is well exemplified in the career of him whose name introduces this sketch. This is a progressive age, and he who does not advance is soon left far behind. Mr. Pryor, by the improvement of opportunities by which all are surrounded, has steadily and honorably worked his way upward and has attained a fair degree of prosperity, being the present superintendent of coke ovens at Whitwell for the Tennessee Coal, Iron & Railroad Co.

A native of Marion county, Mr. Pryor was born in Jasper, July 9, 1865, a son of Philip G. and Temperance (Prigmore) Pryor. The father was born one mile south of Whitwell, in the same county, September 9, 1832, and is a son of John H. and Harriet (Williams) Pryor, natives of North Carolina and Virginia, respectively, who on coming to Tennessee located in Roane county, whence they came to Marion county. Subsequently they lived for two years in Illinois and then returned to Marion county, Tenn., but in 1838 removed to Walker county, Ga., where they made their home for four years. Their next place of residence was in Hamilton county Tenn., where the grandfather died in 1844, his wife sur-

viving him several years and dying in Jasper. Both were consistent members of the Methodist Episcopal church. She was a direct descendant of Roger Williams, who in early colonial days was banished from Massachusetts on account of religious belief, and with his followers founded the colony of Rhode Island. Twelve children were born to John H. and Harriet Pryor, namely: Hayden, Matthew, Mary N., Nancy, Julia, Elizabeth A., Sarah A. and John, all now deceased; Philip G., the father of our subject; Paul N., deceased; William A., who lives near Jasper; and Harriet, deceased.

In October, 1862, Philip G. Pryor joined the Confederate army as a private, but was soon promoted to the rank of second lieutenant, in Captain League's company, Colonel Smith's regiment. After participating in the battle of Richmond, Ky., and other engagements, he resigned in January, 1862, and returned home. In October of that year he married Temperance Prigmore, a daughter of J. O. Prigmore, and the children born to them are J. R., now a merchant of Whitwell; William A., of this review; J. H., a blacksmith, whose sketch appears elsewhere in this work; Ollie, wife of William Richards, of Texas; Annie, wife of James Grayson, who lives near Red Hill, Marion county; and Elizabeth, Ella and David, who are still with their parents. Since a young man the father has engaged in blacksmithing, but is also a millwright by trade, and is now following farming in connection with the former occupation. For six years he capably filled the office of justice of the peace, and for two years served as tax assessor of the Third district of Marion county. In 1870 he removed to Independence county, Ark., and after a residence there of two years located in Boone county, that state, but in 1875 returned to Marion county, and now makes his home at Ketner's Cove. With the Methodist Episcopal church, South, he and his wife hold membership, and their sterling worth and many excellencies of character have gained for them a host of warm friends.

The free schools of Marion county afforded our subject his early educational privileges, but later he was a student in the Looney Creek school and at the Hall in Sequatchie county. Under his father's direction he learned the carpenter's trade during his youth, and then commenced working at that occupation for the Tennessee Coal, Iron & Railroad Company, serving them in that capacity for two years. For the following two years he was in the mines, later was a timberman, and for four years was a weigher of coal. Since then he has most efficiently served as superintendent of the coke ovens, and has the confidence and esteem of his employers to a marked degree.

Mr. Pryor was married November 28, 1886, to Miss Maggie Gott, who was born near Inman, Marion county, a daughter of Rafael Gott, and they now have two children: Alton L. and Eugene A. The parents are both identified with the Cumberland Presbyterian church, at Oak Grove, in which Mr. Pryor is now serving as ruling elder. He belongs to the Masonic order, the Knights of Pythias and the Woodmen of the World fraternities, and as a Democrat has always taken an active part in local politics, doing all in his power to insure the success of his party. He is the present chairman of the executive committee of Marion county and ranks among the most honored counselors of his party, while his opinions and advice are often sought on questions of importance to his city and county. He is well informed on the leading questions and issues of the day, and is a most progressive and public-spirited citizen.

STEPHEN A. PARKINS.—Among the men who are gaining a good support by tilling the soil of Sequatchie county, and incidentally laying aside something for a rainy day, there is no better representative than the gentleman whose name introduces this brief sketch. His home is in the Sixth district, not far from the city of Dunlap.

Mr. Parkins was born in Roane county, Tenn., January 27, 1857, a son of Levi J. and Amanda M. (Owings) Parkins. The father was born in Roane county, Tenn., and when thirty years of age he went to Cumberland county, Tenn., and made that his home fourteen years. From thence he moved to Sequatchie county, bought a farm which he worked until about the year 1886, and then moved to Spencer, Van Buren county, Tenn., where he is still making his home. He had a family of thirteen children: Almyra T., deceased; Louis A., deceased; Stephen A., the subject of this sketch; Robert S., deceased; Mary E., deceased; Eliza C., deceased; Martin L., a farmer of Sequatchie county; Sallie V., wife of Henry C. Franklin, of Spencer, Tenn.; James A., deceased; Maggie L., at home; Corah A., at home; and William and Wilber, twins, both deceased.

Stephen A. Parkins, the ,subject of this sketch, was educated in the public schools of Sequatchie Valley, and on February 6, 1887, he was united in marriage to Miss Mary E. Hatfield, a native of Sequatchie county, born April 19, 1867, daughter of Mrs. Jane Hatfield. She is the second in a family of five children, of whom we have the following record: Maggie E., wife of G. A. Layne, of Ocala, Fla., Mary E., Mrs. Parkins; Martha A., wife of Luther Parkins, of Sequatchie county; Ada A., at home; and William H., at Pelham, Tenn. To Mr. and Mrs. Parkins have been born four children, as follows: Maud, born October 12, 1887; Samuel, born October 14, 1889; Lillie E., born June 9, 1892; and Henry, born October 12, 1894. Mr. and Mrs. Parkins are both members of the Christian church. Our subject has traveled considerably and has become well and widely known, and wherever he has been he has never failed to make friends. Throughout his whole life his occupation has been that of a farmer, and he is now recognized as one of the prominent and leading farmers of the Sixth district. He is a very pleasant neighbor, genial, warm-hearted, and has an agreeable family, and resides in one of the most hospitable homes in the district.

JOHN C. SPARKMAN is one of the younger members of the Van Buren county bar, but his prominence is by no means measured by his years; on the con-

trary he has won a reputation which many an older practitioner might well envy. In public affairs he has also taken the lead, and has efficiently served his fellow citizens in a number of political positions of honor and trust.

Mr. Sparkman was born December 17, 1867, on Caney Fork, in the Second district of Van Buren county, and is a worthy representative of one of the pioneer families of this region, his parents being Thomas Bryant and Sarah (Dodson) Sparkman, also natives of Van Buren county. The paternal grandfather, George W. Sparkman, was born in White county, and was a son of Thomas Bryant Sparkman, who came to Grainger county, this state, from North Carolina, moving from Grainger county to White county, now Van Buren. The maternal grandfather, William Dodson, better known as Buck Dodson, was also one of the early settlers of the county, coming here with his father from the Big Sandy region in West Virginia. He located on the farm now occupied by the parents of our subject and there spent his remaining days.

Thomas B. Sparkman, the father, who is now fifty-seven years of age, has always followed the occupation of farming as a means of livelihood. During the war he volunteered in the Confederate army as a member of Ben Hill's regiment, the Thirty-fifth Tennessee, going to the front in time to participate in the battle of Shiloh, which was followed by the engagements at Stone River, Murfreesboro, Perryville, Ky., and Chickamauga. At the last named place he was captured by the Federal troops and taken to Rock Island, Ill., where he was retained as a prisoner of war until hostilities ceased. He was married in 1860 to Sarah Dodson, and before entering the service one child was born to them—Melinda Jane, who married Andrew J. McBride and died in 1888 at their home in the Second district of Van Buren county. Later the family circle was increased by the birth of four sons, namely: Thomas B., a farmer of White county, Tenn.; Francis V., a farmer of Beech Cove; J. C., of this review; and William L., who is married and lives at home with his father.

During his boyhood and youth, John C. Sparkman was not fortunate in being provided with good educational privileges, he having to take advantage of poverty, and winning the sympathy of his genial teacher, W. N. Billingsley, then at Onward Seminary, who took the risk of trusting the ambitious boy for his tuition fees, which were eventually paid by the grateful youth. At the age of eighteen he began teaching. This profession he followed at Stony Point and Cummings Chapel, in Van Buren county, and at Findley's Institute, White county. He now entered Burritt College, then under the presidency of his old friend and instructor, Prof. Billingsley, and from that institution was graduated in 1893.

Mr. Sparkman began his public career soon after attaining his majority, being elected county court clerk in August, 1890, and was re-elected without opposition in 1894. He has also efficiently served as deputy register of deeds and deputy circuit clerk, proving a most competent and trustworthy official. Politically he is a Democrat, and socially is a member of the Masonic order, at present serving as junior deacon of his lodge.

On the 30th of August, 1896, Mr. Sparkman married Miss Lizzie Charlotte Greer, who was born in Bledsoe county, Tenn., July 24, 1871, a daughter of Clay Greer, of that county. They now have a little son, Elam Harris, born November 24, 1897. Mr. Sparkman, after due preparation, was admitted to the bar July 24, 1894, the anniversary of his wife's birth, and has since successfully engaged in the practice of his chosen calling. From the success he has already achieved in life we predict for him a brilliant future.

He is now the Democratic nominee to represent the Seventh Floterial district, comprising the counties of Cumberland, Bledsoe, Sequatchie, Grundy and Van Buren, in the next general assembly of the state of Tennessee. His district has a small Democratic majority and unless the unexpected occurs he will be elected.

WILLIAM CARROLL SHIRLEY is a well-known and honored citizen and member of the farming community of the Third district, Marion county, and is also the postmaster at the village of Shirleyton. He was born February 18, 1840, in the Third district, Marion county, a son of Jesse and Sarah (Grayson) Shirley. The father was born in White county, Tenn., March 18, 1808, and died August 24, 1894. Jesse Shirley was a son of John Shirley, who was born in South Carolina and married a Miss Frost. John Shirley migrated from his native state to White county, Tenn., and in 1818, moved from thence to the Sequatchie valley. His brother, Thomas, went to

White county at the same time and moved with him to the Sequatchie valley in 1818. He, Thomas, and his son, William, sold goods to the Indians where Whitwell now stands, and the house they built and occupied as a residence is still standing and in use as such.

John Shirley, our subject's grandfather, settled on a farm near where Whitwell now stands, and five years later he moved to Jackson county, Ala., where he died in 1845. He reared a family of eleven children, of whom the father of our subject was the oldest. Jesse Shirley was educated in the common schools of the valley and was twice married. His first wife bore the maiden name of Brandon, and one child, Wilson, was born to them. He died in Osage county, Mo., at the age of fifty-six years. The mother died in Tennessee, and the father subsequently married Sarah Grayson, who was born in Buncombe county, N. C., and died in 1880. They were both members of the Methodist Episcopal church, South, and are buried at Red Hill. Politically he was a Democrat and for eighteen years was magistrate and also served for some time as chairman of the county court. To this union were born ten children, of whom we have the following record: Jane, wife of Joseph Anderson, a farmer of the Third district, Marion county; John, deceased; William Carroll, the subject of this sketch; Thomas was a Confederate soldier under Forrest, and was killed at Fort Donaldson; Elizabeth died in infancy; Francis M. married Miss Emma King; Henry died at the age of fifteen years; Nancy, wife of James Smith, of Sequatchie county, Tenn.; Christopher C., married Miss Laura Condra and

is living in Whitwell; and Jesse L. married Miss Sallie Thacker, and is making his home in Graysville, Ga., where he is engaged in the practice of medicine.

William Carroll Shirley, the subject of this sketch, was educated in the public schools at Cheekville and Red Hill, after which he taught school fourteen sessions, in Marion county, Tenn., and Jackson county, Ala., both before and after the war. He enlisted in Rice's command of cavalry, in the Confederate army, at Shellmound, June 3, 1862, and was sent first to New Albany. From there he went to Athens, Tenn., and from thence to Murfreesboro, and was in the battle at that place. From there he went to Bridgeport, Ala., and, at the battle of Chickamauga he was wounded in the right arm. At the battle of Philadelphia, Tenn., he was wounded in the left arm, breast and shoulder and went to the home of a friend on the Coosa river, Ala., and stayed five months until he recovered from his wounds. He then rejoined the army at Dalton, Ga., and was all through the Atlanta campaign. He was wounded in the left hand at Noonday church. He served until the close of the war, surrendered with the army near Whiteside, Tenn., and was paroled at Nashville, May 27, 1865. He then returned to his home and resumed his teaching.

September 2, 1869, Mr. Shirley was united in marriage with Miss Semiramis Andes, who was born in Marion county, Tenn., in 1836, a daughter of Alexander and Sarah (Lewis) Andes. Mrs. Shirley was educated in the public school at Red Hill. After their marriage they first settled on a farm not far from their present home and lived there eight years, and then moved to where they now live. In 1879 Mr. Shirley began selling goods at his home, and later moved to Whitwell, following that occupation there until 1892, but since then has devoted more of his attention to farming. In 1883 he secured the establishment of the postoffice of Shirleyton at his home and has been its postmaster ever since. Mr. and Mrs. Shirley are members of the Methodist Episcopal church, South.

JOSEPH J. SANDERS, a well-known general merchant of Tracy City, and a business man of known reliability, enjoys to-day the reward of his painstaking and conscientious work. By his energy, perseverance and fine business ability he has secured a comfortable competence. Systematic and methodical, his sagacity, keen discrimination and sound judgment have made him one of the prosperous business men of the place.

Mr. Sanders was born in Holmes county, Ohio, July 29, 1849, a son of Joseph and Josefine Sanders. The father was born in France of German parentage, while the mother was a native of the same country, but of French lineage. In 1847 they emigrated to America and settled in Holmes county, Ohio, where Mrs. Sanders died. Subsequently, in 1860, the father brought his family to Grundy county, Tenn., and here his death occurred in 1888, when in his sixty-fourth year. For his second wife he married Margaret Note, a native of Germany, who is still living and is a resident of Grundy county. By trade he was a brick and stone mason, and in that capacity was in the employ of the French government for fourteen years, working on forts. After coming to the United States he engaged in contracting and building in both Ohio and Tennessee, and was a successful business man in the way of money making, but lost much by going security for supposed friends. He was a communicant of the Catholic church, and an ardent Democrat in politics.

Our subject has three sisters: Emily, the widow of Chris Jenette, of Holmes county, Ohio; Mary, wife of George McCoslin, a farmer of that county; and Lizzie, wife of John McCoslin, of the same place. He also had two brothers, Frank and Paul, but they died at the same time during boyhood.

The public schools of Holmes county, Ohio, afforded our subject his educational advantages. At the age of fifteen he commenced learning the brick and stone mason's trade under the able direction of his father, and soon thoroughly mastered every feature of the business. He continued to work under his father until coming to Tennessee, and in Tracy City became a leading contractor and builder, of whose skill many notable examples are to be seen. He built most of the coke ovens, the round house and machine shops at Tracy City, the stone bridge at Altamont, and many other substantial structures. Retiring from that business, he opened a general store in Tracy, in January, 1898, and has already succeeded in building up a large and lucrative trade.

In 1874, Mr. Sanders married Miss Callie Sweeton, a daughter of Joseph Sweeton, and they now have four children: Roy, who is with his father in the store; Ida, Joseph, and Mary Emma. The wife and mother is a member of the Methodist Episcopal church, South, and a most estimable lady. Socially, Mr. Sanders belongs to the Masonic order, and is a Democrat in politics.

RUBEN BROWN HUTCHESON, a prominent citizen of Bledsoe county, and one of its prosperous and popular farmers, was born on the farm he now owns and makes his home, May 6, 1840, and is a son of Philip S. and Sallie (Brown) Hutcheson.

Philip S. Hutcheson was also born near where our subject now lives, January 15, 1812, and died August 31, 1890. His wife was born January 25, 1813, and died June 5, 1891. They were married in 1832. They were both members of the C. P. church, with which the mother connected herself when she was a child, and the father at the age of thirty-five years. He was also a member of the Masonic fraternity for many years. He was justice of the peace of the Fourth district for thirty-five years, and for many years was chairman of the county court. Politically he was a Whig during the early part of his life, but later he was identified with the Democratic party. Five of his brothers and two sisters migrated from Bledsoe county to the state of Texas. Their father, William Hutcheson, was a native of the upper part of North Carolina.

The subject of this sketch is one of a family of seven brothers and three sisters, all of whom lived to rear families and attain advanced ages except two who were cut off

when about thirty years of age. James L. is a farmer of Bledsoe county; W. F., a prominent citizen of the Fourth district, Bledsoe county, where he was born and reared; Matilda, widow of John Wilson, a soldier in the Confederate army, who died while in the service; she afterward moved with her family to the state of Washington; Ruben Brown, the subject of this sketch; Sallie, wife of Jack Dawson, a merchant of Dayton, Tenn.; Margaret, wife of Carter Drake, a farmer of Van Buren county; Zerenia, wife of Martin Worthington, a prominent citizen of the Fourth district, Bledsoe county; Louisa, wife of Marion Little, a well-known stock dealer of Bledsoe county; Annie Hixson, wife of Henneger Hixson, a farmer living near Pikeville; James was a soldier in the Confederate army, enrolled in the Fifth Tennessee Infantry, and was captured at Chattanooga while acting as a scout; Frank served in the Second Tennessee Cavalry, in Ashby's regiment; he was captured in Kentucky in 1863, and was confined in the prison at Johnson island until the close of the war, which resulted in the destruction of his health.

Ruben Brown Hutcheson, whose name appears at the head of this article, enlisted June 4, 1861, in the Second Tennessee (Confederate) Cavalry, and was mustered in at Knoxville, and served in the capacity of sergeant with that command until the spring of 1865. He participated in the battles of Murfreesboro, Chattanooga, and all of the battles between the last-named place and Atlanta, Ga., a campaign of continuous fighting for ninety days. This command was mustered in with one hundred and twenty-six men, and at the time of its surrender at Davistown, Ala., our subject was one of seven of the original number that escaped without injury or capture. After the close of hostilities Mr. Hutcheson returned to his home in Tennessee and made his home with his parents until 1870. During that year he was united in marriage with Miss Roena E. Woods, a native of Meigs county, Tenn. Mrs. Hutcheson died August 1, 1892, and he subsequently married Josephine Passen, who was reared in White county, Tenn., and to this union has been born one daughter, Gladys. Mr. Hutcheson owns one of the fine farms of Bledsoe county, and his home is a place of social and mental refinement, and he well deserves to be classed among the prominent and influential citizens of the community. He is a member in good standing of the Cumberland Presbyterian church, and in the political world he is identified with the Democratic party.

WILLIAM CLARK RENFRO is one of the prominent and energetic agriculturists of the Twelfth district, Cumberland county. Mr. Renfro was born March 27, 1850, in Cumberland county, Tenn. His parents were Robert A. and Lucinda (Clark) Renfro, both natives of Tennessee, the former of Cumberland county and the the latter of Roane county. Robert Renfro was born on Daddy's Creek in Cumberland county, Tenn., and died in his native county, March 8, 1895. His father, William Renfro, was a Virginian, and went to Tennessee when Cumberland county was first opened to settlement. He took an active

32

part in the early affairs of the county, and was for many years a justice of the peace. Robert Renfro was one of the largest farmers of that part of the state in his day, and for a long period had charge of the Crab Orchard estate of Mr. Burke, as well as the store which the latter had established upon his property. This Crab Orchard farm attained great celebrity in days gone by. The great toll road, and the only means of traveling from Knoxville to Nashville, ran by the side of the farm, and as a consequence the latter was a very public place at times, and the inn and store were nearly always filled with wayfarers, and many of them famous personages. Mr. Renfro, therefore, had a considerable task to look after these large interests, and it is quite superfluous to say that he was a successful business man and a practical farmer. He got to be one of the best known men in Cumberland county, and finally went into local politics. He was elected to the office of justice of the peace, and then became circuit clerk. He served several terms in this office, and after retiring was again selected as a justice of the peace. He was always a strong Democrat. He married Miss Lucinda Clark in Roane county. Mrs. Renfro is still living and resides in Cumberland county, Tenn. She is a member of the Methodist church. There were ten children in the family, nine of whom are now living. William C., the subject of this sketch, was the second child in order of birth. Mary J. is the wife of "Black Bill" Hamby, a resident of Cumberland county. George W. is a farmer in the Twelfth district, Cumberland county. Amanda is the wife of W. H. Pleming of Knoxville. Margaret resides with her mother. Mattie, who is now deceased, was the wife of John Rose, of Dayton, Tenn. Tennie is married to Sewell Howard, of Rockwood, Tenn. Harriet lives with her mother, as do also John and Alice. Our subject was educated at Crab Orchard, and ran his father's farm while the latter was filling the office of circuit clerk. He has since been engaged in farming, at which he has been very successful. Mr. Renfro is a Democrat, but is rather independent at times, and in 1896 refused to vote for Bryan. In 1890 he was elected a justice of the peace, and held the office for six years. He has always been interested in school and educational matters, and is a member of the Missionary Baptist church at Haley's Grove, in which he is a deacon.

In 1879 Mr. Renfro married Mrs. Permelia Wheeler, who is a native of New York, and was the widow of Charles J. Wheeler, the owner of the Crab Orchard House, a well known hotel at Crab Orchard. Mr. and Mrs. Renfro are the parents of three children, Cora, Robert and Clifford.

L OONEY LAFAYETTE JANEWAY, M. D., a successful practicing physician of Whitwell, was born near Tazewell, Claiborne county, Tenn., and is a son of Joseph and Mary (Smith) Janeway, both natives of Jefferson county, Tenn. They were born in 1806, the father being seven days the senior. He was a hatter by trade and followed that pursuit till the last few years of his life. He married Miss Smith in the county of their nativity whence they removed to Claiborne county and later located in that part of Grainger county, which afterward became Union county. In early life they were members of the Primitive Baptist church and on the division of that church united with that branch known as the Missionary Baptist, with which they were connected until death. Mr. Janeway gave his political support to the Democracy, and in matters of business he was very successful, He died December 14, 1887, and his wife passed away in December, 1894. They traveled life's journey together as man and wife for sixty-one years, and their home was blessed with ten children, five sons and five daughters, of whom seven are now living namely: Nancy, widow of Valentine Sharp, and a resident of Union county, Tenn., their home being on Clinch river; Luvisa, a resident of Texas; Joseph, a minister of the Missionary Baptist church, of Sweetwater, Tenn.; Mary, wife of Alfred Wolfe, who resides near Jasper, Marion county; Sarah, wife of Mr. Loftus, of Grainger county, Tenn.; Minerva, widow of James Condra, who is living near Shell Mound, Marion county; and the Doctor. Those who have passed away are: William, who was a farmer of Claiborne county and minister of Missionary Baptist church, and died in 1897; and John, who was a member of the First Tennessee Federal Artillery, and died at Fort Negley; and Pryor, a farmer and minister of the Missionary Baptist church, who had formerly been a merchant, and died in Union county in the summer of 1897.

Dr. Janeway pursued his education in upper east Tennessee and afterward successfully engaged in teaching, but desiring to enter the profession to which he now devotes his energies he took up the study of medicine and later attended a course of lectures in Nashville, and in 1890, 1891 and 1892 was a medical student in Chattanooga. In 1870 he went to Sullivan and Green counties, Ind., and after several months visited the state of Arkansas. Subsequently he returned to the Sequatchie Valley and since that time has engaged in the practice of medicine in Marion county. He has a comprehensive and accurate knowledge of the science of medicine and in the application of its principles to the needs of suffering humanity has demonstrated superior skill and ability. He is now in the enjoyment of an extensive patronage, and has gained a reputation that ranks him among the leading physicians in this part of the state. The Doctor was married in March, 1871, to Miss Margaret, daughter of Josiah Burnette. She was born in Marion county in 1852, and died January 15, 1883. Of her three children, two are living: Dora, now the wife of Joseph Ridge, a farmer residing near Springfield, Tenn., and Joseph, who is living at Chattanooga; while Pryor Henry died in childhood. Mrs. Janeway was a member of the Methodist church and a lady of many excellencies of character. On the 27th of June, 1883, the Doctor was again married, his second union being with Miss Mary J. Ridge, who was born near her present home in 1861, and is a daughter of David Ridge. They have an interesting family of five children: James Robert Graves, Josie Viola, Marshal Foster, Paris David, and Florence Virginia.

Dr. Janeway gives his political support to the Democracy and socially is connected with the Independent Order of Odd Fellows at Whitwell. When sixteen years of age he joined the Missionary Baptist church and has since engaged in preaching the gospel. His life has been well spent in devotion to the physical and moral needs of his fellow men and no man in Marion county is held in higher regard or is more deserving of the confidence and friendship of those with whom he comes in contact.

JULIUS C. HOODENPYLE.—Among the farmers in the prime of life in Sequatchie county, a good station has been attained by the gentleman above named, whose career has been marked with energy, proudence and persistent effort. His well-directed labors have resulted in the attainment of a good farm in the Sixth district, where he is surrounded with those improvements and home comforts which make life enjoyable. Mr. Hoodenpyle was born on the farm he now owns and in the house he now occupies, November 15, 1864, the son of Robert and Delilah (Pickett) Hoodenpyle.

Robert Hoodenpyle was born on the Tennessee river, near Chattanooga, where he grew to maturity, and died July 13, 1890, at the age of fifty-eight years, nine months, and sixteen days. The mother was a daughter of Jesse Pickett, and was also born in the valley. Robert was a son of David Hoodenpyle, and David was a son of Philip Hoodenpyle who came from Holland and settled in North Carolina, and moved from thence to the Sequatchie Valley and settled near Pikeville. Robert

Hoodenpyle made farming his principal occupation and was quite successful in the pursuit of that calling. He also operated a still, making brandy and some whiskey. He was a soldier in the Northern army, serving in a Tennessee regiment, and was discharged at Nashville, Tenn. He was married before the war and a family of eighteen children were born to them, thirteen of whom are still living: Margaret, wife of John Davis; Martha Jane, wife of E. M. White; Jesse, a farmer of Sequatchie county, on the west side of the valley; Mary, wife of E. J. Barber, on the east side of the valley; Lettie, wife of Thomas Mosley, a farmer in the Cumberland mountains; Sallie, wife of Thomas White, of the west side; Luverna, wife of W. F. Hicks, Sequatchie county, Tenn.; Julius C., the subject of this sketch; Malissa Sains, wife of T. Sains, of Marion county; Lydia, wife of W. H. Bryant; Sophronia, deceased, was the wife of S. B. Pickett; Hester, deceased, was the wife of Taylor Layne, of Marion county, Tenn.; William was at Sanger, Cal., when last heard from; Vergie, wife of T. B. Narramore, living on the Hoodenpyle farm; Minnie Nora, deceased, was the wife of Clyde Reeves; Miss Lu; Delia Lee is single and living at the old home place; Elizabeth died in infancy; Johnnie also died in childhood.

Julius C. Hoodenpyle was educated in the common schools of Sequatchie county. He was reared on the farm on which he was born, and helped his father to operate the place until the death of the latter, after which our subject assumed the entire management. In 1895 he moved to the northwestern part of Texas, settled in Baylor county, and conducted a sheep ranch, but with the exception of this time, he has made his home on the old farm. No man in the district has taken a more active interest in the welfare of the community than has Mr. Hoodenpyle. All matters pertaining to the business welfare or the upbuilding or strengthening of good local government have met with his earnest support, and he is always willing to lend a helping hand for the development of the resources of Sequatchie county. Politically he is identified with the Democratic party.

BRYANT SEAMANS, ex-trustee of Van Buren county, and a leading agriculturist of the Second district, is a man whose genial temperment, sound judgment and well-proved integrity have brought him the esteem and friendship of a host of acquaintances far and near.

Mr. Seamans was born in the Second district, December 28, 1834, a son of Micajah and Nancy (Sparkman) Seamans, the former probably a native of North Carolina, the latter of Virginia. The father, who was a soldier of the war of 1812, served as justice of the peace in Van Buren county for quite a number of years, and took an active interest in public affairs, giving his support to the men and measures of the Democratic party. He died in Warren county, Tenn., when past the age of eighty years, and his wife departed this life in Van Buren county, at the age of sixty-five. Both were earnest, conscientious Christian people, the mother holding membership with the Methodist church until a short time before her death, when she united with the Baptist denomination. Of the fourteen children born to them only three are now living, our subject being the youngest, while the others are Micajah, a farmer of Iron county, Mo.; and Martha, a resident of Arkansas.

Bryant Seamans was born on the place now owned by T. J. Shockley, and attended school at Stony Point, Van Buren county. When his school days were over he engaged in milling on Cane creek until after the war, and then turned his attention to farming upon a place in the First district. In 1881 he moved to Pulaski county, Ark., where he was interested in the raising of cotton for nearly three years. On his return to Tennessee, he located in the Second district of Van Buren county, where he now owns a fine farm of two hundred and thirty acres, upon which he has made many useful and valuable improvements that add greatly to its attractive appearance.

In September, 1859, Mr. Seamans was united in marriage with Miss Frances Hunter, who was born in Van Buren county, and died here in 1872. Her father, James Hunter, was for the long period of twenty-four years sheriff of the county. The children born of this union were Martin A., a farmer of Pulaski county, Ark.; Violet, wife of Marion Heard, a farmer of the same county; Reasey, wife of Arthur Granbury, a farmer of Lone Oak county, Ark.; and Lucinda, who was the oldest of the family and died in childhood. For his second wife, Mr. Seamans chose Arminda Hodges, daughter of Joseph Hodges. She was also a native of Van Buren county, and died in 1885. She was the mother of three children: Fanny, who married Michael Roller and

died in Kentucky shortly after her marriage; James, a farmer of the First district of Van Buren county; and William H., at home. In July, 1886, Mr. Seamans wedded Matilda Stewart, a native of Bledsoe county, Tenn., and a daughter of Alexander Stewart. By this marriage our subject has one daughter, P. G.

Before going to Arkansas, Mr. Seamans held the office of justice of the peace for a number of years, and on his return served in the same position. In 1890 he was elected county trustee and so acceptably did he fill that office that he was re-elected two years later. In his political views he has always been a Democrat, and in his social connections is identified with the Independent Order of Odd Fellows. He is a worthy member of the New Hopewell Baptist church, located in the Second district, and as a citizen he ever stands ready to discharge every duty devolving upon him.

JOHN H. GILBREATH, M. D., is one of Marion county's popular and efficient physicians who has gained an enviable reputation and placed himself in the front rank among the medical practitioners of southeastern Tennessee by years of faithful and persistent effort. He has striven to improve upon his early methods, as every physician must who would keep pace with the new discoveries in medical science, and profit by his own experience and observations. His studies did not cease with the beginning of his practice, but have continued year by year, and this is no doubt one of the reasons why he occupies the prominent place he does in the minds of the people.

Dr. Gilbreath was born in Bradley county, Tenn., March 15, 1860, a son of Thomas H. and Dialtha (Hooper) Gilbreath. Thomas H. Gilbreath moved with his parents, when a boy of ten years, from Cocke county, Tenn., to Bradley county, Tenn. He taught school during the early part of his life and was also a farmer. He served for a time as a member of the county court, and was conservative in his political views. Dialtha Hooper was born in Bradley county, Tenn., and they were both members of the Cumberland Presbyterian church. They both died in February, 1894, the father on the eleventh and the mother on the thirteenth, and the former at the age of sixty-two years and the latter at the age of fifty-six years. The family is of Irish descent but several generations have been born in America.

Dr. Gilbreath, the subject of this sketch, is the fifth in the order of birth of a large family of children, five of whom are now living. He spent his school days in Bradley county, Tenn., and at Charleston and Calhoun, in McMinn county, Tenn. He then taught one term of school and then began the study of medicine under Dr. Lee, at Birchwood, and then under Dr. Dunham, of Bradley county. He began his practice in Bradley county, but in 1883 he moved to the Sequatchie Valley and located just above Whitwell. On the opening of the coal mines he moved to the city of Whitwell, and during the years 1887 and '88, he was engaged in selling goods in that city in partnership with W. C. Shirley. In 1894 he returned to Bradley county, his old home, but stayed only a few months, and since that time has made Whitwell his home and base of operations. Socially he affiliates with the Masonic fraternity in the capacity of Master Mason, and in politics he is a conservative Republican. As a man and citizen he is held in the highest respect and esteem by all who have the pleasure of his acquaintance, and as a physician and surgeon he is recognized as one of the leaders of his profession.

March 18, 1888, Dr. Gilbreath was united in marriage to Miss Darthula Jane Andes, daughter of W. L. Andes, and their home has been blessed by the advent of a family of three children, upon whom they have bestowed the following names: William Walter, Elbert Hughston and Bula.

THOMAS C. CENTER, who resides in the Twelfth district, Cumberland county, not far from the village of Northville, is one of the best known and most popular agriculturists of that section, and one of its most influential citizens. Mr. Center was born in Roane county, Tenn., near the Clinch river, within one and one-fourth miles of Kingston, on the 2nd of October, 1828, and is a son of Willis S. and Jane M. (Gallaher) Center, both natives of Roane county. They removed from Tennessee to Trenton, Ky., about the year 1867, where Mr. Center died in 1880, in his eightieth year. His wife's death occurred at Kingston, Tenn., in 1884, soon after she had attained her seventy-sixth year. Mr. Center pursued farming for many years, and also operated a number of stage lines which carried the government mail. For a considerable period he owned the mail route between Knoxville, Tenn., and Springplace, Ga., and that between Knoxville and Sparta, Tenn. It was on one of his stages that Robert Burke, the owner of the Crab Orchard place, was riding when he fell from his seat and was ground to death beneath the wheels. Mr. Center remained in the business until the war, and was a mail contractor nearly all of his life. He was a justice of the peace in Roane county for several years and an ardent Democrat. He was a colonel in the state militia, and prominent in local military circles. Mrs. Center was a member of the Cumberland Presbyterian church. The Center family came originally from Virginia, where they were among the early colonists. Mr. and Mrs. Center had twelve children, six of whom are living: Thomas C., the subject of this sketch, is the eldest. Frank is also a farmer and resides in the Twelfth district. George W. is a merchant at Hopkinsville, Ky. Mollie G. is also a resident of Hopkinsville, and Andrew J. is a general merchant of Albany, Texas. Jennie, the youngest of those living, now makes her home at Hopkinsville, Ky. The deceased children are: Nancy J., who was the wife of E. A. Yost, of Trenton, Ky.; S. M., who died at Kingston, Tenn.; Willis S., who was a Confederate soldier and died in one of the federal prisons; Felix, who died in Texas; Sarah, who was the wife of Hugh Martin, of Kingston, Tenn., and died at Cincinnati, Ohio, in 1895. Thomas was educated in the schools of Kingston, Tenn., Rittenhouse Academy and East Tennessee University. At the same time he assisted his father in the management of the stage lines and thus continued until the war. In 1859 he removed to his present home, which was then in the woods. The place was entirely without improvements, and the land in poor condition, but Mr. Center set to work and soon succeeded in making a splendid farm out of what was before almost worthless property. He now owns forty-five hundred acres of land, all of which contains coal beds of much value, and is but a short distance from the proposed railroad through Cumberland county. Mr. Center is a Democrat in politics, and has held a number of local offices. Upon the organization of Cumberland county he was chosen as its first superintendent of public instruction, holding that office for two years. He is now a notary public for Cumberland county, and has been for several years past. Mr. Center is a master Mason, and is prominent in the affairs of that order. On the first of September, 1857, he married Miss J. C. McEwen. Mrs. Center was born in Roane county, Tenn., on the 12th of March, 1840, and is a daughter of J. C. and Nancy McClung McEwen, both natives of Roane county, Tenn. The McEwens are one of the old families of Roane county. Mr. and Mrs. Center are the parents of thirteen children, four of whom, May E., J. Willis, T. A. and J. P. are deceased. The first two were each twenty-three years old when they died. T. A. was thirty-one and J. P. was twenty-three. Those now living are: Nannie J., the wife of S. P. Sparks, president of the Bank of Kingston; William S., a traveling salesman who lives at Kingston; George G., a merchant of Hopkinsville,

Ky.; Charlie M.; M. A., J. C., Ira, Felix, and Hugh, all at home. Mr. Center and family are members of the Methodist Episcopal church, South, and he has always taken a lively interest in religious matters. He has built a church near his house, which is known as the Center church, and he is one of its deacons. He is also a class leader and superintendent of the Sunday school.

JONAS CLARK.—The gentleman whose name introduces these few brief paragraphs is a respected and prosperous citizen of Pailo, Bledsoe county, and was born and spent the greater part of his life in this county.

Mr. Clark was born about six miles above Pikeville, February 21, 1819, the son of Charles and Hannah (Denton) Clark. Charles Clark was a son of Norris Clark, and moved to the Sequatchie valley from Sevier county, and settled where L. T. Billingsley now lives. Norris Clark was a native of County Down, Ireland, and died in Bledsoe county, Tenn., at a very old age. Charles Clark, our subject's father, was among the first blacksmiths to locate in the valley and operated a shop there for many years. He died there at a very old age. Mr. and Mrs. Charles Clark were the parents of a family of thirteen children, four of whom are now living: Jonas, the subject of this sketch; Francis, a blacksmith of Warren county, Tenn.; Bird is a farmer and blacksmith on Rocky river, in Warren county, Tenn.; and Bird's twin brother, Jacob; on the west side of Waldens Ridge,

a sketch of whom appears on another page of this volume. The deceased are: Jonathan, who died in the vicinity of his birthplace; Isaac N. died on Brush creek, Sequatchie county; James died at Tanbark, Bledsoe county, Tenn., and was postmaster at that place at the time of his death; William died in Missouri; Nancy first married Larkin Swafford, and after his death, she was united in marriage to Thomas McKinney, and both died near Tanbark; Tobitha went west with her husband soon after their marriage; Jerusha died at the old homestead; Clarrissa was the wife of James Clendennin, and died in VanBuren county; and the other died in infancy.

Jonas Clark, the subject of this sketch, began to learn the blacksmith trade in his father's shop when he was so small that he had to build a scaffold to stand on in order to reach the anvil, but learned the trade perfectly in all of its branches. Later he conducted a shop six miles above Pikeville, until 1860, when he moved down the valley, nearer to the city. One year later he bought his present home and since that time has worked at his trade in connection with farming, milling, stock-raising, etc., and has also done some gunmaking. Our subject taught his brother, Jacob Clark, the trade of blacksmithing, and also his sons, Joseph and Charles E., who now have charge of the business. Mr. Clark was county sealer of Bledsoe county before the war, and for most of the time since the war he has been a member of the county court. Since the establishment of the postoffice at Pailo in 1875, he has been its postmaster.

May 25, 1856, Mr. Clark was united in marriage to Mary B. Acuff, who was born

February 15, 1825, a daughter of James Acuff, and died March 11, 1896. To this union were born seven children, three of whom are now living, and of whom we have the following record: Sallie, born April 14, 1857, is the wife of John McReynolds, a farmer living near Chickamauga Station; Annie Jane, born November 17, 1858, and died August 8, 1880; Joseph, born December 16, 1860; James H., born December 29, 1862, and died January 29, 1863; Charles E., born November 28, 1864; and Ida E., born February 24, 1870, and died March 16, 1888. Joseph Clark married Ader, the daughter of Jacob Clark, who was born in Bledsoe county, Tenn., and they have become the parents of five children: Ethel, Dallas, Robert, Hettie and Mabel. Charles E. married Florence Merriman, also a native of the Sequatchie valley, and a daughter of Margaret Merriman. They also have a family of five children: Pearl, Cleo, Clyde, Charles and Sallie Popy. Politically our subject is identified with the Democratic party, and some of the members of his family are members of the Christian church.

EDWARD VON BERGEN. — Tracy City, Grundy county, Tenn., is the seat of several thriving business enterprises, and among the most successful of these may be mentioned the mercantile establishment which is presided over by the gentleman whose name heads this sketch. The store is well-stocked with a carefully selected assortment of such goods as meets the wants of the citizens in the city, as

33

well as those in the surrounding country. The business is conducted in a very able manner, and honorable dealing is accorded to all who patronize the establishment. Mr. Von Bergen, therefore, enjoys an extensive trade, as well as entire confidence and esteem of the residents of the community.

The parents of our subject, Caspar and Anna Barbara (Ruef) Von Bergen, were both natives of Switzerland. Caspar Von Bergen when a young man entered the service of the King of Naples. He also fought under the first Napoleon, as a second lieutenant. After his marriage to the mother of our subject he engaged in mercantile pursuits, though he was always more or less connected with military matters. About the year 1845 he emigrated to the United States. He landed at New Orleans, from whence he proceeded up the Mississippi river to the then territory of Illinois, where he located a home for his family, and then returned to his native land to bring them to their new location. But it is supposed that he died at New Orleans of the yellow fever, as he had written to his family stating that this dreaded epidemic was then prevalent in that city. He was fifty-three years of age, and his wife failing to hear from her husband, died soon after from grief. They were members of the Zwingle Reformed church, and were the parents of the following children: Edward, the subject of this sketch; Caroline, wife of Casper Ott, a tanner in Switzerland, who later made a trip to the United States, visiting Chicago, Chippewa Falls, the states of Pennsylvania, Ohio, Tennessee, and all the western states, and then returned to his native land; Mary Anna was the wife of Beat

Tannler; Margueritta emigrated to the United States when a young woman, located in Pennsylvania, and was there married to John Shisrling, who was in the United States army, later she returned to her native land where she died; Louisa was the wife of John Baud, a French Swiss, and died in her native land; Rosena died when a child.

Edward Von Bergen, was born December 25, 1834, in Switzerland, where he attended school until his seventeenth year, and then learned the brewer's trade. He followed this line of business for two years, and then turned his attention to car building, at which he worked for three or four years. In 1861 he emigrated to the United States, landed at New York city, and then proceeded to Jeffersonville, Sullivan county, New York. He next located at Scranton, Penn., where he worked in the car shops for seven years. He served in the Home Guards during the war of the Rebellion. Later Mr. Von Bergen traveled all over the United States in search of a suitable location, and finally came to the Swiss Colony in Grundy county, Tenn., where he purchased a farm. He followed agricult-. ural pursuits for awhile and then secured a position in the Tennessee Coal, Iron & Railroad Company's shops, where he worked for fifteen years. In 1878 he moved to Tracy City, and made that his home for two years, and then moved to Chattanooga, where he worked six months in the car shops for H. Clay Evans. The climate there did not agree with Mr. Von Bergen, so he returned to Tracy City, and established a furniture store in 1880 in partnership with Mr. Fred Wenger, of Winchester. Mr. Wenger sold his interest in the business to a Richard Hunt, who subsequently purchased the controlling interest in the concern from Mr. Von Bergen, who then opened a business of his own. He still continued in the furniture business until 1895, when he closed out this line of business, and opened a grocery and produce store, which he has since successfully conducted.

Mr. Von Bergen was married in Grundy county, Tenn., to Miss Julia Roth, who was born in Cleveland, Ohio. There have been three children born to bless this congenial union, namely: Eda, now the wife of E. C. Norwell, of Tracy City; Emily and Emil, at home. Both he and his wife are members in good standing of the Episcopal church. Socially Mr. Von Bergen is a member of the I. O. O. F., K. O. P., F. A. M. and the Royal Arcanum. In his political views he stanchly supports the principles of the Republican party.

A LAWRENCE ROBERSON is a young and energetic lawyer of Jasper, and a gentleman who holds a conspicuous position among the members of the bar of Marion county, Tenn., both for his legal ability and forensic power.

Mr. Roberson was born December 6, 1871, at Pikeville, Tenn., a son of James and Penelope P. (Spears) Roberson. The mother is a daughter of Gen. James G. Spears, who was a general in the Union army, and the father, James Roberson, was a son of Col. Isaac and Elvira (Cole) Roberson. Col. Isaac Roberson was a man of strong character and extraordinary intelligence. He was a stanch Democrat and represented his district for two terms in the state legislature. He was too old to take an active part in the war between the states, though his sympathies were with the south. Our subject's father was born in Bledsoe county, Tenn., in 1837, and his wife was born in Rhea county, Tenn., in 1847. He received his primary training in the common schools of his native county and supplemented same with a course in Emory & Henry College in Washington county, Va. He was reared on a farm near Pikeville and spent considerable time at farm work. After leaving school he studied law with James G. Spears and commenced the practice of law at Pikeville. Soon afterwards he was appointed clerk and master for Bledsoe county, and held the office for six years, and then resumed his law practice, and after following with marked success the practice of his profession at Pikeville for twenty years he moved to Sequatchie City, Marion county, and there combines the practice of law with the work of operating a farm. He enlisted in the Confederate army at the beginning of the war as the captain of a company which he gathered and organized in the Sequatchie valley. He was taken prisoner and was kept eighteen months, after which he was exchanged and then continued as a Confederate soldier until the close of the war, completing his education after the war. Mr. and Mrs. James Roberson are the parents of a family of ten children, of whom the subject of this sketch is the second in the order of birth, and of whom we have the following record: Isaac G., a farmer and stock raiser in Texas; Alexander L.; Addie E., wife of J. F. Hoge, a merchant at Litton, Bledsoe county, Tenn.; James N., in college at Jasper; Spears, in college at Jasper; Samuel T., in college at Jasper; Florence, who died at the age of two years; William, also attending the Jasper College; John R. and Brown, both still living at home.

A. Lawrence Roberson, the subject of this sketch, attended the public school in the district in which he spent his boyhood and then entered the Pryor Institute at Jasper. After completing the literary course in 1892, he went to the Emory & Henry College, in Virginia, where his father was educated. He afterward studied law under his uncle, Col. A. L. Spears, who is now our subject's partner in the practice of law. He completed his course and commenced practice in Jasper in 1894. Politically he is a Democrat and cast his first presidential ballot for Grover Cleveland. Socially he is a member of the Knights of Pythias, and is also a member of the Methodist Episcopal church, South. He is a man of excellent business qualifications, public-spirited, possessed of broad ideas, and enjoys the confidence and esteem of a large circle of business and social friends. He is still a young man and has every prospect of becoming one of the leading attorneys and business men, not only of the county but of eastern Tennessee. He is yet unmarried.

JOHN E. PEARSON, who is engaged in the manufacture of leather, and in making boots and shoes, harness and saddlery in Spencer, was born on Flat creek, one of the affluents of Duck river, in Bedford county, Tenn., April 23, 1826, and is a son of Kindred and Sidney (Watson) Pearson. His father was born in Union district of South Carolina, and during his boyhood accompanied his father, William Pearson, from that state to Tennessee, the family locating on Flat creek, a tributary of Duck river. The grandfather of our subject was one of the heroes of the Revolution and after his removal to Tennessee devoted his energies to agricultural pursuits. His capable management, perseverance and industry brought to him a comfortable competence.

Kindred Pearson spent the greater part of his life in Bedford county and was engaged in military service during the Seminole war in 1818. He was a prosperous farmer who also engaged in other business pursuits, which he carried forward to successful completion. He served as a member of the county court both under the old and the new constitution and in his political views was a Democrat. He and his wife held membership in the Christian church, and their many excellencies of character won them the high regard of all. The former died in Bedford county at the age of seventy-two years, his wife having passed away the year previous. They were married in 1818 and reared a large family, of whom John E. is the eldest living; J. K., second of the living sons of the family, was formerly engaged in the sawmill business and carried on a spoke and handle factory at Manchester, Tenn., but is now engaged in farming in Bedford county, Tenn.; E. W. follows agricultural pursuits in Texas; C. N. is operating a sawmill near

Waverly, Tenn., but makes his home in Bedford county; Sidney Jane is the widow of John W. Reagor, a resident of Bedford county; Sarah is the wife of A. J. Wamack, of the same county; William B. died in Bedford county at the age of twenty-four; Thomas died at the age of fourteen; Rosannah was the wife of William C. Hicks and died at her daughter's at Tullahoma and was buried near her home in Bedford county; Charles was engaged in the lumber business in Sparta at the time of his death; Isaac went to Illinois in the '50s and at the commencement of the war, with three companions, crossed the Ohio river into Kentucky, where he joined a Kentucky regiment for the Confederate service. He was lost during the Johnston retreat through Georgia; Joseph was a miner and followed that pursuit in California, British Columbia and Idaho.

John E. Pearson, whose name introduces this review, was reared in the county of his nativity and attended the public schools until twenty years of age, when he began working in a tan-yard established by his father, under whose direction he mastered the business and then became a partner in the enterprise. Some years later he removed to Tullahoma, where he engaged in business for four years, as a dealer in groceries, hardware and drugs.

In April, 1861, at the first call to arms, he joined Company A, Seventeenth Tennessee Regiment of Confederate troops under Col. Tazewell W. Newman. After participating in the battle of Fishing Creek he was transferred to the commissary department and was detailed to make liquor for the Confederate hospitals. Finally the

Federal troops captured Tullahoma, and he left his still, rejoining his old command. While in front of Petersburg, Va., in 1864, he was captured and taken to City Point, whence he was transferred to Point Lookout, and later to Elmira, N., Y. where he was held until the latter part of February, 1865, when he was sent to Richmond for exchange, but arrived one day too late for the regular quarterly exchange. He was then given his liberty and told to make his living the best way he could. Accordingly he commenced work in a tan-yard for his board, but as soon as Lee surrendered he returned to Bedford county, where he began the operation of a tannery on his own account He afterward enlarged his field of labor by engaging in the manufacture of harness, saddlery, boots and shoes, and in 1875 he came to Spencer, where he has since engaged in business. He manufactures for the local trade and is now enjoying a liberal patronage which he well merits.

Mr. Pearson was married November 18, 1849, to Jane Newson, who was born in Shelbyville, Tenn., April 6, 1834, and is a daughter of Thomas Newson. They have three children: Mary, widow of E. T. Floyd, residing at her father's old home in Moore county; Isaac N., a stock-dealer of Tullahoma; and George T., who is assisting his father in business in Spencer. He was for one year United States deputy marshal under J. N. McKinzey.

Mr. Pearson is a stalwart Democrat in his political views and during his residence in VanBuren county has served for six years as a member of the county court. He and his wife hold membership in the Christian church, in which he formerly served as deacon, and is now filling the office of elder. He is a man of exemplary habits and upright life, whose career, public and private, entitles him to the high regard of his fellowmen.

JAMES MONROE LOCKHART holds a conspicuous position among the members of the agricultural part of the Fifth district, Grundy county, Tenn. He was born in Wills Valley, near Trenton, Ga., July 25, 1848, a son of John Calhoun and Cynthia (Bailey) Lockhart.

John C. Lockhart, our subject's father, was born in what is now Grundy county, Tenn., but which was then known as Warren county. He was born in 1815 and was reared in the county of his nativity, and during his lifetime, held several official positions of trust. He was trustee of Sequatchie county, justice of the peace in Grundy county, and was chairman of the county court of the last named county for one term. Upon the breaking out of the Civil war he was forced into the Federal service, preferring to serve in the ranks instead of going as a prisoner of war to Camp Chase, Ohio, but he only served a short time. Politically he was a life long Democrat. He was a member of the Primitive Baptist church, and during the latter years of his life was a minister in that organization. He died on the farm that is now the home of our subject in the year 1887. He was twice married. His first wife bore the maiden name of Miss Martha Walker, and after her death, Mr. Lockhart was united in marriage to Miss Cynthia

Bailey. After his death, Mrs. Lockhart married Daniel Lane, and is now living near Daus Station, in Sequatchie county. To Mr. Lockhart's first marriage were born two children, A. J. and G. W., and the names of the children born to his second marriage appears in the sketch of A. J. Lockhart, on another page of this volume. The Lockhart family came to Tennessee from North Carolina.

James Monroe Lockhart, the subject of this sketch, was reared in Grundy and Sequatchie counties, and was educated in the Langleyford School. He made his home with his father until 1887, and had charge of his father's business until the latter's death. He has made the pursuit of agriculture his principal occupation, and, although he is a thorough and systematic farmer, he has found time to devote to the service of his fellow citizens and looking after the political interests of his adopted district and county. He was justice of the peace for eighteen years, was chairman of the county court for one term, and is now performing the duties of deputy sheriff. In politics he is identified with the Democratic party.

June 30, 1878, our subject was united in marriage to Miss Janie Lockhart, who was born near Beersheba Springs, Grundy county, Tenn., April 8, 1860, a daughter of H. Lockhart. This union has been blessed by the advent of a family of nine children, seven of whom are now living. The names of the living children in the order of their birth are as follows: Cynthia B., Myrtle Viola, Lilly Alice, Sarah Willis, Maude, Pearlie and Lassie Burton. George W. and Edgar M. died in childhood.

HON. WILLIAM PRYOR, an honored resident and a wealthy and prominent farmer of Marion county, whose home is situated in the Fifteenth district, near Whitwell, was born in Marion county, February 27, 1821, a son of Green H. and Obedience (Halloway) Pryor. Green H. was a son of Matthew and (Miss Neely) Pryor.

Matthew Pryor, the grandfather of our subject, was a soldier in the Revolutionary war, and drew a pension while he lived for his services. He moved with his family to Tennessee in an early day and settled on a farm in Roane county, and later moved to Marion county, settled on a farm in the valley, and died near Whitwell. Green H. Pryor, our subject's father, was a farmer and stock trader by occupation, and died June 2, 1862, and his wife died a few years before. She was a member of the Cumberland Presbyterian church. They were the parents of a family of twelve children, viz.: Jackson, who is living in Jasper, Tenn.; Sampson, deceased; Mary, deceased; William, the subject of this sketch; John, deceased; Washington, a farmer and stock raiser living in the Seventh district, Marion county; Preston, who died while young; Anderson, deceased; Jeremiah, deceased; Benjamin F., deceased; Eliza, widow of I. P. Alexander, is living with her brother Jackson in Jasper; and Caroline, deceased.

William Pryor, the subject of this sketch, was educated in the public schools of the Sequatchie valley, and afterward taught school for a few terms. He was married February 27, 1845, to Miss Amanda Prigmore, who was born June 22, 1822, in Marion county, Tenn., a daughter of Ephraim and Margaret (Kelly) Prigmore. Her father was born in Pennsylvania, and went to Tennessee when a young man and died there about the year 1844. His wife died in 1864. They were the parents of a family of ten children, all of whom are now dead except Mrs. Pryor, and whose names in the order of their birth were as follows: James O., Anna, Joseph K., Eliza, Malinda, Amanda, Keziah M., Nancy K., Margaret D. and Ephraim L.

After his marriage our subject settled near the location of his present home, in the Fifteenth district, in a little cabin. In the fall of the same year he moved to Battle Creek, in the Tenth district, bought a farm there and made that his home two years. He then sold out and moved to Little Sequatchie Valley, in the Fourth district, bought a farm and lived there six years. This farm he traded to his father for the one he now owns and occupies, at once moved to it and has since made that his home. The farm originally comprised about one thousand acres, but Mr. Pryor has divided with his children and has also sold a part, and he now has scarcely five hundred acres. He deals very extensively in cattle and hogs, and both in his agricultural and stock-raising business he has been eminently successful. A few years ago he erected a saw and planing mill, and for several years did a large and profitable business. Later he added to it a cabinet factory, and he and his sons control the entire plant.

Mr. Pryor is also an old soldier, having joined the Union army in 1864, enlisting in Company C, Sixth Regiment of Tennessee Mounted Infantry, and was mustered in in Hamilton county, Tenn. He was stationed in Hamilton county for some time, and was then made provost marshal. He also acted as a scout, and was in a great many skirmishes, but participated in none of the regular battles. He was at Dalton, Ga., Resaca, Ga., and at Nashville, Tenn., and was there mustered out June 30, 1865. Politically he is a Republican, and by that party has three times been elected justice of the peace and once a member of the legislature.

Our subject and Mrs. Pryor are the parents of a family of three children, of whom we have the following record: Mary A., born February 27, 1846, is the wife of William B. Hilliard, living on a part of Mr. Pryor's original farm. To them have been born seven children, five of whom are living, viz.: Carry A., Alexander W., James G. (deceased), Edgar L., Luther W. (deceased), Anna and Myrtle. The second child, Ephraim G. H., who was born August 20, 1849, lives not far from his father's home, married Miss Icy Foster, and four children—Hallie, William, Dora A. and Samuel L.—have been born to them. The third child, Samuel L., was born October 26, 1852, and is also living in this district. He married Miss Lucy Williamson, and six children have been born to them, five of whom are still living: Maud E., Mary A., Milton, William (deceased), John and Eva.

LEVI J. PARKINS is an honored resident of Spencer, Van Buren county, where he is living, retired from active business, in a comfortable home that is the center of true and generous hospitality. He was born and spent his entire life in this section of Tennessee, and has been one of the most successful farmers and stock raisers in the Sequatchie Valley, and is now passing the evening of his life enjoying the fruit of his labor.

Mr. Parkins was born in Hinds Valley, Roane county, Tenn., a son of Lewis and Mary (Hinds) Parkins. The father was born in Blount county, Tenn., was a farmer by occupation and died at the age of twenty-eight. They were the parents of a family of two children, Levi J., the subject of this sketch, was born January 25, 1830, and Sarah A., deceased, was the wife of Levi Sevils. After the father's death, the mother was married to William Hickey, and two children, Lewis C., and Susan, were born to them. Our subject's mother died in Roane county, near Rockwood.

Levi J. Parkins received his primary training in the free schools of Hinds Valley, and afterward paid his own tuition to the academy at Postoak Springs, Roane county, Tenn., and attended there several months. June 22, 1853, he was united in marriage to Miss Amanda M. Owings, who was born in Roane county, Tenn., May 30, 1833, the daughter of Samuel and Sarah (Randolph) Owings, the former also a native of Roane county, Tenn. Mr. and Mrs. Owings were the parents of a family of fifteen children, two of which died in infancy. We have the following record: William J., deceased; Clarinda is still living; William J. died at the age of eighty years; Martha, deceased; Manerva, deceased; Mary J., deceased; Sarah is now living in Missouri; Rebecca, deceased; Ellen, deceased; Amanda M., the wife of our subject; Elihu, deceased;

Robert, deceased; Eliza and Albert. To our subject and Mrs. Parkins have been born thirteen children, as follows: Elmyra T., deceased; Lewis A., deceased; Stephen A.; Robert S., deceased; Mary, deceased; Eliza C., deceased; Martin L.; Sarah E.; James A., deceased; Maggie L.; Cora A. A.; and Willie and Wilber, twins, both deceased.

Mr. Parkins has spent the greater part of his life on a farm. He first located on a place twelve miles east of Crossville, in Cumberland county, and made that his home for fourteen years. Here he carried on farming operations, but made a specialty of raising and buying and selling stock. While looking after his stock he usually went on horseback and carried his gun, and during the fourteen years he spent on this place he killed one hundred and six deer and immense quantities of small game. During this time, however, he saw but one wild wolf, and succeeded in killing it. He afterward sold his farm in Cumberland county and bought another situated about five and a half miles south of Dunlap, Sequatchie county. Here he continued the cattle raising business and made his home until 1886, and still owns the farm. In the year 1886, however, he moved to Spencer, Van Buren county, for the purpose of educating his children, and now owns property in that city. He is a very pleasant neighbor, genial, warm-hearted, and has an agreeable family.

GEORGE WASHINGTON ALLEY, one of Marion county's prominent and prosperous farmers, who is now making his home in the city of Jasper, was born one mile east of that city, February 9, 1838, the son of Erasmus and Mary (Kelly) Alley. The father was born in Overton county, Tenn., in the year 1801, and the mother in Marion county, Tenn., in July, 1808. Erasmus Alley was a son of Watson Alley, who was born in Virginia and grew to manhood and was married there. He moved to Overton county, Tenn., with his family when Erasmus, our subject's father, was a small boy, and settled at Battle Creek, now South Pittsburg, where he and his wife both died at the home of their son, Erasmus.

Erasmus Alley, our subject's father, is the oldest of a family of five children. He was educated in Overton county, and worked at farming and trading in stock. He bought a farm one mile east of Jasper and made that his home for several years, being married a short time before buying the farm. He afterward gave this place to his son, Alex, and moved to South Pittsburg, bought a farm near there, and in connection with his farm work, operated a mercantile business in the city, and also a ferry across the Tennessee river. He left there about the year 1850, and went to Running Water, Marion county, Tenn., and was there engaged in getting out railroad timber until 1859, when he returned to his farm at South Pittsburg. At the breaking out of the war he left his home as a refugee and stayed in Cedartown, Ga., until the close of the war. He then made his home on his farm at South Pittsburg until 1873, and then sold out everything and moved to a farm one mile west of Jasper and remained there until his death, which

34

occurred in 1878. His wife died in 1871. They were both members of the M. E. church, South, and are both buried in South Pittsburg. They were the parents of a family of twelve children, as follows: James, John and Levan, deceased; Alex K., who operates a hotel business at Tucker Springs, Bradley county, Tenn.; Thomas, who died while young; Nancy, deceased; George W., the subject of this sketch, James K. P., a farmer in Texas; Valentine K., deceased; Mary E., deceased; Hattie T., wife of Rev. John Burnett, of Whitfield county, Ga.; and Erasmus, deceased.

The subject of our sketch received his primary training in the public schools of the district in which he spent his boyhood and supplemented the same with a full course in the Burritt College at Spencer. Mrs. Alley, who bore the maiden name of Miss Mary J. Bybee, was born February 24, 1838, in Van Buren county, Tenn., the daughter of George D. and Sarah (Wood) Bybee. She was educated in McMinnville and Spencer, and taught school for a few years. They were married July 15, 1858, and five children have been born to them, namely: Leaven L., of Jasper; Mary I., wife of S. O. Bradley, a farmer near Jasper; George E., at Bridgeport, Ala.; John C., at home, and Sallie H. is at home and is attending school. Mr. Alley is an old soldier, having enlisted in 1861, in Company K, Twenty-fifth Tennessee Infantry, under Captain Alex K. Alley, his brother, and participated in the battles of Murfreesboro and Cumberland Gap, and after that he was appointed wagon and forage master, and therefore did not participate in any more of the battles. Socially he is a Mason, and holds his membership in Jasper, and is also a member of the Knights of Labor. Politically he is a Democrat and cast his first presidential ballot for James Buchanan. Mr. Alley has also served as justice of the peace of Marion county since the year 1871 with the exception of about two years. He was elected chairman of the county court in 1885 and held that office seven years. In 1885 he moved from his farm, one mile west of Jasper, and since then has made his home in Jasper, but is still working his place. As a farmer he is thorough and systematic, and as a friend and neighbor he is pleasant, genial, warm-hearted, and has a very agreeable family.

JOHN E. GILLIAM.—The Tenth district of Marion county is not without its share of well-regulated farms, the incomes from which form so large a part of the wealth of that county. One of these carefully cultivated tracts of land belongs to the gentleman whose name introduces these paragraphs. The farm consists of two hundred and eighty acres of choice land, and the situation and the improvements upon it are well adapted to the conducting of a first class dairy farm, and its thrifty owner is a man who thoroughly understands the details of that line of work.

Mr. Gilliam was born October 28, 1834, in the same district and county in which he now makes his home, and is a son of Joseph and Sarah (Brown) Gilliam, the former born in Knox county, Tenn., in 1805, and the latter born in Sullivan county, Tenn., in the year 1805. Joseph Gilliam was a son of Hincha Gilliam. Hincha Gilliam moved to Tennessee and settled on the farm now occupied by our subject in the year 1832, and made that his home until the time of his death. His occupation was that of farming. Joseph Gilliam, our subject's father, moved to Tennessee and located on his father's farm in 1834, a short time before our subject was born. A few years later he bought a farm, settled upon it and made that his home for many years. Politically he was a Democrat, and, upon the breaking out of the Civil war, he was in sympathy with the Southern cause. On that account he was arrested and taken to Chattanooga and from thence he started for Shelbyville and died on the way, in June, 1862. His wife died February 14, 1876. They were the parents of a family of five children, as follows: Lottie, deceased; Carter, deceased; John E., the subject of this sketch; Samuel N., a farmer in Arkansas; and Jane, deceased.

John E. Gilliam was educated in the public schools of the district in which he spent his boyhood, and June 22, 1857, he was united in marriage to Miss Samantha C. Hise, who was born March 14, 1836, a daughter of Henry and Elizabeth (Bryson) Hise, the former a native of North Carolina, and the latter a native of Franklin county, Tenn. Henry Hise is of German descent and the name was originally spelled "Hoss." He was born in a fort at Charleston, S. C., during the Revolutionary war, as his father was a soldier and participated in that struggle for independence. Henry Hise died in 1886 at the age of one hundred and two years, and his wife, who was of Irish parentage, died February 18, 1897.

After his marriage, our subject lived for a few years about four miles above his present home, and then returned to the farm on which he was born and has since made that his home. In the year 1890 he began a dairy business in connection with his farming, and, as it proved a profitable business, he has given it special attention and is now making that his principal business. Mr. Gilliam took no part in the war, but was in sympathy with the Southern cause. In politics he is usually identified with the Democratic party and endorses its platform, although he invariably uses his elective franchises in the support of the man best qualified for the position he seeks, regardless of party lines. The house in which our subject makes his home was erected by William Watson, over one hundred years ago, and is the first house built by a white man in the Battle Creek Valley. Our subject and Mrs. Gilliam are both members of the M. E. church, South.

The home of Mr. and Mrs. Gilliam has been blessed by the advent of a family of seven children, six of whom are now living, viz: George W., a merchant at Pratt City, Ala.; West M., Fort Payne, is a moulder by occupation; Leon E., deceased; Lizzie, wife of Harry Quinn, a resident of the Tenth district, Marion county; Osira L., wife of Harry Barnes, a farmer near Sherwood, Franklin county, Tenn.; James B., Fort Payne, Ala., is a moulder by occupation, and is considered the finest workman in the house with which he is connected; Anna R., wife of Edward Garner, a farmer of Franklin county, Tenn. Mr. and Mrs. Gilliam are also raising and educating a granddaughter, whose name is Daisy L.

Barnes. She was born at Cowan, Tenn., July 1, 1880. She is the daughter of John R. and Leon E. Barnes, and granddaughter of John E. and S. C. Gilliam. Her mother died when she was but fourteen months old.

JOHN W. NORWOOD, of Whitwell, Tenn., a son of S. C. and Catharine J. Norwood, of Pikeville, Tenn., was born March 28, 1852, who in addition to the education received in the common schools of his county closed his course of studies at the famous institute, Burritt College, at Spencer, Tenn., under the tutelage of the renowned instructor W. D. Carnes, familiarly known as old "Pop" Carnes.

From his earliest childhood he developed strong and well defined traits of sterling integrity, with a love for business and strong hatred for unfair and crooked dealings. With these strong constitutionally defined characteristics as a boy, it did not take long to mature and develop these traits when manhood and circumstances called for them, and a few years of mercantile experience with his father, brought him to the attention of large corporations, who are always seeking such characters as safe-guards to their business, and for nearly ten years he has managed and controlled for the Tenn. Coal, Iron & R. R. Co., at Whitwell, one of their many large stores, to their entire satisfaction and profit, having at all times his employers' interest at heart, even to the smallest details of the business he manages.

Fortunately for him, that in the midst of his unceasing energy and love for his business, he has a great lever or balancing power combined with his native ability, by which he gathered much of his wonted physical element in preserving a normal equilibrium—that is his love and devotion for the chase—which is a part of his existance and being, and his pack of thoroughbred fox hounds gives him many hours of recreation after business hours. With his pack of bear and deer dogs he usually spends a vacation from business in some of the wilds of the swamps of Mississippi or Cumberland mountains, and such occasions usually reward him well in restored physical energies, and his many trophies of the chase, consisting of bear and deer rugs, deer antlers and fox skins proclaim him the David Boone of his county. He is a great lover of good horses, deals largely in registered Berkshire hogs, and is perhaps the best posted man in his section on the blood lines of all thorough bred stock.

He married in 1893 Miss Callie Garrett, of Nashville, and a son and daughter to them have been born.

REECE BRABSON PATTON, contractor and builder, at Chattanooga, Tenn., since 1895 has made his home at Highland Park. Mr. Patton was born at Sweeden's Cove, Marion county, December 6, 1859, and is a son of Judge William O. and Millie (Raulston) Patton.

Judge William O. Patton was born in Marion county, Tenn., the date of his birth being 1836, and was reared in Sweeden's Cove. His wife was born in Sweeden's Cove in 1842, and they were married there. They then removed to Chitty's Cove, Marion county, and lived on a farm there until 1876, at which time they removed to what is now known as Patton's Addition to South Pittsburg. During a part of the Civil war Mr. Patton held a position as detective in the Federal employ at Nashville. After the close of the war he was circuit clerk for eight years, and was chairman of the county court until the office of county judge was instituted, at which time he was elected to that office. After his installation in this position, he moved to Jasper, where he died while yet in office, in 1894. His wife is still living, making her home in South Pittsburg. They were both members of the Primitive Baptist church, and he was also a member of the Independent Order of Odd Fellows. In politics he was a Republican. To him and his wife were born five children, all of whom are living, and of whom we have the following record: B. F., of South Pittsburg, was the real promoter in the development of the Battle creek coal mines and was the first president of the Battle Creek Coal Company; Reece Brabson, the subject of this sketch; William M., a machine moulder at the stove foundry at South Pittsburg, and a member of the Marion county court; Robert O., a moulder at Shuster Foundry; and Thomas L., a traveling salesman for the last-named institution.

Our subject attended the public school in South Pittsburg, and in 1876–77 was a student at the Hiwassee College, in Monroe county, Tenn. After leaving the latter he entered the railroad office at South Pittsburg, but a short time after found employment in the Southern States Coal, Iron & Land Co.'s store for one year. At the expiration of that time he was employed by

Mr. John F. Fletcher as paymaster in the construction company of the Cincinnati Southern Railroad Co. The Duck River Valley railroad was the next scene of his labors, and later on the Sparta extension of the same line engaged his attention. He next worked on the bridge across Lake Pontchartrain for the Northeastern or Queen & Crescent Company. In 1884 he quit railroad construction work and turned his attention to general contracting, which has since been his vocation. He has put up many of the best buildings in South Pittsburg, Bridgeport and other places.

December 9, 1879, Mr. Patton was united in marriage with Miss Sallie Bradshaw, daughter of William Bradshaw. She was born in Dade county, Ga., but grew to womanhood in Jasper, Tenn. This union has been blessed by the advent of a family of seven children, six of whom are now living, as follows: Hal T., William H., Ruth, Mary, Sarah and Reece R. Gus died when a child. Mrs. Patton is a member of the Methodist Episcopal church, South, and our subject is a member of the Knights of Pythias, being one of the charter members of the lodges at South Pittsburg, Tenn., and Bridgeport. Politically, he is a Republican.

GEORGE W. MOORE is one of the honored residents of Marion county, and has been a promoter of the varied interests which tend toward its advancement and upbuilding. The educational, moral and material welfare of his district has been promoted through his effective labors, and

no movement for the public good ever seeks his aid in vain. In business he sustains an irreproachable reputation and over his life record there falls no shadow of wrong. Endowed by nature with a sound judgment and an accurate, discriminating mind, he fears not that laborious attention to the details of business so necessary to achieve success, and this essential quality is ever guided by a sense of moral right which will tolerate only the employment of those means that will bear the most rigid examination by a fairness of intention that neither seeks nor requires disguise.

Mr. Moore was born at Red Hill, Marion county, Tenn., September 21, 1833, and is a son of George W. and Nancy Eliza (Davis) Moore. The former, it is supposed, was a native of southwestern Virginia, and was a son of John Moore, who was born in Virginia, and was of Irish lineage. Representatives of the family loyally served their country in the war of the Revolution. John Moore was a farmer by occupation, and was one of the honored pioneers of the Sequatchie valley who came to Marion county about the time of its organization and before Cheekville was made the county seat. He died in 1820, at an advanced age. George Moore, the father of our subject, was a surveyor and civil engineer, and it is thought was a student in a college in upper east Tennessee. In connection with surveying he also followed school teaching to some extent. He served as deputy sheriff of Marion county and also belonged to the militia, being quite noted as a drill master. In politics he was a Democrat, and socially he was connected with Olive Branch lodge, A. F. & A. M., of Jasper, while religiously, his wife was connected with the Cumberland Presbyterian church. They were the parents of ten children, of whom the following is the record: J. D. died in infancy. N. B. was a farmer and served in the Third Confederate Cavalry of Tennessee. Martha J. is the wife of P. H. Grayson, of Whitwell, Tenn. Millie Ann is the wife of Calvin Maxwell, a farmer of Grayson county, Texas. George W. is the next of the family. M. D., who died in 1888 and was a farmer by occupation, served in the Third Confederate Regiment, and was wounded at Fort Donelson and Stone river; Emeline, who married James M. Grayson, and who is living in Texas; Thomas J., who was a member of the Third regiment, died in Sequatchie county. He participated in the battles of Fort Donelson, Chickamauga, Stone River and other important engagements, and in the first named was wounded. James M., now in Texas, was a member of the Fifth Tennessee Regiment of Confederate troops, under Col. B. H. Hill, and at Shiloh was taken prisoner. He was wounded in that engagement and was reported dead, but being captured by the Union forces was sent as a prisoner of war to Camp Douglas, Chicago, where he remained for a year, his family supposing he had been killed until, after his release from prison, he visited his home while on his way to the army. He was afterward detailed as one of the Whitworth sharpshooters in Gen. Pat Clebourne's command and valiantly battled for the cause in which he so firmly believed. Later he attended the People's College and then engaged in teaching school in Texas. He was elected to represent San Saba and Barnett counties in the state legislature of Texas

and was a most prominent citizen of that community. Becoming a minister of the Cumberland Presbyterian church, he filled many important pulpits in the south. He was again called to public office to serve as probate judge of Barnett county, elected on the Prohibition ticket and filled that office in a most acceptable manner for a long period. The youngest member of the family is Rev. Richard Moore, of Whitwell.

George W. Moore, whose name begins this review, was reared on his father's farm near Red Hill and supplemented his preliminary education by a two years' course in Altine Seminary, then under the presidency of Professor Mobery. He afterward engaged in teaching for two years at Sulphur Springs, Shiloh and other places in the Sequatchie valley, and in 1858 secured a clerkship in the store of Washington Turner, of Jasper. The following year he was elected register of Marion county. For some years he has taken a deep and active interest in the raising of fine horses, cattle and other stock, and has done much to improve the grade of stock in this part of the state. His fine farm, known as Prospect Hill, is one of the best improved in Marion county, and its well tilled fields and substantial buildings plainly indicate the thrift and enterprise of the owner.

Although Mr. Moore has led a busy life, he has yet found time to devote to outside interests which concern his duty to his fellowmen. He became a member of Olive Branch lodge, A. F. & A. M., of Jasper, in 1859, and also belongs to the Ancient Order of United Workmen, several times representing the local lodge in the grand lodge. In 1852 he became a member of the

Methodist Episcopal church, South, and has since been one of its most prominent and zealous workers. He has many times served as lay delegate from the Chattanooga district to the Holston conference and is a member of the joint board of finance. He is also recording steward of the Etna circuit, and a member of the board of trustees of McDaniel Chapel. That house of worship was erected by Mr. Moore in 1886-7, the original building having been destroyed by Federal troops during the war. He has also been a delegate to the state Grange in its meetings at Knoxville and Jackson, and has been reporter to the state agricultural department for twelve years, also to the department in Washington, D. C.

On the 19th of September, 1861, Mr. Moore was united in marriage with Miss Nancy Eliza McDaniel, a daughter of the Rev. Goodson McDaniel. She was educated under the direction of her father and her stepmother, both of whom were teachers of superior ability, and is a lady of culture and refinement. Four children have blessed this union: Goodson McDaniel, a prominent farmer of the Eighth district of Marion county and a member of the county court; Ara A., who was educated at People's College, at Pikeville, Tenn., and at Centenary College, of Cleveland, Tenn., and is now the wife of Rev. J. F. Wampler, of Holston conference of the Methodist Episcopal church, South, who for four years was pastor of the church at Jonesboro, Tenn., but is now at Fincastle, Tenn.; William O., who is on the home farm; and Charles C. The family are all members of the Methodist church and are very active workers. In politics Mr. Moore is a stalwart Democrat and has been a valued and efficient member of the county court for a number of years. In business circles he is progressive and enterprising, but yet retains the courteous, gentlemanly manner of the old school, and his home is noted for the true southern hospitality. In all the relations of life he has been true and faithful to the trust reposed in him and his noble example should serve as a source of inspiration and encouragement to representatives of the younger generation.

HON. JOHN J. DYKES is one of the most important factors in the public and business life of Marion county, Tenn., and stands to-day in a prominent place among her leading men. His has been a well-spent life, and the success he has achieved is due entirely to his own efforts. Success comes not to the man who idly waits, but to the faithful toiler whose work is characterized by sleepless vigilance and cheerful alacrity. It is the result of earnest, diligent labor, and it is such qualities that have gained Mr. Dykes his standing in business circles, while his true worth and fitness for leadership have brought to him recognition in the form of political honors, of which he is well deserving.

Mr. Dykes was born in Grundy county, Tenn., July 25, 1863, a son of Andrew Jackson and Mary (Barker) Dykes. His father was born in Grundy county, September 22, 1837, and died March 2, 1898. He was a son of John Dykes, who was a son of Ishem Dykes, and who died in Warren county, Tenn., on his return from Bowling

Green, Ky., whither he had gone during the war in order to care for his son, who was ill. The ancestors of our subject removed from North Carolina into northeastern Tennessee, and thence came to Grundy county. Andrew J. Dykes followed farming and trading throughout his active business career, and won a fair competence. Like his father, his sympathies went out to the Union during the Civil war, and he gave his political support to the Republican party. From Grundy county he removed to Sequatchie county, and in 1890 took up his residence in Whitwell, where he engaged in trading and in the livery business. In his religious belief he was a Methodist, and during his residence in Grundy county was a member of the Masonic fraternity.

Andrew J. Dykes was married in February, 1858, to Miss Mary Barker, who was born in Sequatchie county, Tenn., March 15, 1837, and died February 1, 1889. Her father was Howell Barker, and the Barker family removed from North Carolina to eastern Tennessee, whence they finally came to Sequatchie county. Mr. and Mrs. Dykes became the parents of three children: Elizabeth, wife of N. T. Eagle, of Sequatchie county; John J.; and Elijah, who was formerly engaged in merchandising, and was in the employ of the Tennessee Coal, Iron & Railroad Company's store for quite a period, but is now carrying on farming in Sequatchie county.

Mr. Dykes, whose name introduces this review, acquired his preliminary education in Altamont, Grundy county, and later attended Irving College, in Warren county. For six years he successfully engaged in teaching school and then spent some time in Texas and the southwest. When he and his father embarked in the livery business in Whitwell he became manager of the enterprise, and still carries on the business. He has a splendidly equipped stable, supplied with a large number of fine horses and excellent carriages and other vehicles, and his earnest desire to please his patrons, combined with his straightforward dealing has brought to him a large and profitable business.

On the 8th of January, 1888 Mr. Dykes was united in marriage to Miss Amanda Hudson, a daughter of Isaac Hudson, and a native of Marion county, Tenn. She is a member of the Cumberland Presbyterian church, and a lady of social qualities who presides with gracious hospitality over their pleasant home. They have four children: Robert Anderson, Mamie, Oscar, and Myrtle. They also lost one, Edgar, who died in infancy.

In his social relations Mr. Dykes is a valued and popular member of the Knights of Pythias fraternity. He exercises his right of franchise in support of the men and measures of the Republican party, and so well and favorably is he known in the ranks of that political organization that in 1896 he was nominated by acclamation to represent his county in the state legislature, where he served in a most creditable and acceptable manner. He was a member of the committees on emigration, labor and centennial, and to his duties he gave the most earnest and thoughtful consideration. He is a public-spirited, progressive citizen, deeply interested in everything pertaining to the welfare of county, state and nation. Loyal and true to every duty of public and private life, honorable in business, faithful in friendship, he commands the respect and esteem of all who know him, and is well deserving of mention among the representative and valuable citizens of Marion county.

PATRICK L. STONE, post master and dealer in general merchandise, living and doing business at Grapevine, Bledsoe county, was born in what is now Cumberland county, and in the Third district, June 6, 1848, the son of James C. and Caroline H. (Nail) Stone, the former also born in what is now Cumberland county, December 27, 1819, and the latter born April 15, 1820.

James C. Stone made his home in Cumberland county, Tenn., until 1859, and then moved with his family to Texas, where he died May 12, of the following year. He was a farmer in his younger days, and also did some distilling, and teaching school. He helped to move the Cherokee Indians in 1836-7, to their reservation in the Indian Territory. His father moved to Tennessee when a young man. Mrs. Caroline Stone was a member of the Methodist church. After the death of her husband, she moved with her family to Tennessee in 1861, and died November 23, 1889. Of her family of five children, four are now living, viz: The subject of our sketch, who is the oldest of the family; Mrs. Eliza Walker, wife of Stephen Walker, of Cumberland county; Perry V., a farmer of Cumberland county; Leroy, also a farmer of the above county; and Mitchell, deceased.

Our subject's schooling amounted to only three months, but he has been a constant and studious reader and has secured quite an extensive education, and after the war taught school for some time in Cumberland and Bledsoe counties. Early in the year 1865 he enlisted in Company G, Sixth Tennessee Mounted Infantry, in the Union service, and served until July 11, 1865, and was mustered out at Nashville. At the close of hostilities, Mr. Stone commenced farming, and later, engaged for a time in teaching school, as before stated. He lived with his mother on the farm that Stephen Walker now owns for a number of years. August 24, 1874, he was united in marriage to Miss Mary Ann Hale. She is a daughter of Thomas Hale, and was born in Cumberland county, Tenn., November 15, 1856. To this union have been born nine children, five of whom are now living, and of whom we have the following record: Monrovia Dallas, wife of Reuben Worthington of Bledsoe county, was born October 28, 1878; William is still living with his father; he was born April 20, 1886; Lillie G., born October 18, 1889; H. Clay, born May 20, 1892; Walter E., born August 18, 1894. The deceased are: Mary Caldona, born February 15, 1876, and died September 26, 1886; Eugene L., born March 8, 1880, and died October 7, 1886; James Thomas Arthur, born July 11, 1882, and died September 22, 1886; Mitchell S., born November 4, 1884, and died March 12, 1890.

Shortly after his marriage our subject moved to his present location, built a home, and has since resided there. He has a fine farm, good improvements and an elegant home, and is one of the representative farmers of the district. He has served three

35

years as justice of the peace of his district, and was instrumental in the establishment of the road running to the village of Grapevine, thus making it possible to establish a post office in that place, and as was his just dues, he was appointed postmaster of that office in 1891 and has had charge of it since. In connection with the duties of the office of postmaster, Mr. Stone has recently embarked in the mercantile business, and considering the short time he has been engaged in the business, he has a large and extensive trade, which is steadily increasing, and as the village develops into a prosperous city, we expect Mr. Stone to be the leading and substantial merchant and the backbone of the business interests of the place. He is a member of the G. A. R. at Crossville and a member of the Freewill Baptist church. In political matters he endorses the policy of the Republican party, but at local elections he uses his elective franchise in support of the candidate best fitted for the position he seeks regardless of his party connections.

DR. ANDREW J. McLARNEY, one of Cumberland county's best known and most popular physicians, resides at Crossville. Dr. McLarney was born on the 23rd of February, 1854, near Mouse creek, McMinn county, Tenn., and is the son of James and Isabelle (Lunsford) McLarney, the former a native of North Carolina and the latter of Virginia. James McLarney went to Bradley county, Tenn., when a youth, and was there married. He was a farmer and trader by occupation, and did business all through the south before the war. He was a veteran of the war of 1812, and a prominent man of his time. Politically he was a Whig, and always professed the warmest allegiance to the Union. Mr. McLarney died in 1872, at the remarkable age of ninety-six. Mrs. McLarney died in McMinn county, Tenn., in 1857. There were four children in the family, all sons. William, the eldest, is now a resident of Willard, Ill., and is a farmer and miller. James is a stonemason of Bledsoe county, Tenn. Henry is a farmer in Missouri, and our subject is the youngest. The latter spent the earlier years of his life in the Sequatchie Valley, in Tennessee, attending school at Pleasant Hill, Meigs county. for some time. He then engaged in farming until 1878, when he began to study medicine. In 1881 he entered the Chattanooga Medical College and after completing the course commenced practice in the Valley. He was very successful there, and soon had established an enviable reputation as a physician and surgeon.

In 1893 he removed to Crossville, the county seat of Cumberland county, and is now one of the most prosperous and popular medical men in that section, enjoying a large and remunerative practice, and a flattering record as a professional man. He attends cases all the way from Pikeville to Jamestown, and often beyond these villages. He is a member of the Upper Cumberland Medical Society and of the Melvina Masonic lodge, in which he has held various offices. Dr. McLarney's success is all the more remarkable from the fact that he had little or nothing when he began life. His father, who was at one time in very easy circumstances, lost heavily by the war, and the young man was obliged to make shift for himself. His energy, perseverance and ability, however, supplied what Dame Fortune had denied him, and he is to-day a remarkable example of what the poor young man may make of himself if he only wills it.

On the 31st of December, 1875, Dr. McLarney married Miss Martha Swofford, who was born in Bledsoe county, Tenn., and is a daughter of John D. and Elizabeth Swofford. Dr. and Mrs. McLarney have one child, a son, John D., who is now preparing to study medicine at Herriman College. He has imitated his father and very wisely adopted the medical profession. If he continues to follow the example of his parent, there will, no doubt, be two excellent physicians in the McLarney family.

EDWARD EVERETT BULL.—"History is the essence of innumerable biographies," said Carlyle, and the record of a county or state is best told in the lives of its representative citizens. The efficient postmaster at Whitwell, E. E. Bull, has long been an important factor in the public life of Marion county and is a public-spirited citizen who has contributed largely to the material growth and progress of the community. He has also been an advocate of education and moral interests and co-operates in every movement that tends to advance the welfare of the county. In business his reputation is unassailable, and in private life he commands the respect and regard of many friends.

Mr. Bull was born in Tracy City, Tenn.,

January 13, 1867, and is a son of James Everett and Susan (Sherrill) Bull. The father was born in Morristown, then in Grainger county, Tenn., December 9, 1831, and died March 31, 1896. His parents were Elisha and Sarah (Davis) Bull, and his paternal ancestry came from England to the United States, locating near Baltimore, Md. Elisha Bull served his country in the war of 1812. He was a splendid mechanic and a famous gun-maker, following that pursuit through the greater part of his life. From Maryland he removed to eastern Tennessee and thence to Coffee county, this state, in 1858. There his death occurred in August, 1873, at the age of eighty-six years. He first married Sarah Davis, and after her death wedded Louisa Ladd, who is still living in Coffee county, and is one of the few who receive a pension on account of services rendered in the war of 1812.

James E. Bull attended school in Morristown, and under his father's direction learned the trades of a gunsmith and blacksmith. With the family he removed to Coffee county, and in 1866 went to Tracy City, where for twenty-five years he held a position as blacksmith in the works of the Tennessee Coal, Iron & Railroad Company. During the Civil war he was connected with the United States quartermaster's department under General Milroy, at Nashville and Tullahoma. He was also prominent in civil affairs and served as chairman of the county court of Grundy county for eight years and as one of its members for an additional seven years, while for four years he was deputy county court clerk. He held membership in the Methodist Episcopal church, South, and was a prominent Mason, representing the lodge of Tracy City in the grand lodge. In politics he was a Whig until the organization of the Republican party, when he joined its ranks.

James E. Bull was married November 10, 1863, to Miss Susan Sherrill, daughter of Uriah and Eliza (Brixey) Sherrill. The Sherrill family is of Scotch-Irish descent, and the grandfather, George D. Sherrill, was one of the heroes of the Revolution, probably a member of General Marion's army. He had a sister, Catherine, who became the wife of Governor Sevier, the first governor of Tennessee. Uriah Sherrill was born in North Carolina, November 13, 1802, and died at Tracy City, April 28, 1871. His wife, who was born in Georgia, May 26, 1807, also died in Tracy City, April 21, 1879. They were married June 8, 1840. The former came with his parents to this state, the family locating in Washington county, whence they removed to Coffee county, where the maternal grandfather of our subject remained until 1860. He then took up his residence in Tracy City and was the first bookkeeper for the Tennessee Coal, Iron & Railroad Company at that place. He married Lucinda Camden, a native of Virginia, and after her death wedded Miss Brixey, daughter of Thomas Brixey, a farmer and a native of Georgia. Mr. Sherrill held membership in the Freewill Baptist church, and was a highly educated gentleman. His wife belonged to the "old school" Presbyterian church.

The father of our subject was also twice married, and by Adaline Inman, his first wife, had one son, John H., who died in childhood. The children of his second marriage are: Emma Viola, who is living with her mother in Whitwell; Edward E.; Louella, who is with her mother; Ada, wife of W. C. Adams, a merchant of Whitwell; Rosella, who died in childhood; and one who died in infancy. The mother is a member of the Methodist Episcopal church, South. She still survives her husband, and in the community where she lives is held in the highest regard for her many estimable qualities.

E. E. Bull, of this review, attended school in his native city, and almost from the time that he was tall enough to reach the top of the anvil he has worked at the blacksmith's trade and through the entire period has been connected with the company in whose employ he remains at the present. In 1887 he came to Whitwell and took charge of their shops here. He is an expert mechanic and his ability is shown by the important position he now occupies. He is one of the most faithful and trusted employes of the company and has the respect of all who serve under him.

On the 3d of October, 1889, Mr. Bull married Miss Maggie J., daughter of William Walton and Margaret (Johnson) Garrett, who removed from Robinson county to Davidson. Mrs. Bull was born November 28, 1867, and by her marriage has one son, John Garrett. Her brothers and sisters are: John B., who is grand secretary of the grand lodge of Masons for Tennessee; William W., a merchant of Birmingham, Ala.; Nettie, wife of Dr. Worsham, of Knoxville, Tenn.; Mary, wife of B. F. Stratton, a prominent citizen of Nashville; Alvin, a lawyer who went to Texas; and Callie, wife of J. W. Norwood, who has charge of the store of the Tennessee Coal, Iron & Railroad Company, at Whitwell. The father of this family died at the age of sixty-three years, and the mother at the age of forty-six.

Mr. and Mrs. Bull have a wide acquaintance in the community where they reside, and are held in the highest regard. They hold membership in the Methodist Episcopal church and Mr. Bull belongs to the Knights of Pythias fraternity and in 1895 represented the local lodge in the grand lodge. He is a Republican in politics, and in April, 1897, was appointed postmaster of Whitwell, assuming the duties of the office on the 1st of June, following. He was chairman of the Republican executive committee in 1896–7 and is a loyal and efficient worker in the party. As a citizen he is true to every duty that devolves upon him, and in all the relations of public and private life his reputation is unassailable. Honorable in business, faithful in friendship, of kindly manner and sterling worth, he is one of the popular residents of Marion county.

TYRE A. HAVRON, the subject of this sketch, is the eldest son of James P. and Martha J. Havron. He was born in Marion county, Tenn., February 10, 1860. His grandfather, Col. John M. Havron, was born in Knox county, in 1792, and was a prominent man in the politics of his day. He was an ardent Democrat, and generally successful in his contests. He subsequently moved to Jasper, and served two terms in succession in the state senate. His personal popularity is evidenced by the fact that the Whigs were in the majority in the district. He died June 15, 1856.

James P. Havron was born May 15, 1832. He was married some time in 1858 to Mattie J. Taylor, of Dade county, Ga. To this marriage were born eight other children: Reuben L., Henry A., William E., Samuel L., Septemma, Russell, Arthur V. and James B. Havron. The mother died at the home to which they had moved in Georgia, December 7, 1878, at the age of thirty-six. The two second children, Rubby and Henry, died in infancy. Russell died shortly after the family moved to Jasper, in 1888. Septemma, the only daughter and sister, was married to Charles E. Wyrick, in Jasper, some time in 1891. She died about a year afterward.

James P. Havron, the father, engaged in farming immediately after he married, which vocation he has followed to the present time, excepting the nearly four-years' service in the Confederate army and confinement in Camp Chase and Rock Island prisons. He joined Company H, Fourth Tennessee Confederate Cavalry, in the early part of 1862. He was wounded and taken prisoner while on picket duty, at which time his comrade, Matt Griffith, was killed. He participated in the battles of Fort Donelson, Parker's Cross Roads, Spring Hill and other minor engagements. He was paroled and returned home after hostilities ceased. In 1874 he moved to the southern part of Dade county, Ga., returning to his farm in Marion county in 1885. He moved to Jasper in 1888, where some of the boys are now engaged in merchandising. He is a Mason, and a member of the Cumberland Presbyterian church.

Tyre A. Havron, the eldest of the children and subject of this sketch, served his apprenticeship on the farm. His school advantages were in common with the vast majority of other boys—the public school "between seasons;" but he cultivated a habit and taste, through the sacred offices and influence of a now sainted mother, to read every historical and religious book that came in his way in early life. The fund of information then gained has been of invaluable service to him in his subsequent life. But it was his very good fortune to get the last year or two of his school life in an academic course under a fine instructor, the Rev. W. J. Callan, Sulphur Springs, Ala. At the age of twenty-one he was employed as salesman in a general store at Trenton, Ga. He spent his leisure time for about three years reading law. He was admitted to the bar, and did some practice. In 1883 a little paper in Trenton fell into his possession. It was a new and untried experience, but he made it "swim," and invested some of his time looking after a little law practice and clerking in a store. These experiences covered a period of seven years, from 1881 to 1888. About three months of this time was spent in Texas, and about three months clerking in a store at Rising Fawn. He sold the paper at Trenton in January, 1888, came immediately to Jasper and established the "Marion County Democrat." The "Democrat" has enjoyed ten years of very successful experience. Shortly after it was established it absorbed its predecessor, "The Valley Herald," by purchase. In politics it has been uncompromisingly and aggressively Democratic. In 1896 it very much mystified the vast majority of its

party readers by repudiating the Chicago platform and ticket. The pressure was very heavy, but the editor stood his ground and supported the Palmer and Buckner ticket. It has never wavered in its admiration of Mr. Cleveland and in support of his entire administration. The editor, Mr. Havron, also served as postmaster at Jasper under the Cleveland administration. He also entered the hardware and agricultural business in Jasper in 1894. In this effort he has been very successful. The confidence and respect in which he is held by the citizens of the county is proven in many particulars.

Mr. Havron was married January 2, 1890, to Miss Minnie H. Cowan, daughter of Dr. J. B. Cowan, of Tullahoma. To them have been born two children, Tyre Harton and Howard Taylor. Mr. and Mrs. Havron are both members of the Cumberland Presbyterian church, he being a ruling elder.

WILLIAM HARRISON GURNEY.— It is a pleasure to record the main events in the life of one who has attained an enviable position solely through his own efforts and exertions, and who, though he has persistently pursued his calling for nearly forty years continuously, can look forward to many years of usefulness in his chosen field of labor. It is, therefore, gratifying to place before the readers a brief outline of the life struggles of the superintendent and foreman of the South Pittsburg Stove and Foundry Company.

Mr. Gurney was born at Taunton,

Mass., September 22, 1845, a son of Charles H. and Nancy (Ashley) Gurney. C. H. Gurney was the son of Rev. John Gurney, and he was a son of a Mr. Gurney who served in the Colonial army in its struggle for independence, and the United States government still owes the family for mules that were taken for service during that war. Rev. John Gurney lived and died at Freetown, near New Bedford, Mass. C. H. Gurney was an iron worker for sixty-two years. He operated a blast furnace at New Bedford for a time and was conceded one of New England's best moulders. In politics he was first a Whig but later joined the Republican party. He died in Taunton, Mass., in 1876, at the age of seventy-six years. His wife died in 1889 at the age of eighty-nine years. She was for many years a devout member of the Methodist church. They reared a family of eight sons and four daughters, of whom our subject is the youngest and the only one now living. His brothers and sisters are as follows: James was a sailor, starting from New Bedford. He was a soldier in the Crimean war and also in the Mexican war. Henry was also a sailor and was a first mate on a whaler from New Bedford and was drowned at sea. He was a soldier in the Mexican war. John was an orderly in Colonel Fletcher Webster's regiment during the late war. His home was at Taunton, Mass. Oliver, deceased. Horace went to California in 1849 and it is supposed that he died there. Ephriam and Martin were also moulders. Lois died when quite young. Louisa was the wife of Fred Cushman, a ship carpenter of New Bedford, Mass. Susan was the wife of Horace Peck, a shoe manufacturer of Brock-ton, Mass. Annie was the wife of Earnest Draper, and died in Massachusetts.

William Harrison Gurney, the subject of this sketch, received his education during the evenings of his boyhood at the public library. When thirteen years of age he began working in iron, first in Wilcox & Gibb's sewing machine factory, and since that time has worked in eighty-eight shops and factories, in eight of which he was foreman and is thoroughly posted in all lines of iron work and moulding. In 1868 he went to Norwich, Conn., and after spending eleven years there he went west and worked at different times in St. Louis, Chicago, Cleveland and other cities throughout the west. He then entered the Peekskill foundry at Poughkeepsie, N. Y. He next worked in the Abendrouth Brothers shops at Port Chester, N. Y., and then in J. L. Mott shops in New York city. Mr. Guerney then went south and helped to build and establish the Perry Stove Works, at South Pittsburg, which was the first foundry in that city. From there he returned to Massachusetts and started the Pipe and Fitting foundry at Dighton, and from thence to Bessemer, Ala., and established the Pipe and Fitting works of that place. Our subject then returned to South Pittsburg and assumed charge of the Schoster foundry, and later took an active part in the establishment of the South Pittsburg Stove and Foundry Company, of which he is now superintendent and foreman. Mr. Gurney is a man of ready address, quick thinker and talker, with a repartee that he says he gets from his Huguenot ancestors, a thorough student of nature, men and history and a knowledge of affairs both local and national that is amazing in a man whose time is so thoroughly taken up with business cares and responsibilities. As a Democrat he is of the thoroughbred variety, he neither asks nor grants favors, but is a Democrat for conscience sake. In the New England states he was one of the founders of the Greenback Labor party at Norwich, Conn., and the only time he was discharged was at this place, for upholding the principles of his party. He is a member of the Knights of Pythias, the I. O. O. F., and also of the Moulder's union, with which he has been identified for fifteen years.

In 1881 Mr. Gurney was united in marriage to Miss Martha Wacob, who died April 5, 1898. Mrs. Gurney moved to South Pittsburg about the year 1888, and with the exception of about two years, has since resided there. She was a woman of many sterling qualities, which were fully recognized and gained the highest esteem and regard of all. Retiring, not given to many words, her deeds will live after her and she will long be remembered as one who tried to do and did her whole duty in the community in which she was placed. She was a faithful and consistent member of the Episcopal church. Mr. and Mrs. Gurney had no children, but had adopted and taken into their heart and home an orphan who was as their own.

ROBERT H. WHITE, ex-county superintendent of schools of Grundy county, Tenn., is one of Pelham's prominent and popular citizens and able instructors. Attention, method and industry are the foundation stones of success in any busi-

ness, and these combined with integrity of word and deed have been the corner stone of all the ventures in which he has embarked, and during his residence in the Ninth district, near Pelham, he has made many warm friends in that city and throughout the county.

Mr. White was born near Pelham, October 14, 1856, and is a son of Charles T. and Mary Caroline (Elliott) White. The father was born in Rutherford county, Tenn., January 26, 1826, and died January 27, 1897. The mother was born in Danville, Va., October 3, 1830, and died October 29, 1896. Charles T. White had three brothers in the Confederate army, Hall, Robert G. and Walter. Walter was killed at the battle of Missionary Ridge, Hall died during the war at Shelbyville, and Robert G. is still living and is making his home in Coffee county, Tenn.

Charles T. White, our subject's father, came to Grundy county in about the year 1854, after his marriage. His parents had moved to Rutherford county, Tenn., and had located on a farm two miles north of Carlocksville. Charles T. White was also a farmer by occupation, and both he and his wife were for many years members of the Methodist Episcopal church, South, and he was steward, class-leader and trustee of the society in whch they held their membership. He was also a Mason, being a member of Felix Grundy lodge, No. 284, and represented that lodge many times at the grand lodge. In politics he was originally a Whig, and upon leaving that party, he joined the ranks of the Democratic party, later the Prohibitionists, and his last presidential ballot was cast for W. J. Bryan.

Mr. White was a son of Robert Gilbert White, who, when a boy, moved to Tennessee with his father from North Carolina. The family is of Dutch descent. Our subject's mother was of Scotch and Irish descent. Her parents, Hiram and Susan Elliott, came to Tennessee from Virginia. Her father was a blacksmith by occupation and died in Rutherford county, Tenn. He had a son, Richard Elliott, who was a veteran in the Mexican war.

Robert H. White, the subject of this sketch, is one of a family of nine children, of whom five sons are now living, as follows: T. M. is a farmer of Grundy county; Robert H., the subject of this sketch; J. C., a farmer of Grundy county; H. H., a farmer near Pelham; and C. W., also a farmer living near Pelham. The deceased are: Mary R., who died when quite young; W. B. White was born November 22, 1866, and died January 2, 1892; William D., who died in childhood; and one other died in infancy. Our subject received his primary training in the district school near Pelham, but later attended the Manchester College. Upon leaving that institution in 1877, he entered the Irving College, and later the Tullahoma and Goodman Business College at Nashville. At intervals during that time he taught school, and after completing his studies, he entered the battle of life as a school teacher and has been thus engaged for twenty years at Pelham, Tracy City, Mont Eagle, Altamont, and one term outside the county. For a term of two years, from 1888 to 1890, he served as county superintendent of schools of Grundy county. He is a member of the Methodist Episcopal church, South, at Pelham, and is superin-

36

tendent of the Sunday-school. In politics he has always been identified with the Democratic and Prohibition parties. Mr. White is not married.

REUBEN SMARTT, the well-known chairman of the county court of Grundy county, and a prominent representative of the agricultural interests of this section of the state, was born September 25, 1844, on a farm only a mile from his present home, and is a son of William C. and Esther (Green) Smartt. The father was a native of Warren county, Tenn., born in 1819, and was a son of Reuben Smartt, whose birth occurred in North Carolina. From the latter state the family came to Tennessee during pioneer days. The mother of our subject was probably born in Warren county, June 16, 1822, a daughter of Samuel Green, who was also a native of North Carolina and was a soldier in the Creek Indian war under General Jackson.

William C. Smartt, our subject's father, grew to manhood in Warren county and later came to what is now Grundy county, in 1843, locating in the woods, where he cleared and developed a good farm. By trade he was both a carpenter and cooper, but throughout the greater part of his life he devoted his time and attention to farming. During the Civil war his sympathies were with the Union cause, and in September, 1863, he joined an independent regiment, known as the First Regiment, Independent Vidette Cavalry Volunteers, which was made up of Tennessee and Alabama troops. Being taken sick he was honorably discharged at Madison, Ind., in June, 1864, by special order of the secretary of war, and January 18, 1867, he died from the effects of measles contracted in the service. He was a true and earnest Christian gentleman, a faithful member of the Cumberland Presbyterian church, in which he served as elder. His political support was given the men and measures of the Republican party.

In his family were eleven children, of whom eight are still living namely: Sarah J., wife of Alexander Hobbs, a farmer of Grundy county; Reuben, of this sketch; Mary, wife of Hiram Fults, also a farmer of Grundy county; Calvin, an agriculturist of Stone county, Ark.; Martha S., wife of John Fults, of the same county; Noah and Carroll C., also farmers of Stone county, Ark.; De Ida, wife of Charles C. Hobbs, a farmer of Cleburne county, Ark. Those deceased are Rachel, who married William Drake and both died in Independence county, Ark.; Barsha A., who wedded J. B. Martin and died in Grundy county, Tenn.; and Isaac L., who was the youngest of the family, died in Grundy county.

In the locality where he still resides Reuben Smartt attended school during his boyhood and youth, pursuing his studies in the school at Beech Grove. His education was not yet completed when the Civil war broke out, but in September, 1863, he enlisted in the same company and regiment as his father, being under the command of Capt. James E. Shannon until mustered out at Stephenson, Ala., June 16, 1864. He then served as captain of the home guards under General Milroy until after the close of the war. When his father died he be-

came head of the family and cared for the younger children until they were able to care for themselves. He has always followed the occupation of farming, and in his chosen calling has met with excellent success.

On the 12th of March, 1869, Mr. Smartt married Miss Sarah Munley, who was born August 24, 1852, and is a daughter of Alexander Munley. Ten children graced this union, of whom one, Martha, died in childhood. Those still living are: Frances M., Henry Clay, Benjamin F., Lyman Beecher, Olive, Alfred T., Louie, James B. and Thomas R.

Like his father, Mr. Smartt is an ardent Republican in politics, and has always taken a deep and commendable interest in local affairs. Just after the war he served as school commissioner for a few years, and in 1872 was elected justice of the peace, a position he has most creditably filled ever since with the exception of the years 1888 and 1891, inclusive, when he refused to accept the office. In 1879 and 1880 he was chairman of the county court, and was again chosen to that position in 1898, being the present incumbent. He is thoroughly impartial in meting out justice, his opinions being unbiased by either fear or favor, and his fidelity to the trust reposed in him is above question. He also served for one term as coroner of the county. He is a prominent member of Alto lodge, No. 478, F. & A. M., has served as master for about eight years, and was a representative to the grand lodge of the state in 1895. He is regarded as one of the leading and most highly respected citizens of Grundy county, and it is, therefore, consistent that he be represented in a work whose province is the portrayal of the lives of the prominent men of this section of the state.

THOMAS PATTERSON HALL, whose beautiful home overlooks the Tennessee river, is one of the most popular and highly respected citizens of the Seventh district, Marion county, where he is successfully engaged in general farming and stock raising. He is a native of the county, born eight miles east of Jasper, near Oates Island, August 31, 1840, and is a son of Ignatius and Esther (Kelly) Hall, the former a native of Kentucky, the latter of East Tennessee. When a young man the father came to Marion county, and subsequently married and settled near Oates Island, where he purchased a farm and engaged in agricultural pursuits until life's labors were ended. His wife, who was an earnest and consistent member of the Cumberland Presbyterian church, died several years later, and was laid to rest by his side in the Kelly cemetery, near Kelly's Ferry. In politics he was an old-line Whig and in early days served as colonel of the militia. Their family consisted of nine children, namely: Nancy, Rebecca, James, Adaline, Mary, Martha, John, William and Thomas P. Besides our subject, Mary is the only one now living.

After attending the common schools for some time, Thomas P. Hall became a student in the Sam Houston Academy at Jasper, where he completed his literary education. Early in life he became thoroughly familiar with agricultural pursuits, and is to-day one of the most skillful and systematic farmers of his district. During the war his sympathies were with the Confederacy, and he was a volunteer in the Confederate army. Just after the war he embarked in merchandising at Shellmound, and for several years, off and on, he was interested in that business. He was agent for the N. & C. R. R. at Shellmound for quite a while. About a year and a half ago he took charge of the Pierson tanyard in Dade county, Ga., and is still conducting it in connection with his farm work. As a business man he has been eminently successful, and his upright, honorable course in life commends him to the confidence and esteem of all. His religious views are in accordance with the teachings of the Cumberland Presbyterian church, but he holds membership with no religious organization. He is a Master Mason, belonging to the lodge at Jasper, and is a Democrat in politics. On an independent ticket he was elected sheriff of Marion county, receiving 197 more votes than both of his competitors—one a Republican, the other a Democrat. In that position he served for one term with credit to himself and to the entire satisfaction of the general public. Mr. Hall's household consists of himself, his sister Mary, who acts as his housekeeper, and their niece, Miss Carrie Love, whose parents are deceased. The family have many warm friends throughout the community.

GEORGE E. KELL.—One of the busiest, most energetic and most enterprising men of Van Buren county is Mr.

Kell, who has been identified with the agricultural interests of the Sixth district for many years. Since 1871 he has resided upon his present farm, comprising one hundred and eighty-four acres of rich and arable land under a high state of cultivation and well improved. In addition to general farming and stock raising he is also interested in milling in connection with his son Henry.

Mr. Kell was born August 17, 1830, on the west side of the valley in what is now Sequatchie county, Tenn., and was named for two pioneer Baptist ministers of East Tennessee—Rev. George Walker and Rev. Moses Easterly, his name being George Easterly Kell. His parents, Thomas and Lydia (Lakey) Kell, were both natives of North Carolina, where their marriage was celebrated, and from there they later removed to the Elk river country, Tennessee. They subsequently came to the Sequatchie Valley, where the grandfather, William Kell, had purchased a large tract of land but had received a fraudulent title to the same. He was afterward forced to sell his slaves to pay for this land the second time. Upon his own land he built the first Baptist church in the valley. When well advanced in years he went to Illinois and there his death occurred. Thomas Kell and family moved from the Sequatchie valley to Warren county, locating near McMinnville, where he and his wife both died, the former when in his eighty-ninth year, the latter in her eighty-fourth. They were devout members of the Baptist church, and most highly respected people. The father was a successful farmer and was a Whig in politics. Although very young he volunteered to assist his country in the war of 1812, and was in the battle of New Orleans, but soon afterward was discharged by General Jackson on account of his youth.

To Thomas and Lydia (Lakey) Kell were born nine children, and of the four still living our subject is the oldest. Sarah is the wife of John Cardwell, of Warren county; Nancy is the widow of Joseph Clark and a resident of the same county; and Anna is the wife of Charles Forrest, a captain in the Confederate army and a minister of the Baptist church, who formerly lived in Warren county, Tenn., but now makes his home in Texas.

Until twenty-five years of age George E. Kell remained with his parents. He was then married to Miss Amanda Thomas, a native of what is now Van Buren county, and a daughter of Isaiah Thomas. They became the parents of six children, as follows: Charles T., a farmer of Warren county and a member of the county court; Henry, who is a partner of his father in the mill and postmaster and lives in Laurelburg; Josephine, deceased wife of Richard Russell, a prominent farmer of Van Buren county; Frank, a merchant and deputy postmaster at Laurelburg; America, the present wife of Richard Russell; and Asa, who is still upon the home farm.

During the war Mr. Kell was located on the railroad between McMinnville and Tullahoma, and as he conducted a wood yard at that time he supplied wood to the railroad when it was in the hands of the Confederate army, and also after the federal forces took possession, thus suffering no loss. In early life he was a Whig and since the war has generally supported the Democratic party, but is not strictly partisan, at local elections often supporting the candidate of the other party if he considers him best qualified to fill the office. He is a strong temperance man, and in fact gives his support to all measures which he believes will advance the welfare of his fellow men. He and his wife are leading members of the Baptist church at Laurel Creek, with which he has been connected for forty-two years, and is now serving as deacon.

SAMUEL M. McREYNOLDS is one of the leading farmers and stock raisers of Bledsoe county, wherein he is a large land owner. His real estate amounts to about seven hundred and thirty-one acres, all fine land, and is situated in the Seventh district. Mr. McReynolds was born in the Eighth district, Bledsoe county, Tenn., October 8, 1829, a son of Samuel and Jane (Hale) McReynolds. The father was born in Tazewell county, Va., in June, 1797, the son of Samuel and Margaret McReynolds. The mother was born in Blount county, Tenn., the daughter of Alexander Hale, formerly of Virginia. Samuel McReynolds moved to Bledsoe county with his parents in the year 1806, settled in the Eighth district and made that his home until 1840, when he moved to the Sixth district, near Pikeville, where he lived until his death, which occurred February 13, 1865. He was a very successful farmer, and a popular and respected citizen. He was twice married. To his first wife were born eight children, of whom our subject is the fifth in the order of birth, and upon whom they bestowed

the following names: Margaret (the second died in infancy and was not named), Alexander, Mary Jane, Samuel M., Sarah J., Clayborn Delaney and James W. Mrs. McReynolds died in February, 1843, and he subsequently married Miss Anna D. Stephens, a native of Bledsoe county, and to them were born five children, three of whom are now living: Isaac S., Martha Josephine and Thomas S.

Our subject was educated in the common schools of his native county and the academy at Pikeville. He then formed a partnership with T. J. Wilson, in 1851, and began the mercantile business in Pikeville. He was thus engaged until 1862, when the entire stock was taken by the Federal soldiers, thus inflicting upon the firm a heavy loss. In March, 1887, Mr. McReynolds again engaged in business in the same town in partnership with W. S. Loyd, and three years later he bought out the interest of his partner and continued the business alone until 1892. He then sold out to Mr. G. W. Awlt, who still continues the business. After selling out his stock of merchandise, our subject moved to his present farm in the Seventh district, where he has a beautiful home and is surrounded with such improvements and home comforts as go to make life enjoyable.

Mr. McReynolds was married May 2, 1858, to Miss Elizabeth E. Henson, a native of Bledsoe county, Tenn., born in September, 1839, and their wedded life has been blessed to them by the advent of a family of four children, as follows: Charles, living in Montana; Joseph, also in Montana; James, deceased; and Hallie, wife of D. F. Spring, of Bledsoe county, Tenn. June 16,

1875, Mrs. McReynolds died, and May 30 of the following year our subject was united in marriage to Miss Kate Bell, of Bledsoe county, Tenn., and who was born in Rhea county, October 15, 1843. His present wife is the daughter of Rev. William H. and Nancy (Rainey) Bell, of Bledsoe county, Tenn. Mr. and Mrs. Bell reared a family of seven children, whose names are as follows: Martha, David, Clarissa, Kate, Robert, James T. and Hattie. The mother —Mrs. Nancy Bell—died in Gainesville, Texas, where she made her home with her children after the death of her husband. The father, Rev. William H. Bell, was a Cumberland Presbyterian minister of considerable ability, and did much good for the church, for which he was a zealous worker. He had many friends. He died at his home in Bledsoe county, Tenn., February 19, 1876. Our subject and his present wife have no children. She was educated in the academies of Rhea and Hamilton counties, and later taught school for a few years. She is a member of the Cumberland Presbyterian church. Mr. McReynolds is a loyal citizen, a man of excellent business qualifications, is genial, warm-hearted and generous, and is highly esteemed by all who know him.

JAMES K. HOWLAND, clerk of the circuit court of Grundy county. Among the prominent men now living in Altamont who have won for themselves enviable positions and reputations as honorable and highly respected citizens of that thriving town, none is better deserving of represen- tation in a volume of this nature than James K. Howland. He was born in Rutherford county, Tenn., on a farm, June 6, 1857, a son of Lewis H. and Isabel (Daughtry) Howland.

Our subject's father was born in North Carolina, February 1, 1800. His mother moved with her family to Rutherford, Tenn., in 1812. Here he grew to maturity, pursued the calling of a farmer, and died April 18, 1875. He served in the Mexican war, being a non-commissioned officer, and served in the commissary department a part of the time. In 1861 he enlisted in the Second Tennessee Infantry, in the Confederate army, and served about a year under Captain Newman, and was then dismissed on the account of his age. Politically he was a Democrat. Our subject's mother was born in Rutherford county, and died in Carlocksville, at the age of forty-five years. She was her husband's second wife. Mr. Howland first married Miss Elizabeth Jacobs, and to this union were born eleven children, of whom we have the following record: Amanda was the wife of W. Jacobs, and is now living in Crittenden county, Ky.; Kit, wife of William Phelps; both she and her husband died in Kentucky; Mollie, wife of Grundy Sumner, died near Glass, Williamson county, Tenn.; Richard was a soldier in the Confederate army and is now living in Rutherford county; John died during the war, in the Federal army; Rebecca was the wife of Thomas Brady and died in Rutherford county; Martha, wife of Pinkney Alexander, is now living in Rutherford county; Ellen, wife of J. K. P. Robinson, of Noah, Coffee county, Tenn.; Clinton, at Rucker, Tenn.; Fannie, wife of Joseph

Parker, of Coffee county, Tenn. To his last marriage six children were born, viz.: James K., the subject of this sketch; Sarah Doak, wife of T. J. Robinson, of Manchester, Tenn.; Robert T., who died in childhood; Lydia J., wife of Drewy Gowin, of Bonham, Fannin county, Texas; William H. is in Crandall, Kauffman county, Texas; and Wilcome H., also of Kauffman county, Texas.

James K. Howland, the subject of this sketch, spent his school days in Rutherford county, and attended the public school in the district in which he lived. In 1881 he left Rutherford and moved to Tracy City, and was there employed as a clerk in a store until 1883. He then went into business in partnership with Mr. W. B. Holt, and was thus engaged for eighteen months. He then sold out and went to Texas, and, after spending six months in different places in Texas, Louisiana and Alabama, he returned to Tracy City, and was there employed to guard the convicts at the branch prison at that place. A few months later he accepted a position as tip boss and timekeeper at the mines, up to May 15, 1890. He was elected clerk of the circuit court in August, 1890, and has held that position continuously since, being re-elected in 1894.

November 27, 1886, Mr. Howland was united in marriage with Miss Flora Tipton, daughter of Stephen and Louisa E. (Griswold) Tipton. Mrs. Howland was born in Grundy county, Tenn., March 15, 1864. To this union have been born five children, as follows: William H. died January 21, 1888, when but one month of age; Vera E., Alfred Herbert, Louis P. and Ruth. Our subject and Mrs. Howland are both

members of the church, and while at Tracy City Mr. Howland performed the duties of elder of the society at that place. Socially he affiliates with the Masonic fraternity, the Independent Order of Odd Fellows and the Knights of Pythias. He twice represented Alto Masonic lodge, No. 478, at the grand lodge, has filled all the chairs in the Independent Order of Odd Fellows, and is now past grand. In politics he is a Democrat.

DR. DAVID CARAH SHELTON.— Marion county has few more energetic or wide-awake men among the younger members of its professional population than this gentleman. His name will be readily recognized by the citizens of Whitwell and vicinity, and even throughout the greater part of the county, as a physician and surgeon who, in partnership with Dr. Alton T. Peay, has built up a lucrative practice in the town of Whitwell and the northeastern part of Marion county.

Our subject was born September 3, 1868, in Shelton's Cove, Marion county, Tenn., and is a son of Richard Elijah and Mary (Thatcher) Shelton, the father born in the Fifth district of Marion county, Tenn., December 31, 1838, and the mother born near Soddy, Hamilton county, Tenn., May 24, 1838. Richard Elijah Shelton, father of our subject, graduated from the University of Nashville in 1860, and at once began the practice of medicine at the village of Soddy, Hamilton county, Tenn., and was thus engaged until the breaking out of the Civil war. He enlisted in 1861 in the Confederate army, under Bragg, and was employed in Georgia, Alabama, Kentucky and Virginia in the capacity of a surgeon. After the close of hostilities he returned to his home in Soddy, and remained there one year, and then moved to the Sequatchie valley and settled in Shelton's Cove, and there spent the remaining years of his life. He was a Master Mason and held his membership in Altine lodge, No. 477, at Sulphur Springs. He served as school commissioner for two years, and died near Victoria Mines, at the home of Mr. Holecamp, while making a professional call, January 29, 1885. His wife died December 26, 1896. Both were members of the Cumberland Presbyterian church. To them were born eight children, whose names and the dates of their births are as follows: William F., born September 19, 1862; George S., born April 13, 1866; Dr. David Carah, the subject of this sketch; Wathan Dudley, born October 10, 1870, and died January 20, 1871; Sallie Malinda, born December 30, 1871, the wife of Fred Keller, an attorney living in St. Louis, Mo.; Esther E., born June 2, 1874, and died May 18, 1890; Joseph T., born August 19, 1876, and died August 26, 1885; and Alta Icie, born October 9, 1879.

Dr. Shelton first attended the public schools of the Valley and then the high school at Chattanooga. He entered the University at Nashville, from which he graduated with high honors in 1897. He began practicing medicine at Inman in 1893, before graduating, and remained there about two years. In 1897 he went to Whitwell and September 11, of that year, he formed a partnership with Dr. Alton T. Peay, and they have built up an extensive and profitable patronage.

November 17, 1897, Dr. Shelton was united in marriage with Miss Bertie Bennett, who was born in the Fifth district, Marion county, Tenn., December 25, 1872, a daughter of Samuel and Sallie (Pryor) Bennett, and eldest grandchild of Washington Pryor. She was educated at Centenary College and Pryor Institute, Jasper, Tenn. Both the Doctor and Mrs. Shelton are members of the Cumberland Presbyterian church, and he is a member of the Modern Woodmen fraternity and also of the Alumni Association of Nashville. Politically he is a Democrat but has never aspired to public office. He is a man of excellent education, of marked ability and bids fair to become one of the leading physicians of eastern Tennessee.

———

HON. MOSES E. DEAKINS, ex-representative of the Seventh Floterial district, composed of the counties of Bledsoe, Cumberland, Sequatchie, Grundy and Van Buren. Perhaps no man in all of Sequatchie county is better known for his intelligence, active public spirit and thorough appreciation of the wants of his locality than is the gentleman whose name heads this article. He was born and has spent nearly his whole life in Sequatchie county, and since arriving at maturity has been identified with all matters which pertain to the improvement and upbuilding of the better interests of the locality in which he lives. Being a man of excellent business qualifications, and a character of the highest order, he has been called upon by his fellow-citizens to occupy some of the important official positions. In every instance he has proven his efficiency and has administered the duties of his various offices with rare fidelity and with increasing popularity. He was born near his present home, in what was then Marion county, November 30, 1840, the son of Franklin and Lydia (Easterly) Deakins, both of whom are natives of the state of Tennessee.

Franklin Deakins was born February 18, 1819, and is a son of Absalom Deakins. The latter was born in Lee county, Va., in the year 1802. The family moved to the Sequatchie Valley in the year 1812, and settled six miles below Pikeville. Franklin Deakins served as clerk of the county court from 1860 until 1864, and then served one term as deputy clerk of the circuit court under Dr. Smith, and subsequently served four years as chief clerk. Moses E., the subject of this sketch, was educated in the public schools of his district, finishing his course of study in 1856, after which he taught school for a number of years in Marion and Warren counties. September 5, 1861, he joined Company H, Thirty-fifth Tennessee Infantry, and served in that command under General Bragg until April, 1865. As an old soldier he can look back over an honorable military career in which he served his cause well and faithfully, and to-day he is a true and faithful citizen and is always ready to lend a helping hand to everything that will in any way tend to the protection and building up of the better interests of the communitty in which he lives. While in the legislature he was a member of the committees on education and elections, and was chairman of the committee on new counties and county lines. Politically he is a Democrat.

37

ROBERT FOSTER is one of Marion county's native sons and a representative of one of her most prominent and honored families, whose identification with her history dates from an early period in the development of the county. His father was born January 30, 1802, near St. Stephen's Chapel, London, England, and in 1835 crossed the Atlantic in the packet Philadelphia, landing in New York City in September of that last year. He first located in Detroit, Mich., but at an early day came to Marion county, Tenn., where he engaged in farming until his death, which occurred February 25, 1889. Though entirely self-educated, he was a very intellgent and well-read man, and possessed a very fine library, and one of the finest collections of pictures in the state, many of which were the work of his own hands. He was a natural artist, and in early life was employed as an engraver and draftsman. Prior to coming to this state he had lived for a time in Cincinnati, Ohio, where as editor, he published the "Western Farmer and Gardener." After traveling to some extent through the south, he finally decided on Marion county, Tenn., as his future home, and in 1843 located upon the farm, where he spent his remaining days, giving his time and attention wholly to farming and stock raising. During the Civil war he served as chief engineer under Gen. S. B. Buckner, and at its close was a member of the county court for many years.

Charles Foster was twice married, the first time in England, to Miss Gusta Smith, by whom he has one son, Charles, who recently died in Arkansas. He had traveled all over the world, and was with Walker in his Central American Revolution. After the death of his first wife, Mr. Foster was again married, in 1852, his second union being with Miss Martha Shrum, who was born in Bledsoe county, Tenn., August 14, 1828, and is a daughter of Moses Shrum, an honored pioneer of this section of the state. Seven children were born of this union, of whom Francis, the eldest, died in childhood. Those still living are Mary J., wife of Benjamin Harris; Martha, wife of G. W. Harris; Robert, of this sketch; Ellen, wife of Newton Fults; Sarah A., wife of William Price; and Elizabeth, wife of Dr. W. R. C. Booher, a physician living near Bristol, Tenn. The father was originally a Whig in politics, but in later years espoused the cause of the Democratic party and during the latter part of the war was sent as a prisoner to Fort Delaware, where he was retained for a few months. He was one of the most prominent and influential citizens of his community and was widely and favorably known throughout this section of the state. Religiously he was a member of the Episcopal church, to which his estimable wife also belongs.

Robert Foster, whose name introduces this sketch, was born in Marion county, May 15, 1860, and acquired his literary education at home and in the public schools of the neighborhood. Since starting out in life for himself he has been interested in the sawmill business and stock-raising, and has also worked at the carpenter's trade as a contractor and builder. In his undertakings he has met with fair success. He was married May 26, 1892, the lady of his choice being Miss Maggie Almany, a native of upper East Tennessee, and a daughter of Frank Almany. They now have five children: Charles, Robert, William, Ruth and Nellie. Mrs. Foster is a sincere member of the Methodist Episcopal church, South, and both she and her husband are held in high regard by all who know them.

HON. JAMES WORTHINGTON.—The history of a county, as well as that of a nation, is chiefly the chronicles of the lives and deeds of those who have conferred honor and dignity upon society. The world judges the character of a community by those of its representative citizens. Among the most distinguished and influential men of Van Buren county is Captain Worthington, who now resides upon a farm in the Sixth district.

He was born in Hickory Valley, the same county, on the 5th of November, 1833, and is a son of William and Elizabeth Worthington, both natives of East Tennessee, the former born in Anderson county, the latter in Bledsoe county. His paternal grandparents, James and Elizabeth (Carney) Worthington, and their parents, were from Virginia. The grandfather took part in the Seminole war in Florida and died in Alabama on his way home. The father of our subject was a well-educated man and successfully engaged in teaching school in early life, later following farming. In politics he was a Democrat, and served as justice of the peace, chairman and clerk of the circuit court. Both he and his wife believed in the doctrines of the Primitive Baptist church and had the friendship of all who knew them. He died April 15, 1875, and she passed away in 1891. Their children were Mary, now deceased; Lodeima; James; Sarah C.: Samuel; Margaret R., deceased; William T.; and Angeline, deceased.

The primary education of Captain Worthington, acquired in the free schools of this county, was supplemented by a course in York Academy at Spencer, and also at Burritt College, of the same place, where he graduated with the degree of A. B. and later the degree of A. M. was conferred. For several years he was a popular and successful teacher, first in the subscription schools, and later for four years in Burritt College. In 1861 he entered the Confederate service, enlisting at Spencer in the Sixteenth Tennessee Volunteer Infantry, for one year, under Captain York and Colonel Savage. On the expiration of that period he re-enlisted for the remainder of the war with Captain Reynolds, and when the latter was promoted to the rank of major our subject was commissioned captain of Company I, in which capacity he served until the war was over. He participated in the battles of Murfreesboro, Chickamauga, and took part in the Atlanta campaign. Near the close of the war the ranks had become so thinned that several companies were consolidated into one and the supernumerary officers were sent to Macon, where they remained until hostilities ceased, Captain Worthington being paroled at that place.

He then returned to his home in Van Buren county, and on the 1st of January, 1866, was united in marriage with Mrs. Emma L. Brown, daughter of James T. and Malinda (Rowland) Clenney. They have one son, William, who was born September 1, 1886, and is now attending school. After his marriage Captain Worthington went to Benton county, Ark., where he engaged in teaching for two years and then on account of his father's ill health, he returned to this county and located on a farm in the Sixth district, where he has since resided. To the cultivation and improvement of his place he devotes his energies and is meeting with excellent results.

Since reaching man's estate the Captain has always taken an active and commendable interest in public affairs of a political nature, and has most efficiently served as road overseer, justice of the peace and chairman at different times. In 1890 he was honored with an election to the legislature, and became quite a prominent and popular member of that body. Socially he is a member of the Independent Order of Odd Fellows, and the Masonic fraternity. He has several times served as master and has represented the lodge in the grand lodge of the state. In religious belief he is a Methodist.

CAPT. JOHN FRATER.—Only those lives are worthy of record that have been potential factors in the public progress, in promoting the general welfare or in any way advancing the interests of the community. As an expert mining engineer Mr. Frater was for many years prominently identified with the development of the coal districts of this section of the state, but has now retired from that business and devotes his time and attention to the improvement and cultivation of his farm in the Fifteenth district of Marion county. He is ever faithful to his duties of citizenship, and by the successful conduct of his business interests not only promotes individual success but also advances the general prosperity.

Mr. Frater was born December 10, 1832, in Penshaw, County Durham, England, a son of William and Hannah (Stobart) Frater, the former born in 1804 near Chatershaugh, the latter at the Ship House at Ravensworth, County Durham, in 1808, on the estate of Lord Ravensworth. Their marriage was celebrated in 1831, at Lamesley church on the same estate. The mother, who was the daughter of a farmer, died at her home in England at the age of forty-eight years. She was a devout member of the Wesleyan church, and was buried in the Chesterly street churchyard. Our subject was the oldest of her children, the others being: Bessie, who died in childhood; Lizzie, now the widow of Charles Scott, and a resident of Birmingham, Ala.; Aaron, who died at the age of eight years; Willie, who died of typhoid fever at the age of six years; Hannah, who now keeps house for our subject; James, who died at the home of our subject and was buried in the Pryor cemetery, Marion county. In 1856 the father crossed the Atlantic and located in Allegheny county, Penn., where he followed his old line of occupation, that of sinking coal pits. In 1860 he came to the Etna mines in Marion county, Tenn., where he remained twelve years, and then went to Coal Creek, Anderson county, dying there in 1874. His remains were interred in that county.

At the early age of eight years the subject of this sketch commenced working in the mines of his native land, and was thus employed for two years before he decided to procure an education. He then entered a night school, where he pursued his studies until he attained his majority, in this way acquiring a good practical education while still continuing his work as a miner. By a semi-special license he was married at Liverpool, England, in 1854, to Miss Mary Watson, and the following day the young couple started for America on the " City of Philadelphia." After being out eight days they were shipwrecked off the coast of Newfoundland. The vessel was lost but the passengers were all saved and taken to St. Johns, Newfoundland, where they remained for ten days. Mr. and Mrs. Frater then proceeded to Halifax, Nova Scotia, and two days later to Boston, and from the latter place to McKeesport, Penn. There they made their home until 1857, while Mr. Frater found employment in coal mining and coke burning. The latter year they removed to Illinois, but after working for about two years in various mines in that state, they removed to Marion county, Tenn., in 1859. They located at the Etna mines, where the following twelve years were passed. Mr. Frater opened up the mines there and also at Castle Rock, Ala., near Shellmound; Anderson County Coal Company's mines at Coal Creek, and the Victoria and Whitwell mines. He is the oldest and the most successful mining engineer in this section of the country. About sixteen years ago he purchased his present farm in the Fifteenth district of Marion county, and has now retired from mining, giving his undivided attention to his farming operations, in which he has also met with marked success, becoming a well-to-do and prosperous citizen.

Mr. Frater has been called upon to mourn the loss of his estimable wife, who was a devoted member of the Methodist Episcopal church, and died in May, 1894, being laid to rest in the Pryor cemetery. Politically Mr. Frater is what may be termed a conservative Republican, and socially is a Master Mason, belonging to the lodge at Whitwell. His career has ever been such as to warrant the trust and confidence of the business world, for he has ever conducted all transactions on the strictest principles of honor and integrity. His devotion to the public good is unquestioned and arises from a sincere interest in his fellow men.

ROBERT EARL DAVIS, one of Marion county's thrifty and hard-working farmers, is now making his home in the Fifth district of that county, near the city of Whitwell. He was born on the farm on which he is now making his home September 21, 1854, the son of Robert Earl C. and Amanda (Carmack) Davis, both born near Abington, Va., the father May 24, 1820, and the mother September 24, 1825. They were quite extensively acquainted in the county of their nativity, and it was there that their courtship began. They both moved to Tennessee when young and were married where the mother now makes her home. The father died August 8, 1885, and is buried on the farm that for many years was his home and is still the home of his companion. They were both members of the Cumberland Presbyterian church. To them was born a family of six children as follows: The first born, who died in infancy; John L., living on a farm north of Whitwell; Robert Earl, the subject of this sketch; James K., a farmer of Marion county, Tenn.; William E., a farmer in Arkansas; and Mary J., deceased.

Robert Earl Davis, the subject of this sketch, was educated at Sulphur Springs, Marion county, Tenn., and, after finishing his study, engaged in farming in that vicinity until the year 1877. He then went to Texas and located in Commerce, Hunt county, and for about a year worked in a livery barn; at the end of that time he began for himself at Brackenridge the same line of business. About a year later he returned to his home in Tennessee and was united in marriage with Miss Nancy Bailey, a native of Marion county, and a daughter of Benjamin J. and Emily West Bailey. After their marriage they removed to Texas, but Mr. Davis discontinued his livery business and worked at farming in that vicinity for two years. He and his estimable wife then returned to Tennessee and have since lived in various places in Marion county but have each time been engaged in farming. They bought their present home in 1895. Mr. and Mrs. Davis are the parents of a family of six children, four of whom are now living, and whose names in the order of their birth are as follows: Ethel, Joseph, William, Talmage, Curry and Kelly. William and Kelly are dead, but the rest are all making their home with their parents.

Mr. Davis is a member of the Cumberland Presbyterian church, but his wife is not a member of any denomination. He is loyal and determined in his adherence to the right and to his friends, and has shown himself to be a man in whom all might place the highest confidence. He has been quite successful in life and has gained for himself, his companion and his children a comfortable and pleasant home. He is a loyal citizen, and an earnest and enthusiastic supporter of everything which tends to develop and bring prosperity to the locality in which he lives.

CAPTAIN GEORGE WASHINGTON HEARD.—As an all around prominent man of Sequatchie county, there is probably no one of its citizens who more justly deserves the title than does Mr. Heard. For an occupation he combines milling and farming and has been quite successful in both of these vocations. He has also taken an active part in public matters and some of the important offices of the county have been entrusted to his care. He is intelligent, well educated, and is held in high respect and esteem wherever he is known.

Mr. Heard is a native of Sequatchie county, and was born within two miles of his present home, October 26, 1836, a son of William and Artelier (Webb) Heard. William Heard moved to the Sequatchie Valley from Virginia, and his wife's people were Irish emigrants. Our subject's grandfather, John Heard, upon arriving in the valley, first located on the farm now occupied by Joseph Davis. He was a very successful farmer. William Heard lived for a time on Brush Creek, and from there he moved to the foot of the Cumberland mountains. In 1874 he moved with part of his family to Texas county, Mo., and made that his home until March, 1895, when he died at the extreme old age of ninety-three years. His wife also died at a very old age in the year 1890. He was a member of the Missionary Baptist church, but his wife affiliated with the Christian denomination. Of their family, three sons and two daughters are now living: John M., a farmer of Sequatchie county; Sarah, wife of James Billingsley, a farmer of Marion county; George Washington, the subject of this sketch: James, a farmer of Bledsoe county, where he also owns a mill; Nancy, wife of William Wheeler, a farmer of Texas county, Mo. The deceased are, Thomas, a farmer by occupation, died in the state of Arkansas in 1876, and Matilda, who died at the age of sixteen years.

Captain Heard attended school on the "Ridge" near his father's home, and, very early in life, assumed the management of one of his father's two stills. January 12, 1860, he was united in marriage to Miss Adaline Pankey, a native of Sequatchie county, and a daughter of Thomas Pankey. After his marriage he moved to the Pankey farm and made that his home for several years. In 1862 he joined the Federal army, enlisting in the Fourth Tennessee Cavalry, but never joined the command. General Rosecrans, learning of his acquaintance with that section of the country, detailed him for the escort service in which he served until 1864, when General Thomas gave him an order to recruit a company, which was known as Company E, Sixth Tennessee mounted Federal Infantry. Captain Heard participated in the battle of Chickamauga, and was wounded in the battle of Mission Ridge, Chattanooga, Tenn.

After the war our subject bought the farm on which he now lives, and in connection with the work of conducting it, he has plied the carpenter trade, and built the finest house in Jasper, or in the valley. Captain Heard is a man of mark in the community, and his standing as a good citizen is irreproachable. At the close of the war Governor Brownlow appointed him clerk of the circuit court of Sequatchie county. In the G. A. R. fraternity (post No. 49, department of Tennessee) of which he has long been a member, he is the present adjutant, and has performed the duties of commander. Politically he is a Republican, but before the war was a Whig.

HON. LEVI VERNON WOODLEE. It is a well attested maxim that the greatness of a state lies not in the machinery of government, nor even in its institutions. but in the sterling qualities of its individual citizens, in their capacity for high and unselfish effort and their devotion to the public good. Rising above the heads of the mass there have always been a series of individuals, distinguished beyond others, who by reason of their prononuced ability and forceful personality have always commanded the homage of their fellow men, and to this class belongs Mr. Woodlee, a prominent lawyer and statesman of Grundy county. He is regarded as one of the most popular citizens of his community and Altamont, where he makes his home, is proud to number him among her residents.

Mr. Woodlee is one of the native sons of Grundy county, his birth having occurred at Tarlton, on the 8th of February, 1861, his parents being Enoch and Mary (Reed) Woodlee. The father was born at Irving College, Warren county, Tennessee, November 3, 1824, and was a son of Jacob Woodlee, also a native of the same county. The grandfather was probably of Irish descent, and his parents came from North Carolina to Tennessee, casting in their lot with the pioneer settlers of Warren county. The various representatives of the family have always followed farming. That was the occupation of the grandfather and father of our subject, and the latter was married in Bledsoe county in April, 1852, to Miss Reed, who was born in that county in 1831. Both held membership with the Missionary Baptist church, and for over twenty years the father was a member of its ministry and had charge of Baptist churches in quite a large district. His political support was given the Democracy, and he was a progressive citizen and upright man who won the respect of all by his honorable life. In April, 1870, he was called to the home beyond, but his widow still survives Their children were as follows: Savannah, wife of P. M. Barnes, a farmer of Tarlton; A. H., ex-state senator and editor of the Tracy City News; James B., who followed farming on Collins river and died at the age of twenty-four years; L. V.; Victoria, wife of James Cathcart; and M. J. D., who is living with his mother.

Levi V. Woodlee spent his boyhood days on his father's farm at Tarlton on Collins river, and early learned to handle the plow and perform the other labors of the fields. This service was interspersed with attendance at the neighboring schools and afterward he pursued his education at Chapel Hill and Irving College, Warren county. For two years he successfully engaged in teaching school, which profession he followed at Shiloh, Warren county, Beech Grove and Northcuts Cove. While attending and teaching school he continued to make his home with his mother, but in 1886 left home, going to Fayetteville, Lincoln county, where he entered upon the study of law in the office and under the direction of Judge A. B. Woodard, a distinguished jurist. On the 1st of January, 1887, he was admitted to the bar and locating at Altamont, he has since been numbered among the able and successful practitioners at this place. He has a keenly analytical mind, a comprehensive knowledge of the principles of jurisprudence, is thorough in the preparation of his cases and has won many notable forensic victories.

In 1888 Mr. Woodlee was appointed back tax collector and acceptably filled that position until 1895, during which time he succeeded in collecting about thirty thousand dollars, at one time collecting sixteen thousand dollars net for the county from the Tennessee Coal, Iron & Railroad Company on back assessments, after fighting it through the supreme court. The able manner in which he handled the litigation excited favorable comment among the legal profession throughout the state. Mr. Woodlee was county attorney in 1893, and in 1891 was elected county superintendent of schools, filling the position for six years, during which time he greatly raised the standard of the schools. In 1896 he was elected floterial representative to the state legislature, and as a member of the house won distinction by his masterful handling of important questions which came up for disposal. He served as a member of the committees on finance, ways and means, judiciary, education, new counties and county lines, and his record in the law-making body of the commonwealth is one which reflects credit upon himself and his county.

On the 25th of April, 1889, Mr. Woodlee was united in marriage to Miss Bettie Willis, daughter of Hence and Susan (Van Zant) Willis, of Pelham. She was born in Grundy county, Tenn., and by her marriage has become the mother of three children: Mary Sue, Ida Blanche and L. Vernon. The parents are members of the Missionary Baptist church, and our subject is also a prominent Mason, having represented his local lodge in the grand lodge. In all the relations of life he has been found true and faithful to the trust reposed in him, and his strong mentality, force of character and genuine worth well fit him for leadership in the important affairs of life.

MEYER & SCHILD.—This firm carries on one of the prosperous business enterprises of Tracy City, Grundy county, Tenn., their stock in trade being adequate to fill all the demands in the vicinity. They conduct a general blacksmithing, wagon making, and are manufacturers of agricultural implements. The establishment ranks well among the dealers, and those who have occasion to patronize the shop are sure to received courteous treatment and meet with a careful consideration of their wants.

JACOB MEYER, the senior member of the firm, was born December 6, 1858, in Switzerland, and is a son of George and Margaret (Rueger) Meyer, who were both natives of Switzerland. The father followed farming all his life, and died in 1883, at the age of sixty, but his good wife still survives. They were members of the Christian Reform church, and were the parents of the following children: Lizzie, deceased; Robert is a farmer and resides in Ohio; Lydia lives in Iowa; Jacob, of whom this brief sketch is written; Godfrey makes his home in Switzerland; Bertha is a resident of Iowa; and Barbara is making her home in Switzerland.

Jacob Meyer attended the schools in his native land until he had attained his fourteenth year, when he started to work at his trade of a blacksmith. After becoming proficient in the profession of his choice, he followed his calling in the various shops in his native land. In 1878 he came to the United States, landed at New York, and then went to Cleveland, Ohio, where he remained for a few years. His next location was at Pittsburg, then followed Cincinnati, Ohio, St. Louis, Mo., and finally settled in the Swiss colony in Grundy county, Tenn. Upon his arrival here Mr. Meyer started to work for L. R. Von Lohr, with whom he remained for two years, and then opened a shop in Tracy City, in connection with John Henry Schild. By strict attention to business and faithful discharge of their several duties, they have since built up a profitable trade. The wife of our subject was known in her girlhood as Miss Julia

38

Born, a daughter of Fred Born, and she was born in the Swiss colony in Grundy county. They are the parents of the following children: Jacob, Elsie, Robert, and the baby, who is not yet named. Mr. and Mrs. Meyer are members of the German Reform church, and he is a member of the Royal Arcanum. He is independent in his political views, and casts his vote invariably for the best man fitted for the place.

JOHN HENRY SCHILD, the junior member of the firm of Meyer & Schild, was born March 2, 1862, in Switzerland, and is a son of Peter and Margaret (Ruef) Schild, a short sketch of whom will be found in the biography of J. Schild, on another page of this volume. J. H. Schild was but seven years of age when he accompanied his parents to the United States, and attended school in the Swiss colony in Grundy county, Tenn. When he became of age he learned the woodworker's trade in the same shop with his present partner, and later worked at his trade four and one-half years, when he formed a partnership with Mr. Meyer, under the firm name of Meyer & Schild. On December 15, 1889, Mr. Schild was united in marriage to Miss Bertha Werner, who was born in New York city and was a daughter of Samuel Werner. There have been three children born to bless this happy couple, namely: Samuel, Willie and Martin. He and his wife are members in good standing of the Episcopal church. Socially he is a member of the Royal Arcanum and the I. O. O. F., and he is independent in his political views, as he believes in purity in politics.

A thorough knowledge of the business in which they are engaged, combined with practical skill in its mechanical departments, and a large amount of energy and tact, conspire to give promise of a prosperous future to the firm of Meyer & Schild. Both gentlemen receive a due measure of respect and esteem, on account of their private characters, and are sought after by society for their many social qualities.

JOHN L. DAVIS, one of Marion county's thrifty and industrious agriculturists who owns a farm and pleasant home in the Third district of that county, was born near Sulphur Springs, Marion county, Tenn., January 3, 1851, a son of Robert Earl C. and Amanda (Carmack) Davis, both born near Abington, Va., the father May 24, 1820, and the mother September 24, 1825. Both moved to Marion county, Tenn., when young, and were married on the farm on which they lived for so many years. The father died there August 8, 1885, and is buried in the family cemetery, on the farm, and the mother is still making the old farm her home. He was an elder in the Cumberland Presbyterian church, and in politics was identified with the Democratic party.

The subject of our sketch is the second in the order of birth of a family of six children. He was educated in the public schools of Sulphur Springs and was married September 14, 1875, to Miss Sarah D. Condra, who was born near Red Hill church, July 29, 1855, a daughter of Howell and Delilah (Cowan) Condra. Her father was a soldier in the Confederate army during the Civil war. He was a member of the Cumberland Presbyterian church and

died November 15, 1897. The mother is living with her daughter, Maggie Jones. Mrs. Davis was educated in the common schools of Red Hill and Cedar Springs. After his marriage our subject first settled on a farm near Sulphur Springs, and, after making his home there for five years, he sold out and went to Johnson county, Arkansas. He only stopped at the latter place about ten months, however, and, on his return to Tennessee, he stopped near Victoria for about a year. He then bought the farm on which he now resides in the Third district.

Politically our subject invariably uses his elective franchise in the support of the candidates of the Democratic party, but has never aspired to public office, and he and his wife are both members of the Cumberland Presbyterian church. Their home has been blessed by the presence of a family of four children upon whom they have bestowed the following names: Ellen A., Arthur D., Lena B. and Lulu F.

JOSEPH H. WALKER, a member of the county court from the Fourth district of Van Buren county, and a progressive agriculturist, was born on the Cumberland mountains, December 4, 1839, and is a son of David and Polly Ann (Stultz) Walker. His father was born in Hawkins county, Tenn., in 1804, and died on Cane creek when fifty-two years of age. His wife was of German descent, her parents having emigrated from the fatherland to eastern Tennessee, where her birth occurred in 1811. The parents of our subject were married in

Hawkins county and began their domestic life upon a farm there, the father carrying on agricultural pursuits until his death. His political support was given to the Whig party. His children were Jefferson J., of Van Buren county; K. D., a Confederate soldier, who died in Kentucky during the war; David A., who died in Spencer; J. W., an agriculturist of Monroe county, Ark.; Jane, who married Sam McCormack, and died on Cane creek; Joseph H., of this review; G. W., who went from Tennessee to the far west and is probably deceased; Polly Ann, who became the wife of Clayton Shockley and died in the Sequatchie valley in Bledsoe county; Sarah A., who was burned to death in girlhood; Abner M., of Hunt county, Texas; and Wilburn F., also a resident of Hunt county.

Joseph H. Walker acquired his education mostly at home and in the Sunday-schools, which he regularly attended for twenty-five years during the summer seasons, rarely missing a Sunday. In early life he started out to make his own way in the world, and his success is attributable entirely to his well-directed efforts. On the 15th of May, 1861, he enlisted in Captain York's company, Colonel Savage's regiment, for the Confederate service, in which he remained twenty-six months. He participated in the battle at Cheat Mountain, was in several skirmishes in South Carolina, below Charleston, was on picket duty at Corinth, and participated in the battles at Perryville, Wild Cat and Collins Station. At Cheat Mountain he was wounded in the side of the neck, and after his return home was shot by some northern troops in the other side of the neck and in the arm.

When about twenty-two years of age Mr. Walker married Nancy Jane Haston, a native of Van Buren county, and to them have been born eleven children: Martha F., wife of Stanton S. Graham, a resident of Big Bottom, in White county; James A., who for six years was sheriff of Van Buren county, and now resides near his father; Sarah, wife of W. J. Rogers, of Turkey Cock Cove, Van Buren county; John J., of Laurel Cove; Amy, wife of William Wilson, of Turkey Cock Cove; J. L., of Laurel Cove; Melvina, wife of Joseph Humphreys, also of Laurel Cove, and William B., at home; Rachel, wife of G. S. Marsh, of Turkey Cock Cove; Ellen, who died at the age of seven years; and Isaac C., who completes the family.

After his marriage Mr. Walker engaged in farming on the mountain, and in 1867 removed to Todd county, Ky., but after two years returned to Van Buren county, locating in Turkey Cock Cove. In 1888 he purchased his present farm, whereon he has now made his home for ten years. He is an enterprising, progressive agriculturist, who keeps his land under a high state of cultivation. Starting out in life empty-handed, he has overcome the difficulties and obstacles in his path and worked his way steadily upward to success, for which he is certainly deserving of great credit. He is a member of the Christian church, and belongs to the Masonic lodge in Spencer. Before the war he was a Whig, but is now a Democrat, and for ten years has creditably and acceptably filled the office of justice of the peace, discharging his duties in a fair and impartial manner, which has won him the high commendation of all concerned.

MATT COPE, one of the most efficient locomotive engineers in the employ of the Nashville & Chattanooga railroad, and a highly respected citizen of Tracy City, was born in Grundy county, May 8, 1861, and is a son of W. M. and Piney (Sanders) Cope. The father, who engaged in farming as a life work, died about five years ago, but the mother is still living and now makes her home in Marion county, Tenn. Both were earnest and consistent members of the Methodist Episcopal church, South. Of their ten children those still living are Rosie, a resident of Ætna, Tenn.; Rhoda, wife of John Nunnely, of Tracy City; Harris, a miner of Whitwell, Tenn.; Lewis, an agriculturist of Marion county; Amos, a miner of Tracy City; Matt, of this sketch; and Vester, of Marion county. The deceased are J. P., a railway fireman; Mark, a miner; and Jennie, who died in girlhood.

When a boy, Matt Cope commenced working on a switch engine as fireman, later was brakeman, but afterward returned to firing, and when the Nashville & Chattanooga railroad bought the Tracy City branch from the Tennessee Coal, Iron & Railroad Company, he became engineer, and is still serving in that capacity, being one of their most faithful and trusted employes.

On the 1st of March, 1883, Mr. Cope was united in marriage with Miss Mollie Berry, a sketch of whose family is given in the biography of J. W. Berry, on another page of this volume. The children born to them are Wilcia Alma and Oma Lee. The wife and mother is an earnest member of the Methodist Episcopal church, South, and a most estimable lady. Fraternally Mr. Cope belongs to the Knights of Pythias, the Royal Arcanum and the Brotherhood of Locomotive Engineers. In politics he is independent, voting for the man whom he considers best qualified to fill the office regardless of party affiliations. Being of a social, genial disposition, he makes friends readily, and is highly respected by all who know him.

GEN. JACKSON PRYOR is an honored and well-known citizen of Jasper. He was formerly one of its leading merchants and is one of the men to whom that city owes much of its present state of growth and prosperity. He is now living on a beautiful farm of three hundred acres situated scarcely outside of the limits on the north side of the city.

Mr. Pryor was born in Morgan county, Tenn., January 15, 1816, a son of Green H. and Biddy (Halloway) Pryor, and the father was a son of Matthew Pryor. Matthew Pryor was a native of Virginia and moved from there to North Carolina, but soon after settled in Marion county, Tenn,. where he spent the remaining years of his life on a farm. Green H. Pryor, the father of our subject, was born in North Carolina about the year 1787, and moved from thence to Marion county, Tenn., with his parents when a child. He served in the Creek Indian war under General Jackson, was a farmer by occupation, and died June 4, 1862, four years after the death of his wife. They were the parents of a family of twelve children, of whom we have the following record: Jackson, the subject of this sketch; Polly A., deceased;

Sampson, deceased; William, a farmer near Whitwell, Tenn.; Preston, who died in infancy; John, deceased; Washington, a farmer living on the old homestead; Anderson M., deceased; Jeremiah, deceased; Benjamin F., deceased; Eliza J., widow of Isham P. Alexander, and is now living with her brother, Jackson, the subject of this sketch; and Caroline Z. died in Arkansas.

Jackson Pryor was educated in the public schools of Marion county, and for a time was engaged in farming. He began selling goods in Jasper in the year 1838, and a few years later he formed a partnership with W. S. Griffith. About two years later Mr. Pryor bought out his partner and carried on an extensive mercantile business alone until 1857. He then sold out to W. S. Griffith, his former partner, and I. P. Alexander, and returned to his farm, which is situated just north of the city, and has made that his home since 1861. He is a man of the very best character and of good business qualifications and as such is well and widely known and highly respected throughout the county, and, as a token of the respect in which he is held, his fellow citizens have bestowed upon him the title of "General," although he took no part in the war. Politically he is a Democrat, and, although he has never sought public honor, he once accepted the office of entry taker. In business matters and all matters tending to the welfare and improvement of Jasper and vicinity he has always proved a valuable factor. He has always sanctioned and given material aid in the development of all financial matters which tended to the better establishment of the business interests of Jasper. The Pryor Institute was established here in 1889 by General Pryor, Col. A. L. Spears and Washington Pryor, and the institution was named "Pryor Institute" in the honor of the subject of this sketch.

General Pryor has been twice married. He first met at the hymeneal altar Miss Beersheba L. Perkins who, became his wife June 28, 1841. She was a daughter of Isam Perkins who moved, during the early part of his life, to Dade county, Ga., and sent his daughter to the Sam Houston Academy, in Marion county, Tenn., and it was while there that she formed the acquaintance with and was united in marriage to Mr. Pryor. She was born in Warren county, Tenn., in the year 1822, and died in Jasper, January 17, 1881. She was a consistent member of the Methodist Episcopal church, South. To this union were born four children: The first died in infancy; John, William G. and Elizabeth, all of whom died while young. July 18, 1882, our subject was united in marriage to Miss Mary A. Hornbeck, who was born in Marion county, in 1839, the daughter of James H. Hornbeck. Mr. and Mrs. Pryor are both members in good standing of the Methodist Episcopal church, South.

J W. THAXTON.—A prominent position as a citizen and member of the farming community of Sequatchie county is held by the gentleman above named. He was born January 15, 1837, in Warren county, Tenn., the son of John and Frances (Hammond) Thaxton, both natives of Warren county, Tenn. The family moved to Tennessee from Kentucky in an early day.

The parents of our subject, Mr. and Mrs. John Thaxton, made their home in the county of their nativity until the date of their deaths. The father died at the home of our subject in the year 1890, at the age of eighty-two years, and was taken to his home and buried at Mount Zion. The mother died several years previous to the death of her husband. By occupation John Thaxton was a farmer and trader, and in religious matters he and his wife were both members of the Methodist church. They were the parents of a family of eleven children, seven of whom are now living, and of whom our subject is the sixth in the order of birth: Houston J., a farmer of Warren county, Tenn.; John B., a farmer of Grundy county, Tenn.; J. W., the subject of this sketch; F. K., a resident of Huntsville, Ala., and a manufacturer of brooms; T. B., a miller by occupation, is making his home in Texas; Sarah, widow of F. J. Bell, is living in Dunlap; and Fanny is in Warren county, Tenn. The deceased are: Mary, wife of Francis McDonough, a cousin of Andrew Johnson, died in Warren county; Rebecca, wife of John Northcut; Martha, wife of Greek Brawley; and William M., all of whom died in Warren county, Tenn.

J. W. Thaxton spent his boyhood near Mount Zion, Warren county, Tenn., where he lived with his parents until he was twenty-four years of age. He then went to Sequatchie county and located in Dunlap, where he was engaged in the mercantile business until about 1885 or 1886, and then moved to his present home near Delphi. In the year 1885 he began the manufacture of fruit brandy in partnership with David Tate. For sixteen years he served as justice of the peace, and for a number of years was also chairman of the county court. He is a man of excellent business qualifications, and whatsoever enlists his assistance is almost sure of meeting success. He is careful and systematic in all details, and the general outcome of all his dealings is assuredly desirable and profitable.

In 1863 Mr. Thaxton was united in marriage with Miss Achsah Deakins, a native of Sequatchie county, and a daughter of John Deakins. Mrs. Thaxton died in 1883, leaving a family of two children—Maggie, who died while quite young, and William K., deputy revenue collector. September 21, 1884, our subject was united in marriage with Mrs. Flora Teresa Layne, daughter of Thomas Pankey, and to this union have been born two children, Bob and Mattie. Socially our subject is affiliated with the Masonic fraternity at Dunlap, and in politics he uses his elective franchise and influence in the support of the candidates of the Democratic party. Mrs. Thaxton is a member of the Baptist church.

ISAAC HICKS holds a prominent position as a citizen and member of the farming community of the Sixth district, Sequatchie county. He was born February 28, 1830, on the farm he now owns and operates, and which was then a part of the Second district, Marion county, a son of Isaac and Martha (Ashburn) Hicks. The father was a son of Elijah and Nancy (Keith) Hicks, and Elijah was a descendant of English parents, who settled in Maryland.

Elijah Hicks, grandfather of our subject, moved to eastern Tennessee in an early day, and later settled in Bledsoe county, and from there he moved to the farm our subject now owns, and spent the remaining years of his life there. Isaac Hicks, our subject's father, was born in May, 1796, and moved to this section of Tennessee with his parents. He was in the war of 1812, and participated in the battle of Horse Shoe Bend. By occupation he was a merchant and farmer, and, politically, he was a Whig. He was a member of the Baptist church, and died August 5, 1852. He was the second in the order of birth of a family of six children, whose names were as follows: Stephen, Isaac, John, Borden, Elijah M. and Mary. To Mr. and Mrs. Isaac Hicks were born ten children, of whom we have the following record: Stephen, a retired merchant and stock dealer of Marion county, Tenn.; Elijah, who died in childhood; Thomas died in Marion county, Tenn., at the age of sixty-nine years; Martin, who died in childhood; James H., who died in 1853, on the farm our subject now owns; Isaac, the subject of this sketch; Nancy, widow of William Bennett, is living in Jasper, Marion county; J. O., a farmer in Williamson county, Tenn.; Elizabeth, deceased, was the wife of Joseph Bennett; and Martha, deceased, was the wife of William Kell. She died in Warren county, Tenn.

Isaac Hicks, the subject of this sketch, was educated in the common schools of the Sequatchie valley. In the fall of 1862 he enlisted in the Confederate army, under General Bragg, and served in the commissary department. He operated in Tennes-see and northern Georgia, and, after the battle of Chickamauga, went to Florida and operated there, being engaged in procuring cattle for beef for the soldiers. He was discharged at Chattanooga, Tenn., May 25, 1865, returned to his home in Sequatchie county, Tenn., and has since been engaged in farming and dealing in cattle in that county. Before the war he served two years as deputy sheriff of the county, and has since served as a member of the county court. As an officer and leader in local political affairs he has made many friends by his honorable, just and straightforward manners, and his name is honorably connected with the history of the growth and development of the county.

January 19, 1855, Mr. Hicks was united in marriage to Miss Laverna C. Mercer, who was born in Jackson county, Tenn., September 11, 1829, a daughter of Edward and Jane (Billingsley) Mercer. To this union have been born eight children, seven of whom are now living, and upon whom they have bestowed the following names: James H., Martha J., Eliza L., deceased, Nancy C., Joel Whitten, Edward A., Martin L. and Stephen L.

THOMAS E. MABRY, one of the honored and highly respected citizens of Grundy county, is a native of Virginia, born in Brunswick county, January 5, 1828, and is a son of Nathaniel and Martha (Elliott) Mabry, also natives of the Old Dominion. The father was a farmer, and also served as sheriff for some time. He died in that state during the childhood of our subject, after which the family removed to Mississippi, later to Montgomery county, Tenn., near Clarksville, and in 1840 to Warren county, same state, where the mother's death occurred two years later. Of their five children, Thomas E. is the youngest and the only one now living. Mary wedded John Cunningham and died in Warren county. Hinchia died in Grundy county, in 1876, at the age of sixty years. John E., a farmer, died near Clarksville, Tenn., leaving two sons—Thomas and John. Harriet became the wife of William Cunningham and also died in Grundy county.

The subject of this sketch spent his school days in Montgomery and Warren counties, Tenn., obtaining the greater part of his education in an academy near Clarksville. At the age of eighteen he accepted a position as salesman in a store in Christian county, Ky., and at the end of three years became a member of the firm, remaining in business there until coming to Grundy county, Tenn., in 1862. At that time he located upon his present farm, to the cultivation and improvement of which he has since devoted his energies with most gratifying results.

In November, 1859, was celebrated the marriage of Mr. Mabry and Miss Julia Gwyn, who was born January 25, 1843, a daughter of Ransom Gwyn. Nine children have been born to this union, all of whom are still living: Margaret, now the wife of S. W. Talifarro, a farmer and blacksmith of Viola, Tenn.; Mary, at home; William R., a dealer in dynamite and strong powder at Birmingham, Ala.; R. N., a salesman for the wholesale hardware firm of Moore & Handley, of Birmingham; Martha, wife of A. G. Brown, of Ladonia, Texas, where he is engaged in merchandising; Hudie and Myrtle, at home; Robert, a salesman for the Arms & Cycle Company, of Birmingham, Ala; and George, at home.

Mr. Mabry is a prominent and active member of the Methodist Episcopal church, South, and is now serving as trustee of Wesley Chapel and as superintendent of the Sunday school. By his ballot he usually supports the Democratic party, but is not strictly partisan, always voting for the man whom he thinks best qualified to fill the office. For four years he has creditably filled the office of justice of the peace, and in 1865 was elected circuit court clerk, a position he filled for six years with credit to himself and to the entire satisfaction of his constituents. His honorable, upright career has gained for him the confidence and respect of all with whom he has come in contact, and his circle of friends and acquaintants is extensive.

————

MATHIAS DIETZEN enjoys the well-earned distinction of being what the public calls "a self-made man." He started out in life with no capital, but possessing sturdy determination, good judgment and resolute purpose, he has steadily worked his way upward, overcoming the many difficulties and obstacles in his path, until he has achieved a brilliant success. He is not only numbered among the leading citizens of Marion county, but is also deserving of their gratitude for the introduction of a new line of business into this section of the state. He is the pioneer horticulturist of this region, and in opening up a new industry he has largely promoted the material welfare and prosperity of the county. He is therefore deserving of prominent mention among those whose labors have brought about the present advanced condition of the county, and this record would be incomplete without a sketch of his useful and honorable career.

Mr. Dietzen was born near the celebrated city of Trier, Germany, December 3, 1843, and is a son of John and Margaret (Williams) Dietzen, who were also natives of the same locality, where they spent their entire lives, both dying in 1860. The mother passed away before her husband and his death was undoubtedly occasioned by grief at her loss. He was a farmer and machinist, and possessed much natural ability as a mechanic, being able to make almost anything in wood. He manufactured wagons and cider mills, and was very useful in all lines of mechanical work. He also owned land and was a thrifty agriculturist. Both he and his wife were members of the Catholic church. Their family numbered nine children, six of whom are now living. John, the eldest, is still living in the house where he was born. He is an excellent worker in wood, and in addition to farming manufactures wine barrels, cider mills and wagons. Mathias is the next of the family. Nicholas is in the wholesale fruit and confectionary business at Chattanooga and has one of the finest and most extensive fruit farms in the south, comprising one thousand acres at Fort Valley, Ga. His opinion concerning fruit culture is always regarded as authority on the subject. Peter is a tailor of Louisville, Ky. Katie is the wife of John Ruhl, a cooper of Louisville, Ky. Joseph

39

is with his brother in Chattanooga. Margaret, who was the wife of a Mr. Ollinger, died in her native land.

Mathias Dietzen, of this review, attended school in the Fatherland, where he learned the shoemaker's trade, which he followed in Germany for about six years. In 1866 he came to the United States locating in Louisville, Ky., where he followed his trade for three years, when in 1869 he removed to Chattanooga, Tenn. In 1876 he became one of the pioneer settlers of South Pittsburg, where he opened a shoeshop and grocery store, carrying on this dual enterprise until 1888, when on account of failing health he took up his residence in his mountain home. Ten years previous, in 1878, he embarked in the fruit-growing business, and to-day he is one of the most extensive and best known horticulturists of Tennessee. His excellent fruit farm is located at a point on the Cumberland mountains overlooking South Pittsburg, the Tennessee river, Battle Creek and the Sequatchie Valley, and here, at an elevation of about fifteen hundred feet above the valley, he owns seven hundred acres of land, constituting one of the finest and most valuable fruit farms in the state. When he began its development, he had only an unbroken tract of forest land, but he at once began to clear and cultivate it, and to-day the mountain side is a splendid orchard containing five thousand apple trees, about one thousand peach trees, of many varieties, one hundred and fifty bearing cherry trees, many German prune trees, several varieties of plums and some pears. He has been very careful in the selection of his trees and raises fruit only of the finest quality, size and flavor. He has also been successful in the cultivation of the smaller fruits, such as gooseberries, raspberries and strawberries, but his attention is given mostly to the cultivation of the larger fruits; and with what success is shown by the fact that at the Centennial Exposition in Nashville, in 1897, he won ten prizes, including the first prize on early apples, on the best plate of apples, on early peaches, the second prize on a plate of peaches, the second on plums, the first prize on the best plate of plums, the second on grapes (Tennessee fruit), the first prize on German prunes when competing against a California exhibit, the first prize on the best plate of prunes, and the first prize on "grand fruit display." This was certainly a very creditable showing, and Marion county may well be proud of her commissioner to the Exposition,—Mathias Dietzen. In addition to the fruits already mentioned, he is also extensively engaged in the cultivation of grapes, having some two thousand vines, including the Concord, Delaware, Catawba, Niagara and Ives seedling, and the latter fruit compares favorably in size, quality and flavor, with those before alluded to.

When Mr. Dietzen began the cultivation of fruit he had no experience in that line save some little training received on his father's farm in early boyhood, but he is very observing, studied closely, profited by his mistakes as well as his failures and was soon conversant with the best methods to be followed and understood thoroughly the needs of different kinds and varieties. He is now regarded as authority on all matters connected with fruit culture, and for his success he is certainly deserving of great credit. He has now added a nursery to his business, having fifty thousand trees,—apples, peaches, pears, plums, and cherries, besides grape vines,—all of the best varieties, both ingrafted and budded. This has proved to him a profitable source of income and has yielded very satisfactory results. From the beginning success has attended his efforts, and the fine fruit which he raises has enabled him to command the highest market prices. His largest yield was sixteen bushels of Ben Davis apples to the tree which he sold for from a dollar and a half to two dollars per bushel. He has always had a home market in South Pittsburg, Bridgeport, Suwanee and Mont Eagle, and has shipped extensively to the cities. Every facility for the cultivation and care of his fruit has been secured. In addition to his fine residence, he has upon his farm a stone wareroom and cellar. The former is built of rock with a rock floor and double ceiling, the walls twenty inches thick, the ceiling twelve feet high, and the building twenty by twenty-two feet. It is also well ventilated and is an excellent store-house for the fruit both winter and summer. In addition to this he has an excellent cellar forty-two by sixteen feet. A fine wine is also another product of this fruit farm, and in this, as in the cultivation of the various fruits, Mr. Dietzen cannot be surpassed. His fruits are always the first upon the market and they cannot be excelled for size, variety, flavor or quality.

Mr. Dietzen was married June 2, 1868, to Miss Mary Kallenbach, a native of Cincinnati, Ohio, while her parents were natives of Germany. To this union have been born nine children, all living: Joseph, who is engaged in horticultural pursuits near his father and is meeting with excellent success; Theodore, proprietor of a saloon in South Pittsburg; Josephine, wife of John Luke, of South Pittsburg, Rosie, Annie, Maggie, Katie, Mamie and Lula, all at home. The family belong to the Catholic church, and in the community where they reside are highly respected for their many excellencies of character. Mr. Dietzen is a Democrat in his political views, but has never been an aspirant for office, preferring to devote his time and energies to his·business, in which he has met with signal success. He started out in life without capital, and his resolute spirit, sound judgment and unflagging industry have brought to him a handsome competence, which numbers him among the substantial citizens of Marion county.

JOHN SCHILD.—Among the foreign-born residents of Grundy county, Tenn., who are thoroughly identified with American civilization and progress, may be noted John Schild. He is one of Gruetli's thrifty merchants, and has made that town his home and place of business for several years.

Mr. Schild was born in Switzerland July 8, 1858, a son of Peter and Margaret (Ruef) Schild. The parents were both born in Switzerland and came to America with their family of seven children in the year 1869. They settled first at Jeffersonville, N. Y., for a few months and then bought the farm on which Peter Schild now lives. They all set to work to clear their new home of its timber, and soon developed it into one of the fine farms of the community. The mother is now dead, but the father is still living and is making his home with Martin Marugg, his son-in-law, living at Tracy City. The family is identified with the German Reform church. Of the family of seven children, we have the following record: Peter, living on the old home farm; Margaret, wife of Henry Schlapback, a butcher at Atlanta, Ga.; John, the subject of this sketch; Henry, whose home is at Tracy City, is engaged in the blacksmith and wagon-making business in partnership with Mr. Meyer; Lizzie is the wife of Martin Marugg, of Tracy City; Rudolph is married and lives in St. Louis, Mo., where he carries on the butcher business; and William is a telegraph operator at Tracy City.

John Schild, the subject of our sketch, attended school in his native country until he migrated with his parents to America. At the age of sixteen he left home and went to Nashville, Tenn., and was engaged in the butcher business at that place for about fifteen years. He then returned to the Colony and opened a store in Gruetli, the operation of which has occupied the greater part of his time and attention since that date. In connection with his mercantile interests, however, he was postmaster at Gruetli during Cleveland's second administration.

In 1886 Mr. Schild was united in marriage to Miss Barbara Marugg, also a native of Switzerland, and a daughter of Christian Marugg. This union has been blessed by the advent of a family of six children, whose names in the order of their birth are as follows: John M., Christian P., George W.,

Anna Margaret, Rudolph H. and Elizabeth Anna. Our subject and his wife are both members of the German Reform church, and Mr. Schild is also a member of the Royal Arcanum at Tracy City. He is also a member of the Swiss Relief Society at Nashville, Tenn., and in politics is identified with the Democratic party.

SIMON P. HODGES, a citizen of the Third district, who has served with distinction in several official positions, is a representative of one of the oldest and most honored families of Van Buren county. His grandfather, Abner Hodges, with his family, came to Tennessee about the beginning of the present century, from the Big Sandy region in what is now West Virginia, being accompanied by the Dodson and Hollingsworth families. Mr. Hodges located on Caney Fork in what is now Van Buren county, where he died many years ago at quite an advanced age. His wife was also quite old at the time of her death, which occurred in 1862. Although now Van Buren county, their home in early days formed a part of the Third district of White county.

William Hodges, our subject's father, was born on Caney Fork, Van Buren county, about 1818, and after reaching manhood he successfully engaged in agricultural pursuits in this section of the county, owning and operating a good farm just below the one on which his son Simon is now located. He wedded Mary McBride, also born on Caney Fork. Both were identified with the Separate Baptist church, and were held in high regard by the entire community in which their lots were cast. The father, who was a Whig in politics, died in 1854, and the mother passed away in 1888, at the age of seventy-four years. Of their six children, Jasper, a farmer by occupation, died May 11, 1881, at Hodges Ferry on Caney Fork; Simon P. is next in order of birth; Martha J. became the wife of John Hollingsworth and died at the same time as her brother Jasper; Lydia is the widow of William B. Sparkman, and lives in the same neighborhood as our subject; John and William are both farmers of the Third district of Van Buren county.

Mr. Hodges, whose name introduces this sketch, was born March 21, 1842, and spent his early life like most farmer boys, assisting in the labors of the farm and attending the common schools of the neighborhood when his services were not needed at home. As his father died when he was quite young he started out in life for himself at a tender age, and soon became of great assistance to his mother in caring for the younger members of the family. After his marriage he located upon his present farm, whose well-tilled fields and neat and thrifty appearance testifies to the careful supervision of the owner.

On the 28th of January, 1869, Mr. Hodges was married to Miss Martha E. Seitz, who was born in Warren county, Tenn., July 31, 1847. Her father, Lawson Seitz, was a twin brother of Logan Seitz, a prominent citizen of Van Buren county. To Mr. and Mrs. Hodges have been born five children, as follows: Edward, who is engaged in farming on his father's place; Fanny, wife of A. B. Denney, living near Temple, in Bell county, Texas, ; Jennie, wife of Morgan Lewis, whose home is on Cane Creek, Van Buren county; and Florence and Iola, both at home.

In 1869 and 1870, Mr. Hodges served as deputy sheriff under James Hunter, and the following year was elected register of deeds, being re-elected to the same position four years later. He has also served as justice of the peace for twenty-one years, and his official duties have always been discharged in a most capable and acceptable manner. He has always taken an active interest in educational affairs and materially assisted in the building of Burritt College, which is one of the best educational institutions in this section of the state. Since attaining his majority he has been unswerving in his allegiance to the Republican party, and he is an honored and prominent member of Mountain lodge, No. 261, A. F. & A. M., which he has represented in the grand lodge, and also belongs to the Independent Order of Odd Fellows. His estimable wife is connected with the Christian church.

JACOB ROLAND PARTIN, cinder yard engineer at the Tennessee Coal, Iron & Railroad furnaces, at South Pittsburg, is one of the pioneers of that thriving city, having located there when it was a mere hamlet. His career has been marked throughout with persistent and faithful effort to advance his own interests and the interests of those by whom he was employed, and he has been rewarded by the acquisition of a good property and a high reputation.

Mr. Partin was born November 25, 1854, a son of Ales and Nancy (Jones) Partin, both natives of Tennessee, the former born either in Marion or Franklin county, and died in 1890, at the age of sixty-four years, and the latter born in either Marion or Sequatchie county, and died in 1888 at the age of fifty-four years. The mother was a member of the Baptist church. The father was a farmer by occupation, and was a son of Thomas Partin. The Partin family were among the pioneers of this section of Tennessee. Our subject is one of a family of seven children, five of whom are living. Of his brothers and sisters we have the following record: Thomas is a carpenter in South Pittsburg; John is a brick mason, also making his home at South Pittsburg; Claiborne is a farmer, living in Jackson county, Ala.; Mrs. Mahalla Jane, wife of Wade Goolsby, of Madison county, Ala.

Our subject spent his boyhood on a farm in Jackson county, Ala., and after farming there on his own responsibility for a few years, moved to South Pittsburg, Tenn., and entered the employ of the company he is still serving, and worked for a time in the stock house. He was next employed for a time in the cinder yard and after that, for about eighteen months, at the carpenter's trade. Since about the year 1891 he has been an engineer in the cinder yard.

February 13, 1876, our subject was united in marriage with Miss Annie Linch, a native of Franklin county, Tenn., and to this union have been born nine children, seven of whom are now living. Their names in the order of their birth are as follows: Amanda, Ada, Maggie, Maude, Lila, Adam Worth and Thaddis May Amanda, the oldest of the family, is the wife of John McKinzie, who is in the employ of the Eagle Pencil Co., at South Pittsburg, and the rest of those named are all living with their parents. Willie and George W. are dead. Socially Mr. Partin affiliates with the Independent Order of Odd Fellows, and in political matters he invariably uses his franchise and influence in the support of the candidate who, in his estimation, is the best qualified for the position he seeks regardless of party lines. He is a man of much energy, industrious and is careful and systematic in his work. He has been in the employ of the company he is now serving for many years, has performed the functions of the various positions he has filled for them with rare ability and is recognized as one of the most trustworthy and reliable men in the employ of the Tennessee Coal, Iron & Railroad Co.

JAMES C. KELLY, a prominent and prosperous citizen and a member of the agricultural district of Sequatchie county, was born in Mullins Cove, Marion county, Tenn., and has spent his entire life in the eastern part of that state. He was born October 12, 1842, the son of Alexander and Elizabeth (Oatts) Kelly, and is now making his home in the Fifth district, Sequatchie county, not far from the village of Delphi.

Alexander Kelly was a son of Col. John Kelly. The latter had two brothers, William and Alexander, who also lived in the valley. He was a surveyor by occupation,

and was quite widely known, and died in Marion county. Of his family we have the following record: Thomas was a resident of Georgia, but probably died in Florida; James was living in Texas when last heard of; Valentine died in Texas; Alexander, our subject's father; Maj. William J. is a civil engineer and lives east of Jasper. The daughters were: Esther, wife of Ignatius Hall, died in Marion county, Tenn.; Polly, wife of Erasmus Alley, died in Marion county, Tenn.; Mrs. James Hoge died in Georgia; and Jane died, unmarried, in Marion county, Tenn.

Alexander Kelly was ruling elder at Ebenezer, which is the location of the old camping ground. By occupation he followed farming all his life, and, in connection with that vocation, he kept store at different times, and also kept the Kelly ferry. He was a slave-owner before the war, owning twenty-five negro slaves. He was a man of large means, but was very generous. He died about 1878, at the age of seventy-five years, in Marion county, Tenn., which had been his home since early boyhood, and his wife died in 1871, at the age of about seventy years. They were both members of the Cumberland Presbyterian church. The Oatts family is one of the oldest families in the valley. Elizabeth (Oatts) Kelly, our subject's mother, was a daughter of Col. David Oatts, who moved to the valley from Virginia. To Mr. and Mrs. Alexander Kelly were born the following children: David, who died in Jasper, Marion county, was a farmer for many years; he also served as register of deeds and clerk of the circuit court, and was postmaster for many years at Jasper; Nancy M., still living near Inman, in Marion county, widow of Dudley C. Peck; John G., of Jasper, is now the judge of Marion county, Tenn.; Eli T. is a farmer of Marion county, Tenn.; James C., the subject of this sketch; William E., who died at Kelly's Ferry; Abigail, deceased; and a child who died in infancy.

James C. Kelly, the subject of this sketch, was reared at Kelly's Ferry, near Jasper, Marion county, Tenn. Before the war he attended school in Mullins Cove, and after the war he entered Sam Houston Academy, but made his home with his parents until twenty-seven years of age, and helped his father in the management of his farm. In 1867 he was united in marriage to Miss Martha Early, daughter of Rev. A. P. Early, a noted minister of the Cumberland Presbyterian church who was engaged for many years in preaching throughout eastern Tennessee. Rev. Early was a near relative of Gen. Jubal A. Early. Mrs. Kelly was born in the state of Georgia, in 1848, and her wedded life has been blessed by the advent of a family of seven children, all of whom are living, viz: Albert O., of Whitwell, Tenn., connected with the coal company of that city; William A. is also with the coal company at Whitwell, Tenn.; Henry W. is with his father on the farm; Elizabeth J., Early C. and Ida M. and Thomas C., still at home. At the time of his marriage our subject began farming in Marion county, and made his home there until 1875, when he bought his present home and moved to it. He has served the citizens of Sequatchie county in the capacity of register of deeds, was elected in 1884, and held the office one term. Politically, he is a Republican and is one of the few

followers of that party that have held office in Sequatchie county. He and his wife are both members of the Cumberland Presbyterian church and our subject has held the position of ruling elder of the same for many consecutive years. During the war the Kelly family sympathized with the North and Alexander Kelly was in a position where he had considerable influence with some of the men in power in the Federal army, and served on the board of claims at the close of the hostilities.

MAJOR WILLIAM J. KELLY—There are few men in the entire south who have taken a more important part in the substantial development and improvement of that section of the country than Major Kelly, who in his work as a civil engineer has largely advanced the welfare, not only of this native state, but of many other of the southern states. Jasper claims him among her valued citizens and has honored him with public office, at the same time holding him in the highest respect for his many sterling characteristics.

The Major was born near Jasper, May 8, 1823, a son of Col. John and Nancy (Mayo) Kelly. His grandfather, Alexander Kelly, was born in County Armagh, Ireland, and during his infancy was brought to America by his parents. He served as a colonel either in one of the Indian wars or the war of the Revolution. After his son John located in the Sequatchie valley, he removed thither and was accidentally drowned in the Sequatchie river near Dunlap.

Col. John Kelly was born in Greenbrier, Va., June 2, 1779, and was married April 8, 1798, to Nancy Mayo, a native of North Carolina, and of Scotch-Irish descent. The marriage was celebrated in Monroe county, Tenn., and in 1808 they came down the Tennessee river to Lowry's Landing, in Marion county, at which time the Indians were still in possession of this part of the valley. They located on land that is now owned by the Lamb family in Bledsoe county, there remaining until 1817, when they moved to Liberty, in Marion county, lived there until 1820, when they took up their residence near Jasper, Marion county. In 1838 they removed to Kelly's Ferry on the Tennessee river, where the father spent the residue of his days. In 1826 he was granted a charter by the state to build a turnpike road to Ross' Landing, and at the same time he constructed the first bridge across the Sequatchie river. He was the first to advocate the building of a road around the base of Lookout Mountain, the same to follow the route which is now used by the Nashville & Chattanooga Railroad. He made a bid to build that road if the state would give him control of it for a term of fifty years, but as some one else put in a lower bid he did not get the contract. He was a most progressive and public-spirited man, always advocating and supporting some measure that would develop the country and add to the general prosperity. He was government contractor to remove obstructions in Tennessee river. He was a man of considerable means and owned a large number of slaves, but instead of being a source of income for him his endeavor to provide for their best interests made their labor more of an expense than a source of profit. In politics he was a Whig, was a member of the constitutional convention of 1834, and served for a time as circuit clerk and in other public offices. He aided in the organization of Olive Branch lodge, F. & A. M., at Jasper, and held to the religious faith of the Presbyterian church, while his wife was a member of the Methodist church. His name is indissolubly connected with the best development of the state, and for many years he was one of the most important factors in the public life of his section of Tennessee. He died November 26, 1845, and his wife passed away October 14, 1857, at the age of eighty years. They were the parents of thirteen children, namely: Esther, Nancy, Alexander, Polly, Adaline and Thomas, twins, Martha and Jane, twins, Valentine, James, Margaret, William and one who died in infancy.

Major William Kelly is now the only survivor of the family. He was educated in the Sam Houston Academy at Jasper, the academy at Franklin, Ala., and under the private instruction of Rev. James Gamble, of La Fayette, Ga., taking special interest in the study of mathematics in the last named place. After leaving school he read medicine for two years and then accepted a position as teacher at Cedar Springs, Tenn. Later he became a member of the faculty of the academy in Pikeville, and then taught for a number of terms in the Sam Houston Academy at Jasper, which was erected by his father, the Major himself carrying brick for the structure.

In 1852 Major Kelly began working as a civil engineer on the survey for the Rome & Columbus Railroad from Chattanooga through La Fayette, Ga., to the Alabama state line. On the completion of that labor he went to Gadsden, where he began the survey of the Will's Valley Railroad along the Coosa river, now known as the Alabama & Great Southern road. Entering the employ of the Nashville & Chattanooga Railroad Company he began work at Stevenson, Ala., engineering its construction. In 1867 he built the bridge across the Tennessee river to replace the one which had been washed away by a freshet and accomplished this in such a remarkably short time that the Nashville & Chattanooga Railroad Company made him a present of five hundred dollars; the Bridge Company gave him a gun and a two-hundred-and-seventy-five-dollar watch. Soon afterward he built the Jasper branch of the same road and made the survey to Pikeville. He then made a survey for the Cincinnati Southern railroad from Dunlap, Tenn., to the Kentucky line, by way of Sparta, and from Rockwood, Tenn. to Big Creek Gap, in Claiborne county, Tenn., also opened coal mines near Boyd's Switch in Alabama and built five miles of railroad from the main line to the foot of the mountain and the incline road to the mine. This was followed by the construction of the incline at Whitwell, which is a marvelous piece of engineering, winning high commendation from those best able to judge of such work. In the meantime he constructed the railroad from Jasper to Victoria and for a time was superintendent of the line.

When the convention was held at Chattanooga to petition Congress to do away with the obstructions in the Tennessee river at Muscle's Shoals, Major Kelly, General
40

Wilder and Captain Byrd were selected to compose the committee on resolutions and they wrote the petition which was adopted by the convention and presented to Congress. The result of this was the construction of the canal around the shoals, thus opening up navigation for many miles toward the head of the Tennessee river. The Major's next work was on the Birmingham & Columbus railroad, followed by a survey from Columbus, Miss., to Decatur, Ala., connecting the Tennessee and the Tombigbee rivers. He opened the Corono coal mines in Alabama, made the survey from Kimball to the Beaver creek coal fields in the lower part of Cumberland county, Tenn., and when the town of Kimball was laid out he was the chief engineer. In 1876 Major Kelly made for the Centennial at Philadelphia a map 17 x 14 feet showing the mineral district around Chattanooga, ninety-four miles east and west of that city and seventy-four miles north and south. This map was afterward exhibited at Paris and Vienna and was the means of bringing to the state millions of dollars which had been invested in the development of this mineral district. This map was also exhibited at the Nashville Centennial and now hangs in the Chamber of Commerce at Chattanooga.

It would be impossible to determine the far-reaching influences and benefits of Major Kelly's life work. There is probably no industry or line of business that has not been benefited thereby and mining and commerce particularly have been greatly advanced through his labors. He has opened up to civilization various districts of the country, whither men have gone and in the development of the natural resources have secured wealth and comfort. He who places before his fellowmen the means of personal achievement and success may well be termed a benefactor of his race and such indeed is Major Kelly. His more direct duties of citizenship, too, have also been ever faithfully performed. During the Civil war he entered the Federal service in the engineering department and under the authority of Generals Thomas and Grant he constructed the military warehouse and depots at Bridgeport and other points, continuing in the service until December 31, 1863. In 1869, 1870 and 1871 he was a prominent member of the state legislature and served on the railroad committee. During that time he was instrumental in securing the defeat of Andrew Johnson, who was a candidate for the United States senate. He also introduced into the legislature and secured the passage of the bill prohibiting the sale and giving away of liquor on election days. His political support is given the Republican party.

On the 20th of January, 1846, Major Kelly married Sarah Ann Hoge, who was born near Jasper, October 28, 1826, and died January 2, 1897. She was a daughter of John Hoge, a native of Virginia. Major and Mrs. Kelly became the parents of seven children, four of whom are now living: J. Crittenden, a farmer residing near his father; David Corry, a farmer and civil engineer of the same neighborhood; Alexander Scott, also a civil engineer and agriculturist; and Emma J., who is living with her father. The Major and his family are members of the Cumberland Presbyterian church, in which he has held the office of deacon.

There are few men whose lives have been more eminently useful and while he is modest and unassuming in manner it is but just to say of Major Kelly that his labors have been of the greatest benefit to his fellowmen and that he is therefore deserving of their highest gratitude and regard.

RILEY BRADFORD ROBERTS. —The subject of this sketch finds an appropriate place in the history of those men of business and enterprise in Grundy county whose force of character, whose sterling integrity, whose fortitude amid discouragements and whose good sense in the management of business affairs, have not only secured for him a comfortable competence, but have contributed in an eminent degree to the general prosperity. His career has not been helped by accident, luck, wealth, family or powerful friends. He is, in the broadest sense, a self-made man, being both the architect and builder of his own fortune, and is to-day one of the leading mine contractors of Tracy City.

Mr. Roberts was born near Pelham, Grundy county, May 1, 1861, and is a son of Philip and Asenath (Pearson) Roberts. The father was born in North Carolina, in 1806, but in 1812 was brought by his parents to Grundy county, Tenn., where he engaged in farming after reaching manhood until his death, which occurred May 30, 1888. He was a soldier in the Seminole war in Florida, and during the Civil war was commissioned captain of a Confederate company, but before hostilities ceased he was honorably discharged on account of his extreme old age. He was one of the most distinguished and honored citizens of Grundy county, was elected its first sheriff and filled the office for many years, and was also for a long time judge of Grundy county. He was twice married, his first wife being in her maidenhood Miss Susan R. Smith. His second wife, Asenath Pearson, was born near Pelham in 1833, and is still living, making her home near that of our subject. All of his children were of the second union, and are as follows: Isaac, who died at the age of six years; Alexander P., a farmer of Grundy county; Riley B., of this sketch; Susan, wife of Henry M. Mitchell, a miner of Tracy City; Annie, wife of Peter McGovern, of the same place; William P., a miner of Tracy City; Betty, wife of L. J. Campbell, a miner of Tracy City; and Philip H., also a miner.

Upon the home farm Riley B. Roberts was reared until nineteen years of age, acquiring his literary education in the public schools of the neighborhood. On leaving home he began work in the mines, first driving mules, and later digging coal in Rattle Snake mine. For one year he was overseer of the convict laborers, next engaged in contracting in Rattle Snake mine for for eighteen months, was foreman of drivers four years, then engaged in contracting in East Fork mine, but soon transferred his operations to the Lone Rock mine, where he is still an extensive contractor. He is an upright, reliable business man, who commands the respect of all with whom he comes in contact.

On the 26th of June, 1884, Mr. Roberts was united in marriage with Miss Jennie McGovern, a daughter of James McGovern, and to them have been born five children: Lizzie, Isaac, Carl, Cora, and Everett. The parents are leading members of the Mt. Pleasant Methodist Episcopal church, South, in which Mr. Roberts is now serving as steward, while socially he affiliates with the Independent Order of Odd Fellows and the Royal Arcanum, and politically is indentified with the Democratic party.

———————

ELI T. KELLY, whose name appears in the sketch of Judge John G. Kelly, as a brother of that gentleman, was born November 29, 1838, a son of Alexander and Elizabeth (Oatts) Kelly.

Our subject attended the best schools of the country where he received a good, practical education, thus equipping himself for the battle of life. He then turned his attention to farming and operating a saw mill. December 23, 1868, he was united in marriage to Miss Caroline Foster, who was born in Bledsoe county, March 16, 1847, a daughter of William and Rhoda (Roberson) Foster, who were early settlers of Bledsoe county. To this union have been born four children, as follows: Foster A.; Elizabeth G., wife of Rev. James Jones, of Wilson county, Tenn., a Cumberland Presbyterian minister; Rhoda I. and Charles H. are still making their homes with their parents.

Mr. Kelly is a very pleasant neighbor, genial, warm-hearted, and has an agreeable family. He has labored hard on his farm to make it one of the best stock and grain farms in that part of the country, and has become one of the substantial and prosperous citizens of Marion county. He and his family are all members of the Cumberland Presbyterian church.

ALEXANDER HALE McREYNOLDS, one of Bledsoe county's prominent and respected citizens and retired farmers, was born June 20, 1826, about seven miles below Pikeville, a son of Samuel and Jane (Hale) McReynolds.

Mr. McReynolds is the second son of a family of nine children, seven of whom are now living. He was educated at Lafayette Academy at Pikeville, and taught school for a time. While attending there, he was appointed teacher in the institution to fill a vacancy for the balance of that year, which was about five months. He afterward taught public school for a number of years and was engaged in farming at the same time. In 1857 he formed a partnership with his brother, Samuel M., and T. J. Wilson, and was engaged in business at Pikeville for five years. In June, 1862, the store was destroyed by the Federal soldiers, and Mr. McReynolds moved to his farm of three hundred and twenty acres which had been given him by his father in 1848, and has since made that his home.

Mr. McReynolds was married December 2, 1847, to Miss Emily C. Greer, who was born September 30, 1827, in Franklin county, Va., the daughter of Weatherston S. and Mary (Kyle) Greer, a brief history of whom will appear in the sketch of William Henry Greer, on another page of this volume. This union has been blessed by the birth of nine children, one of whom, Elizabeth A., the second in the order of birth, is now dead. Of those still living we have the following record: Mary J., Weatherston S., John S., Margaret F., Alice, Marthy, Gather A. and Ida. The youngest is still living with her parents, but the rest are all married and live to themselves. Mr. McReynolds did not enlist in the war, but he was taken prisoner by the Union soldiers on account of his sympathy with the south. Besides his store and business in Pikeville, he lost seven slaves, a great deal of stock and grain, and, in fact, everything but his land. Politically he is a Democrat, but has never entered the race for a political office. He has now rented his farm, and is living in practical retirement.

JOHN CRITTENDEN KELLY occupies a prominent place as a well-to-do and progressive member of the farming community of Marion county, Tenn. He has spent the greater part of his life in the county, and has been one of the potent factors in the business and political history of the county. He was born on the farm he now makes his home, April 6, 1848, a son of William J. Kelly, whose sketch appears on another page of this volume.

Mr. Kelly spent his school days at the Winchester branch of the Sewanee University, and also at the Sam Houston Academy at Jasper, and in both institutions he made a specialty of mathematics. Upon leaving school he helped his father on the farm for a time, and then helped in the construction of the Jasper branch of the Nashville, Chattanooga & St. Louis railroad, working in the capacity of bookkeeper and overseer about one year. In 1884 he moved to his father's old home place, three miles east of Jasper, and has since made that his home. He was clerk of the circuit court of Marion county for four years, being elected in 1882.

In August, 1867, our subject was united in marriage with Miss Laura Ann Turner, daughter of Washington Turner, who was born at South Pittsburg, Marion county, Tenn., in July, 1852. To this union have been born seven children, six of whom are living, and of whom we have the following record: Charles W. died in April, 1887, at the age of eighteen years; Sarah Ann, wife of T. R. Hockworth, a school teacher at South Pittsburg, Tenn.; William Atwood is living with his parents; Mary Etta, wife of Andrew Pryor, a mill owner and operator living above Jasper; Melville Clyde, a miller, is living with his parents; Scott P. and Hershel Corry both are still making their home with their parents.

H ENRY OVERTURF. — As an all-around prominent man of Grundy county, there is probably no one of its citizens who more justly deserves the title than Mr. Overturf. He is a farmer by occupation and is making his home and base of operations near the town of Tatesville. Together with his agricultural interests, he has ever been mindful of the interest of the community and has always been found ready to lend a helping hand in all projects that tend to the upbuilding or strengthening of good local government or the improvement

of the status of his adopted county. Several important offices have been entrusted to his care and he has never failed to justify the confidence placed in him by the people.

Mr. Overturf was born in Warren county, Tenn., January 2, 1835. His father was born in Virginia, and moved with his father to Warren county, Tenn., in an early day and became one of the early settlers of that section. Our subject's mother was born either in White or Warren county, Tenn., and spent the last few years of her life with the subject of our sketch. Henry Overturf was educated at Altamont Academy, and during the early part of his life he lived at a number of places in and around Altamont, and was engaged in farming and trading. In November, 1861, he joined Company A, of the Fifth Confederate Tennessee Regiment, and was appointed lieutenant of that company. After its organization, this regiment was known as the Thirty-fifth Tennessee, and Mr. Overturf became a member of Company F. At Shiloh this company sustained a very heavy loss, nineteen of its men being killed in the space of three minutes. Our subject participated in the battles of Shiloh, Corinth and Plum Orchard. At Shiloh he received a slight wound in the neck, had his ear cut by a passing ball, and three times bullets passed through his hair. He then returned to his home and was soon after captured by the Federal troops and was sent as a prisoner of war to Camp Chase, Ohio, and from there was transferred to Rock Island. After spending some eighteen months in the prison at that place, he enlisted in Company A, Second

United States Volunteer Infantry, to fight the Indians and was sent to the frontier. He was afterward detailed to serve in the quartermaster's department at Fort Leavenworth. Upon receiving his discharge, in April, 1865, he returned to Tennessee and located on a farm on the present town site of Gruetli, and in April, 1880, he moved to his present home in the Fifth district, Grundy county, where he now owns a fine farm. He is a very heavy land owner, and has an interest in about seven thousand acres of land. Our subject has also taken a wholesome interest in local political matters and has served the citizens of his adopted district and county in many different capacities. He was constable for several years and was sheriff of the county for a term of two years. He was county surveyor seventeen years, justice of the peace ten years, has been postmaster at Tatesville continuously since 1880, has been county coroner and held other minor offices.

January 1, 1857, Mr. Overturf was united in marriage to Miss Nancy Scruggs, who was born in Marion county, Tenn., in November, 1840, a daughter of Carter Scruggs. To this union has been born fourteen children, eight of whom are now living, and of whom we have the following record: J. H., living at Altamont; F. D., an engineer at Richland, Tex.; E. F. is a a farmer of Grundy county; W. R. is a farmer living near Maroa, Ill.; H. B., also a farmer; Mary Lou and Nancy Edna, both still living with their parents; and Sarah Della. The deceased are: James, who died in childhood; Lintchia, wife of William Stump, died at Altamont; Lucy Belle died in childhood; Thomas Gordon and Richard M. both died in childhood; and an infant, deceased. Socially Mr. Overturf affiliates with the Masonic fraternity, and in 1896 he represented the lodge in which he holds his membership at the grand lodge. In politics he is a Democrat.

JOSEPH D. CUMMINGS.—This gentleman is one of the leading and most influential farmers and stock men in the Third district, VanBuren county. He was born and reared on the farm which he still makes his home and has always been identified with all matters pertaining to the improvement and upbuilding of the better interests of the locality in which he lives.

Mr. Cummings was born January 1, 1841, the son of Judge William B. and Martha A. (Denny) Cummings. The father was also born on the farm now occupied by the subject of this sketch, the son of Joseph Cummings, a Revolutionary soldier who was born in Virginia, and moved to White county, now VanBuren county, Tenn., about the year 1800. He settled on the farm now occupied by the subject of our sketch, and died at the home of his son, Joseph, in the same county. The father of our subject, Judge William Cummings, was born, educated and married in VanBuren county, the date of his birth being May 10, 1810. He enlisted in the Confederate army at the beginning of the Civil war, and raised and partly equipped a company and joined the Fifth Tennesse Infantry, under the command of Col. Ben Hill. This company was reorganized at Corinth; the captain was discharged on the account of his age and poor hearing, and his son, Capt. Gabriel Marion Cummings, was elected in his place. After his discharge he returned to his home and engaged in farming and in the practice of law. In politics he was a Whig previous to the Civil war, but at that time he affiliated with the Democratic party. He performed the duties of the office of justice of the peace, was judge for several terms and for several years was clerk of the circuit court. He died in VanBuren county and was buried at Cummings Chapel. He reared a family of twelve children as follows: Capt. Gabriel Marion; William J.; Martha, deceased; Lucinda E.; Joseph D.; John L.; Mary J., deceased; Sarah A.; Margaret A., of White county, Tenn.; Azalie, deceased; Budge, deceased; and Malachi A., of White county, Tenn.

Joseph D. Cummings, the subject of this sketch, is the fifth in the order of birth of this family. He was educated at Burritt College, and afterward taught school in connection with his farm work for four years, and for two years held the position of county superintendent of public schools. May 20, 1861, he enlisted in Company I, Sixteenth Tennessee Infantry. After the battle of Murfreesboro he was transferred to the Fifth, afterwards the Thirty-fifth Tennessee Infantry, and served until the surrender of General Johnston. He participated in the battles of Cheat Mountain, Port Royal, S. C., siege of Corinth, Perryville, Ky., Murfreesboro, Chickamauga, Bentonville, N. C., and a great many minor engagements. He was wounded slightly at the battles of Perryville and Murfreesboro, and severely at Chickamauga. During the campaign at Atlanta our subject was on detached service, and did not participate in the engagements from Dalton to Atlanta, but was in all of the other contests in which his command was engaged during the war. At the close of hostilities he returned to his home in Tennessee, arriving May 28, 1865, after an absence of four years and eight days.

November 25, 1866, Mr. Cummings was united in marriage with Miss Jane Fraser, daughter of Thomas and Nancy (Tucker) Fraser, and their wedded life has been blessed by the advent of a family of eight children, upon whom they have bestowed the following names: Alice D., Mary A. C., Pattie L., Nannie U., Daisy I., Sarah E., Effie L. and Malachi Gooding, all of whom are at home except Alice, who is married, and Pattie L., who died in infancy. The family is closely connected with the Methodist Episcopal church South. Mr. Cummings is an earnest supporter of the ordinances and institutions of his church, and has served the church in official capacity, as recording steward, trustee and superintendent of the Sabbath-school for twenty-seven years continuously, and has been ex-officio member of each quarterly and district conference since his connection with the church. It is said of him that in all this time he has never missed a service held at his church, by any denomination, except as prevented by sickness and when a few services were held by some Mormon elders. He has willingly and liberally contributed both time and money in every cause for the upbuilding of the church and the uplifting of the people. Mr. Cummings has been connected with the Masonic fraternity for many years, having been made a Master Mason some twenty-five years ago, in Mountain lodge, No. 261. With them he remained and affiliated for one and twenty years, filling various offices and stations. He represented that lodge a number of times in the grand lodge of Tennessee, and for one year was grand marshal of the latter body. He is now connected with Hickory Valley lodge, No. 555, and has been worshipful master of the same for the past four years. He has also for twenty-three years been a member of the Independent Order of Odd Fellows, and has filled the position of secretary of Altus lodge, No. 200, of that order, for ten consecutive years. Politically he is a Democrat, and cast his first presidential vote for Jeff. Davis. He is a valued and respected citizen and a representative man of the community, in which he owns a large farm of about five hundred and ten acres of land, which he makes his home.

Capt. Gabriel Marion Cummings, the eldest brother of the subject of this sketch, was born January 10, 1834. He was married May 20, 1860, to Miss Martha L. Morgan, a native of Pope county, Ga., born January 13, 1840. To this union have been born twelve children. Captain Cummings was reared on a farm, but, after arriving at maturity and completing his education, he went to Georgia and taught school for a few years, and while there he met the lady who became his wife. At the breaking out of the war he returned to his home and joined the Confederate army, enlisting in Company I, Sixteenth Tennessee Infantry, under Capt. H. York, and was mustered into service at Camp Harris. From there he was at once sent to Summer county. He partici-pated in the battle of Shelton's Hill, Miss., Richmond, Perryville, Ky., Stone River, Chickamauga and Bentonville, N. C. When his father was discharged he was elected captain in his place at Corinth, Miss. He was soon after appointed military conductor on the railroad from Dalton to Atlanta, and thus missed many of the hard-fought battles of that bloody campaign. He was in the battle of Perryville, Ky., and was there slightly wounded in the left side, and was also wounded in the battle of Chickamauga, slightly, in the face and neck. He was discharged just before the surrender of Johnston, and returned to his home May 23, 1865. He and his father lost heavily by the war, as they were quite extensively engaged in the mercantile business at Cummingsville. He is now occupied in farming and is living a quiet, peaceful life, and, although he is a stanch Democrat, he takes little interest in political affairs.

THOMPSON A. SHELTON resides on the ancestral homestead of the Shelton family which for a century has been occupied by those bearing his name. His grandparents, Richard E. and Temperance Shelton, removed from Virginia to North Carolina, and thence came to the Sequatchie valley, where Mr. Shelton secured a tract of unimproved land in the midst of the forest. This he at once began to improve and succeeded in making it a good farm which has been still further cultivated by his son and grandson until it is one of the best properties in this county.

George W. Shelton, father of our subject, was born on this farm in 1812, and throughout his life carried on agricultural pursuits. His father was a Whig and he supported that party until the organization of the Republican party when he joined its ranks. For twelve years he filled the office of justice of the peace with credit to himself and satisfaction to his constituents and was a worthy, progressive citizen. Both he and his wife held membership in the Ebenezer Cumberland Presbyterian church, in which he held the office of ruling elder. His death occurred December 22, 1870. Mrs. George W. Shelton bore the maiden name of Sarah Hornbeack and was probably a native of Bledsoe county, Tennessee. Her death also occurred on the Shelton homestead. To this worthy couple were born eleven children, four of whom are yet living: Temperance, wife of Spearman Brown, a prominent citizen of this community; Thompson A.; Esther C., wife of A. L. Anderson, of Chattanooga; and Dr. A. K., a practicing physician of Olliver Springs, Anderson county, Tenn. Those deceased are: Mary A., who became the wife of L. D. Westcott, and died in Chattanooga, Tenn.; Dr. R. E., who served as a surgeon in the Confederate army, died in January, 1885; Martha J., who became the wife of G. W. Lewis, and died in the Fifth district of Marion county; Prudence M.; Nancy E., who married J. J. Kelly, and died in Bledsoe county, Tenn.; Ruth B. and Delilah, who died in infancy.

Thompson A. Shelton was born on the farm which is now his home, June 14, 1847, and spent his boyhood under the parental roof. When twenty years of age he started out in life for himself and began operating

41

an adjoining farm. In 1870 he returned to the old home place and afterward purchased the farm comprising two hundred and fifty acres of rich and valuable land, much of which is under a high state of cultivation. The buildings were all erected by Mr. Shelton and in the cultivation of his land he has shown a progressive advancement that classes him among the substantial and leading farmers of the county.

On the 17th of November, 1870, Mr. Shelton married Miss Nancy J. Bryson, a daughter of J. M. and Keziah (Prigmore) Bryson. Her father was born on Battle Creek, January 26, 1824, and died March 1, 1893, while his wife, who was born April 7, 1825, passed away June 20, 1883. Mrs. Shelton was born August 19, 1850, and by her marriage has become the mother of six children as follows: Rev. George W., who is pastor of the First Cumberland Presbyterian church, of Clarksville, Tenn.; J. M., who is attending the University of Nashville, medical department; W. J., who is studying for the ministry in McKinzie; R. E., Eudora S. and Arthur G., at home.

Mr. Shelton, his wife and all of the children, with the exception of the youngest, are members of the Cumberland Presbyterian church of Oak Grove, and the family is one of prominence in the community, enjoying the hospitality of the best homes in this section of Marion county. Mr. Shelton is a stanch Republican in his political views and exercises his right of franchise in support of the men and measures of that party. He has been honored with public office and an incumbency of twelve years as a member of the county court plainly indicates the efficient and prompt manner in which he discharged the duties of that position. Socially he is connected with the Altine Masonic lodge, in which he is serving as senior warden, and in his life he exemplifies the noble principles of that time-honored fraternity. His interest in public affairs is that of one who does not lightly regard the duties of citizenship, but rather seeks to perform them fully, always with an eye single to the public welfare and with a clear appreciation of the value of example.

REV. JAMES ROBERT HUNTER, principal of the Pryor Training School, of Jasper, is one of the city's ablest and most popular educators. Attention, method and industry are the foundation stones of success in any business, and especially in that of teaching, and these combined with integrity of word and deed have been the corner stone of all the enterprises in which he has embarked, and during his residence in Jasper he has made many warm friends throughout the city and county.

Our subject was born on a farm in Polk county, Tenn., January 25, 1864, the son of Rev. Andrew Caldwell and Emeline (Wingard) Hunter, the former born August 26, 1820, in Buncombe county, N. C., and the latter born April 22, 1831, in Charleston, S. C. Andrew Caldwell Hunter was a son of Samuel and Catharine (Poteet) Hunter, both natives of Buncombe county, N. C. Samuel Hunter was a farmer by occupation, but served one term as sheriff of his county. In 1833, he moved with his family to Georgetown, Meigs county, Tenn., where he died a short time before the war,

and his wife died soon after the close of the war. They were both members of the Missionary Baptist church.

Rev. Andrew Caldwell Hunter, our subject's father, grew to manhood in Meigs county, Tenn., and acquired his education in the public schools of that county. He commenced preaching for the Methodist Episcopal church, South, in the year 1844, just as the division in the church occurred. His first sermon was before Rev. G. W. Brownlow, who afterward became governor. Reverend Hunter traveled as a minister until the year 1862, and then located in Ducktown, Polk county, Tenn., where our subject was born. This he made his home until 1887, when he moved to Jasper where he now resides. He has been an earnest and zealous worker in the ministry, and to realize that many souls have been brought to the foot of the cross as a result of his efforts is a source of satisfaction to him in his declining years. His faithful wife is not only a judicious manager of the household and the kindest of mothers, but has been of much assistance to her husband in his chosen life work. Reverend Hunter was first married in Blount county, Tenn., to Miss Martha Ann Humphreys, a native of that county, and three children were born to them: Thomas, deceased; Samuel M., a physician in Hope, Kan.; and the third child died in infancy. Mrs. Hunter died in 1856, and her husband subsequently married Miss Emeline Wingard, his present wife, near Gadsden, Ala., and they have become the parents of a family of seven children, as follows: John, deceased; Mattie, wife of I. J. Stamper, of Ducktown, Tenn.; William H., a miner living in Alma,

Colo.; Rev. James Robert, the subject of this sketch; Ellen, wife of J. E. Jolly, telegraph operator; Emma, who died at the age of nineteen years; Edward, attending school at the Pryor Training School.

In 1882 James Robert Hunter, the subject of our sketch, went to Colorado and engaged in mining for four years and thus secured money enough to pay his way through college. He accordingly supplemented his public-school education with a course at Hiwassee College, Monroe county, Tenn., from which he graduated, receiving the degree of B. A., and then entered the Vanderbilt University at Nashville, Tenn., taking the B. A. course at that institution also. He taught one year while attending school in the college at Nashville. In 1892 he was appointed chaplain of the penitentiary at Nashville and held that position for three years, and, although attending school, averaged over three sermons per week. He was licensed to preach in December, 1888, and took charge of the Cherry Street church, in Chattanooga, in April of the following year to fill the remaining five months of an unexpired term. In the following October he joined the conference and was sent to Citico Mission, at Chattanooga, and served there two years. He then entered Vanderbilt University at Nashville, and, after graduating from that institution, went to Bridgeport, Ala., and organized a school known as the Bridgeport Training School, which institution is still running. In 1896 he leased for five years the Pryor Institute, a property of the Methodist Episcopal church, South, and took possession of it in July of that year.

August 25, 1885, our subject was married in Chattanooga, to Mrs. Ada F. Woodhead, who was born in Yorkshire, England, September 5, 1854, the daughter of Dan and Frances (Exley) Furniss, both natives of England. At the time of her marriage to our subject, Mrs. Hunter had three children from a previous marriage: Lawrence, in Chattanooga; and Harry and Grace, now living with their parents and attending school. Mrs. Hunter is also a member of the Methodist Episcopal church, South. Socially our subject affiliates with a Greek letter fraternity, and in politics he is identified with the Prohibition party. He is a man of excellent business ability, has not only a quick but a comprehensive mind and is especially endowed with the faculty of making a subject clear to his pupils, and is held in the highest respect and esteem by them.

REV. WILLIAM McGLOTHEN.—The subject of this sketch may be truly classed as one of the leading members of the rural population of Sequatchie county. He was one of the earliest settlers of the Second district, and is now one of its oldest citizens, and has devoted almost his whole life to agricultural pursuits. In prosecuting his farm work he has been very industrious, progressive in his ideas, and ready to take advantage of every turn of the tide to improve his circumstances.

Mr. McGlothen was born in Virginia in the year 1818, the son of Elias and Polly (Cadel) McGlothen, the former a native of Virginia, and the latter a native of North Carolina. They moved from Virginia to

Tennessee when our subject was quite young, and located, first, in White county, near Sparta. In 1852 they moved to what is now Sequatchie county, where the parents both died, the father at the age of eighty-two years, and the mother at the age of seventy years. Upon leaving Virginia, the family stopped on French Broad river, near Knoxville, long enough to raise one crop, and then moved on horseback to their new home in Sequatchie county by the way of Crab Orchard. They were members of the Primitive Baptist church, and the father was a Jackson Democrat. They reared a family of twelve children, of whom our subject is the ninth in the order of birth and the only one now living.

William McGlothen made his home with his parents until he reached the age of twenty-one years, and then went to Meigs county, Tenn., and made that his home for four years. From there he moved to the Sequatchie valley, where he spent two years, and then located in the woods, where he has since made his home. In 1841, Mr. McGlothen was united in marriage to Mrs. Lucinda Seals, a native of North Carolina. She died August 20, 1896. To this union were born seven children, four of whom are now living, and of whom we have the following record: Catharine lives with her father; Margaret, at home; Mary, widow of William Whitlow, of the Second district, Sequatchie county; and William Taylor, of the Second district, Sequatchie county. The three deceased are as follows: James, who died during the war; Lucinda, wife of Charles Cagel, died near Huntsville, Ark.; and Thomas, who died at the age of seven years. Our subject has served several years as school director and has also been a member of the county court. He is a member of the Primitive Baptist church, and has been a minister in that organization since the war, and now has charge of the Mount Pleasant church. He preached thirteen years at Tracy City. Mr. McGlothen is loyal and determined in his adherence to the right, and is a zealous and devout Christian worker, and carries these characteristics into his everyday life. He is a man of earnest, practical nature, of much culture, and is very popular with his people and greatly loved by them. Politically, he was formerly a Whig, but is now identified with the Democratic party.

———

DAVID M. TATE occupies a prominent place as a well-to-do and progressive member of the farming community of Marion county, in the Seventh district of which he has an elegant farm. He is one of that county's public-spirited citizens and is always ready to lend a helping hand to everything that pertains to the interest of the county, and has become one of its leading politicians.

Mr. Tate was born near South Pittsburg, Marion county, Tenn., May 23, 1857, a son of Samuel M. and Catharine (Anderson) Tate. The father was born May 1, 1820, in Jackson county, Ala., and his wife was born in Franklin county, Tenn., June 5, 1824, and died March 21, 1895. She was a member of the M. E. church. Samuel M. Tate is a son of John K. and Rachael (Alsup) Tate, the former born in Granger county, Tenn., and the latter born in Lincoln county, Tenn. After their marriage they moved to Jackson county, Ala., but remained there but a short time until they moved near South Pittsburg, in 1829, bought a farm there and made that their home until their death. He was a soldier in the Creek war. Samuel M. and Catharine Tate, the parents of our subject, were married in Marion county, Tenn., and always lived on a farm in that county. He was a Methodist minister, beginning his ministerial work in 1858, in Marion county, and has since followed that line of work in connection with his farming. Socially he is a Master Mason, and holds his membership at Jasper. Mr. and Mrs. Samuel M. Tate are the parents of a family of nine children, of whom we have the following record: Sina, deceased; Rachael, deceased; Anna, deceased; John K., a farmer living on Battle Creek, Marion county, and is the present nominee on the Republican ticket for sheriff; Abigal C., deceased; Margaret A., wife of Jasper Dawson, a merchant at South Pittsburg; David M., the subject of this sketch; Virginia, wife of T. W. Anderson, a prominent farmer living near Battle Creek; and James B., who died at the age of two years.

David M. Tate, the subject of this sketch, received his primary training in the public schools of the district in which his boyhood was spent and supplemented the same with a course in the William & Emma Austin College at Stevenson, Ala., and was married there April 8, 1879, to Miss Tennie R. Tate. She was born in Jackson county, Ala., July 13, 1860, the daughter of Judge David and Martha A. (Winn) Tate, both natives of Marion county, Tenn., the father born at Battle Creek, December 5, 1824, and the mother born May 11, 1835, in Swedens Cove. They were the parents of a family of nine children, as follows: Maggie J.; Tennie R., wife of Mr. Tate; John K.; Edward C., deceased; Samuel, whose home is at Scottsboro, Ala., is the judge of the city court of that city and of Bridgeport; David M., deceased; George B., M. D.; Mary C. and Mack.

After his marriage, our subject made his home at Stevenson, Ala., until 1886, and for six years was at the same time a student, a teacher and a farmer. In 1889 he returned to South Pittsburg and settled on a farm. He was soon after elected, on the Republican ticket, to the office of trustee and moved to Jasper and performed the duties of that office two terms, or four years. He then bought a farm a short distance northwest of the city of Jasper, in June, 1895, moved to it and has since made that his home. Mr. Tate is a well-informed man, being particularly well-versed on topics of education and economy, and is widely and favorably known as a citizen devoted to his county's best interests. Mr. and Mrs. Tate are both members of the M. E. church, and Mr. Tate is also a Master Mason, holding his membership in the lodge at South Pittsburg. They are the parents of a family of eight children, whose names and the dates of their births are as follows: Clarence E., born July 27, 1881; John K., born August 16, 1883; Katie C., born August 25, 1885; Martha A., born February 26, 1888; Maggie J., born January 25, 1890; Miltie M., born March 20, 1892; and Una T., born July 16, 1896. David S., born April 18, 1898.

ELI W. HAMBY, one of the representa- tive and prominent agriculturists of Grundy county, has spent almost his entire life there, his birth occurring in Burrass Cove, August 8, 1860. His parents are Eli W. and Rachel Arkansas (Sartain) Ham- by. His paternal grandfather, who also bore the name of Ely Hamby, was born and reared in North Carolina, and was a small boy during the Revolutionary war, being too young to enter the service. In 1818 he came to Tennessee, and first located in War- ren county, but afterward lived in several different places until buying land at the head of Elk river, where he made his home until called to his final rest at the age of seventy years. He was a farmer and stock- raiser and was very successful financially.

The father of our subject was one of the prominent self-made men of Grundy county, for he started out in life for him- self in limited circumstances, but became one of the most prosperous citizens of his community, and all that he acquired was obtained through industry, perseverance and good management. He was born October 5, 1826, on Hickory creek, probably in Warren county, and died at his home at the head of Elk river, in Grundy county, in 1884. During the Civil war, he enlisted, in 1861, in the Forty-fourth Tennessee Con- federate Infantry, and assisted in organizing his company. He remained in the service until 1863 and participated in the battles of Shiloh, Perryville and others. On his re- turn home he had to begin life anew as he was without means, but success at length crowned his efforts and he became one of the most prosperous farmers and stock raisers of his community, being worth twelve

thousand dollars, and owning between six and seven hundred acres of valuable land at in the Elk river valley, and the greater part of Robert's Cove. In politics he was a stanch Democrat, and being a public- spirited, enterprising citizen, he gave his support to all measures for public good.

In his family were five children, namely: James H., who owns and operates a farm at the head of Elk river; Eli W., of this review; Jesse R., also a farmer on Elk river; Clarissa, wife of Charles B. Wamack, of Pelham, Tenn.; and George F., also an agriculturist. The mother of the children was a native of Arkansas, born November 5, 1839, and died at her home in Coffee county, Tenn., August 2, 1892. After the death of her first husband she married P. H. Bost and removed to Coffee county. She was a consistent and faithful member of the Christian church.

Mr. Hamby, whose name introduces this sketch, pursued his studies at the Camp Ground government school during his boy- hood and youth, and at the age of twenty years began his business career as a farmer upon his father's farm on Elk river. He continued to successfully engage in agri- cultural pursuits until December, 1895, when he removed to Tracy City, with whose official interests he has since been promi- nently identified. He has always made his home in this section of the state with the exception of about a year, having spent a portion of 1882 and 1883 in Arkansas, In- dian Territory, Kansas and Missouri, and he then returned to his old home on account of the illness of his father.

On the 29th of October, 1885, Mr. Hamby led to the marriage altar Miss Allie

Hawk, who was born on Elk river, and is a daughter of Alexander B. Hawk. They have an interesting family of four children, namely: Henry A., Cora May, Roy Briggs and Dora Belle. The parents hold membership in the Methodist Episcopal church, South, with which Mr. Hamby has been officially connected, and they take an active part in all church work. Socially he affiliates with the Independent Order of Odd Fellows, and politically is identified with the Democracy.

JESSE THACH, a well-known harness and saddle maker, and a prominent citizen of Jasper, has been identified with the business interests of that city longer than any other man still residing there. He was born in Jasper, May 13, 1830, a son of Josiah D. and Lydia (Parks) Thach, both natives of North Carolina, the former born at Edenton, the county seat or courthouse of Chowan county, the latter in Buncombe county. When a young man the father learned the harness and saddler's trade, which he continued to follow throughout life. With the Russie family he removed to Franklin county, Tenn., while his future wife went with her people from North Carolina to Grainger county, this State, then floated down the Tennessee river to Mattison county, Ala., where she remained until after her father's death. She then went to Beene creek in Franklin county, Tenn., where she gave her hand in marriage to Mr. Thach. In 1826 they came to the Sequatchie valley, where they resided until 1835. In the latter year they removed to Wauhat-

chie within six miles of Ross' Landing, but after a short stay returned to Jasper. There the father died in 1840, at the age of forty-five years, but the mother, who was born September 20, 1792, long survived him, dying March 6, 1891, at the extreme old age of ninety-nine years. Until a short time before her death she was still quite active and well preserved. For many years she was a faithful member of the Methodist church. In politics the father was a Whig.

In the family of this worthy couple were eight children, the living being as follows: George, a farmer of Milam county, Texas; Jesse, of this sketch; Joseph, a farmer and carpenter of Alpine, Pulaski county, Ky.; Sarah, widow of John Mattox, of Butler county, Mo.; and William, a resident of Jasper. The deceased are Olliver P., who died in Kimball; Elizabeth, who married A. B. Johnson and died in 1842; and Caroline, who became the wife of William Guinn and died in Jasper of recent years.

The schools of Jasper afforded Jesse Thach his educational privileges, and in early life he learned the trade of harness and saddle making. Prior to the war he and his brother O. P. engaged in that business in Jasper. In 1863 he went to Chattanooga and also to Nashville, where he worked for the Federal government. At the close of the war he resumed business in Jasper, and has successfully carried on operations in that place ever since.

Mr. Thach was married, October 8, 1871, to Miss Martha O'Neal, a daughter of Andrew O'Neal, who was born in Dublin, Ireland, and was a blacksmith by trade. He died in the Sequatchie valley and is buried at Jasper. Mr. and Mrs. Thach have five children: Samuel, chief mail clerk on the Louisville & Nashville railroad between Nashville and St. Louis; Julia, at home; Thomas, a baggage and express messenger on the Jasper branch of the Nashville & Chattanooga railroad; Patrick, who is studying law in Jasper; and Andrew, at home. The wife and mother is a devout member of the Methodist church. Socially, Mr. Thach affiliates with the Masonic fraternity, and politically is identified with the Republican party.

DAN T. THACH, one of Marion county's best and most prominent citizens, was born in Jasper, Marion county, Tenn., September 4, 1858, a son of Oliver Perry and Annie Caroline (Henson) Thach. The father was born May 4, 1819, and during childhood was brought by his parents to Marion county, the family locating in Jasper, where he grew to manhood and attended school. He was a saddle and harnessmaker by trade and as such was very proficient. He and his brother, George W. Thach, now living in Cameron, Milam county, Texas, were soldiers under General Scott in the war between the United States and Mexico. For a time during the Civil war, while located at Bridgeport, Ala., he worked at his trade in the employ of the Federal government. After the war he served three terms as tax collector of Marion county with credit to himself and to the entire satisfaction of the public, and was also a member of the county court for a time. His death occurred February 6,

1887, and after surviving him for two and a half years, the mother of our subject also passed away. She was twice married, her first husband being Andrew O'Neal, by whom she had three children: James L., of Gurdon, Ark.; Julia, wife of W. F. Gilliam, of Battle Creek; and Martha, wife of Jesse Thach, of Jasper. The children born of the second marriage are Millard Fillmore, who is engaged in farming three miles below Jasper; Jesse Johnson, also an agriculturist; Dan Trewhitt, of this sketch; and Oliver Perry, George W., Tennessee and Alice, who all died in childhood.

During his youth the subject of this sketch was provided with good school privileges, being a student in the Sam Houston Academy and other schools until nineteen years of age. After quitting his studies he successfully engaged in teaching for a time, and also learned the carpenter's trade, at which latter he worked at times in both Arkansas and Texas, but throughout the greater part of his business career his energies have been devoted to agricultural pursuits, owning and operating a small, fertile farm three miles west of Jasper, on the public road leading from Jasper to South Pittsburg, and midway between the two places.

On the 17th of April, 1881, Mr. Thach wedded Miss Sarah D. Doss, who was born in Marion county, Tenn., August 12, 1862, a daughter of John R. C. and Sarah Ann Doss. Six children blessed this union: Bertha Clark, who died in childhood; and Effie Lucretia, Alford Taylor, Vernon Johnson, John Oliver and Robert, all at home. The parents are earnest and consistent members of the Christian church, and Mr. Thach also belongs to the Independent Order of Odd Fellows at South Pittsburg. Politically he has been identified with the Republican party since attaining his majority, and has taken an active and prominent part in local politics. He was appointed the first postmaster at Kimball, Tenn., June 9, 1890, which position he held to the satisfaction of all until he resigned. He has efficiently served as deputy sheriff under William Rankin, and also as deputy county trustee under D. M. Tate, and under the present incumbent, S. B. Raulston. He is a member of the board of trustees of Sam Houston Academy. At the Republican primary election held in Marion county, February 18, 1898, he received the nomination for county court clerk, which is equivalent to an election, as the Democrats did not see proper to oppose him, and virtually endorsed him in their convention at the time they nominated the balance of their county ticket. It is safe to predict that he will prove a very popular and capable official, as he is at all times and under all circumstances prompt, reliable, energetic and courteous.

WILLIAM HENRY GREER, one of Bledsoe county's prominent farmers and stock raisers, was born in Franklin county, Va., October 9, 1821, a son of Weatherston S. and Mary (Kyle) Greer. The father was born in Franklin county, Va., in the year 1801, the son of Moses S. Greer, who is supposed to have also been born in Virginia The mother was born in Ireland, about the year 1804, and came to America when a child with her uncle, Robert Calhoun, by whom she was reared. Mr. and Mrs. Weatherston S. Greer moved to Bledsoe county, Tenn., about the year 1832, and bought a farm in Grassy Cove, which they made their home until the year 1868, at which time they sold the farm and spent the remaining years of their lives with their children. They were the parents of a family of eight children, of whom our subject is the oldest, and of whom we have the following record: William Henry; Elizabeth, wife of Mark Stephens, deceased; Harriet A., wife of Mr. Vernon, of Bledsoe county, deceased; Emily C., wife of Alexander H. McReynolds, of Bledsoe county; Thomas, of Bledsoe county; Moses, of Dayton, Tenn.; Weatherston S., of Texas; and Henry C., of Bledsoe county.

Mr. Greer was educated at the New Market College in Jefferson county, Tenn. He afterward taught school for three terms, and at the same time carried on a farm. He moved to his present home in 1869 and remained until 1872, and then bought another large farm in the same county and moved to it. Hard times came on, however, and he was compelled to return to his former home and forfeit his first payment on the new farm which was a very heavy one, his loss in the transaction being nine thousand dollars. By the war he lost nine slaves, sixty cattle and fifteen horses and mules. His present farm comprises four hundred and seventy-five acres of land and is situated in the Seventh district. In spite of the many reverses, Mr. Greer has been quite successful and now is the fortunate owner of a fine property and is conceded one of the leading and most prosperous farmers of Bledsoe county.

42

Mr. Greer has been three times married. His first wife bore the maiden name of Miss Rebecca M. Hutcheson, and was born August 30, 1835. She became the wife of our subject November 13, 1851, and died July 18, 1885. To this union were born nine children, of whom we have the following record: John; Martha, deceased; Ann, deceased; Nancy; Emma, deceased; Clay; Lou; Addie and William. After the death of his first wife, our subject was united in marriage to Miss Matilda Roberson, also a native of Bledsoe county. They were married September 30, 1885, and Mrs. Greer died April 25, 1897, leaving no children. June 7, 1897, our subject was united in marriage to Mrs. Levina T. Pearsons, who was born in New York, July 9, 1834. She was first married to Thomas E. Pearsons, and they moved to Bledsoe county in an early day and settled on a farm in the mountain. Mr. Pearson was instrumental in securing the establishment of the post office which bears his name and was postmaster there for twelve years, or until his death, and his wife, now Mrs. Greer, managed the affairs of the office for five years. He was a Mason and was buried at Pikeville by the fraternity. The date of his death was May 20, 1892.

Our subject did not participate in the Civil war, but sympathized with the South and is a Democrat in political views. He was deputy sheriff for six years and was elected justice of the peace at the beginning of the war, and after its close was re-elected. Socially he affiliates with the Masonic fraternity. Mr. and Mrs. Greer and the family of eight children are all members in good standing of the Christian church, as were also his first and second wives. Mr. Greer is a man of the very best character, pleasant to meet, and is held in high esteem by all with whom he comes in contact. He has an excellent farm, commodious and comfortable home, and has a pleasant family.

EMMIT M. VICK, switch-yard engineer at South Pittsburg, for the Tennessee Iron, Coal & Railroad Co., is one of the pioneers of that thriving city, locating there when the greater part of it was farm land and under cultivation. He has seen it in all its stages of growth and development and has held quite a conspicuous place among the thrifty and enterprising citizens who have built up South Pittsburg, and made of it one of the principal manufacturing cities of eastern Tennessee.

Our subject was born in Bledsoe county, Tenn., one mile east of Pikeville, July 26, 1856, a son of Robert and Manervia (Nelson) Vick. The father was born in North Carolina in the year 1810, and is now a resident of Knoxville, Tenn. The mother was born in upper east Tennessee, in the year 1822, and died in Knoxville, Tenn., in 1893. The Vick family were among the first settlers of Bledsoe county, having moved there when our subject's father was a small boy. He grew to manhood there and, in 1874, moved to Bridgeport, Ala., and from there he moved to Knoxville, Tenn., which he has since made his home. During the war he was in sympathy with the cause of the North, and in politics he is now identified with the Republican party. His wife was a member of the Baptist church. Her parents settled in Bledsoe county in a very early day. Mr. and Mrs. Robert Vick were the parents of a family of twelve children, of whom we have the following record: Martha died in childhood; Emeline died in South Pittsburg; John died in Bledsoe county at about   eginning of the war; James is a carpenter and is in the employ of the East Tennessee, Virginia & Georgia railroad shops at Knoxville, having served in that capacity since the war; Edward was a soldier in a Federal Tennessee regiment and died of the measles at Flat Lake, Ky., during his service; Mary died when a young woman; Rufus is a carpenter in the employ of the Nashville, Tellico & Charleston railroad shops at Nashville; Ash was a blacksmith and died in Jackson county, Ala.; Virginia is living with her father in Knoxville, Tenn.; Emmit M., the subject of this sketch; Alex died in childhood; Asbury is a blacksmith in Birmingham, Ala.

Our subject spent his school days near Pikeville, Tenn., and attended school in that city. In 1874 he went with his father to Bridgeport, Ala., and helped him on the farm until he was twenty-one years of age, when he entered the employ of the Tennessee Coal, Iron & Railroad Co. His first service for this company was in their sawmill, but he soon was given a position at the furnaces. He next fired an engine for two years, after which he became engineer on the switch engine and was thus engaged for six years. He then went to Waxahachie, Ellis county, Texas, and after farming for four years in that vicinity, returned to his engine in South Pittsburg, Tenn.

December 19, 1888, Mr. Vick was united in marriage with Miss Elizabeth Childres, daughter of Mary Childres, who was a native of upper east Tennessee. Mrs. Vick was born in Washington county, Tenn., November 16, 1854. To this union have been born a family of six children, five of whom are now living: John was born September 22, 1879, and died January 13, 1880. The five living are all making their home with their parents, and the following is a list of their names given in the order of their birth: Ellen, Walter, Allie, Sallie and Rufus. Mr. and Mrs. Vick are both members of the Methodist Episcopal church, South. Socially our subject affiliates with the Independent Order of Odd Fellows and is an officer in that lodge, and is also a member of the Modern Woodmen. Politically he is a Republican.

GEORGE W. HARRIS, one of Grundy county's leading and substantial business men, is making his home and base of operations at Tracy City. He is a manufacturer of lumber and building material, operating two large saw mills, and is doing an extensive business.

Mr. Harris is a son of Martin and Orphia L. (Wilson) Harris. Martin Harris was born November 2, 1826, and his wife was born in Dade county, Ga., April 28, 1828. She died November 21, 1895, and he January 13, 1888. Martin Harris was a son of William Harris, a pioneer of Knox county, Tenn., who moved from thence to Dade county, Ga., and from there to Marion county, Tenn. He died in Dickson's

Cove, in the last named county. He and his family owned a cotton gin and carding factory on the Little Sequatchie river. William Harris was also a farmer. He died March 7, 1878, at the age of sixty-five years. Our subject's father, like his father, was a miller. During his life he moved fifty times. He served in the Federal army, acting as pilot for General Wagner. He was justice of the peace in Marion county a number of times, and was living in Tracy City when it was made a part of Grundy county. He has made one or two trips to the state of Alabama. Politically, he was formerly a Whig, but later, upon the organization of the Republican party, he identified himself with that organization, and he and his wife were both members of the Christian church. They were the parents of a family of seven sons, six of whom are now living, and of whom we have the following record: George W., the subject of this sketch; William H., a well-known lawyer of Tacoma, Wash.; B. E. W., of Marion county, Tenn.; A. C. J., who is now in the gold fields of the Klondike; John, a resident of the Third district, Marion county, Tenn.; Marshall is a contractor of Tacoma, Wash.; and Martin Prince, who died at the age of twenty-six years.

George W. Harris, our subject, was educated at Altamont, and upon arriving at manhood he continued the business to which his father had devoted his life work, that of operating a saw mill, and conducted a mill at Colony and one at Tracy City with marked success. He has done a great deal of contract work, making building and railroad material, and, for a time, operated a saw mill for the Tennessee Coal, Iron &

Railroad Co. He is a man of excellent business ability, and, like his father and grandfather, has done much for the improvement of the community in which he lives in many ways, and, with other things, has done a great deal of building public roads. Socially, he affiliates with the Knights of Pythias, the Independent Order of Odd Fellows, the Royal Arcanum, and the F. & A. M., and, politically, he is a Republican.

In September, 1875, Mr. Harris was united in marriage to Miss Martha Foster, and their wedded life has been blessed by the advent of a family of eleven children, ten of whom are now living, and whose names are as follows: Martin Franklin, William Charles, Arthur L., Clara, Etta, Emma, Virgie, Nellie, George H., Earnest, and Clarence, who died when a child.

JOHN SCRUGGS, clerk of the county court of Grundy county, was born in Marion county, Tenn., on the Cumberland mountains, February 19, 1844, a son of Carter and Lucinda (Kilgore) Scruggs. The father was born in Anderson county, Tenn., July 2, 1810, and died February 1, 1866, at Altamont, Tenn.; and the mother was born in the Sequatchie valley, where Victoria now stands, March 20, 1820 and died at Beersheba Springs in April, 1884.

Carter Scruggs was a son of John Scruggs, who served under General Green in the Revolutionary war, and participated in the battle of Guilford court house, and other important engagements, and John Scruggs, the subject of our sketch, was on the same battlefield of Guilford court house in the Confederate army, during the Civil war. He died in Anderson county, Tenn., being one of the pioneers of that county. Carter Scruggs went to Marion county, Tenn., when a young man, and was married there, and in January, 1850, he moved to Altamont with his family. By occupation he was a farmer, mechanic and also a a saddler. He served one term as clerk of the circuit court, and also taught school for a time. He was a justice of the peace for many years, was chairman of the county court and tax assessor of the county. He and his wife were both members of the Methodist church, South, and he held several offices in the society to which they belonged. Politically he was originally a Whig, but later in life he joined the Democratic party. The Scruggs family is of Irish lineage, but our subject's mother was of Scotch descent. Mr. and Mrs. Carter Scruggs were the parents of a family of ten children, seven of whom are now living, and of whom we have the following record: Nancy, wife of Henry Overturf, a farmer and surveyor of Grundy county; John, the subject of this sketch; Sarah A., wife of J. C. Smith, a farmer of Grundy county; Martha B., wife of William Brown, a farmer of Warren county, Tenn.; James E., a farmer of Grundy county; William M., a farmer of Newton county, Mo., and Thomas J., also a farmer of Newton county, Mo. The deceased are: Milly, wife of William Lathrum, died at Beersheba Springs; George M. died in childhood; and one who died in infancy.

Our subject was educated in the academy at Altamont, and left school to join Company A, Thirty-fifth Tennessee Infantry, Pat Cleburn brigade. Company A was commanded by A. C. Hannah, and the regiment was commanded by B. J. Hill. Mr. Scruggs participated in the battles of Perryville, Ky., Murfreesboro, Tenn., Chickamauga and Atlanta, Missionary Ridge and Bentonville, N. C., but was sick with the measles when the battle of Shiloh was fought. He was also in numerous skirmishes and smaller engagements. At the last named battle, this command was cut to pieces, and Mr. Scruggs, upon his recovery, was transferred to Company D, commanded by Capt. John Macon. At the battle of Chickamauga he was knocked senseless by an exploding shell, and at the same battle fourteen bullet holes were shot in his clothes, but none of them touched him. More than fifty balls during the war penetrated his clothes. At the battle of Perryville, a spent ball struck his knee. He was appointed lieutenant of the company to which he belonged, but the war closed before he received his commission. He was, however, orderly sergeant for two years.

After the close of hostilities, he was employed for two years by Mr. H. B. Northcut as a salesman. He then taught school for a time, and in 1870, he was elected clerk of the county court and served three successive terms, being repeatedly re-elected. After leaving this office, he again engaged in selling goods and teaching school at Tracy City until 1894, when he was again elected clerk of the county court. He was also superintendent of the public schools of Grundy county for ten years. He is a member of the Methodist church, South, and is steward of the society in which he holds his membership, and recording secretary of the Altamont Mission. Socially he affiliates with the Masonic fraternity, and has represented Alto lodge, No. 474, at the grand lodge twice. He is also identified with the Independent Order of Odd Fellows at Tracy City, and has twice represented that lodge at the grand lodge. He also belongs to S. L. Freeman Camp, No. 884, U. C. V., Tracy City, Tenn. Politically he is a Democrat.

Mr. Scruggs was first married January 24, 1867, to Miss Winnie J. Walker, daughter of Zedekiah Walker. She was born in Grundy county, May 24, 1849, and died at Tracy City, Tenn., March 21, 1889. November 8, 1893, Mr. Scruggs married Bertha A. Freudenberg, daughter of John N. Freudenberg, and widow of Albert O'Leary, deceased. Mrs. Scruggs was born in Youngstown, Ohio, August 21, 1866, and came with her parents, when a child, to Tennessee and located in Hamilton county. Eight children were born to our subject's first marriage, four of whom are now living, as follows: James D., a farmer of Grundy county; Joseph H., a miner at Tracy City; Mary C., at home; and Laura Ann, wife of Dan Fults, a farmer of Grundy county. The deceased are: Fannie Lee died in infancy; John Carter also died quite young; Ida Jane died at the age of four years; and Nancy Alice, three and a half years old. To his last marriage have been born four children, viz: Twin sisters, Ida May and Adie Augusta, born August 7, 1894; Robert Bryan, born June 30, 1896; and William Clarence, born May 20, 1898. His present (as well as former) wife is a member of the Methodist church, South. He is much devoted to his wife and children, and commands the respect and esteem of all who know him.

————

CHARLES CARROLL MOORE is one of South Pittsburg's popular attorneys and holds quite a prominent position among the members of the bar of Marion county, both for his legal ability and his forensic power. He was born and reared and has spent the greater part of his life in the eastern part of Tennessee and has gained an enviable reputation, especially in the county in which he has been for a number of years an acting attorney.

Mr. Moore was born in the Eighth civil district, Marion county, Tenn., October 12, 1872, a son of George and Nancy Elizabeth (McDaniel) Moore. Both of these families are among the oldest in the county, and a brief history of the Moore family will appear in the sketch of N. B. Moore, on another page of this work. The McDaniel family moved from Scotland to the north of Ireland, and migrated from there, in an early day, to northern Virginia. David McDaniel was a soldier in the war of 1812, as were also six of his brothers. The father of this family was the first to land in America. David McDaniel moved from Virginia to White county, Tenn., in 1800, but not being suited with that locality, he sold out within a few years and moved to what is now the town of South Pittsburg, and there spent the remaining years of his life. He had a family of ten children, four of whom were sons, viz.: John, a farmer, died when quite young; Goodson; Walter was a minister in the North Alabama conference of the Methodist Episcopal church, South, for fifty-three years; and Andrew T., who died while quite young.

Goodson McDaniel, our subject's grandfather, was born in 1803, and died in 1887. He gained a classical education at a southern Virginia collegiate institution and through his own efforts. He was admitted to the bar, practiced law for a short time, but discontinued the practice of law for the work of the ministry. Joining the Holston conference of the Methodist Episcopal church, South, he was actively engaged in church work until the war, being stationed at Cleveland, Knoxville, and other important places. He afterward retired from the ministry, returned to Marion county and made his home in the Eighth district, on the south side of the river. He was a member of the county court, a Democrat in politics, and socially he was a member of the Olive Branch Masonic lodge at Jasper. He was for many years a teacher and many of the older citizens of the county acquired their education while attending the school over which he presided. His first wife was Naomi Young, a native of North Carolina, and whose brother was for several years a member of congress and was quite wealty. She was killed by a falling limb of a tree, and left a family of four children: William B., Mary Lucretia, Rachael Sophronia and Nancy Elizabeth. Mr. McDaniel subsequently married Rachael B. Longacre, a graduate of and a teacher in Martha Washington College, of Virginia. No children were born to this union. After her death Mr. McDaniel married Elizabeth Blevins, of Rising Fawn, Ga. She is still living and making her home in Rising Fawn.

George W. Moore, our subject's father, was born at Red Hill, Marion county, September, 1835. He received his education at Burritt College, Van Buren county, Tenn., working at various occupations to pay his way through school. He was a clerk in the store owned by Wash Tanner, at Jasper, for several years, and while there he met Miss McDaniel, who became his wife in 1858. After his marriage he began farming in the Eighth district, Marion county, and at that vocation was very successful. He has been justice of the peace and also register of deeds of the county. Both he and his wife are members of the McDaniel Chapel, M. E. church, South, which Mr. Moore rebuilt. The building had formerly been erected by Rev. Goodson McDaniel, for whom it was named, but was burned during the war by Federal troops. Mr. Moore is one of the trustees and the steward of the society in which he holds his membership and also holds an official position in the Holston conference. He belongs to the Olive Branch lodge of the Masonic fraternity, at Jasper, and in politics is identified with the Democratic party. Mr. and Mrs. George W. Moore are the parents of a family of four children, of whom our subject is the youngest, and of whom we have the following record: Goodson McDaniel, a farmer living near his father's farm; Ara Alto, wife of Rev. J. F. Wampler, of the Holston Conference, and is now stationed at Jacksboro, Tenn.; W. O., who is still living with his parents; and Charles Carroll, our subject.

Charles Carroll Moore attended the public school in the district in which his boyhood was spent and then entered the

Pryor Institute at Jasper. After leaving this institution he took a course at the U. S. Grant University at Athens, Tenn. He next entered the law department of the Cumberland University, at Lebanon, Tenn., from which he graduated in June, 1894, and at once formed a partnership with Colonel A. L. Spears, of Jasper, and commenced the practice of law. In October, 1894, he moved to South Pittsburg, where they have since been engaged in the practice of law, continuing his partnership with Colonel A. L. Spears. Our subject has been city attorney of this city and has also been tax attorney for the city. He is a member of the Knights of Pythias, has filled all the chairs in that lodge, and is the present post counsellor. He belongs to the Marion lodge, A. F. & A. M., at South Pittsburg, the Junior Order United American Mechanics, Woodmen of the World, and the Alpha Tau Omega, a college society, and Regents of the White Shield. Politically he is a Democrat.

———

BENJAMIN FRANKLIN PATTON, whose home is situated in the Fourteenth district, Marion county, near the city of South Pittsburg, is one of the popular and influential citizens of that community. He is operating a farm in the Fourteenth district, and is also interested in coal mining, teaming and contracting. Mr. Patton was born in Sweedens Cove, in Marion county, Tenn., May 29, 1858, a son of Judge William O. and Caroline (Raulston) Patton.

Judge Patton was a son of Robert Patton, who moved to Marion county in an early day, and whose wife bore the maiden name of Miss Raulston. Judge Patton made Marion county his home all his life. When a young man he engaged for a time in teaching school. He was later clerk of one of the courts and was also elected justice of the peace several times. He was chairman of the county court. The first judge was by appointment and W. O. Patton was the first elected judge in the county, and was serving in the capacity of county judge at the time of his death, January 25, 1893, when about fifty-five years of age. He was married in Sweden's Cove, and later moved to Chitty's Cove, thence to South·Pittsburg, and upon his election to the office of county judge, he moved to Jasper. His wife, who is still making her home in South Pittsburg, has been for twenty-five years a member of the Primitive Baptist church. The Judge was a member of the Independent Order of Odd Fellows, and in politics, affiliated with the Republican party. They were the parents of a family of five children: Benjamin Franklin, the subject of this sketch; R. B., a sketch of whom will appear on another page of this volume; W. M., a justice of the peace, and is a moulder in the stove works of South Pittsburg; Robert O., a moulder at South Pittsburg; and T. L., a bookkeeper at South Pittsburg.

Benjamin Franklin Patton, the subject of this sketch, spent his school days in Chitty's Cove and in Sweden's Cove, but principally in Sweden's Cove. At the age of eighteen he began farming and logging in Chitty's Cove, being thus engaged for two years. After raising a couple of crops, he again turned his attention to logging and followed that occupation in Chitty's Cove, on the mountain and on Battle Creek, in Doran's Cove and in Sweden's Cove. He then entered the employ of Fletcher Wesenburg & Co., serving in the commissary department of the construction company which was then building the line of railroad known as the Sparta Extension. He then went to Memphis, where he was married, and upon leaving that city he went back to South Pittsburg, and for a time operated a meat market. He then took a contract from R. M. Payne to deliver his coal which had to be hauled from South Pittsburg, for one year. For the following two years he had a contract to mine and deliver coal, and after that he and his brother, R. B. Patton, went in partnership into a general contracting business under the firm name of B. F. Patton & Co. Under this name they did an immense amount of contracting, and took some heavy contracts, among them being those of the stove works. In 1891 he opened the Patton mines at Needmore, and the following year he organized the Battle Creek Coal Co. He was the chief promoter of this company, was its first president and presided over it until April, 1897. This company has also done a very extensive business. Since April, 1897, he has been interested in the Patton mines, and has also turned his attention to farming. His home is very beautifully situated on the top of one of the Cumberland mountains and overlooks the city of South Pittsburg and the Tennessee and the Sequatchie valleys.

Mrs. Patton, who became the wife of our subject December 9, 1880, bore the

43

maiden name of Miss Clara Zweifel. She was reared and educated in Paris, France, and came to the United States in 1877 or 1878. To this congenial union have been born five children whose names in the order of their birth are as follows: William August, Raulie Scott, Wilhelmena, Lilly and Frank T. Mr. Patton affiliates with the fraternity of the Knights of Pythias, holding his membership in the Mystic Circle. Politically he is a Republican.

ROBERT A. PATTON, the present popular postmaster of South Pittsburg, Marion county, has been identified with the interests of that place since its origin, and has contributed to its material progress and prosperity to an extent equalled by but few of his fellow citizens. He early had the sagacity and prescience to discern the eminence which the future had in store for the thriving little city, and acting in accordance with the dictates of his faith and judgment, he reaped, in the fulness of time, the generous benefits, which are the just recompense of indomitable industry, spotless integrity and marvelous enterprise.

A native of Marion county, Mr. Patton was born in Sweeden's Cove, April 10, 1848, and is a son of Robert and Elizabeth (Roulston) Patton. During boyhood the father located in Sweeden's Cove, his parents, John and Elizabeth Patton, with their family, being its first settlers. Robert Patton, Sr., was a farmer by occupation, but also taught school for a time, served as justice of the peace many years, and filled the office of deputy tax collector of Marion county. He was an ardent Republican in politics, was a strong Union sympathizer, and had two sons, James R. and Samuel B., in the Federal service, both members of the Fifth Tennessee Cavalry, and the former, James R., died in the hospital at Murfreesboro, in 1863. The parents were consistent members of the Primitive Baptist church and died in that faith, the father February 24, 1886, at the age of seventy years, and the mother in October, 1876.

Their family consisted of twelve children, of whom eight are still living: Jane, the eldest daughter, married L. J. Beene, a prominent citizen of Sweeden's Cove; William O. married Caroline Roulston, and died in Jasper, Marion county, January 25, 1893, after having been elected judge of the county the previous August; James, previously mentioned, is the next of the family; John died in Mississippi some years ago; Samuel B. married Mary A. Roulston and resides in Jasper; Martha Ann married Sampson W. Roulston, an old resident of South Pittsburg, who died at that place August 2, 1896; Sallie I. married L. R. Lucas; Rhoda C. is the wife of R. C. Powell, of Knoxville, Tenn.; Tennessee is the wife of William R. Bible, of Battle Creek, Marion county; Laura T. married Dr. J. G. Lowber, of Philadelphia, Penn., and died in South Pittsburg, August 28, 1897; and Maggie is the wife of A. H. Blacklock, bookkeeper for the Tennessee Coal, Iron & Railroad Co., at Whitwell, Tenn.

Robert A. Patton, until he attained his majority, remained under the parental roof receiving a good practical education in the schools of Sweeden's Cove. On leaving home he first engaged in farming on his own ac-

count in Marion county, and then removed to Arkansas, locating near the line of the Choctaw nation. Later he lived in the Boston mountains of northwestern Arkansas, but after three years spent in that state he came to what is now South Pittsburg, Tenn. This was in 1875, and here he erected a little three-room cottage on the mountain side, becoming one of the first residents of the place. He took a contract to lay the railroad to the furnace and has since successfully engaged in contracting, not only in South Pittsburg but also in Whitwell, Tracy City and Cowan.

On the 25th of March, 1869, near Jasper, Mr. Patton led to the marriage altar Miss Pemmie C. White, a most excellent lady who has been to her husband a true helpmeet, and to her he attributes much of his success in life. She was born July 16, 1849, in Dadeville, Tallapoosa county, Ala., and is the daughter of Josephus H. and L. A. F. (Hearne) White. By her marriage she has become the mother of eight children, namely: James J., who married Annie Bowler, of Knoxville, Tenn., and resides in that city, being in the employ of the Louisville & Nashville railroad; Mary Elgin, wife of C. M. Hash, a native of Rock Island, White county, Tenn., and a resident of South Pittsburg, who is in the employ of the Nashville & Chattanooga railroad; Bessie, wife of L. K. Downing, a native of Ohio, who is interested in the South Pittsburg Pipe Works; Robert M., who is with his father in the post office; Angus, the youngest daughter, who is now serving as assistant postmaster; and Maurice V., Harry White and Jean Sloan, who are all at home. The wife and mother is a worthy member of the Primitive Baptist church.

Fraternally Mr. Patton is a member of the Masonic order, the Knights of Pythias, and the Heptasophs. Since attaining his majority he has taken an active part in promoting the interests of the Republican party, which he always supports by his ballot, and recently, through the recommendation of his friends, among them the Hon. H. Clay Evans, now commissioner of pensions, he was appointed postmaster of South Pittsburg. The prompt and able discharge of his official duties has won the commendation of the many patrons of the office, and if possible has increased the circle of his friends, which is extensive.

CAPTAIN JAMES W. McREYNOLDS, one of the most prosperous and substantial farmers as well as one of the leading and highly respected citizens of the Eighth district of Marion county, is a native of Tennessee, born February 19, 1836, in Bledsoe county, three miles south of Pikeville, and is a son of Samuel and Mary Jane (Hale) McReynolds. The father was a native of Virginia and during boyhood was taken by his father, Samuel McReynolds, Sr., to Bledsoe county, being among the first settlers of the valley. Samuel McReynolds, Jr., was a very successful farmer and stock raiser, and was probably the most prosperous citizen of Bledsoe county at that time. He died on our subject's birthday, February 19, 1865, on the farm now occupied by I. S. McReynolds, and on the same day the Captain, whose command was

President Davis' escort, was forced to surrender near Washington, Ga. For several years the father was a member of the Masonic lodge at Pikeville, and was a Whig in politics and did not favor secession. He was twice married, his first wife being Miss Mary Jane Hale, a native of Blount county, Tenn., and a daughter of Alexander Hale. She died when our subject was a mere child, and the father afterward married Annie Stephens, a daughter of Isaac Stephens, of Bledsoe county. Her death occurred in 1869 or 1870.

By the first marriage the following children were born: Margaret, wife of Judge Frazier, of Davidson county, Tenn.; Alex H. and Samuel M., both farmers of Bledsoe county; Sarah, wife of Alexander Pope, a farmer of the same county; Claibourne D., farmer and stock raiser of Texas; and James W., of this sketch. The only one deceased is Mary J., who died in girlhood. By the second union the children are Isaac S., who lives on his father's old farm; Martha, wife of W. R. Pope, of Pikeville, Tenn.; T. S., also a farmer of Bledsoe county; and three who died in childhood.

Captain McReynolds attended school at Pikeville, and completed his literary education at Burritt college in 1854. He then engaged in farming in Bledsoe county until 1861, when he enlisted in Company I, Eight Tennessee Confederate Cavalry, being commissioned captain of his company, which was a part of Gen. Joseph Wheeler's command and was in many important engagements. He participated in the campaign in West Tennessee, was in the engagement at Parkers Cross Roads, and the battle of Chickamauga, and the engagement at the

Salt Works in Virginia. He was in the retreat from Chickamauga to Atlanta, and when the war was over returned home. During the siege of Knoxville he was taken prisoner, but a few hours later was re-captured by his own command, and for nearly a month he was one of President Davis' escorts.

In the fall of 1865 Captain McReynolds went to San Antonio, Texas, making that place his headquarters while engaged in the stock business for three years, and then began driving ponies overland from that state to East Tennessee, and as it proved a profitable business, he continued in the same for four years. At the end of that time he came to Marion county, where he now owns seven hundred acres of very fine farming land on the south side of the Ten-nessee river in the Eighth district. His farm should be named Grand View, as from the front steps of his residence he has a splendid view of his large farm, and the Tennessee river and the mountains on the opposite side help to make the prospect a most delightful one. Besides his valuable property the Captain owns other fine farms. Upon his home place is the entrance of the famous Nicojack Cave, which is probably as large as Mammoth Cave of Kentucky, and during early days was a rendezvous of the Indians. Colonel Holt was buried near the entrance of the cave and during the Civil war quite a battle was fought near there and Colonel Orr, a Federal commander, was killed.

On November 26, 1872, Captain Mc-Reynolds was united in marriage with Miss Martha Graham, who was born in Marion county, in 1851, and is a daughter of Pope Graham. They have three children and the only son, Hope, still lives with his parents. Joe and Jim were twins, and the former is now the wife of J. P. Howard, but Miss Jim died in 1894. The parents hold member-ship in the Methodist Episcopal church, South, and in social circles occupy an en-viable position. The Captain is a Democrat in politics, and for twelve years was a prom-inent member of the county court.

ALFRED K. STANDEFER, one of the leading and highly-esteemed agricult-urists of Sequatchie county, was born in Bledsoe county, Tenn., February 24, 1849, and is a worthy representative of one of the oldest and most distinguished families of the Sequatchie valley, his grandfather, James Standefer, and Amos Griffith being among the first settlers here. The latter was born April 19, 1779, and his wife, Patsy Stan-defer, was born January 19, 1783. They were the parents of six children, namely: William S., who was born in 1801, and was a child of five years when brought by his parents to the valley; Luke C., a United States soldier, who was born November 3, 1810, and it is supposed was killed by the Indians; Jesse H., born September 3, 1812; Skelton Carroll, born April 12, 1815; James M., born October 6, 1817; and Eliza Ann, born August 31, 1820. The father of these children was one of the most prominent men of this region, and for two terms he repre-sented his district in the United States con-gress. While on the way to Washington, he died suddenly at Kingston, Roane county, Tenn., August 20, 1837, and his wife departed this life June 15, 1848.

Skelton Carroll Standefer, our subject's father, was born just above the Pope place in Bledsoe county, and has spent his entire life in the Sequatchie valley. He was probably a Whig in early life, but since the Civil war has given his allegiance to the Democracy. He was a soldier in both the Florida and Mexican wars, and is a man highly respected by all who know him. He married Nancy Kane, and the children born to them are as follows: Martha, wife of a Mr. Hornsby, of Yell county, Ark.; Pernina, wife of J. P. Minton, of the same county; Sarah, wife of Josiah Jones, of Clarksville, Tenn.; Polly, widow of John Johnson, and a resident of Dunlap, Tenn.; Lucy, wife of Patrick Lamb, of Dunlap; William, a farmer of Bledsoe county; Alfred K., of this sketch; Tabitha, who married Cass Bice, and died in Texas; and Thomas, who died in Bledsoe county, Tenn.

On leaving the parental roof, at the age of seventeen years, Alfred K. Standefer went to live with the Pope family on the Alex. Pope land, remaining with them until his marriage, Miss Julia Elliott becoming his wife January 28, 1869. She was born October 15, 1847, a daughter of William B. Elliott, a prominent citizen of Sequatchie county, and she died October 28, 1893. Thirteen children were born to Mr. and Mrs. Standefer, as follows: Jane, now the wife of Josiah Harmon, of the Second district of Sequatchie county; Mattie, wife of J. T. Wheeler; John, a farmer of the Second district; Margaret, wife of William Whitlow; Lila, wife of Daniel Boyd; Pernina, wife of Isham Kenner; Myrtle, wife

of Lewis Cordell; Carroll, Ada and Ida, all at home; and William A., Nancy and Florence, all deceased. Mr. Standefer was again married March 18, 1893, his second union being with Miss Polly Monnahan, who was born October 7, 1868, and is a daughter of Daniel Monnahan. Two children graced this union, Phœbe and Rachel, the latter now deceased.

Mr. Standefer prefers living on the Cumberland mountains, and about fifteen years ago he purchased his present farm, to which he removed the following year, making it his home ever since. He deserves great credit for the success that he has achieved in life, for he started out empty-handed, and has succeeded in accumulating a comfortable competence through his own unaided efforts.

REV. ANDREW J. WILLIS, a well-known minister of the Primitive Baptist church, and a prominent citizen of South Pittsburg, Marion county, Tenn., was born July 1, 1849, in Jackson county, Ala., near the Tennessee state line, and is a son of Samuel and Elizabeth (Matthews) Willis, both of whom were born in Hawkins county, upper east Tennessee. The father was born in 1803, and was a son of Larkin Willis and wife, who was a Miss Wilson prior to her marriage. Our subject's mother was some years younger than her husband and in early life went to Jackson county, Ala., with her parents, James and Elizabeth (Hardin) Matthews. Her father was a very successful farmer and at one time owned all of Crow Valley, Jackson county, Ala. In 1823 was celebrated the marriage of Samuel Willis and Elizabeth Matthews, and of the fourteen children born to them the following reached man and womanhood. (1) Larkin, a veteran of the Mexican war, was for many years connected with the Nashville & Chattanooga railroad; was warden of the Alabama State penitentiary; and died in Jackson county, that state. (2) George W., also deceased, was a farmer of that county and was a soldier in the Confederate army. (3) Frances is the widow of W. W. Anderson, who was a farmer of Franklin county, Tenn., where she still resides. (4) James was a member of Bragg's army, and being taken sick with measles was sent home, where his death occurred. (5) Michael was a teacher of ability, who died in Franklin county, Tenn., at the age of twenty-one years. (6) Wilson was also in the Confederate service and is now a farmer of Franklin county. (7) Andrew J. is the next of the family. (8) Alfred is a Cumberland Presbyterian minister, now located in Jackson county, Ala. The father of these children, who was a farmer by occupation, died in 1862, and the mother passed away ten years later, honored and respected by all who knew them.

Andrew J. Willis attended Cecilian College, of Hardin county, Ky., in 1868, 1869 and 1870, thus completing his literary education. At the age of sixteen years he united with the Primitive Baptist church, two years later commenced preaching, and has now for thirty-two years labored as a minister of the gospel. He has preached in all the churches of his denomination within a radius of one hundred miles from his home; had charge of the Crow Valley church twenty years; the Sweden's Cove fifteen years; and now has charge of the churches at Jasper and South Pittsburg. He has been an untiring worker in the Master's vineyard, has received many into the church and has married thousands. For the past four years he has most creditably served as justice of the peace, and on his removal from Jackson county, Ala., to South Pittsburg in 1890, he was the choice of many for the office of postmaster. Politically he is a Republican, and socially is a member of the Woodmen of the World and the American Guild.

On the 25th of December, 1870, Mr. Willis was united in marriage with Miss Eliza, daughter of Rev. James Wagner, of Franklin county, Tenn., and they have become the parents of nine children, as follows: Mary, wife of a Mr. McCallis, of South Pittsburg; James S., who died in childhood; Rena Viola, wife of D. C. Janey, of South Pittsburg; and Luke W., Thomas Arthur, Willie Hudson, Alice Ethel, Ynectker and Ruth Falley, all at home.

ISAAC CLINTON MORGAN, M. D.— Among those who devote their time and energies to the practice of medicine and have gained a leading place in the ranks of the profession is Dr. Morgan, who is the only physician of Cummingsville, Van Buren county. He was born in Polk county, Ga., January 8, 1838, and is a son of J. D. and Martha A. (Payne) Morgan, both of whom were natives of South Carolina, but were married in Hall county, Ga., and later became residents of Polk county, that state, where they spent their last days, the father dying at the age of seventy years, the mother at the age of forty. The elder Mr. Morgan was twice married, his second wife being Nannie E. Crabb, a Georgian by birth, who is still living on the old homestead in Polk county, Ga. He was of Dutch descent, was a life long farmer, but also engaged in merchandising for some time. Originally he was a Whig in politics, but on the dissolution of that party affiliated with the Republicans. Religiously he was an earnest member of the Missionary Baptist church.

Dr. Morgan is the oldest of the nine children, three sons and six daughters, born of the first marriage, the others being as follows: A. L., a mechanic of Polk county, Ga.; Joseph, who was recently killed in Arkansas; Josephine, a resident of Mississippi; Nancy E., of Polk county, Ga.; Martha, of Van Buren county, Tenn.; Mary, of Chattanooga; Elliott, of White county, Tenn.; Cynthia, of Polk county, Ga.; and Lee Ella Alice, of the same place. The children born of the second marriage are B. E., a farmer of Polk county, Ga.: Newton, a farmer, who died in that county, leaving a family; Orvin, who grew to manhood and died in the same county; E. A., who lives on the old homestead; R. J., a Baptist minister of Oklahoma; Lena, of Van Buren county, Tenn.; Cora, of Floyd county, Ga.; and Dela, of Texas.

In the public schools of Cassville, Ga., and at Cassville College, Dr. Morgan acquired his literary education. He commenced the study of medicine with Dr. J. L. Flannagan as his preceptor, and later attended lectures at the medical college of Macon, Ga. He began the practice of his chosen profession in his native county, but in 1857 came to VanBuren county, Tenn., where he soon built up a large and lucrative practice which he still enjoys.

On the 5th of February, 1856, the Doctor was united in marriage with Miss Lucinda E. Cummings, who was born in VanBuren county, in 1837, a daughter of Burrell Cummings, and died May 3, 1884. Seven children were born of this union, namely: Joseph D., a prominent physican of Fort Wayne, Ind., who has represented Allen county in the Indiana state senate; Sarah L., widow of W. C. Haston, Jr., and a resident of White county, Tenn.; Isaac C., Jr., deputy sheriff of Hamilton county, Tenn.; Maggie, wife of James Stipe, a farmer of White county, Tenn.; John L., who is connected with the street railway of Chattanooga; Marion P., a telegraph operator at Dickson, Ohio; and M. B., who is attending Burritt College. Dr. Morgan was again married, January 28, 1885, his second union being with Miss Virginia Brady, a daughter of Colonel Brady, and to them have been born five children: Emma H., Anna J., Brady, Virginia J. and Charles, all at home.

In July, 1861, Dr. Morgan enlisted in Company C, Thirty-fifth Tennessee Confederate Infantry, as lieutenant, but at the end of a year was transferred to the Fifth Tennessee Cavalry as surgeon of the regiment, serving as such until hostilities ceased. He was slightly wounded at the battle of Shiloh, and besides participating in that engagement he was in the battles of Murfreesboro, Parker's Cross Roads and Stone River. At one time he was held a prisoner for a few minutes. After the war he returned to Cummingsville and resumed the practice of medicine. He is the only physician in VanBuren county, and is a prominent member of the Upper Cumberland Medical Society and the State Medical Association (Eclectic) of Nashville. He established the postoffice at Cummingsville, served as postmaster twenty-five years, but being a Republican he was out of office during President Cleveland's administration, though he has since been re-appointed. Religiously he is a consistent member of the Methodist church, and socially belongs to the Masonic order, being past master of his lodge, and is also connected with the Independent Order of Odd Fellows and the encampment at Onward, where he has served as grand chief patriarch.

THOMAS SHOEMATE.—Bledsoe county has many well-to-do and successful farmers who have accumulated what they have of this world's goods through individual effort. Among this class the name of the subject of this notice is entitled to a place. He was born September 18, 1834, upon the farm which he now owns and operates, it being pleasantly situated in the Seventh district, four miles below Pikeville. Here he is industriously engaged in the prosecution of his noble calling, and is meeting with far more than ordinary success.

His parents were William and Hannah Shoemate, the former of whom died before the birth of our subject. At the age of seventeen years he started out in life for himself, and his mother lived with him, dy-

ing at his home in 1883, at the advanced age of ninety-one years. The Shoemate family came to the Sequatchie valley from upper East Tennessee, and has since been identified with the interests of this region.

During his boyhood Thomas Shoemate attended school in the neighborhood of his home, and for one term was a student in a boarding school conducted near the present home of Clay Greer. At the beginning of his business career he worked for J. C. Roberson at eight dollars per month and remained with that gentleman as manager of his farm for fourteen years. Since then he has purchased one thousand acres of his former employer, and being energetic, economical and industrious, he has become one of the most prosperous and substantial citizens of the district.

Prior to the Civil war Mr Shoemate married Miss Rachel Keasey, a native of Bledsoe county, who died in 1883, leaving two sons, namely: R. B., a business man of South Pittsburg, Tenn.; and L. M., a farmer of Bledsoe county. For eighteen years Mr. Shoemate was a prominent member of the county court from the Seventh district, and in his political affiliations has always been a stalwart Democrat.

JAMES MASON COTNAM, M. D., is engaged in the practice of medicine and surgery in South Pittsburg, Marion county, Tenn., and has that love for and devotion to his profession which has brought to him success and won him a place among the ablest representatives of the medical fraternity in this locality.

The Doctor was born in Grundy county, Tenn., February 6, 1847, and is a son of Dr. Thomas T. and Elizabeth (Doran) Cotnam, who were both of Irish parentage. The father was born in Limestone county, Ala., in 1822, and died in December, 1884, while the mother was born in Franklin county, Tenn., probably in 1822, and died July 14, 1895. When a young man, Thomas Cotnam attended college at Portersville, Ala., and subsequently entered the medical department of the old Nashville University, from which he was graduated in 1846. Opening an office at Hawkersville, Grundy county, Tenn., he engaged in practice at that place for a few years, and then removed to Stephenson, Jackson county, Ala. In the latter place he successfully followed his profession until life's labors were ended. During the Civil war he served for nearly three years as surgeon of the Fourth Alabama Cavalry, which was General Forrest's original command, and was with that general all the time he was in the service, but finally had to resign on account of ill health. He was one of the most prominent citizens of his community, and represented Jackson county, Ala., in the state legislature a number of times. He was a Royal Arch Mason and often represented his lodge in the grand lodge of the state. He also belonged to the Independent Order of Odd Fellows, was an ardent Democrat in politics, and, religiously, both he and his wife were sincere and earnest members of the Methodist Episcopal church, South, with which he was officially connected. In their family were ten children, five sons and five daughters, of whom seven are still living, namely: Tennessee E., wife of Jones C. Beene, of South

44

Pittsburg, whose sketch appears elsewhere in this work; James M., of this review; W. W., a resident of Indian Territory; Ida, widow of R. P. Beene, and a resident of South Pittsburg; Maggie, wife of John Duncan, of southern Alabama; Narcissa, wife of W. E. Carter, bookkeeper for the Tennessee Coal, Iron & Railroad Co., at South Pittsburg. Those deceased are Louise, who died in childhood; Gilbert C., a ranchman of Texas, who died at the age of forty-two years; and A. B., a physician of South Pittsburg, who died at the age of thirty-five.

The subject of this sketch was attending the Military Academy at La Grange, Ala., when the Civil war broke out, and in 1862 he ran away from school to join the Confederate army, enlisting in Company E, Third Confederate Cavalry, which was made up of troops from Alabama, Georgia, Tennessee and Texas. He was the youngest soldier in the regiment, but was one of the bravest and most daring. He participated in the battles of Murfreesboro, Fort Donelson and Chickamauga, the siege of Knoxville, which lasted three months, and was with the army on the retreat to Atlanta. After the surrender of General Lee, the regiment disbanded in South Carolina and Dr. Cotnam returned home. He then attended Lebanon College, at Lebanon, Ala., and, on leaving school in 1867, he commenced studying medicine under the direction of his father. In 1872 he graduated with honor at the Louisville Medical College, and was given a place in the United States Hospital at Louisville, where he remained until 1874, when he returned to his old home in Stephenson, Ala., and entered into partnership with his father. Two years later, however, he came to South Pittsburg, Tenn., and soon succeeded in building up an extensive practice, which he still enjoys. He was physician for the Southern States Coal, Iron & Land Co., and then for the Tennessee Coal, Iron & Railroad Co. for a long time. Fraternally, he is a prominent member of the Tri-State Medical Society, the South Pittsburg Medical Society, the Knights of Pythias lodge, and is captain of the Eighteenth Division of the Uniformed Rank, Knights of Pythias. In his political affiliations he is a Democrat, and, religiously, both he and his wife hold membership in the Methodist Episcopal church, South.

On the 11th of December, 1873, Dr. Cotnam was united in marriage with Miss Avis Ellen Jones, a native of Jackson county, Ala., and a daughter of Willis Jones.

THOMAS E. WILSON, a well-known and prominent citizen of Cumberland county, Tenn., was born February 18, 1863, and is a great-grandson of Greenberry Wilson, a native of Buncombe county, N. C., who was the first of the family to locate in the Sequatchie Valley, having as early as 1803 taken up his residence on Wilson's Branch, which was named in his honor. He there built the second house erected in the valley, it being constructed of cedar, and it is now occupied by his grandson, Charles B. Wilson. He was an old man on coming to this region, and in the home above mentioned his death occurred. He was one of the heroes of the Revolutionary war, having valiantly aided the colonies in their struggle for independence. In his family were two sons, Charles B. and Greenberry. The latter was a soldier of the war of 1812, and afterward settled in Morgan county, Ala., where he entered a large tract of land and extensively engaged in the stock business, becoming quite wealthy.

His son, Charles B. Wilson, remained in the valley and died in 1851, in the house erected by his father. By his first marriage he had two sons, Greenberry and William, who went west in 1840, stopping first in Missouri, but later proceeding to California and finally to Oregon. William was a farmer and remained single, while Greenberry was a horse dealer and was married at the age of sixty years. For his second wife Charles B. Wilson married Louvassie McKinney, a native of Hawkins county, East Tennessee, whose death occurred in 1849. Their son, Charles B., Jr., is the present owner of the Wilson creek land. The family located at the head of the Sequatchie Valley on account of the fine soil and the excellent range for stock.

Charles B. Wilson, Jr., was born November 2, 1829, on the old homestead where he was reared to manhood, but later spent a number of years in Alabama. He has since returned to the old farm, however, and there continues to reside. In 1860 he married Miss Nancy Swafford, a daughter of "Big Tommy Swafford." She died in 1867, leaving three sons, Thomas E., whose name introduces this sketch; William G., a farmer of Bledsoe county, Tenn.; and James C., who died in Concho county, Tex., at the age of twenty-six years. In 1872 Mr. Wilson was again married, his second union being with Ellen Robertson, a native of Walker county, Ga., who died October

22, 1892. Five children were born to them: E. G., Mary H., Lula A. and Martha J., all living; and Nancy J., deceased. The father is one of the leading and highly respected ctziens of his community, and has been called upon to fill the offices of deputy sheriff and constable. Politically he is a Democrat, and socially is a member of the Masonic lodge at Melvine, which he once represented in the grand lodge of the state.

Thomas E. Wilson first opened his eyes to the light of day February 18, 1863, and during his boyhood pursued his studies in the Hickory Grove, Stony Point and Red Hill schools, and in them acquired a good practical education which has well fitted him for life's responsible duties. At the age of twenty-one years he commenced farming for himself on the place where he now lives, and for some time was also engaged in getting out walnut logs for the Strawbridge company. He got out many thousand feet of lumber, working in the mountains all the time. Since then he has devoted his energies principally to farming and stock raising.

On the 14th of February, 1884, Mr. Wilson was united in marriage with Miss Martha A. Davenport, a daughter of Clabe Davenport, and they now have an interesting family of five children: Nannie, James C., William Moses, Charles B. and Claiborne F. The wife and mother is a member of the Methodist Episcopal church, South.

Mr. Wilson has always taken an active part in politics, working hard for the success of the Democratic party, and in 1893 he was appointed revenue collector for the East Tennessee district, being recommended by John T. Essary to the internal revenue commissioner. Since then he has received the appointment as internal revenue gauger in a district comprising thirteen counties, and his services have been efficient and given entire satisfaction.

CHRIS BAUMGARTNER.—The subject of this biography, one of the honored sons of Switzerland, and a well-known furniture dealer and undertaker of South Pittsburg, is pre-eminently a self-made man. He began life with a definite purpose in view, worked faithfully, honestly, and with a will for its accomplishment, and is now one of the leading and prosperous business men of Grundy county.

Mr. Baumgartner was born in Berne, Switzerland, April 19, 1856, and is a son of John and Annie (Neuashwander) Baumgartner, also natives of that country, where the father served as a sharpshooter in the regular army for some time. With their family of eight children the parents came to the United States in 1868 and settled in Allegheny, Pa., but the father and sons worked in a glass factory in Pittsburg. In 1873 they came south and the father was the first of the Swiss to buy land in Grundy county, Tenn., purchasing one hundred acres, on which his family located the following year. About 1877 or 1878 he moved to South Pittsburg, Tenn., where he died in 1886, at the age of fifty-four years, and his wife passed away in 1892, at the age of sixty-four. They were faithful members of the Lutheran church. In their family were the following children: Mary, now the wife of

John Zwald, formerly with the Tennessee Coal, Iron & Railroad Co.; John, a carpenter of Brunswick, Ga.; Chris, the subject of this sketch; Charles, a butcher of Brunswick, Ga.; Jacob, a molder, of Birmingham, Ala.; Fred, a truck farmer of Brunswick, Ga.; Nicholas, who until recently was in the grocery and butcher business at South Pittsburg, Tenn.; Henry, a machinist, of Jackson, Tenn.; and one daughter, who died in childhood.

The subject of this review attended school in Switzerland, where he learned to read and write German, and his education was completed by attending night school in Allegheny, Pa., and at South Pittsburg, Tenn. Coming to the latter place in 1876, he worked for T. A. Graham at the carpenter's trade until 1891, when he embarked in business on his own account as an undertaker and furniture dealer. Since then he has taken a course in embalming at Atlanta, Ga., and for the past three years has also engaged in the livery business with good success.

On the 14th of October, 1880, Mr. Baumgartner was united in marriage with Miss Callie Chambers, who was born in Cleveland, Tenn., April 15, 1858, a daughter of Robert Chambers. She was a most estimable lady, a consistent member of the Cumberland Presbyterian church, and died in that faith July 5, 1897. She left a family of six children, namely: Fred, Gertrude, Walter, Ida, Grace and Callie. Mr. Baumgartner is also a leading member of the Cumberland Presbyterian church at South Pittsburg, in which he serves as deacon, and in political sentiment is a stanch Republican.

THOMAS FLEMING WEAVER, a highly respected citizen and well-known mine foreman at No. 10, Tennessee Coal & Iron mines, at Tracy City, is a native of Alabama, born in Cherokee county, February 25, 1855, and is a son of William and Martha Jane (Hill) Weaver, who were born, reared and married in North Carolina and moved to Alabama before the birth of our subject. In 1874, they became residents of Tracy City, where the father died two years later at the age of sixty, and the mother passed away at Pelham, Tenn., in 1878, at the age of fifty-five years. The father was always a farmer by occupation and was very successful, but lost heavily during the war. In political sentiment he was a Democrat, and in religious faith both he and his wife were Missionary Baptists, taking an active part in the work of the church in which he served as deacon. Our subject is the youngest of their five children, all of whom are still living with the exception of Rufus, who died in childhood. Eliza is the widow of David Lindsey, who was killed during the Civil war, and she is now a resident of Mount Eagle, Grundy county; Martha Jane is the wife of William Troy, of Franklin county, Tenn.; and Samuel, formerly a coal miner, is now a farmer of Bevier, Kentucky.

The schools of Tracy City afforded Thomas F. Weaver his educational privileges, and when his school days were over he sought employment in the mines at that place, driving mules for the first five years. The following eight years were spent on a farm at Pelham, Grundy county, but at the end of that period he returned to Tracy City, and was engaged in digging coal at

No. 1 for a time. He was next stable boss of the mines and afterward dug coal at No. 2, East Fork. For two years he had charge of convict laborers, but for the past two years has been mine foreman at No. 10. He has thoroughly mastered every branch of the mining business and is thus well qualified to hold the responsible position which he now so ably fills.

In 1882 Mr. Weaver led to the marriage altar Miss Florence Burroughs, who was born at Burroughs Cove, and is a daughter of Dick Burroughs. They have three children living: Hallie H., Nina and Lucile, and one deceased, Daniel J., who died at the age of two years and two months. For eleven years Mr. Weaver has been a consistent member of the Methodist Episcopal church, South, in which he has served as steward for six years. Socially he affiliates with the Independent Order of Odd Fellows, in which he has held office; and politically is identified with the Democratic party. As a business man and citizen he is justly entitled to the high regard in which he is uniformly held.

MAJOR JEPTHA BRIGHT is one of the most prominent and progressive business men of South Pittsburg, and has won for himself an eminent position at the bar of Marion county. He is a native of Kentucky, born on a farm in Shelby county, September 14, 1862, and is a son of Newton and Dorcas (Helm) Bright, who are, also, natives of that county and now make their home in Eminence, Ky., though the father still carries on farming in Shelby.

county. The Bright family was originally from Holland and went to England with William, Prince of Orange, afterwards William III., of Great Britain. Subsequently two brothers came to America, one settling in Virginia, the other in North Carolina, and from the latter our subject is descended. His grandfather, Jeptha Bright, was also an agriculturist. Aside from voting, Newton Bright never took a very active part in political affairs in early life, but in 1892 he consented to become the candidate of the Democratic party for the state legislature, and was elected by a large majority. While a member of that body he served on the railroad and agricultural committees. For many years he has also served as justice of the peace. He is a graduate of Bethany College, West Virginia, is a well-posted man, and it his religion to be honest and do right, while his wife holds membership in the Christian church.

In the family of this worthy couple were seven children: Charles, who is in the United States Revenue service in Kentucky; Coleman, a farmer of Shelby county, Ky.; Jeptha, of this sketch; George R., wife of A. D. Hudson, a wholesale liquor dealer of Mt. Sterling, Ky.; James C., a tobacco broker at Shelbyville, Ky.; Newton, who is in a commercial establishment at Louisville, Ky.; and Walter, who died in childhood.

Major Bright began his education in a school house built by his father and a few others in the neighborhood of their homes for the benefit of their children, and later in life he pursued his studies in the Kentucky University at Lexington. After teaching for two years, he commenced reading law and in 1885 entered the Louisville Law School from which he graduated in 1887. Prior to entering that institution he served as city attorney of Eminence, Ky. After his graduation he came to South Pittsburg and was the first attorney to open an office in that city. He has since taken a very active and prominent part in the development of the city; was one of the organizers of the Schoster foundry and also the Blacklock foundry, and is a member of the board of directors of both concerns. As a lawyer he has built up quite an extensive and lucrative practice, and from 1891 until 1895 served as tax attorney for Marion county. He was the first city attorney for South Pittsburg, and is now filling the office of city recorder to the entire satisfaction of all concerned.

On the 10th of September, 1888, Mr. Bright was united in marriage with Miss Teresia Marie Fitzgerald, who was born in Nicaraugua, Central America, and was educated on the Island of Trinidad. Mr. Bright has always been quite a prominent and influential member of the Democratic party in his community, and socially is a member of the Knights of Pythias fraternity. He has for eight years represented the local lodge in the grand lodge, and is now grand prelate of the grand lodge of Tennessee. He also belongs to the uniformed rank, and is major of the Third Tennessee Regiment Knights of Pythias Infantry.

THOMAS J. AUSTIN, an industrious and thrifty farmer residing in the Ninth district of Bledsoe county, is a native of Tennessee, born in Sequatchie county August 4, 1849, and is a son of Elijah F. and Phœbe (Minton) Austin. The father was born in Powell Valley, Claibourne county, Tenn., in 1818, and was a son of Jonathan Austin, who was very likely a Virginian by birth. Our subject's great-grandfather was an Englishman, who came to America and joined Washington's army, serving through the Revolutionary war, after which he located in Virginia and there spent the remainder of his life. Elijah F. Austin was the owner of a fine farm in the Ninth district of Bledsoe county, just above Mt. Airy, and was a most successful farmer and stock raiser. He was a Jeffersonian Democrat in political sentiment, and both he and his wife were earnest and faithful members of the Primitive Baptist church. She was born about the same year in which her husband's birth occurred, and is still living. In their family were nine children, namely: Joseph B., a farmer living in the upper part of Sequatchie county; Rebecca, wife of Henry Cagle, of the Ninth district of Bledsoe county; William T., of the upper part of Sequatchie county; Thomas J., of this review; John B., James H. and Joel B., all farmers of the Ninth district of Bledsoe county; and J. L., who was born in 1861, and died at the age of twenty-nine years.

Reared upon the home farm, Thomas J. Austin received his education in the schools of the neighborhood, and early in life became familiar with all the duties which fall to the lot of the agriculturist. On the 22d of July, 1869, at the age of twenty years, he was united in marriage with Miss Sarah Hale, who was born near Pikeville, in Bledsoe county, October 17, 1849, and is a daughter of Rev. James Hale. Of the ten children that blessed this union, eight are still living. They are as follows: J. L , a successful teacher of Johnson county, Texas; E. F., a merchant and barber of the same county; Frances A., wife of J. T. Southerland, a farmer of the First district of Bledsoe county; O. S., who died at the age of fourteen years; Leona E., Walter Cleveland, Melvine, Mabel and Monroe; all at home; and Joseph, who died in childhood.

At the time of his marriage Mr. Austin commenced farming upon his father's place, and in 1885 removed to his present farm, where he has two hundred acres of valuable and well-tilled land, under a high state of cultivation and improved with an elegant residence and substantial outbuildings. By his ballot he always supports the men and measures of the Democratic party, and is one of the most public-spirited and progressive citizens of his district. His estimable wife holds membership in the Missionary Baptist church.

G EORGE FOSTER BROWN, an expert machinist in the employ of the Tennessee Coal, Iron & Railroad Company, at South Pittsburg, was born in Philadelphia, Penn., January 27, 1851, and is a son of George Foster and Jane (Beck) Brown, both natives of England, the former born in the city of Durham, September 12, 1817, the latter in Leeds, Yorkshire, November 1, 1819. Our subject has inherited his ability as a machinist from his father and also his grandfather, Foster Brown, who was a cabinetmaker and also worked with machinery.

In their native land the parents of our subject were married and there they continued to reside until after the birth of their oldest child. It was in 1838 that they crossed the ocean and took up their residence in Philadelphia, Penn., where they made their home until 1856. In that year they came to Loudon, Tenn., but two years later removed to Chattanooga. The father had learned the machinist's trade in shops of Leeds, England, and in Philadelphia went to work for his uncle, who was operating a machine shop, manufacturing heavy sugar machinery for planters in Cuba, and after a time commenced business for himself, but was obliged to close out during the panic of 1847. He then worked in the navy yard at Baltimore for a time, and was afterward examining machinist for the Philadelphia & Savannah steamship line. For a time he was connected with extensive iron works at Richmond, Va., and was sent to Loudon, Tenn., to put in operation the rolling mills at that place. As that venture did not prove a success, he went to Chattanooga and entered the service of the Chattanooga Foundry & Machine shop, afterward known as the Webster Foundry & Machine shop. During the Civil war he was employed by the Federal government as a master mechanic to take charge of the railroad shops at Chattanooga, and later was employed as foreman by Thomas Webster. Socially, he was a Mason; politically a Democrat; and religiously both he and his wife were devout members of the Methodist Episcopal church. He died on his birthday in 1889, and his wife died October 29, 1896, and was buried on her birthday. They were the parents of nine children, six sons and three daughters, but only two are now living—George Foster, and Sarah Jane, widow of Robert Giles, who was in the auction and commission business in Chattanooga, but she now resides in Nashville. Those deceased are William T., who was born in Leeds, England, and died in Philadelphia, Penn., at the age of twelve years; John T., who died in the same city at the age of five years; Charles, who died in Chattanooga at the age of two; William T., who died in Chattanooga in infancy; and Mary E., who was born in Philadelphia, became the wife of John T. Saunders and died in Chattanooga.

During his boyhood and youth, Mr. Brown, of this sketch, attended both public and private schools in Chattanooga, and in 1866 he commenced learning the machinist's trade under his father in the Webster Machine shops of that city, where he remained nine years. The following eighteen months he was employed in the Alabama & Chattanooga railroad shops, and in 1876 came to South Pittsburg, Tenn., in the interest of the Southern States Iron, Coal & Land Company, which afterward sold out to the Tennessee Coal, Iron & Railroad Company, by whom he is now employed. He assisted in the erection of the first engines and boilers for the plant, and remained with the company until 1889, when he returned to Chattanooga and was foreman of the Wagner Machine shops for six years. At the end of that period he returned to South Pittsburg, and again entered the service of the Tennessee Coal, Iron & Railroad Company, of which he is still a trusted and faithful employe.

On the 3d of October, 1872, Mr. Brown led to the marriage altar Miss Lizzie Cowart, a native of Chattanooga, and a daughter of John Cowart. They are leading and prominent members of St. Elmo Methodist Episcopal church, South, and he affiliates with the Ancient Order of United Workmen. In politics he is an independent Democrat, and was one of the first alderman elected in South Pittsburg.

BLACKSTONE OREGON HILLIS.— Honored and respected by all, there is no man in Van Buren county who occupies a more enviable position in agricultural and political circles than Mr. Hillis, who is now the efficient and popular register of deeds of the county. He possesses untiring energy, is quick of perception, forms his plans readily and is determined in their execution, and his close application to business and excellent management have brought to him the prosperity which is to-day his.

On Rocky river, in the Eighth district, upon the farm where he now lives, Mr. Hillis was born March 12, 1854, a son of Isaac and Jane (Loge) Hillis. The father was born near Lexington, Ky., and was one of the first settlers on Rocky river, the country round about being then a vast cane brake. Bear was plentiful and deer and wild turkey abounded. Throughout life he followed the occupation of farming and was very successful. On coming to Van Buren county, he was accompanied by his brother, James Hillis. He was twice married, his first wife being Rebecca Naylor, who died many years ago. His death occurred March 9, 1877, in the house now occupied by our subject, when he was eighty-nine years of age. In politics he was a pronounced Democrat. The mother of our subject, who was a consistent member of the Christian church, was born on Rocky River, Van Buren county, and died here in 1891, at the age of seventy-seven years. By each wife the father had twelve children, but only eight of the twenty-four are now living, namely: Rebecca, widow of Chris Hager, and a resident of McLennon county, Texas; James, who lives at the head of Rocky River in Van Buren county; Roswell, whose home is also in that locality; Squire, a resident of Rocky River valley; Stephen, a farmer of Texas; L. H., who lives near our subject; W. P., who resides in the First district of Van Buren county; and Virginia, wife of Nelson R. Gully, a prominent farmer of this valley. The last three named, together with our subject, are children of the second marriage.

In the schools near his father's home, Blackstone O. Hillis obtained his education. At the age of sixteen years he began earning his own livelihood, and has since successfully engaged in general farming and stock raising, owning a fine farm in the valley and another in the mountains. He was married on the 11th of January, 1875, the lady of his choice being Miss Martha Denney, who was born on Laurel creek, and is a daughter of Preston Denney. To them were born three children, but Revedy is the only one now living, the others having died in infancy.

Since attaining his majority Mr. Hillis has been an ardent Democrat, and on that ticket was elected register of Van Buren county in 1896. His wife holds membership in the Christian church.

45

A J. KEELING, one of the leading and highly esteemed citizens of South Pittsburg, who now holds the responsible position of furnaceman for the Tennessee Coal, Iron & Railroad Co., was born in Walker county, Ga., March 27, 1853, and is a son of James and Mary (Griffin) Keeling, also natives of that county. The mother died in Nashville, Tenn., in 1865, when comparatively a young woman, and the father departed this life at South Pittsburg, in 1875, at the age of fifty-three years. The latter was a mechanic employed in the bridge department of the Memphis & Charleston railroad and later on the Nashville & Chattanooga railroad. He was an ardent Republican in politics and during the Civil war served for three years in the Tenth Tennessee Federal Infantry. In early life he removed from Alabama to Georgia; in 1861 went to Nashville, Tenn.; and in 1869 took up his residence in Marion county, where he spent his last days. Both he and his wife were members of the Baptist church and were held in high regard by all who knew them.

The subject of this sketch is the third in order of birth in their family of eight children, and was educated in the schools of Marion county. His studies were often interrupted, however, by work, for at an early age he entered the track department of the railroad company. Subsequently he engaged in farming for four years on the south side of the river in Marion county, and in 1875, when the Southern States Iron & Coal Co. was organized, he entered their employ at South Pittsburg, learning the business perfectly. When the Tennessee Coal, Iron & Railroad Co. bought the plant, he remained with them and twelve years ago was promoted to the responsible position that he is now so capably filling. He has three hundred men working under him and has the entire confidence and respect of the company.

In 1875 Mr. Keeling was united in marriage with Miss Sarah Horner, a native of Kentucky, and a daughter of Tobias Horner. She died in Marion county in 1884, leaving three children: James, who is with the Tennessee Coal, Iron & Railroad Co., and has charge of the iron yard; and Mary and Willie, both at home. Mr. Keeling was again married in 1886, his second union being with Miss Nannie Smith, who was born in Georgia, and is a daughter of Macajah Smith. One child, Nora, graces this union. The parents are both identified with the Cumberland Presbyterian church, while socially Mr. Keeling is also a member of the Masonic order, the Knights of Pythias and the Woodmen, and politically affiliates with the Democracy.

W R. HENSON, a prominent citizen of Sequatchie county, is a man whose successful struggle with adverse circumstances shows what can be done by industry and economy, especially if a sensible wife seconds his efforts to secure a home and competence. He was obliged to make his way in life without any of the aids which are usually considered essential to success, and is now the owner of a very fine farm, which he is successfully operating.

A native of Sequatchie county, he was born near where he now lives, January 7, 1835, and is a son of John and Zilpah (Cooper) Henson. The father was born in 1794, and died May 27, 1872, on the farm where our subject now resides. He was three times married, his first wife being Susie Thurman. After her death he married Mrs. Zilpah (Cooper) Keys, widow of Washington Keys, by whom she had three children, namely: Nancy, now the widow of Joseph Davis, and a resident of the valley; Julia, deceased wife of Charles Lewis; and Sallie, who married Robert D. Mitchell and died in Polk county, Tenn. The subject of this sketch is the oldest of the three children born of the second marriage, the others being Martha, who died at home, and Zilpah, who married Houston Barker and died in the Sequatchie valley. For his third wife the father married Nancy Lafary, who is still living.

W. R. Henson was educated in the public schools near his boyhood's home, and he remained with his father until the fall of 1862, when he enlisted in Colonel Storm's regiment of Confederate cavalry, which was a part of General Forrest's command. He took part in the battle of Murfreesboro and in many skirmishes, and was never forced to surrender. At the close of the war he turned his attention to farming, and has since successfully followed that pursuit.

On the 12th of February, 1857, was consummated the marriage of Mr. Henson and Miss Sarah Barker, a daughter of William Barker, and they have become the parents of thirteen children, of whom eleven are still living: Ruthie, who first married Samuel Perkins, and is now the wife of Frank Jackson, a farmer of Sequatchie county; Martha Jane, wife of John Deakins;

Mary, wife of W. H. Smith; Sallie, wife of R. E. Kelley; and Andrew, William B., Lodenia, Julia, Charles S. and Lee A., all at home. Those deceased are John and Alice, wife of Frank Jackson. Mrs. Henson is a worthy member of the Baptist church and a most estimable lady, who has proved to her husband a true helpmeet. The Democratic party finds in our subject a stanch supporter of its principles, and in his social relations he is a Mason.

JAMES HOUSTON NORTHCUT, who is connected with the Tennessee Coal, Iron & Railroad Company, at Whitwell, Marion county, was born on the 24th of January, 1857, in Altamont, Grundy county, Tenn., and is a son of Elihu and Mary (Griswold) Northcut. His father went south in 1859 with some stock and the supposition is that he was murdered for his money as he never returned. He had previously served as tax collector of Grundy county. He was a son of Gen. Adrian Northcut, who was a graduate of West Point and a general in the United States army during the war with Mexico. For many years he was a prominent and wealthy farmer and stock-dealer of Grundy county, buying stock which he would drive south and sell. He held quite a number of official positions, and so great was his popularity that he was never defeated for any office for which he was a candidate. After the disappearance of her first husband the mother of our subject married Joseph Sweeden, who is now deceased. She now makes her home in Tracy City, Grundy county. She is a most estimable lady and

a faithful member of the Christian church. By her first marriage she became the mother of five children, of whom four are still living: Stephen A., a resident of Jasper, Tenn.; Sarah F., wife of Robert Campbell, of Chattanooga; Norman Eudoria Idelia, wife of William Meeks, a farmer of Grundy county; and James H., of this sketch. William E. was crippled in a wreck on the Tennessee Coal & Iron Railroad in 1887, which accident ultimately caused his death.

James H. Northcut acquired his education in the school at Altamont. At the age of sixteen years he began to earn his own livelihood as a coal miner at Earlington, Ky., where he remained for four years, and for the following eighteen months he was employed in the mines at Tracy City, Tenn. He was then with the Tennessee Coal, Iron & Railroad Company at that place as a brakesman and fireman, and for a short time ran an engine and was connected with the railroad service there for three years. Subsequently, in connection with Samuel Bennett, he rented the Pryor Tennessee river farm, for which they paid a yearly rent of three thousand dollars cash. The first year they made money, but after that the place proved unprofitable and they gave it up at the end of three years. For two years Mr. Northcut served as deputy sheriff under J. R. Jones, and then began contracting to furnish the Tennessee coal and iron mines at Whitwell with propping timber. He is still extensively and successfully engaged in that business, giving employment to twelve men, and in connection with it he operates a sawmill.

On the 23d of January, 1881, Mr. Northcut was united in marriage with Miss Sallie

Grantham, who was born in Bedford county, Tenn., January 23, 1859, and is a daughter of John Grantham. Though they have no children of their own they have given homes to several, one of whom was Henry, who died recently at the age of seventeen years. His brother William has also been adopted by our subject. Mr. Northcut holds membership in the Christian church, while his wife is a Methodist in religious belief. Wherever known they are held in high regard, and their circle of friends and acquaintances is extensive. Politically he is identified with the Democratic party, and socially is connected with the Independent Order of Odd Fellows, the Knights of Pythias and the Royal Arcanum. He is six feet, one inch in height, and is well proportioned physically.

J C. BROWN, a prosperous, enterprising and highly respected farmer of Bledsoe county, belongs to one of the honored pioneer families of the Sequatchie Valley. His grandfather, Reuben Brown, came here many years ago and was the first to bring a wagon into the valley, but was forced to bring it in in pieces as there were no roads. He located where Thomas Brown now lives, cut out the cane and planted a small crop. He returned to Anderson county, Tenn., for his family, and settling in Bledsoe county he there made his permanent home. He was born in South Carolina and died here at the age of fifty years. He married Sallie Worthington, who died in 1873 at the age of ninety-one years and seven days. He was a very successful farmer and both he and his wife were earnest members of the Cumberland Presbyterian church. In their family were eleven children, three sons and eight daughters, all now deceased. They were as follows: Nancy, who first married Samuel Close and after his death wedded Johnson Clark, and who died in the Valley; Disa married Samuel Rankin and died in the Valley; Peggy was the wife of William Worthington and died many years ago; Betsy was the wife of William Brown and died in the Valley; Fannie was the wife of Jerry Dorsey and died in Mississippi, Sallie was the wife of Philip Hutcheson and died in the Valley; James R., who served as justice of the peace, also died in the Sequatchie Valley; Minerva first married James Worthington and after his death wedded Easterly Swafford, and she died in the Valley.

Jesse C. Brown, who completes the the family and was the father of our subject, was born May 31, 1815, and spent his entire life in Bledsoe county, where his death occurred May 3, 1876. He was married April 1, 1841, to Miss Sarah Jane Swafford, a daughter of Thomas Swafford. She was born November 19, 1823, a twin sister of Samuel Swafford, and they are the only ones of the family now living. By her marriage she has become the mother of ten children, of whom seven still survive, namely: Rebecca Ann, wife of Dick Johnson, of Marion county, Tenn.; Samuel, a farmer living near Big Spring; Elizabeth, who lives on the old homestead; Thomas, who operates the old home farm; I. E., a farmer living near Big Spring; J. C., the subject of this review; Sallie, wife of T. J. Swafford, of the third district of Bledsoe county; and Martha J., wife of John Swafford, of the fourth district. Those deceased are Reuben, who died in infancy; and Joseph, who died in childhood. At the time of his marriage the father of these children moved to a farm just below the Big Spring, and in the midst of the forest made for himself a home, where he spent the balance of his life. There his widow is still living. Both were connected with the Cumberland Presbyterian church, and he cast his ballot with the Democracy.

J. C. Brown, whose name introduces this sketch, was born on the 20th of December, 1856, and during his boyhood and youth pursued his studies in the Cedar Grove school. On attaining his majority he started out to make his own way in the world and due success has not been denied him. He was married, October 14, 1886, to Miss Sallie Swafford, a daughter of Major Swafford. She died September 6, 1896, and her death was widely and deeply mourned. To them were born four children, Kitty, Samuel and Pearl, all living; and Luther, who died in childhood. In politics Mr. Brown is a stanch Democrat, and in his social relations is a Mason, belonging to the lodge at Melvine, in which he has served as junior warden.

———————

JOHN H. PRYOR, a well-known general blacksmith and highly respected citizen of Whitwell, Marion county, was born at Jasper, November 4, 1867. After attending the common schools of his native city for some time he became a student in the Sam Houston Academy and later in Forest Hill College. During his boyhood and youth he became quite familiar with blacksmithing in his father's shop, and in 1887 went to Chattanooga, where he accepted a position in the blacksmith and carriage shop of A. Fachtnech, remaining there three years and becoming thoroughly proficient in his chosen calling. On leaving Chattanooga he went to Harriman, Tenn,, but shortly afterward came to Whitwell and entered the employ of the Tennessee Coal, Iron & Railroad Co., working in their blacksmith shop for two years. He then established a shop of his own at that place, and so successful has he been that he now gives employment to two hands and enjoys an excellent trade. He carries on both general blacksmithing and wagon making and the work turned out of his shop is first class in every particular.

Mr. Pryor was married on the 26th of August, 1888, the lady of his choice being Miss Fannie Miller, a daughter of Jacob Miller, of Dayton, Tennessee. They have two children living, Gracie and Lillie, and have lost one, Edley, who died at the age of three years. The parents are both worthy members of the Methodist Episcopal church, South, while politically Mr. Pryor is identified with the Democratic party, and socially is a member of the Independent Order of Odd Fellows, and the Woodmen of the World, having held office in both.

———————

HARRIS GILLIAM THOMPSON, a prominent contractor at the mines No. 1 and No. 2, Tracy City, has led a life of honest toil. Throughout his career of continued and far-reaching usefulness his duties have been performed with the greatest care, and his business interests have been so managed as to win him the confidence of the public and the prosperity which should always attend honorable effort.

A native of Grundy county, Mr. Thompson was born at Altamont, March 5, 1858, and is a son of John and Lucy (Griswold) Thompson, the former also a native of Grundy county and a farmer by occupation. At the commencement of the Civil war, the father joined Colonel Carnes' Confederate Regiment, and participated in many important engagements, including the battles of Murfreesboro and Missionary Ridge. At the battle of Chickamauga he was killed while serving as an artilleryman. He was one of Grundy county's leading and most influential citizens, and was often called upon to fill various official positions of honor and trust. He was a member of the county court and deputy sheriff. The mother of our subject is a native of Indiana, whence she came to Tennessee with her parents. She is now the wife of Abner Street and a resident of Tracy City.

During his boyhood and youth Mr. Thompson, of this review, pursued his studies in the school at Altamont, and at the age of twenty years began his business career as a farmer in Warren county, near McMinnville. Coming to Tracy City he entered the employ of the Tennessee Coal, Iron & Railroad Company, as a coal digger, in 1878, and has been with that corporation ever since in one capacity or another. He commenced operations at the East Fork mines; was next foreman over convicts at No. 2 for two years; subsequently was bank foreman at Nos. 1 and 2 for twelve years; and has since engaged in contracting with good success. In 1881 he was crippled by slate falling upon him, and the same year while mining coal fell upon him. He now has in his employ from forty-five to one hundred seventy-five men and is doing an extensive and profitable business.

On the 4th of November, 1880, Mr. Thompson was united in marriage with Miss Maggie Farrell, a native of Tracy City and a daughter of Patrick Farrell. They have four children, namely: Beatrice, Henrietta, James and Lucile. They have also lost three—Nellie, who died at the age of eight years; Jessie, who died at the age of three; and Walter, who died at the age of four. The parents are both members of the Methodist Episcopal church, South, in which Mr. Thompson serves as steward. Socially he is identified with the Masonic order, the Royal Arcanum, and the Knights of Pythias, and has represented the local lodge of the last named order in the grand lodge. His political support is always given the Democracy, and was serving as a member of the school board at Tracy City at the time the school house was erected.

JAMES S. PANKEY is an influential and distinguished citizen of Bledsoe county, who throughout life has devoted his energies principally to farming and stock raising. He is a worthy representative of a prominent family, which was founded in the Sequatchie Valley by his grandfather, James Smith Pankey, who was also a farmer by occupation, but late in life, when his health failed, he removed to Pikeville, where he lived with his son until his death, which occurred in November, 1847, when over seventy years of age. In his family were two sons, the younger being James S., who was born in 1822, and died in 1860. He was a merchant, and a soldier in the Mexican war. After that struggle was over he served as county clerk of Bledsoe county for sixteen years, resigning the position to go to Florida for his health.

Bird Pankey, the older son, was the father of our subject. Agricultural pursuits claimed a part of his attention, but he was also engaged in driving stock south for a number of years and was interested in merchandising. He died in 1856, honored and respected by all who knew him. He was a very energetic and influential man and was often called upon to serve in responsible official positions, being at one time a member of the county court and postmaster at Pikeville, while as justice of the peace his decisions were never reversed by the higher courts. He was a Democrat in politics and a very intimate friend of General James D. Spears.

As a companion and helpmeet on life's journey Bird Pankey chose Mary Story, a daughter of Dr. Samuel Story, who was prominently identified with the early history of Sequatchie Valley. The Doctor was a native of Kentucky and when a young man came to Tennessee, where he successfully engaged in the practice of medicine throughout the remainder of his life. He built the Sequatchie Hotel and was the prime mover in many enterprises, which materially advanced the interests of this region. For many years he also served as circuit clerk

of Bledsoe county. He died in the prime of life in 1839. Two of his children are still living—Mary, who was born August 15, 1828, and is now Mrs. Pankey; and Matilda, who was born in 1838, and has never married. The Story family is closely related to the Montgomery family, one of whom made himself famous at Quebec during the French and Indian war, and another fell at the Battle of Horse Shoe and the City of Montgomery, Ala., was named in his honor. Mrs. Pankey has for many years been a devoted member of the Methodist church and is a most estimable lady. She is the mother of four children, of whom our subject is the second in order of birth and the only one now living. Samuel S., born March 22, 1848, died October 5, 1887. Nettie, born January 1, 1853, married James Henry and died April 8, 1882. Hugh Montgomery born March 18, 1855, died April 5, 1856.

James S. Pankey, whose name introduces this sketch, was born April 24, 1850, and was educated at Sequatchie College, of Bledsoe county, and the State University at Knoxville. His school days being over he commenced farming upon the place where he now lives, and to agricultural pursuits and stock raising he has since devoted the greater part of his time. For a few years he also engaged in teaching, and taught for two terms in Rhea county, Tenn.

On the 23d of December, 1886, Mr. Pankey married Mrs. Cena Rankin, who was born in Bledsoe county, March 24, 1857, and was the widow of J. M. Rankin. Her father, Rev. F. J. Hutcheson, was a prominent citizen of the county and an elder in the Christian church for many years. By her first marriage Mrs. Pankey had one son, J. B., who now lives with his mother. There are four children by the second union, namely: Birdie E., Beula M., Benton J. and Annie S., and the parents have also reared Eugenia Maud Henry, a niece. They are leading and active members of the Christian church at Smyrna, and Mr. Pankey is now one of the trustees of the same. He has always been an ardent Democrat in politics, and though the county is strongly Republican he was elected, in 1882, county clerk, a position he filled most creditably for one term.

JAMES S. GARRISON, the sheriff of Cumberland county, was born in the Eleventh district, near Swaggarty's Cove, in 1858 and is a son of Garrett and Sarah (Reed) Garrison. The senior Garrison is still living, and resides on the head waters of White creek. His wife, the mother of the subject of this article, died some two years since, but the father is still hale and hearty. He has vivid memories of the Civil war. During its first year he acted as guide to parties seeking to escape from Tennessee into Kentucky that they might join the Union forces. He was in this most dangerous service for about two years when he succumbed to its hardships, and became an invalid, nor did he recover his health until after the war had ended. He was a hard-working farmer, and a man of upright character. He has been a Republican from the organization of the party, and with his wife was a member of the Missionary Baptist church. He was the father of nine children, of whom seven are now living, and the Cumberland county sheriff is the oldest. John H. is a farmer, and has his home in the Eleventh district. Eliza Jane is the wife of John Mullins, a farmer, of Cole's Creek, Ky. Betsy is the wife of Alex Logan, a farmer in the Eleventh district. David is in Kentucky, and Burt and Doc are on the old home place with their aged father. Abraham and Albro both died young.

James S. Garrison grew to manhood under the parental roof and received such educational advantages as the times afforded, from which he profited beyond the run of lads. He early attained a manly character, and before reaching his seventeenth birthday, took a wife, and set up a home. Mary Emeline Monday, who was born and raised in Rhea county, did not hesitate to link her fortunes in with his, and to them have come a numerous family, of whom four daughters and three sons are now living: Abraham L., Arminta J., Hattie Belle, Maude, Vernie, James and William Mc. Three are dead, John, Selia Ann and Milo. When he was married, Mr. Garrison immediately began to clear up a farm in Rhea county, but a year later sold out, and moved to the Eleventh district, and located one mile from the farm on which he was raised, and where he made his home until he came to Crossville to take charge of the office of sheriff. Before his election to this important position he had served as constable for four years, and had been justice of the peace for eight years, and had acquired a very necessary familiarity with legal processes. He was first elected in 1894, and was re-elected in 1896, carrying every district in the county, something that no other candidate has ever been able to do. In the position of sheriff Mr. Garrison has made a model record. He has been quick and accurate in every department of his work, and his administration has been a constant terror to evil doers. Cumberland county makes a good showing in the police records of the state, and the credit is very largely due to its efficient sheriff.

Sheriff Garrison stands high in social and fraternal circles of the community. In religious matters he is a member of the Missionary Baptist church, and is much respected by his fellow members. In fraternal relations he is associated with Crossville Masonic organizations, and is an active and zealous worker. Politically he works with the Republican party from which he has received many honors. He is a leading man and may well be pronounced one of the prominent citizens of Cumberland county.

CHARLES RAINES ROGERS, a prominent and highly respected citizen of Marion county, was born November 5, 1833, on the farm where he still resides, it being pleasantly located three miles east of Jasper, and he is a worthy representative of one of the leading families of the county. With him resides his sister Emily, who was born on the same farm August 17, 1838, and she now acts as his housekeeper. Their parents were Emanuel C. and Martha (Smith) Rogers. The father was a native of Hawkins county, Tenn., and the town of Rogersville probably took its name from his family. He was born April 8, 1794, and
46

was a son of William Rogers, who died near Sparta, in White county, Tenn., and a grandson of Dauswell Rogers.

It was in 1814, that our subject's father came to the Sequatchie Valley and located in Bledsoe county, where he was married to Miss Martha Smith, whose people lived in that county near Pikeville. She was born, however, in Anderson county, Tenn., May 3, 1798. After their marriage the young couple continued to make their home in Bledsoe county until 1832, when they took up their residence upon the farm in Marion county now owned and occupied by their son and daughter of this sketch. Upon this place they spent their remaining days, the father dying November 22, 1851, the mother July 15, 1885, and the remains of both were interred upon the farm. For many years the father was a prominent and influential local preacher of the Methodist church, and of him it may be said the world is far better for his having lived. In his political affiliations he was a Whig.

To this worthy couple were born seventeen children, but only four are now living, namely: Sallie, the widow of Andrew Dame and a resident of the Seventh district of Marion county, her home being near the old homestead; Charles R., of this sketch; Emily, who is with our subject; and Martha, wife of Carroll Rainey, of Jackson county, Ala. Those deceased are, John A., a farmer who died on the old home place in 1888, at the age of seventy-three years; Rhodie, who died in July, 1888, at the age of seventy-two years; A. H., who died in Jackson county, Ala., in April, 1892, at the age of seventy-two years; E. T., a farmer, formerly a merchant of Trenton, Ga., and other places, who died near the old homestead March 16, 1893, at the age of sixty-six years; Aaron B., a farmer, who was born in 1824, and died in the neighborhood of the home farm, November 18, 1851; R. M., a farmer, who died April 23, 1858, at the age of twenty-eight years; T. F., who died at Vicksburg, Miss., during the siege, having been forced into the Confederate service and belonging to the company commanded by his brother, E. T. Rogers, though his sympathies were with the North; Elizabeth A., who married Levi Webb and died March 30, 1897, on her sixtieth birthday, in the house where she was born; David C., who died in boyhood, Nov. 13, 1851; and Allen, Alfred, Pleasant and Dauswell, who all died in childhood.

Having never married Charles Rogers and sister Emily have always remained on the old homestead, and he has successfully managed the same for many years, being a painstaking and skillful agriculturist. Both he and his sister are leading members of the Methodist church at Pleasant Grove, and are held in high regard by all who know them. Being forced into the service, Mr Rogers was a member of the Confederate army for just one week, but he has always been an ardent Republican in politics and was opposed to secession.

JAMES M. RIGGLE.—Prominent among the successful farmers and stockraisers of Marion county may be named the subject of this historical notice, who now resides in the Thirteenth district, and who, by his enterprise and energy in the direc-

tion of his chosen industry, has given to his work a significance and beauty of which few deemed it capable.

A native of Marion county, he was born March 22, 1835, in the Seventh district on land now owned by William E. Hamilton, and he is a son of Jacob and Jane (Smith) Riggle, who were born, reared and married in Virginia, whence they came to this section of Tennessee, locating first at Rankin's Cove. Subsequently they removed to the Thirteenth district and located on the farm now owned by C. C. Anderson, and upon that place both died when well advanced in life. The father always engaged in farming and met with a well-deserved success. He was a Whig in politics, and as a soldier of the war of 1812 participated in the famous battle of New Orleans. His wife was a worthy member of the Cumberland Presbyterian church, and both were honored and respected by all who knew them. Of their large family of children only two are now living: James M., of this review; and Mrs. Elizabeth Anderson, who now lives with her son, C. C. Anderson, mentioned above.

During his boyhood and youth James M. Riggle attended school near Jasper, and, laying aside his text books at the age of eighteen years, he took up the more responsible duties of business life, choosing the occupation of farming with which he had become thoroughly familiar upon the home farm. At the time of his first marriage he located at Rankin's Cove, and on coming to the Thirteenth district lived for a time on the farm now occupied by Jacob Cyphers. From that place he removed to his present farm, where he owns one hundred and seventy-five acres, principally on the Tennessee river bottom, and is meeting with excellent success in its operation.

On the 24th of August, 1854, at the age of twenty years, Mr. Riggle was united in marriage with Miss Ruthie Stovall, who was born in Sumner county, Tenn., November 20, 1835, and was a daughter of James Stovall. They became the parents of eleven children, namely: Josephine B., who died in infancy; Rosaline, who died at the age of sixteen years; Thomas J., a conductor on the Nashville & Chattanooga railroad, living at Nashville; Louisa Jane, wife of William Beddow, of Nashville, a passenger conductor on the same road; James B., who is also in the employ of the Nashville & Chattanooga railroad, and a resident of Nashville; Ellen O., widow of James M. Davis, living with our subject; William M., who died in childhood; Laura, a resident of Nashville; Margaret, who died in infancy; Simon, who was killed at the age of twenty-three years by an engine on the Nashville & Chattanooga railroad blowing up at Bridgeport; and Cora, who died in infancy. The wife and mother, who was a consistent member of the Methodist church, died April 18, 1879. Mr. Riggle was again married, February 26, 1882, his second union being with Mrs. Sarah Elizabeth (Cyphers) Brophy. She was born November 18, 1835, and departed this life July 12, 1897. There were no children by this marriage.

During the Civil war, in 1863, Mr. Riggle joined Company H, Third Confederate Cavalry, and was with General Forrest on several raids in middle and west Tennessee. Politically, he is a Democrat, but at local elections always supports the man whom he believes best qualified for office, regardless of party affiliations. Religiously, he is a member of the Methodist Episcopal church, South, belonging to the Hale Chapel congregation.

ROBERT E. KELLEY is a prosperous farmer residing near Delphi, Sequatchie county. He is still a young man but has won a good standing by both personal and business qualities. He was born April 2, 1864, and is a son of Joseph B. and Mary J. (Carmack) Kelley.

The senior Kelley was a man of mark in his day, and began life for himself as a country merchant on Looney Creek, but after a few years sold out his store and went on a farm. He continued farming the rest of his life. He was born December 1, 1819, in what is now a part of Sequatchie county, but was then a part of Marion, and died August 26, 1874. He became the head of a household March 7, 1848, by his union with Miss Mary J. Carmack. She was a native of Virginia, where she was born in 1829, and was a daughter of John Carmack. He was married near Dunlap, Tenn., and he and his wife were members of the Cumberland Presbyterian church. To them were born eight children: Jackson, born November 21, 1849; John A., April 6, 1852 (died an infant); Amanda, May 7, 1854; Thomas L., November 24, 1856 (died at the age of ten years); Mary Alice, February 26, 1859; Albert S., February 19, 1862 (died an infant); Robert E., April 2, 1864; Joseph F., April 2, 1865.

Robert E. Kelley received a very good

education in the public school of his district, and supplemented its instructions by attendance upon the high schools at Spencer and Pikeville. Growing into manhood he embraced the profession of a farmer, and is devoting his life to the cultivation of the soil. He finds a satisfaction in a sound and healthy country life that he could not expect anywhere else, and is regarded as one of the most capable and reliable men of his community. He has been called to several positions of trust and honor by his fellow townsmen, and is classed among the best citizens of the county. He is a successful farmer, and makes his farm not only grain producing but stock raising, and derives a good profit from its cultivation. He is a Democrat in his party associations, and is deeply interested in its fortunes. Mr. Kelley was married December 20, 1895, to Miss Henson, who presented him with a son, Joseph F., September 17, 1896. She is a daughter of Riley and Sallie (Barker) Henson, and belongs to the Methodist church. Mr. Kelley is a member of the Cumberland Presbyterian church, and both himself and wife are prominent people in the community.

HON. AUGUSTUS HENRY WOODLEE, one of the most prominent and representative citizens of Grundy county, and editor of the "Tracy City News," was born on Collins river, in the northern part of that county, March 1, 1855, and on the paternal side is of English descent. His father, Enoch Woodlee, was born near Irving College, in Warren county, Tenn.,

November 3, 1825, and was a son of Jacob Woodlee, a native of North Carolina, who came with his parents to this state, being among the earliest settlers of Warren county, where his death occurred. He was a farmer, and Enoch Woodlee also followed that occupation in connection with his work as a minister of the Separate Baptist church, for which he preached for several years before his death, being pastor of the church at Philadelphia, Tenn., and other churches in that neighborhood. Soon after his marriage, or about 1851 or 1852, he came to Grundy county, and here died April 16, 1870. In political sentiment he was a Democrat. His wife, the mother of our subject, bore the maiden name of Mary Reed, and was born in North Carolina March 20, 1831, a daughter of John Reed. She is still living on the old homestead on Collins river, and is a faithful member of the Missionary Baptist church. Of her six children, five are still living, namely: Savannah Magness, wife of P. M. Barnes, who operates the old home farm; Augustus H., of this sketch; L. V., an attorney and farmer, who is now representing Grundy county in the state legislature, and has also served as back tax attorney and superintendent of public instruction in the county; Mary Victoria, wife of J. A. Cathcut, a farmer living on the old Woodlee homestead; and M. J. D., a farmer and teacher, who lives with his mother. The one deceased is J. B., who was born in 1856, and died in Grundy county in January, 1881. He, too, was an agriculturist.

The early education of our subject acquired in the schools near his childhood's home, has been supplemented by his attendance at the schools of Chapel Hill and

Shiloh, Warren county, and by one term at Burritt College and at the schools of Altamont, Grundy county. He successfully engaged in teaching at Cedar Bluff, New Union and Altamont, and in 1882 was appointed circuit court clerk by Judge Williams. The same year, at the regular election, he was elected to the same office, and so acceptably did he fill the position that he was re-elected without opposition in 1886. Four years later he was elected on the Democratic ticket to represent the ninth district in the State senate, and as a prominent and influential member of that august body he was made chairman of the committee on enrolled bills, and a member of the finance, ways and means committee, committee on charitable institutions and committee on public buildings and grounds. For one year after his retirement from office he engaged in merchandising at McMinnville, but in July, 1893, came to Tracy City and bought the "Tracy City News," which he has since successfully published. He is a recognized leader in the ranks of the Democratic party in his locality, and has done much to insure its success, both by personal effort and through his paper. He holds membership in the Missionary Baptist church, in which he has served as clerk; and is a prominent member of the Masonic lodge at Altamont, of which he has served as master, and which he has represented in the grand lodge, where he was grand sword bearer. He was also secretary of the local order for some years.

Mr. Woodlee was married, January 1, 1879, to Miss Emily C. Walker, who was born on Collins river, in Grundy county, and was a daughter of Rev. F. M. and Martha Walker. She died October 7, 1885, leaving one child, Hallie E., who is with our subject. On January 18, 1888, Mr. Woodlee was again married, his second union being with Miss Metta E., daughter of J. M. Burger, of McMinnville. Two children grace this union—Lena B. and Elmer G.

CHARLES P. TAYLOR.—The men who belonged to the generation that preceded and included the period of the Civil war in the border states, have strangely interesting memories of that stirring time. Mr. Taylor was but a mere lad when it broke out, but he was old enough to serve in the home guard, and in these far away times he has valuable and instructive recollections of that great struggle.

Charles P. Taylor was born January 14, 1845, at Parker's Ford on the Obed river. He was a son of Isaac N. and Elizabeth (Vickery) Taylor, both natives of Kentucky. The senior Taylor was born in 1812, and brought his family into Bledsoe county in 1845, settling first at Brown's Gap, upon a farm now belonging to Major Tallett. He removed to a place now owned by W. B. Swafford, and from there to the farm now the property of Samuel Swafford, where he died in 1882, surviving his wife one year. He was a saddler and farmer, a hard working man, moderately successful in a financial way, and sustained a good reputation throughout his part of the county. He was a Democrat, and with his wife was a member of the Methodist church. In his family were nine children, six of whom are now living. Mary is the widow of J. P. Swafford, and lives in the valley. Eliza J. is the widow of Aaron Swafford, and also has her home in the valley. Charles P. is the subject of this writing, and Salina, the wife of Benjamin Franklin, has her home in Dayton, Tenn. Amanda married William Day, a farmer of Rhea county, where W. G. is also engaged in farming. John A. died in 1867 at the age of twenty-five years. Stacy died at the age of eighteen, and Virginia died after she had become the wife of Thomas Swafford.

Charles P. Taylor spent his boyhood days in this county attending school, and when the war broke out was enrolled in the home guard. After the war was over, he set up for himself on the Millard farm, with an old sway-back horse for his entire capital. Pluck and energy did wonders, and in the intervening years he has been very successful. For a time he was on the William Wood farm, and in 1893 located where we find him. Here he has a fine farm which is well stocked and thoroughly improved.

Mr. Taylor was married December 31, 1878, to Miss Emeline Swafford, a daughter of William Swafford. She was born in Hamilton county, August 24, 1855, and belongs to one of the oldest families of the valley. Her parents spent some years in Arkansas, but returned to Hamilton county, where he spent the earlier years of her life. She is the mother of seven children, Eliza, William T., Cleurta Anna, Amanda E., Charles G., Gailaird V., and Celia E. She is a lady of many excellent traits, and commands the esteem of those who know her

best. She is an active and devoted member of the Methodist church, where her presence and assistance are much appreciated. Mr. Taylor is a Mason and is affiliated with the order at Melvine. He was in business in the years from 1892 to 1895 at Litton and had at first a partner by the name of J. C. Thurman. Later on the partnership was dissolved and our subject is now in business at Nine Mile. He is an affable gentleman, and is highly respected by a wide circle of acquaintances.

BALIS LADD, a leading representative of the agricultural interests of Marion county, Tenn., was born in 1833, upon the farm where he still continues to reside. It is a well-improved place, pleasantly located near Mont Eagle, at the head of Battle creek, and, being a thorough and skillful farmer, he has placed it under a high state of cultivation. His father, Washington Ladd, settled at what is now known as Ladd's Cove many years ago, and throughout life followed the occupation of farming. He reared a large family of children, ten in all, and died in 1894, at the ripe old age of eighty-six years.

Balis Ladd, who is the oldest of the family, joined the Confederate army in 1861, and participated in many important battles and skirmishes, including the engagement at Fort Donelson. During his service he was taken prisoner, and was held in captivity for some time. In 1864, when the war was over, he returned home to resume agricultural pursuits.

At the age of thirty-five years Mr. Ladd

was united in marriage with Miss Jennie Reed, who was born in Franklin county, Tenn., and is a daughter of Isaac Reed. Of the ten children born of this union, only five are now living. The parents are earnest and consistent members of the Methodist Episcopal church, South, and Mr. Ladd is a stalwart supporter of the Democratic party. Wherever known they are held in high regard, and their friends in Marion county are many.

EPHRAIM WILLIAM PRIGMORE, a leading and representative agriculturist of Marion county, Tenn., has spent all his life there, his birth occurring January 25, 1850. His father, Joseph K. Prigmore, was born March 20, 1815, a son of Ephraim and Margaret (Kelly) Prigmore, who were of French descent. Before the war the father engaged in merchandising near Whitwell, Marion county, but later removed to Oats Landing and turned his attention to farming. From early boyhood he made his home in Marion county, and was here married, February 20, 1840, to Miss Mary Pryor, who was born March 21, 1818, of Irish descent. They became the parents of eight children, namely: Margaret and Melinda J., both deceased; Louisa A., wife of J. S. Richmond; Ephraim W., of this sketch; James G., who married Laura Stafford and is engaged in merchandising at South Pittsburg, Tenn.; John A., who married Florence Heiskell and lives on a farm adjoining our subject's; Mary, wife of Robert Richards, who lives near our subject; and Ruth, wife of John Ely, of Moore county, Tenn. There parents were both sincere and faithful members of the Presbyterian church and died in that faith, the father November 12, 1889, the mother November 6, 1865, being laid to rest in Gotts cemetery, where the remains of their parents were also interred.

Mr. Prigmore, whose name introduces this sketch, obtained his education in the Sam Houston Academy, and when his schools days were over he returned to the old homestead, where throughout life he has successfully followed agricultural pursuits. On the 7th of January, 1886, he led to the marriage altar Miss Lizzie Mitchell, who was born December 25, 1853, in Marion county, and is a daughter of Preston and Mary A. (Deakins) Mitchell. Her father was a native of the same county, born November 19, 1819, but the birth of her mother occurred near Dunlap, Sequatchie county, Tenn., September 26, 1826. They were the parents of six children: James A., Lizzie, John F., Mary A., Mattie and Laura E. The mother, who was a worthy member of the Methodist Episcopal church, died August 19, 1873, and was burried at Shiloh. Mr. Mitchell as again married, July 15, 1877, his second wife being Mary J. Hudson. He is a prominent farmer of the Fifth district of Marion county, where he has lived for many years.

To Mr. and Mrs. Prigmore have been born three children, namely: Joe M., who was born March 13, 1890, and died October 23, 1895; Mary A., born June 21, 1892; and Victor E., born March 2, 1894. The parents hold membership in the Methodist Episcopal church, South, and socially Mr. Prigmore is an active and prominent member of the Masonic fraternity. As a Democrat he has been prominently identified with local political affairs, and in 1886 he was triumphantly elected trustee of the county by a large majority, though the county is usually strongly Republican. The fact that he was elected plainly indicates his personal popularity and the confidence and trust reposed in him by his fellow citizens.

M L. TAYLOR.—It would be difficult to find a character superior in honor and reliability to that of M. L. Taylor among the men of Cumberland county. He is justice of the peace at Pleasant Hill, and sustains a reputation far and wide as an upright and trustworthy man. He was born November 17, 1866, and is the only child of his mother, Barbara Ann Broyles, who was the second wife of his father, Leroy Taylor. The mother is still living.

The Taylors are a distinguished family in the state. The present governor of the state belongs to this family, and it has given other capable men to the public service. Leroy Taylor, the father of the subject of this article, was born in Overton county, October 8, 1812. He was a son of Isaac Taylor, and a grandson of Captain George Taylor of Revolutionary fame. The latter fought at King's Mountain, and bore an active part in the great struggle that gave the United States to the world. Isaac Taylor went into Overton county when it was a wilderness. He located in a little village that afterward became the city of Livingston, the present county seat. He died in 1862 at a very great age. In the war of 1812 he served under General Jackson, and

worthily sustained his father's fame. Leroy Taylor spent the first fifteen years of his life in his native county, and then followed his father into Fentress county. There his father died and was buried, and there he spent all the remaining years of his life, dying March 8, 1892. He was twice married. Margaret Campbell was his first wife, and she bore him eight children, four of whom are now living. Eliza, the wife of J. A. Brown, living in this county. Rebecca, Mrs. W. T. Erwin, of White county, and Armilda, Mrs. E. G. Hamby, of this county; Mahala the wife of E. W. Wiley, of this county. Richardson was a soldier in the Confederate army, and died during the war. This was also the destiny of his brother Evan. Alvin C. was in the prime of his life at the time of his death. He was a farmer and stone mason. William died in infancy. Leroy Taylor was a man well known in this part of the county. He was a Democrat politically and religiously a member of the Methodist church.

M. L. Taylor received an excellent education in the Pleasant Hill schools, and finished at Hiawassee College, a well-known institution of learning near Madison, Monroe county. In 1887 he began teaching school near where he was born, at Pleasant Hill, which has been the principal scene of his labors in that line. In 1894 he was was elected justice of the peace, and still serves the public in that capacity. In 1892 Miss Ollie Vandever became his wife. She is a daughter of George and Martha Vandever, and is a native of this county. They are the parents of one son, Charles. Mr. Taylor and his wife are members of Taylor chapel, which latter was built by his father, and it bears his name. He is conservative in his political actions, and seeks the good of the public rather than partisan and personal ends.

JUDGE JOHN G. KELLY.—We are now permitted to touch briefly upon the life history of one who has retained a personal association with the affairs of Marion county throughout life, and is to-day one of its most distinguished and honored citizens, a worthy representative of a prominent old pioneer family. His grandfather, Col. John Kelly, a native of Virginia, and a well-educated gentleman, came to Marion county, Tenn., at an early day, and as a surveyor laid out and chartered the old Chattanooga & Nashville pike, the charter now being in the possession of our subject. He was a Whig in politics; was a delegate to the first state convention, served as county court clerk of Marion county, and also filled the office of justice of the peace. He married Miss Nancy Mayo, also a native of the Old Dominion, and both lived to quite an advanced age. They were Presbyterians in religious faith, belonging to the church at Ebenezer, and he took an active part in the organization of the Masonic lodge here, which he afterward represented in the grand lodge.

Alexander Kelly, the father of the Judge, was born October 7, 1803, at Old Liberty, in the upper part of Marion county, and was educated in the common schools of the valley. Though his advantages in this direction were rather limited he made the most of them, became a great reader, was a man

47

of sound judgment and was always very industrious and enterprising. He started in life as a mechanic, and helped to build the first court house in Marion county at Jasper, but later in life removed to a farm three miles east of Jasper, and to agricultural pursuits devoted considerable attention throughout the remainder of his life. After living upon the farm for a number of years, he took charge of Kelly's Ferry, which he conducted until some time during the '50s. He served as justice of the peace and county court clerk before the Civil war; was first a Whig and later a Republican in politics. Socially he was identified with the Masonic fraternity; and religiously both he and his wife were earnest members of the Cumberland Presbyterian church. In early manhood he married Miss Elizabeth Oates, who was born in November, 1803, and died at Oates Landing, on the Tennessee river, at the age of sixty-four years. His death occurred upon his farm, three miles east of Jasper, when he was sixty-seven years of age. In their family were eight children, six sons and two daughters, of whom four are now living: Nancy M., widow of P. C. Peck, and a resident of Marion county; John G., of this sketch; Eli T., a farmer living three miles east of Jasper; and James Clay, a resident of Sequatchie county, Tenn. Those deceased are, David O., who served as circuit court clerk, register and postmaster at Jasper; Abigail who died at Oates Landing during girlhood; and Thomas, who died at the same place.

Judge Kelly was born on the old home farm east of Jasper, December 29, 1832, and was educated at Sam Houston Academy. Hunting was his chief delight during boyhood and youth, and with a pack of hounds he hunted from Chattanooga to Stephenson, Ala. After reaching man's estate he commenced farming and continued to follow that pursuit until the outbreak of the Civil war. Loyal to the Union, in 1861, he joined Knight's company, Swain's division, and was in the secret service all through the war, acting as scout, carrying messages, and guiding men through to the Federal lines when they wished to join the Union service. He was with General Rosecrans and Thomas most of the time. This was a very valuable as well as a very dangerous service, and he was twice arrested by Confederate troops, once by Captain Alley's company, but he escaped from the soldier that was guarding him. He was present at the battles of Lookout Mountain, Wauhatchie and Missionary Ridge, but he carried no gun and took no part in the engagements as his services were not in the ranks, being back and forth through the lines many times.

After the war was over, Judge Kelly operated a farm east of Jasper given him by his father, but in 1876 removed to South Pittsburg, and for one year was connected with the Coal & Iron Company. He then engaged in farming and speculating, later conducted a meat market, and served as postmaster at South Pittsburg during President Hayes' administration. He established the South Pittsburg "Republican," the first Republican paper published in the Sequatchie valley. His fellow citizens recognizing his worth and ability have often called upon him to fill important official positions. He was the first mayor of South Pittsburg, has been justice of the peace, and in 1894

was honored with an election to the office of county judge for a term of eight years.

In 1859 Judge Kelly was united in marriage with Miss Barbara Jane Bean, a native of Sweden's Cove, Marion county, and a daughter of Owen R. Bean, who was born in Middle Tennessee. She died October 15, 1894. Of the seven children born to this union six are still living, namely: Martha E., who is a successful teacher residing at home with her father; Nancy F., wife of B. A. Heard, an attorney of South Pittsburg; A. O., who is connected with the iron and coal mines at Inman: Mary Abigail, wife of S. R. Ransom, a prominent citizen of South Pittsburg; John C., postmaster at Jasper; and Joseph B. H., at home.

For generations some of the Kelly family have held membership in Olive Branch lodge, F. & A. M., of Jasper, and the Judge has affiliated with that fraternity since 1858. He also belongs to the Ancient Order of United Workmen and is one of the leading and prominent members of the Cumberland Presbyterian church at Jasper, in which he is serving as elder. In his political affiliations he is a stanch Republican.

———

JEROME GRAVES BLALOCK, justice of the peace and editor of the "Tribune" at Dunlap, Sequatchie county, was born in Gordon county, Ga., October 28, 1867, and is a son of Newborn W. and Martha J. (Cannon) Blalock, both natives of Georgia, the former born in that part of Gilmer county which now forms Pickens county, and the latter born near Clarksville in White county. They were married in

Gordon county, that state, and both are now past fifty years of age. From their native state they removed to Green Pond, near Birmingham, Ala. The father has been a minister of the Missionary Baptist church since a young man, is also a physician, and has been interested in merchandising and in newspaper work, editing the "Gospel Trumpet," a Baptist paper. He has also served as president of the Ooltewah Normal, Ooltewah, Tenn., and the Crew Normal College, at Crew's Depot, Ala. His political support is always given the men and measures of the Republican party, and his aid is never withheld from any enterprise which he believes calculated to prove of public benefit. He served nearly all through the Civil war as a member of the Eighth Georgia Battalion; participated in the sieges of Vicksburg and Knoxville, and was wounded at the battle of Chickamauga. He had a brother killed in the same battle. His children are as follows: Emma, wife of Prof. B. F. P. Jones, superintendent of public instruction of Sequatchie county, and principal of the Ben Jones Training School at Dunlap; Jerome Graves, of this review; Bart M., who assists in the publication of the Dunlap "Tribune," being a member of the firm of Blalock Brothers; Rose, at home; Alla Viola, deceased; David, a druggist; and Roscoe, at home.

The subject of this sketch was provided with excellent educational privileges during his youth, having been a student at the Winchester Normal under Prof. J. W. Ferritt. On leaving school he adopted the profession of teaching, and taught for three terms at Ooltewah Normal and for a part of two terms at Crew Normal College in Ala-

bama. Coming to Dunlap five years ago, he purchased the "Tribune," and has shaped its policy since. Personally and through the editorial columns of his paper he supports the Democracy, and has always taken quite an active and prominent part in political affairs.

D R. NAPOLEON BONAPARTE MOORE is a capable and successful dentist of Whitwell, Marion county, where he has won an enviable standing in his chosen profession. He belongs to a family that has long been identified with the history of the state, and well sustains its honor and dignity.

Dr. Moore is a son of Reverend Richard Jackson and Lizzie (Condra) Moore, and was born in the northern part of the county, June 2, 1869, just one hundred years after the birth of his illustrious namesake. His father has been for many years a venerated clergyman of Marion county, and still makes his home on the farm where he was born July 6, 1842, and here he is peacefully passing the last years of a a useful life. His wife, a daughter of James A. Condra, did not long survive her marriage, but early entered into the heavenly life, leaving two children behind her as a consolation to her bereaved husband, the subject of this writing, and a younger son, Abner L., who is still in school and as yet unmarried.

George W. Moore, the paternal grandfather of the Whitwell dentist, was born January 25, 1799. He had a long and eventful life and his remains are interred in the Red Hill cemetery. Here also repose the ashes of his wife, Nancy Davis, who was born July 19, 1806, and died January 13, 1882. He was a public-spirited and generous man, and contributed the land on which the Red Hill church and school house stand, and the cemetery is established. He had little opportunity for instruction in early life, but an indomitable spirit pushed him on, and he became a leading man in the affairs of this part of the state. He was a surveyor, and served Marion county as sheriff. He was a major of the militia, and assisted in the removal of the Indians to their new quarters in Indian Territory. He was a Master Mason at Jasper, and prominent in the Democratic party. His father, John, came from North Carolina, where his ancestors had settled on coming from Ireland. He had one brother, Richard W., who went into Benton county, Arkansas, and died during the Civil war, leaving a large family. Nancy Davis, mentioned above, had a varied and eventful history. She was the daughter of Major Davis, a veteran of many wars who died at Pulaski, Tennessee. She was born at Jonesboro, Tennessee, and married, when only thirteen years of age, to a Mr. Bacon, who was killed by falling from his horse. She was the mother of ten children, of whom all but one attained maturity. John was the name of her first born, who died while still an infant. Napoleon B. died July 6, 1865, just after his return from the Confederate army. Martha J. is the wife of Patrick H. Grayson, a prominent farmer whose home is not far away. G. W. has his home near Shellmound, Marion county. Millie A. is the wife of Calvin Maxwell, an eloquent clergyman of the Protestant Methodist church,

whose field of work is now in Texas. M. D. L. died in Nashville. Emeline is the wife of James Grayson, and is with her husband in Montague county, Texas. Thomas J. died March 31, 1896, in Sequatchie county. James M. lives at Llano, Texas, where he is widely known as a minister of the Cumberland Presbyterian church. The esteem in which he is held by the community is evidenced by his election as a probate judge. He has also been in the state legislature. Richard Jackson, the father of the subject of this sketch, had an exciting career as a member of Company H, Fourth Tennessee Confederate Cavalry, in which he served nearly four years as a private under Captain Rankin. He was on detached service much of the time, but participated in the battles of Perryville, Chickamauga, and Stone River. He was taken prisoner at Van Buren, Ala., but was in captivity only eight days. He escaped by jumping from a rapidly moving train as he was being carried northward, and rejoined his command. When the war closed his sole possessions were a poor horse and a ragged uniform. But he had a strong heart, and faced the problems of destitution as he had the dangers of war. He soon made a place for himself, and dared to marry within two years, Lizzie Condra becoming his wife August 15, 1867. She died April 27, 1878, and two years later, August 27, 1880, he took to himself a second wife, Nancy J. Andes. He united with the Cumberland Presbyterian church at the age of fifteen years, and almost immediately began preaching the gospel, and for twenty-five years has been regularly connected with the ministry. During that time he has had charge of many churches and has preached in fifteen surrounding counties. He is a member of the Masonic order at Whitwell, and is a Democrat.

Dr. Napoleon B. Moore, whose name introduces this article, has enjoyed unusual educational advantages by which he has greatly profited. He has made the most of the public schools, and is a graduate of the dental department of the Vanderbilt University at Nashville. He graduated in 1893, but had been engaged in practice at Whitwell since the spring of 1891. Dr. Moore was married June 7, 1893, to Miss Alice Ashburn. She is a daughter of B. F. and Susan (Price) Ashburn, who first drew her breath November 29, 1871, at their home near Whitwell. She was educated in the public schools of the valley, and is the mother of two promising children, Henry Grady, born January 7, 1894, and Randolph Judson, April 25, 1896. Dr. Moore and his wife are members of the Cumberland Presbyterian church, and have a host of friends. He is a member of the fraternal order of the Knights of Pythias, and as a consistent Democrat cast his first vote for Grover Cleveland for president.

NATHAN BOULDIN.—Prominent among the energetic, progressive and successful business men of VanBuren county is the subject of this sketch—a well-known merchant and hotel man of Spencer. He is a native of North Carolina, born November 27, 1840, and is a son of Elisha and Elizabeth (Southerland) Bouldin, who with their family removed from North Carolina to Al-

abama in 1846, and subsequently became residents of the Seventh district of Van-Buren county, Tenn., settling in the woods at Laurel Cove, six miles west of Spencer. The father, who was a farmer and distiller by occupation, was born June 11, 1808, and died at Laurel Cove, October 28, 1867. In his family were the following children: Rachel, wife of Jesse Martin, sheriff of Van-Buren county; Jane, wife of Tolbert Grissom, of the Seventh district of VanBuren county; Nancy, wife of William Johnson, of the Seventh district; Eliza, who first married J. Argo, and after his death wedded a second cousin, Thomas Bouldin, and died in VanBuren county; Fanny, deceased wife of Samuel Grissom, who was county court clerk of VanBuren county for three terms; Eliza, a resident of the Fifth district of VanBuren county; and Nathan, whose name introduces this sketch.

Nathan Bouldin was provided with excellent school privileges during his youth, completing his education at Burritt College. Although he did not join the Confederate army during the Civil war, he was taken prisoner by the northern troops and sent to Camp Chase, Ohio. Before and after the war he engaged in farming and distilling, but finally turned his attention to merchandising and to the management of his hotel. Misfortune overtook him, however, in 1887, his store and hotel being totally destroyed by fire. With characteristic energy he at once rebuilt and at the end of four months was carrying on business on a more extensive scale than before. By fair and honorable dealing he has built up an excellent trade, and has gained the friendship of his many patrons and the confidence of all with whom he comes in contact.

In 1867 Mr. Bouldin was united in marriage with Miss Anna Safley, who was born in Warren county, Tenn., in 1847, and they have become the parents of three children: Amanda, wife of David L. Haston, a stock-dealer of VanBuren county; America, wife of A. W. Lauter, a merchant of Chattanooga; and D. L., who is at home. The son attended Burritt College until nineteen years of age, after which he learned telegraphy and was employed as operator at Rock Island, Tenn., Sparta, Bon Air, Flintville, and at the union depot at Nashville, Tenn. He was then appointed circuit clerk of VanBuren county, by Judge M. D. Smallman, and is now acceptably filling that position.

Mr. and Mrs. Bouldin are both faithful members of the Christian church, while socially he is a Mason, and politically he and his son are stanch Democrats. For one term he served as trustee of VanBuren county, and he is now trustee of Burritt College.

PATRICK HENRY GRAYSON, one of the most prominent and highly respected farmers of the Third district of Marion county, was born September 4, 1828, and is a son of Henry and Mary (Hixon) Grayson, whose sketch appears elsewhere in this volume. Our subject is indebted to the public schools of the county for his educational privileges, and being reared to farm work he became a most thorough and skillful agriculturist.

On the 26th of September, 1850, he led to the marriage altar Miss Martha J. Moore, who was born in the Third district of Marion county, in June, 1830, and is a daughter of George and Nancy E. (Davis) Moore. Her mother was twice married, her first husband being a Mr. Bacon, who was killed by a horse. Mrs. Grayson was also educated in the public schools, and by her marriage she has become the mother of nine children, as follows: Nancy L., now the wife of John W. Andes, of the Third district; Sarah A., wife of John Lasater, of Tracy City, Tenn.; Fannie E., wife of John Lasater, a farmer of Pelham, Tenn.; George W., who married Effie Myers and lives in the state of Oregon; Henry C., who married Ruth Bryson, and is a farmer of the Fifth district of Marion county; Ada L., wife of George W. Bryson, an agriculturist of the same district; Tula H., at home; James M., who married Anna Pryor, and is a farmer of the Third district of Marion county; and Amanda, who died at the age of ten years.

During the Civil war, Mr. Grayson's sympathies were with the South, and in September, 1862, he joined the Confederate army, becoming a member of Capt. Patrick H. Price's company, Third Tennessee Cavalry. He first went to Kentucky, then to Chattanooga, later to middle Tennessee, and participated in the battles of Fort Donelson and Beech Grove, besides several skirmishes. He was captured in Marion county, in 1863, was paroled and sent home, where he afterward took the oath of allegiance to the United States government. His father lost several slaves during the war, and he lost two, besides considerable other property, including horses, mules, cattle and sheep, amounting to several thousand dollars.

After his return from the war Mr. Grayson resumed farming in the Third district of Marion county, where he continued to carry on operations until 1880, when he removed to Yamhill county, Ore., but three years later he returned to Tennessee, and has since successfully engaged in farming in the Third district of Marion county. Since his return he has served for six years as justice of the peace with credit to himself and to the entire satisfaction of the general public, and prior to the war also filled that office for eight years. He is a Democrat in political sentiment, and a Master Mason, belonging to Altine lodge, at Sulphur Springs. Religiously both he and his wife are worthy members of the Methodist Episcopal church, South.

ISAAC E. SWAFFORD, is one of that thrifty and energetic race of young men who are doing so much to make the new south a fact. He was born January 12, 1869, and is known far and wide in Beldsoe county as a pushing and successful stock dealer, whose judgment is good and whose word is reliable. He lives in Melvine, Bledsoe connty, where he was born. He is a son of Isaac E. and Martha T. (Roberson) Swafford, both of whom are now dead. His father was born February 6, 1827, and died December 27, 1891. His mother was born February 8, 1832, and died August 21, 1871.

The paternal grandfather of the subject of this article was Thomas Swafford, who was born March 10, 1783, and died November 2, 1856. He married for his second wife Elizabeth Nicholas, who was born September 26, 1788, and died January 14, 1878. She was the mother of four children. Samuel Swafford, her oldest son, is a well-known and highly respected citizen of this county. Sarah married Jesse Brown and has her residence on the Brown homestead, which is situated on the east side of the valley. Fannie was twice married. Her first husband was a Mr. Lloyd, and on his death she married Mr. Stone, and moved to Texas, where she died.

Isaac E. Swafford, Sr., was only twenty-two when he married, his wife being the sister of James Roberson, who at one time paid the largest tax of any man in Bledsoe county. He continued to occupy and improve the place where the subject of this notice now dwells all his life, and there he died. He was a successful farmer and stockraiser, and manifested on every occasion good business qualities. He was made justice of the peace at the age of twenty-six, and was chairman of the county court a number of years. He and his wife were members of the Methodist Episcopal church, South, and he served many years a steward. He and his brother Samuel practically built Swafford chapel, which bears their name, and of which they were liberal supporters. He was a Mason at Melvine, and a Democrat. He was the father of nine children, of whom four are now living. Samuel H. L. lives in Abilene, Texas. Aaron E. is a prominent farmer in the Fourth district of this county. Elizabeth is the wife of Prof. W. E. Stephens, who is·connected with the Dayton high school. Isaac E., the youngest child, is the theme of this article. T. J. R. was a lawyer and was killed at Sparta. He was a man of marked ability, and was the partner of Supreme Judge Snodgrass. F. H., A. M., T. L. died when children.

Mr. Swafford spent several years at Sequatchie College and at the Tennessee Valley College, but quit school at the age of sveenteen, feeling quite well prepared to take care of himself. He remained with his father until the latter's death, and then he and his sister came into possession of the family homestead, which has since entirely come into his hands by purchase. He has achieved marked success in his comparatively brief career, and in 1894 was elected a member of the county court. Miss Sallie S. Worthington became his wife April 22, 1891. She is a daughter of C. C. Worthington, of the Fourth district of this county, and is a lady of unusual talents. They are members of Swafford chapel, where Mr. Swafford acts as steward. They are the parents of two children, Thomas J. R. and M. T. N. Mr. Swafford is a Democrat, and is one of the leading spirits of the party in his community.

JOHN A. BURNETT, for the past eleven years register of Cumberland county, was born in Knox county, Tenn., December 1, 1860, and is a son of E. D. G. and Nancy A. E. (Adams) Burnett. The Burnett family was identified with the earliest beginnings of settlement of East Tennessee. The father of the subject of this writing is still living in Grassy Cove, and has had his home in this county for the last twenty-seven years. His wife has been dead for nine years. She was a member of that illustrious Adams family that contributed two presidents to the United States. Her father, John Quincy Adams, went to the Mexican war, but died on his way home. Her mother was Nancy J. Fryas, who died quite recently at a very advanced age.

John A. Burnett was the oldest of a family of nine sons and three daughters. He attended school in Knox county on the French Broad or river seven miles north of Knoxville, and profiting by his opportunities, was able to teach school very successfully when it afterward seemed necessary. Among the schools he taught were those known as the Forrest Hill, Big Lick, Hyder and Bethlehem schools. In the month of October, 1879, Mattie E. Hamby, a daughter of James M. Hamby, and a native of Cumberland county, became his wife. To this marriage there have been born seven children, all but one of whom are living. May A. died in childhood. The names of the other living children are Martin H., James Douglas, Verdie Tennis, Henry Preston, John Baxter and Rosa Victoria. At the time of his marriage Mr. Burnett was engaged in farming, but an accident forced him to seek another means of earning his living, and so taking a little more instruction to fit himself for it he became a teacher, and only left the school room to go into his present position. His career is that of the typical American, who finding one door closed does not hesitate to open into another and very different line of labor from that to which he has been accustomed. He relies upon himself, and feels that honesty and candor and faithful service will win anywhere. As a farmer he did well, he was a good school teacher, and nobody thinks of trying to win the office of register from him. During the last few years he dealt quite largely in real estate, and in that time has bought and sold many thousand acres of land.

Mr. Burnett is an active Mason, holding membership in Crossville lodge, No. 483. He has been delegate to the grand lodge, and is now senior warden of the local order. Personally he is a genial gentleman, and is the fortunate possessor of many friends throughout the county, as his stronghold upon the office of register abundantly attests.

JOHN W. GREER owns and operates a fine farm of two hundred acres pleasantly located in the Fifth district of Bledsoe county, five miles above Pikeville. It invariably attracts the eye of the passing traveler as being under the supervision of a thorough and skillful agriculturist, and a man otherwise of good business qualifications.

Mr. Greer was born in that district, September 27, 1853, and is a son of W. H. and Mahala (Hutcheson) Greer, the latter a daughter of John Hutcheson, who died in Bledsoe county. Our subject's father is a native of Virginia, and during early life came with his parents to Bledsoe county, taking up his residence in that part of the county now known as Grassy Cove, Cumberland county. After his marriage to

48

Mahala Hutcheson he removed to the Sequatchie Valley and located on land now belonging to George W. Ault, but now makes his home in the Seventh district of Bledsoe county. He was sheriff of the county before the war and later served as justice of the peace with credit to himself and to the entire satisfaction of the general public. He has always been a stanch Democrat in politics, is identified with the Masonic order, and is a consistent member of the Christian church, to which the mother of our subject also belonged. Throughout life he has followed the occupations of farming and stock raising with excellent success. His first wife died about twelve years ago, and of the eight children born to them, three are also deceased—Martha, who married Charles Hart and died in Pikeville; Ann, who married J. P. McGarr; and Emma, who died when a young lady. Those living are John W., of this sketch; Nancy J., wife of John Hall, of Pikeville; H. C., who is married, but is still with his father; and Lou and Moses, both at home. For his second wife the father married Matilda Roberson, of Bledsoe county, and when she died about a year ago, he married a Mrs. Pearson, of the same county.

John Greer spent his school days at Peoples College, and when not in the schoolroom aided his father in the operation of the home farm. On leaving the parental roof his father gave him his present farm of two hundred acres, of which one hundred and fifty were cleared and ready for cultivation. He takes considerable interest in the stock business, buying and selling, and as a general farmer he has also been very successful.

In 1887 Mr. Greer was united in marriage with Miss Nannie Farmer, a daughter of William Farmer, of Bledsoe county, and they have become the parents of an interesting family of five children: Mahala, Willie, Joseph, Leonard and Audley. Mr. and Mrs. Greer are both active and prominent members of the Smyrna Christian church, in which he is serving as deacon, and in social circles of the community they they occupy an enviable position.

ABRAHAM DALLAS HARGIS.—Not alone is there particular interest attaching to the career of this gentleman as one of the leading citizens of Tracy City, Grundy county, but in reviewing his genealogical record we find his lineage tracing back to the colonial history of the nation, and to that period that marked the inception of the grandest republic the world has ever known. His great-grandfather was a drummer boy in the Revolutionary war, and had two brothers who also aided the colonies in their successful struggle for independence. Our subject's grandfather, Abraham Hargis, was a soldier of the war of 1812, and also took part in the Indian war in Florida. He was a native of North Carolina, a farmer by occupation, and a pioneer of Franklin county, Tenn. He was also one of the first settlers near the head of Battle creek, and died in Marion county, being laid to rest at Oak Grove, on Battle creek. The Hargis family is of English and Dutch descent.

Thomas Hargis, our subject's father, was born in what is now Franklin county,

in 1804, and died in Marion county, December 25, 1873. He was a very prominent and influential man; for a quarter of a century was a member of the county court; and for a great many years was a minister of the Primitive Baptist church. Politically, he was a Democrat, and, socially, a member of Olive Branch lodge, F. & A. M. In early life he married Miss Mary Gunter, who was born, in 1804, in Warren county, Tenn., of which county her people were the earliest settlers from South Carolina. Her father was Augustus Gunter, and most of his descendants now live in Jackson county, Ala., or in the west. Mrs. Hargis died in Tracy City, May 12, 1895, at the advanced age of ninety-one years. Her mental and physical faculties were still unimpaired, and no doubt she would have lived to be one hundred had she not been accidentally burned while lighting her pipe by her dress catching fire. For seventy-two long years she was a consistent member of the Methodist Episcopal church, the latter years of her life being identified with the southern branch of that denomination. After her husband's death she found a pleasant home with our subject.

Of the ten children born to this worthy couple six are now living: William L., a minister of the Methodist Episcopal church, South, now located at Tracy City; James G., a resident of the same place; John W., a farmer living near Pelham, Grundy county, who served for over four years in the Confederate army, was orderly sergeant in the Forty-fourth Tennessee Infantry, Army of the Virginia, under General Longstreet, and was captured, and held a prisoner at Elmira, N. Y., for eleven months; Thomas M., a resident of Tracy City, who was in Company A, Fourth Confederate Tennessee Infantry, until 1863, and was in many battles but was never wounded; Melvina, wife of Alfred Spigles, a farmer of Marion county; and A. D., who is the youngest of the family. Those deceased are Jane K., who married Samuel Anderson and died in Marion county; Rebecca, who married Alfred Spigles and died in the same county; Tabitha, who died in girlhood; and Mahala C., who married John P. Henry and died near Pelham in Grundy county.

Abraham D. Hargis, of this sketch, was born on Battle creek in Marion county, January 4, 1844, and was educated in the schools of that locality. In July, 1861, he responded to the call of the Confederacy for volunteers, and enlisted in Company A, Fourth Tennessee Infantry, with which he served for four years, his command being disbanded below Atlanta in May, 1865. His father was the oldest man of the regiment and was lieutenant of Company A. Our subject participated in the battles of Fishing Creek, Richmond, Ky., Stone River, Chickamauga, the Atlanta campaign, and the engagement at Pine Mountain, where the regiment lost their commander, Col. James A. McMurray. Fortunately Mr. Hargis was never wounded, but was taken prisoner at Tullahoma and was on parole for six months. After the war he located at Tracy City, and in 1867 entered the employ of the Tennessee Coal, Iron & Railroad Company, as a coal digger in mines Nos. 1 and 2, being thus engaged for sixteen years. For twelve years he was foreman of the Lone Rock mines; engaged in contracting for two years; and in 1897 was appointed mine inspector, a position he is now most capably filling.

On December 22, 1864, Mr. Hargis wedded Miss Mary Travis, a native of Madison county, Ala., and a daughter of Charles Travis. To them have been born nine children, namely Martha J., wife of T. H. Jackson; Thomas J.; Joseph W.; Augustus G.; Ella, wife of John Myers; Mahala C. and Rebecca, both at home; and Abraham D., who died in childhood. The sons and sons-in-law are all miners of Tracy City. The parents are earnest members of the Methodist Episcopal church, South, and socially, Mr. Hargis belongs to the Masonic fraternity, the Independent Order of Odd Fellows and the Royal Arcanum. He has taken an active and prominent part in promoting the success of the Democratic party in his locality; has been a member and chairman of the Democratic Club; and at the present time is a member of the executive committee; but his present position is the first and only office he ever asked for.

HUGH MANSFIELD is the proprietor of Mansfield's flour mills, which are located three miles above Pikeville, in the Sequatchie valley, and which were built by the Mansfield Brothers, G. J. and Hugh. They put the mill into operation in 1895, with all the latest improvements. This is one of the best mill sites on the river, and on account of its fine products Mr. Mansfield is enjoying an excellent and increasing patronage. He supplies patrons in places far in Georgia and Alabama, and wherever his flour goes it is pronounced equal to the best.

Hugh Mansfield was born at Viola, Warren county, Tenn., September 24, 1863, and is the son of Robert and Martha Mansfield, both of whom are natives of the state. The Mansfields came into the Sequatchie valley from Virginia at the first opening of the country and settled near Dunlap, where Robert was born. He is now at Marysville, Cook county, Texas, where he was recently appointed postmaster. He grew up in the valley, and during the war made his home at Viola. In 1883 he removed to Texas, and, though he has reached a goodly age, he still enjoys the companionship of the wife of his youth. This venerable couple are the parents of a family of nine children, all of whom are still living. Jeff G. is located at Viola operating the Mansfield Milling Company. Hugh is the second oldest child. Mary, the only daughter, is the wife of the Rev. E. W. Garner, a Baptist minister at Viola. Philip H. is in Texas, while Lee is in the Indian territory, a faithful and successful teacher and preacher. Harrison is in Texas, while David and Floyd, the younger children, are still at home with their parents.

Hugh attended the normal college at Viola, but, desiring to strike out early for themselves, he and his brother Jeff went to Birmingham, Ala., where they found employment at carpenter work. They were still boys, but they played men's parts, and early made their mark. They spent some time at Crescent City, Fla., and were engaged in the same business, after which they came north as far as Knoxville, where they still plied the hammer and pushed the plane.

Their first venture in independent work was made at Pikeville, where they began contracting and building on their own account. Much of the town had recently been destroyed by fire, and all the work they could possibly take was offered them. As noted above, they built the Mansfield flour mill in 1895, and immediately put it into operation under the control of the subject of this sketch. In it he has won a large success, and his good fortune is well deserved, for it springs from integrity and business capacity.

JACOB CLARK, who lives on the side of Walden's Ridge, overlooking the Sequatchie valley—one of the finest scenes in the world—owns the ideal apple orchard of this part of Tennessee and is also a worthy representative of the industrial and agricultural interests of Bledsoe county. Before the war he learned blacksmithing, and for some time he and his brother Jonah carried on operations at his father's old shop, but now has a blacksmith and wagon shop upon his own farm. He is a skilled mechanic, an upright, reliable business man, and a citizen of whom any community might be proud.

Mr. Clark was born in the Sequatchie valley, in 1833, and is a son of Charles and Hannah (Denton) Clark, who were born, reared and married in Sevier county, Tenn., whence they came to Bledsoe county, locating where L. T. Billingsly now lives, and upon that place both died. There the father erected and conducted a blacksmith shop, and was also interested in farming and merchandising for a time. At his death he had reached the age of seventy-six years, six months and fifteen days, and his wife only survived him a few years, the remains of both being interred in the Billingsly cemetery. The mother was an earnest and consistent member of the Christian church. Of the twelve children born to them, only four are now living, namely: Jonah, a farmer living in the valley below Pikeville; Francis, also an agriculturist of Bledsoe county; and Jacob and Bird, twins, the latter now a resident of Van Buren county, Tenn.

The boyhood and youth of Jacob Clark was spent upon his father's farm, and in the schools of Smyrna he acquired his literary education. On starting out in life for himself he chose the occupation to which he had been reared, and until after the Civil war operated rented land. He then purchased his present farm, set out a number of apple trees, and to his further development and improvement of the place he has since devoted his energies with most gratifying results. He now has an excellent orchard of over three thousand trees, most of which are bearing fruit and are in a fine condition.

In 1856 was celebrated the marriage of Mr. Clark and Miss Mary Romine, a native of Bledsoe county, and a daughter of Thomas Romine. Of this union the following children were born, namely: Sylvester, who is now the widow of Martin Farmer, and is living on the west side of Sequatchie creek; Trasdine, widow of Robert Gentry, and also a resident of the valley; Thomas Crutchfield, at home; Nellie, widow of David Walker, and a resident of the valley; Sophronia, at home; Ada, wife of Joseph Clark, who lives below Pikeville; and Jonah, at home. Hettie married James Standefer and died in Bledsoe county. The family is one of the highest respectability, and is widely and favorably known.

ELIJAH H. HUDSON, a prominent farmer of Sequatchie county, residing opposite Sunnyside post office, in District No. 5, is a native of Tennessee, born in Marion county, October 20, 1849. His father, John Hudson, was also born in Marion county, March 12, 1826, and is a son of Elijah and Rebecca (Barker) Hudson. The grandfather was a native of North Carolina, and, on coming to this state at an early day, he located on the farm where our subject's father now resides, and there reared his family. He died in Marion county, honored and respected by all who knew him.

Upon the same farm where his birth occurred John Hudson has spent his entire life, and in its operation has met with more than ordinary success. He is an ardent Democrat in politics, and, though never an aspirant for office, he has been called upon to serve as a member of the county court. In religious faith he is a Cumberland Presbyterian. In Marion county he married Miss Isabel Hackworth, by whom he had five children, namely: Elijah H., of this review; John H., a resident of Marion county; Joseph, deceased; Samuel, deceased; and Lizzie, wife of W. H. Cowan, of Nolan county, Texas. After the death of the mother of these children, John Hudson wedded Miss Matilda Heard, a native of Sequatchie county, and to them were born four children: Byron, who married Esther Grayson and lives near his father, in Marion county; Isabel, deceased; Nancy, wife of Joe Carmack, of Sequatchie county; and James L., at home.

In much the usual manner of farmer boys, Elijah H. Hudson was reared upon the old homestead and obtained a thorough knowledge of every department of farm work. On reaching man's estate he was united in marriage with Miss Sophronia Hixon, a native of Hamilton county, Tenn., and by this union he had four children: John H., Foster, Isabel, and an infant, all deceased. The wife and mother also departed this life in 1876. Mr. Hudson was again married, October 6, 1881, his second union being with Miss Nancy M. Grason, who was born in Marion county. Eight children graced this union: Henry E.; one who died in infancy; Edith; Lizzie; William L.; Lula; Siller and Vivian. Those living are all at home.

Mr. Hudson has a well-cultivated and highly-improved place and is justly accounted one of the best farmers in the Sequatchie valley. His political support is always given the men and measures of the Democracy, and he has been a member of the county court one term and deputy postmaster at Sunnyside. Religiously, he is an earnest member of the Presbyterian church, and, socially, is a member of the Masonic order in high standing.

MELVILLE TURNER, M. D., of Jasper, is one of the ablest and most successful physicians and surgeons of the Sequatchie Valley. He was born August 31, 1857, on a farm five miles above Jasper, and is a son of Washington and Mary E. (Haley) Turner, the former of French, the latter of Irish descent. The father was a native of Faulkner county, Va., born in 1816, and was a son of John Turner, also a native of the Old Dominion, who at an early day removed with his family to a farm in middle Tennessee, and there spent the remainder of his life. When a young man Washington Turner came to the Sequatchie Valley, where he continued to make his home throughout life. He did not enlist in the Confederate army during the Civil war, but his sympathies were with the South and he did all in his power to advance the cause. He lost heavily by the Union soldiers stealing goods from his store in Jasper, and horses, mules, cattle and hogs from his farm, and they also burned his dwelling, destroying the Bible containing the family records. He also lost several slaves and was much crippled financially. Being taken prisoner by the Union troops, he was carried to Nashville but nearly died on the way. He finally made his escape, returned home, and took his family to Mt. Pleasant, Fla., where they remained for three years. On returning to Jasper, he resumed farming and merchandising. He affiliated with the Masonic lodge at Jasper, and was a consistent member of the Methodist Episcopal church, South. He died December 15, 1896, honored and respected by all who knew him.

Washington Turner was twice married, first at Battle Creek, Tenn., July 17, 1851, to Miss Mary E. Haley, a native of this state, who died in 1859, a faithful member of the

Methodist Episcopal church, South. Three children blessed this union: Laura A., wife of J. C. Kelly, who lives on a farm near Jasper; John, who married Lizzie Peck and is engaged in farming near Inman, Tenn.; and Melville, of this review. In 1860, the father wedded Miss Mary E. Horn, a native of Jackson county, Ala., and a daughter of Andrew and Dolly Horn. By the second marriage there were seven children, namely: South Carolina, wife of R. T. Simpson, a merchant of Jasper; Marion L., who lives on a farm five miles above Jasper; Calhoun B., born in Florida in 1865, who followed farming for several years, then engaged in merchandising in Jasper, but is now interested in agricultural pursuits; he is a stalwart Democrat in politics and cast his first vote for Grover Cleveland; Mollie E., wife of E. M. Prigmore, a real estate dealer of Chattanooga; Washington C., a farmer living five miles above Jasper; Thomas S., who married Lennie Gant and is engaged in farming five miles above Jasper; and Emma C., who lives with her sister in Chattanooga. The mother of these children, who also held membership in the Methodist Episcopal church, South, also died in 1876.

Dr. Turner began his literary education in the public schools, and in 1880 entered Vanderbilt University at Nashville, where he pursued a medical course, graduating in 1882, with the degree of M. D. Returning home he opened an office in Jasper, but in 1890 took a six weeks' course at the Polyclinic in New York City, where he was granted a certificate. He is a progressive member of his profession, who keeps abreast with the latest discoveries and theories in the science of medicine and surgery by constant study. His skill and ability is attested by the liberal patronage he enjoys, and he ranks among the leading physicians in this section of the state. His political support is always given the Democracy, and both he and his wife are active and prominent members of the Methodist Episcopal church, South.

On the 23d of June, 1888, Dr. Turner was united in marriage with Miss Mary Cook, who was born in Marion county, August 1, 1868, and is a daughter of P. H. and Mary E. (Alley) Cook. She was educated in the common schools of her native county. The Doctor and his wife have two interesting children: Mary B., born April 8, 1889; and Helen, born August 22, 1891.

HUGH WHITE GRIFFITH, a prominent and successful physician and surgeon engaged in practice at Jasper, Marion county, Tenn., was born at that place, June 5, 1838, and traces his ancestry back to two brothers, William and George Griffith, who came to this country from Wales at an early day and settled in Virginia, the former being our subject's great-great-grandfather. His great-grandfather, who also bore the name of William, was a native of the Old Dominion and married Susanna Jones. Their son Amos, the Doctor's grandfather, was born in Virginia, in 1783, and as early as 1806 settled in Sequatchie county, Tenn., six miles above Dunlap, being the first settler in that section. The nearest mill at that time was in Knox county, a distance of one hundred and twenty-five miles. His son, William S., whose birth occurred September 18, 1807, is supposed to have been the first white child born in the Sequatchie valley. Amos Griffith married Miss Polly Standefer.

James Griffith, the Doctor's father, was born October 6, 1811, in Marion county, sixteen miles above Jasper, was educated in the public schools, and at an early day went to Athens, McMinn county, Tenn., where he followed farming until 1832. In partnership with his brother Jehu he then engaged in merchandising at his home, but two years later sold out to his brother and returned to Jasper, where he formed a partnership with another brother, William S., in the same line. Together they conducted the store until 1846, when James sold his interest to William, and returned to his farm, which he continued to operate until the death of his wife. He was married in Marion county, November 12, 1835, to Miss Jane McClain, who was born in Knox county, Tenn., December 2, 1819, and was a daughter of Daniel and Malinda (Yarnell) McClain. She was a consistent member of the Cumberland Presbyterian church, and died in that faith December 31, 1897, since which time Mr. Griffith has made his home with our subject. He is now eighty-six years old, and is highly respected by all who know him. His father, Amos Griffith, was the first register of Marion county, holding that office from 1819 to 1836. The Doctor's father was then elected to the same position, and being re-elected, served for eight years to the entire satisfaction of all concerned. For ten years he was post-master of Checkville, now Cedar Springs, and at the same time served as justice of

the peace. Socially he is a member of the Masonic lodge at Jasper, and politically was first a Whig, and now a Democrat.

Dr. Griffith is the oldest in a family of seven children, the others being as follows: Martha A., deceased; Mary, wife of Robert Price, a merchant of Jasper; William, who married Louisa Condra and is engaged in farming in Marion county; Louisa J., wife of John H. Parrott, a minister of the Methodist Episcopal church, South; Peyton S., who wedded May Briggle and is engaged in the real estate business in Chattanooga; and Susan, deceased.

In the public schools near his childhood home Dr. Griffith began his education, and later attended Burritt College at Spencer, Alpine Seminary in Hamilton county, and the University of Tennessee at Nashville, where he was granted the degree of M. D., in 1860. He then opened an office in Jasper, but during the Civil war was assistant surgeon in the United States hospital at Nashville for two years. Returning to Jasper, he has since successfully engaged in practice there.

The Doctor has been three times married, first on the 4th of May, 1865, in Dade county, Ga., to Miss Kate Paris, who was born at McMinnville, Tenn., June 22, 1843, and was a daughter of R. M. and Elizabeth (Perkins) Paris, at that time residents of Dade county. Four children were born of this union: Ida L., deceased; Albert, who was killed at Cleveland, Tenn.; Milton, who died in infancy; and James, at home. The wife and mother, who was a consistent member of the Cumberland Presbyterian church, died July 3, 1872. On the 22nd of October, 1874, Dr. Griffith was united in marriage with Miss Jane Mitchell, a native of Arkansas, who was brought to Jasper during infancy and was reared by relatives as she was an orphan. By her the Doctor had two children: Betty, deceased; and May, at home. She, too, was a faithful member of the Cumberland Presbyterian church. Her death occurred July 20, 1879. The Doctor was again married, October 14, 1880, his third union being with Miss Amanda C. Lewis, who was born November 10, 1847, and is a daughter of Mordecai and Adaline (Mitchell) Lewis. She died May 28, 1882, in the faith of the Cumberland Presbyterian church, and left one son, Charles M., who was born May 22, 1882, and is now engaged in farming in Dade county, Georgia.

The Doctor cast his first presidential vote for John Bell, and has since been a pronounced Democrat in politics. He is a member of the Masonic lodge at Jasper, which he has represented in the grand lodge of the state, and in the Cumberland Presbyterian church, he, too, holds membership. He has been very successful as a physician, and for several years served as county physician. He owns several tracts of land and is one of Jasper's most prosperous and highly respected citizen, being very popular with all classes.

A L. MANSFIELD is one of the well-known proprietors of the Sequatchie Valley Roller Mills at Dunlap. His career illustrates most forcibly the possibilities that are open to a young man who possesses sterling business qualification. It

49

proves that neither wealth nor social position, nor the assistance of influential friends at the outset of his career are necessary to place him on the road to success. It also proves that ambition, perseverance, steadfast principles and indefatigable industry, combined with sound business principles will be rewarded, and that true success follows individual effort only.

Mr. Mansfield was born within a mile of his mills, March 1, 1837, and is a son of Norman and Jane (Haney) Mansfield, natives of North Carolina. The father was born in 1810, and with his parents came to Sequatchie county, then Marion county, in 1823, locating one mile below Dunlap on the land now owned by L. W. Cordell. Dunlap was then known as Coops Creek, and William Rankins conducted the only store there. The grandfather of our subject afterward moved five miles below that place and there died. In that locality Norman Mansfield spent the greater part of his life buying land three miles below Dunlap on what is now known as Mansfield Creek, on the west side of the valley next to the mountains, and building thereon a little mill which he operated a number of years. Subsequently he removed to Brush Creek and bought a farm and an interest in a mill, which still goes by the name of the Mansfield Mill. At the time of his death, which occurred March 1, 1887, he was living with our subject. Originally he was a Whig in politics, but later in life affiliated with the Democratic party. He was for a long time a local minister of the Methodist Episcopal church, South, and led a true Christian life. His estimable wife is still living and holds membership in the Baptist church.

She was born about 1816, and makes her home alternately with her son William H. and our subject She is the mother of eighteen children, of whom six sons and four daughters are still living, but only three reside in Sequatchie county—Matthew, who lives on his brother William's place; William H., who is rebuilding the old Mt. Airy Mills, which he expects to operate; and A. L., of this sketch. The family control the milling business in this section of the state, five of the brothers being interested in milling up and down the Sequatchie river.

A. L. Mansfield pursued his studies in a school near his father's home, and commenced learning the miller's trade before he was able to carry a sack of grain. On leaving his father's employ, he bought his father's mill on Brush Creek, in the fall of 1859, and during the war successfully operated the same as he was not molested by the armies on either side. Coming to Dunlap in 1866, he worked at the carpenter's trade for one year, and then he and his brother, William H., bought the land, on which the latter now lives. After farming it for three years our subject traded his interest in the same for his present mill, which at that time was of the old-fashioned kind. He rebuilt the dam and the building, put in new and modern machinery, including four sets of rolls and now has one of the best equipped mills in the locality. All his product is disposed of in the valley, and the flour manufactured is equal to the best.

On the 17th of August, 1857, Mr. Mansfield was united in marriage with Miss Lizzie Rains, who was born in Bledsoe county, Tenn., February 16, 1838, and is a daughter of Josiah Rains. By this union five children have been born, namely: William, a farmer living with his uncle William; John, a miller of Salisburg, N. C.; Clayton, a farmer of Oklahoma; Aachac, wife of Gilliam Farmer, a farmer living on our subject's land; Hettie, wife of Samuel Welch, who lives on our subject's land and assists in the operation of the mill. The parents both hold membership in the Methodist Episcopal church at Dunlap, while Mr. Mansfield is identified with the Masonic lodge of that place, and casts his ballot with the Democracy.

ELIJAH SPARKMAN is an enterprising, progressive farmer of Van Buren county, pleasantly located in the Second district, where he owns a fine and well-cultivated farm of one hundred and forty acres. He was born in the First district of the same county, April 12, 1856, and is a son of George W. and Malissa (Hill) Sparkman, also natives of Van Buren county. His paternal grandfather was Bryant Sparkman, while his grandmother was a Miss Comis prior to her marriage. As a life work the father followed farming, and as one of the leading and influential citizens of his community he was often called upon to fill public positions of honor and trust, being a school commissioner for about a quarter of a century, justice of the peace for twenty years, and sheriff of Van Buren county for two years. In his political affiliations he was a Democrat, in his social relations an Odd Fellow, and in religious belief a Baptist. His first wife, who died December 23,

1874, was also a faithful member of the Baptist church. His death occurred in 1886. After his first wife died he married Miss Lena Slaten, but had no children by that union.

The children of the first marriage were as follows: Thomas, who married Sarah Dodson, and lives in the First district of Van Buren county; Helen, deceased; Martha J., wife of a Mr. Breeden, of Alabama; Sarah, deceased wife of Noah Mayfield, of Texas; Mrs. Rosina Forsyth, deceased; Lewis, who is married and lives in Texas; Elijah, of this sketch; Jeremiah, a resident of Texas; George B., who married Eliza Collings, and is now deceased; Vina, deceased wife of Zack Hodge; and Rowin, who married Dean Yates.

The subject of this sketch is indebted to the public schools of the Second district of Van Buren county for his educational privileges, and his business training was secured upon the home farm, where he remained until reaching man's estate. On the 30th of September, 1875, was celebrated his marriage with Miss Nancy Holenwogth, who was born in June, 1855, on the farm where he now resides, and was one of a family of three children. Seven children were born to Mr. and Mrs. Sparkman, namely: Stephen; Mollie, who died October 3, 1897; George L., who died August 20, 1897; Malechi and Sophia, at home; Dallas, deceased; and J. Hodge, at home. The wife and mother was called to her final rest February 28, 1891, and Mr. Sparkman was again married, February 28, 1895, his second union being with Thuley McBride, who was born in 1868, and is a daughter of James and Hallie (Vance) McBride. Of the three children born of this union, Lydia is the only one living, the others having died in infancy.

The Republican party has always found in Mr. Sparkman a stanch supporter of its principles, and he has been called upon to serve as both road and school commissioner. Religiously he belongs to the Separate Baptist church, while his wife holds membership in the Methodist church.

DR. GEORGE REAL was a physician and minister who was for many years a well-known and prosperous citizen of the Sequatchie Valley. He was born in Virginia in 1794, his father's people being of German and his mother's of English descent. He grew to manhood and married Esther Pilson, who was born in Virginia in 1800. They were married in White county, Tenn., and at an early day moved to the Sequatchie Valley and lived on a number of different farms in that region. He traded extensively in land, and when still a young man began the practice of medicine, which latter profession he continued until about nine years before his death. Early in life he experienced religion and began preaching, first in the Methodist church and later in the Baptist. He was decidedly a man of action and served in the war of 1812. In politics he was a Democrat, not an extremest and not in sympathy with the secession movement, but after the commencement of the war his sympathies were all with the South. He died in 1887.

Dr. Real's first wife, Esther Pilson, died in 1851. He later married Miss Jemima

Smith, also a native of Virginia, who died in 1888.   Nine children were born to bless the first marriage, four of whom are now living.   By the second marriage three children were born, all of whom are deceased. Dr. Real was a man of a great deal of ability, a great revivalist, and a man who took an active and prominent part in all public movements.

JOHN W. BERRY, the well-known and popular superintendent of the coke ovens at Tracy City for the Tennessee Coal, Iron & Railroad Company, is one of the self-made men of the community, and his popularity is well deserved, as in him are embraced the characteristics of an unbending integrity, unabated energy and industry that never flags.

Mr. Berry was born near McMinnville, Warren county, Tenn., October 20, 1857, and is a son of Green A. and Martha A. (Miles) Berry.   The father was born in North Carolina about sixty years ago, and is a son of William Berry, also native of that state.   The mother of our subject, however, is a native of Tennessee and a daughter of William Miles.   When a young man Green A. Berry used to frequently visit his uncle, Benjamin Wooten, whose home was on the present site of Tracy City, which at that time was a fine hunting ground, and being a lover of the chase Mr. Berry made a trip to this region every summer.   However, he continued to live in Warren county, this state, until 1867 or 1868 when he moved to Lincoln county, and from there came to Tracy City about 1872.   Prior to the Civil war he was engaged in agricultural pursuits, but during his residence in Tracy City he has followed teaming.   He is an ardent Democrat in politics and he and his wife are earnest and faithful members of the Methodist Episcopal church, South. They are the parents of eight children, and our subject is the oldest of the five who are still living: Mollie F. is the wife of Matthew Cope, an engineer on the Nashville & Chattanooga railroad, whose sketch appears elsewhere in this volume; Josephine is the widow of J. C. Roddy, and a resident of Tracy City; Thomas G. is a miner of that place; and Henry E. is still living with his parents.   Those deceased are Robert L., who died in boyhood; Cora M., who married Thomas Crick; and Lillie, who died in childhood.

To a limited extent John W. Berry attended school in the valley near Pelham, but at an early age became water boy while the first ovens were being built at the old mines.   Later he drove mules in the mines, then had charge of the water boiler and was track man for a time, after which he was foreman over convict laborers.   Subsequently he engaged in contracting on his own account, and on leaving the mines was in business for himself at Tracy City for a few years.   As brakesman he afterward entered the employ of the Nashville & Chattanooga railroad, and was then conductor on the Tracy City branch.   Returning to the mines he was foreman over convicts until January, 1896, when he accepted the position of superintendent of the coke ovens and has since most acceptably filled that post.

In 1884 Mr. Berry married Miss Alice Eller, a daughter of David Eller, and to them were born five children, namely: Bessie L.; Barney Lawrence; Maude Beatrice and Norma Leatrice, twins, the latter now deceased; and Florence. The wife and mother died in 1893, and in 1895 Mr. Berry was again married, his second union being with Miss Mattie E. Morgan, a native of Wartrace, Tenn., and a daughter of Dr. Morgan. They now have a little son, Charles. Mr. and Mrs. Berry are members of the Methodist Episcopal church, South, in which he serves as steward; and fraternally he is connected with the Masonic Order, the Knights of Pythias, the Independent Order of Odd Fellows, the Royal Arcanum, and at one time belonged to the Order of Railway Conductors.

JAMES A. SKILLERN, a leading and prosperous agriculturist of the Sixth district, of Bledsoe county, was born January 29, 1840, on the farm where he still continues to reside, and is a worthy representative of one of the honored pioneer families of this region. His father, James A. Skillern, Sr., was born in Lee county, Va., June 13, 1799, and was a son of John and Mary (Anderson) Skillern, also natives of that county, whence they came to Bledsoe county, Tenn., in 1808, locating here before any roads had been cut through the forest, and having to clear their own path from the mountain to the valley in order to reach their new home. Here the grandfather purchased nine hundred acres of wild land, upon a portion of which our subject now resides. He died in 1846, his wife in 1844, and the remains of both were buried in the Skillern cemetery on the old homestead. They had a family of nine children, six sons and three daughters, of whom James, the father of our subject, is the oldest. On reaching manhood he was married in the Sixth district of Bledsoe county, to Miss Scottie Lewis, a native of Rhea county, Tenn., and they also became the parents of nine children, as follows: Franklin, deceased; Adaline, widow of Stephen D. Thurman, whose home is near Dunlap; John, deceased; Sophronia; Mary, deceased; James A., of this sketch; Orlando L.; Neal S., deceased; and Andrew C.

The early education of James A. Skillern, Jr., acquired in the public schools, was supplemented by a course in Burritt College at Spencer, Tenn. He was married May 2, 1867, to Miss Rebecca C. Hinch, who was born August 19, 1843, in Bledsoe county, now Cumberland county, Tenn., and is a daughter of John and Anna (Parham) Hinch. She is the youngest of their eight children, the others being William, Nathan, Mary, Jackson, Curt, Nancy J. and Harman. Mr. and Mrs. Skillern have a family of six children, whose names and dates of birth are as follows: James R., May 24, 1868; John C., February 28, 1870; Neal S., April 13, 1872; Luther F., April 5, 1874; Mather M., July 18, 1879; and Anna J., January 14, 1882.

Mr. Skillern is the owner of one of the most beautiful farms of the valley, comprising one hundred and seven acres of the original tract purchased by his grandfather in 1808. He is a thorough, systematic and enterprising farmer, and has therefore met with excellent success in the operation of his place. He casts his ballot in support of the men and measures of the Republican party, but has never cared for political honors, though he has most efficiently served as school director in his district for sixteen years. Both he and his wife are active and prominent members of the Methodist Episcopal church, South, and are worthy of the high regard in which they are uniformly held.

COL. ASHLEY LAWRENCE SPEARS. —Few men are more prominent or widely known in Marion county than Col. Ashley L. Spears, a leading attorney of Jasper and one of the honored veterans of the Civil war. He has been an important factor in the business, political and social life of the community; is public-spirited and thoroughly interested in whatever tends to promote the moral, intellectual or material welfare of his town and county.

The Colonel was born March 28, 1842, eight miles below Pikeville, in Bledsoe county, Tenn., and among his ancestors are several that have been prominent in military circles. The family has been well represented in all the wars of this country, his great-great-grandfather having served in the Revolution. His grandfather, Dr. John H. Spears, belonged to General Coffee's command in the war of 1812, and participated in the battles of New Orleans and Horse Shoe. The latter was a native of Buckingham county, Va., and as early as 1796 removed to the head of the Sequatchie valley, being among the earliest settlers of that region. He made his home upon a farm at Grassy Cove, Bledsoe county, and

successfully engaged in the practice of medicine until called from this life in 1860, at the age of seventy-four years.

Gen. James G. Spears, the father of our subject, was born in Bledsoe county, March 29, 1816, was educated in the common schools of the county and successfully engaged in teaching for a number of years. He was elected clerk of the circuit court of Bledsoe county, and while holding that office, he studied law. About 1848 he commenced practice in Pikeville and for many years was one of the leading attorneys of the valley. In 1847 he was commissioned colonel of the militia of Bledsoe county; organized a company for the Mexican war; and tendered his services to the government, but was not needed. At the outbreak of the Civil war, however, his sympathies were with the Union cause, and he and R. K. Bird, of Roane county, Tenn.; organized a regiment in 1861, at Camp Dick Roberson. Mr. Bird was elected colonel and Mr. Spears lieutenant-colonel. With his command he took part in the first battle of the war at Wild Cat Mountain, Ky., which was followed by the engagement at Fishing Creek, where he was promoted to the rank of brigadier-general for gallantry, from which he gets his well-known title of general. His brigade was composed at first of the First, Second, Third, Fourth, Fifth and Sixth Tennessee regiments, but when it was reorganized he had some Indiana and Kentucky regiments in his command. He was in the battles of Cumberland Gap, Stone River and Chickamauga, later engaged in guarding the fords along the Tennessee river, was in the engagement at Missionary Ridge, and then went in pursuit of Longstreet.

Early in 1863 he resigned his commission and returned home to resume the practice of law, which he followed until his death. At the battle of Stone River, General Rosecrans had recommended him for promotion to the rank of major-general. He was a good soldier and an excellent attorney. Politically he was a Douglas Democrat, and was an elector on the ticket when the "Little Giant" ran for president. He died at his summer home at Braden's Knob, July 22, 1869, and was buried at Pikeville.

Colonel Spears, of this review, acquired his primary education in the public schools, and then entered Emory & Henry College, in Virginia, where he was a student when the Civil war broke out. Before completing his college course he returned home and taught school for a short time, but on the 25th of February, 1862, he enlisted as a private in Company D, Fifth Volunteer Tennessee Infantry, at Flat Lick, on the Cumberland river, with Capt. Joe Turner as organizer of the regiment. He was made adjutant and held that position until the close of the war. With his father he was in the battles of Stone River and Chickamauga, and was in all the engagements in the campaign from Chattanooga to Atlanta, under General Sherman. He was wounded in both legs at the battle of Resaca, Ga., but not very severely, and also slightly wounded in the left side, but remained with his regiment. Returning west with General Thomas he took part in the battles of Franklin and Nashville, Tenn., and followed Hood south to the Tennessee river. Shortly after the troops of which he formed a part were shipped for Cincinnati, Ohio, thence to Washington, D. C., in box cars, and on

to Annapolis, Md., and Fort Fisher, arriving at the latter place just after Terry had taken the fort. Colonel Spears was in the siege and capture of Fort Alexander and Town Creek, and then proceeded to Wilmington, N. C. While there the prisoners released from Andersonville arrived, and were escorted by the soldiers to Fortress Monroe, where they were clothed and fed. Our subject then went to Washington, D. C., and from there returned to Nashville, Tenn., where he was mustered out in April, 1865.

Returning to his home in Pikeville, Colonel Spears was appointed clerk of the county court of Bledsoe county, for two years, and was then elected clerk of the circuit court by the people. About a year later he hired a deputy and in 1867 entered law school at Cumberland University, where he completed the law course. While in college he was nominated, in 1869, to represent Bledsoe, Rhea, Sequatchie and Hamilton counties in the state legislature, and on returning home made the race and was elected. In 1871 he was re-elected for two years, and in 1872 was an elector on the Horace Greeley ticket. He commenced the practice of law at Pikeville in the latter year, and in 1878 was elected attorney-general of the Fourth judicial district, a position he most creditably filled for eight years. He is one of the best and most distinguished lawyers of East Tennessee, and is now successfully engaged in practice at Jasper, with his nephew, A. L. Roberson, one of the coming attorneys of the county. The Colonel is now serving as president of the First National Bank at South Pittsburg, Tenn.

On the 9th of April, 1873, Colonel Spears was united in marriage with Miss Mattie J. Pitts, who was born in Bledsoe county, in 1846, and died November 23, 1896. Three children blessed this union: Nellie Pitts, now the wife of William D. Wright, of Knoxville, Tenn.; and Grace Kendrick and Alvin Lawrence, both at home. The Colonel was again married, December 28, 1897, this second union being with Miss Willie Cummins, who was born in Franklin, Tenn., December 15, 1856, and is a daughter of William and Susan (Russell) Cummins. She was well educated in the schools of her native city and at Nashville, became an excellent teacher, and for about twelve years was employed in that capacity in a college. The Colonel and his wife are both active and prominent members of the Methodist Episcopal church, South, while socially he is a Master Mason, belonging to the lodge at Jasper, and politically is a Democrat. He is one of the most substantial citizens in the county, owning over two thousand acres of land, but is very generous with his means, and gave seven thousand and five hundred dolllars to help build the Pryor Institute at Jasper.

Compiled By:
Ella E. Lee Sheffield, Texas City, TX 77590
Lucille Smith Craddock, La Marque, TX 77568